"This book advances the theology of deification in a number of ways. It shows how Luther's theology—read from diverse angles—accords with key insights in ecumenical deification theology. It integrates the important Chinese and Taiwanese church movement fostered by Witness Lee, along with the work of C. S. Lewis. And it fully welcomes Protestant biblical scholars and theologians into the deification conversation. Warmly commended!"

**Matthew Levering,** James N. Jr. and Mary D. Perry Chair of Theology at Mundelein Seminary and coeditor of *The Oxford Handbook of Deification*

"A fascinating collection of studies on the theological and practical meaning of deification. These refreshing essays show how Protestant theology creatively appropriated—and continues to creatively appropriate—traditional notions of deification in light of particular doctrinal commitments and pastoral contexts. The editors and authors are to be commended for challenging the false idea that deification is merely an Eastern doctrine, while also firmly demonstrating the biblical roots, Protestant appropriation, and evangelical possibilities of this foundational Christian teaching."

**Jared Ortiz,** professor of religion at Hope College and editor of *With All the Fullness of God: Deification in Christian Tradition*

"This book will help Protestant theologians, especially evangelicals, see that forensic justification might not be the heart of the gospel or biblical theology. Therefore, this book has the potential of advancing ecumenical understanding among orthodox Christians. Recommended for all those interested in biblical and systematic theology."

**Gerald McDermott,** author of *A New History of Redemption* and *Deep Anglicanism*

"What do you get if you cross PBS's *Antiques Roadshow*, the Protestant Reformation, and one of the trending topics in evangelical theology? The doctrine of deification! This fascinating collection of essays sets out to retrieve the patristic notion of *theosis* by showing its biblical and Protestant bona fides as well as its potential for ecumenical dialogue about the nature of salvation—and more. I particularly appreciated the suggestion that believers are deified by being transformed into the image of Christ, the God-man: not simply deified but Christified."

**Kevin J. Vanhoozer,** research professor of systematic theology at Trinity Evangelical Divinity School

"The doctrine of deification was first neglected in modern Western theology, and then enthusiastically rediscovered by Lutheran, Calvinist, Methodist, and Pentecostal scholars. Now the time is ripe for a critical and constructive reassessment. The present volume undertakes a differentiated evaluation of biblical and historical evidence and makes a number of fascinating new proposals. With the help of this book, the relative importance of deification in Christian soteriology is outlined in a solid and inspiring fashion."

**Risto Saarinen,** professor of ecumenics at University of Helsinki in Finland

"In recent decades, the doctrine of *theosis* ceased to be an exclusive preserve of Orthodox thinkers and gained traction among thinkers of all Christian traditions. Yet its position remained tenuous, like that of an unexpected houseguest who arrives and then intends to stay on indefinitely. *Theosis* was admitted but not welcomed. *Theosis*, so to speak, had to sleep in the woodshed. Copan and Reardon's volume shows that *theosis* is capable of encompassing and integrating such classical Western soteriological themes as conversion, justification, sanctification, etc., without effacing their distinctness or violating their integrity. Perhaps a 'theotic' turn in soteriology will facilitate the sort of ecumenical renewal that has already occurred in trinitarian and Christological reflection. This volume will be of great interest for those who feel stymied by the seemingly unbridgeable chasms between East and West, Catholic and Protestant, Evangelical and Charismatic, on the crucial questions regarding Christian salvation."

**Michael McClymond,** professor of modern Christianity at Saint Louis University

"This collection of well-written and groundbreaking essays by a diverse array of fine scholars provides a number of fascinating perspectives on the doctrine of *theosis*. With a unique (but not exclusive) focus on a spectrum of Protestant viewpoints and ways of approaching deification, this work significantly advances the discussion and is sure to spark further research and dialogue on, among other things, what it means for Christians to be in Christ by faith and reflect the glory of God."

**John C. Peckham,** research professor of theology and Christian philosophy at Andrews University in Berrian Springs, Michigan

"*Transformed into the Same Image* is a timely gift for Protestants who seek to grasp the biblical, theological, and historical roots and fruits of deification. This expansive and breathtaking treatment examines the conceptions of *theosis* from the Lutheran, Reformed, Baptist, Wesleyan, Pentecostal, Evangelical, and nondenominational traditions. Special attention is focused on the often misunderstood but insightful contributions of Watchman Nee and Witness Lee. Copan and Reardon are to be congratulated on enlisting both prominent scholars and new and promising researchers to guide readers in this fresh and stimulating exploration of being partakers of the divine image. May this outstanding work continue the conversation on this often-neglected topic."

**Tom Schwanda,** associate professor emeritus of Christian formation and ministry at Wheaton College

"It is wonderful to see how Protestant scholars have reconnected with the patristic exegetical tradition. Even the Hesychast emphasis makes its contribution. These excellent essays show that evangelical reflection on *theosis*, with its view of deification not just as salvation for the individual but as the return of the whole of creation to its divine fullness, is of much more than intra-confessional interest. This is a book of truly ecumenical significance."

**Norman Russell,** honorary research fellow at the University of Oxford and author of *The Doctrine of Deification in the Greek Patristic Tradition*

PAUL COPAN *and* MICHAEL
M. C. REARDON, *eds.*

# TRANSFORMED
*into the*
# SAME
# IMAGE

CONSTRUCTIVE
INVESTIGATIONS
*into the* DOCTRINE
*of* DEIFICATION

FOREWORD *by* MICHAEL J. GORMAN

An imprint of InterVarsity Press
Downers Grove, Illinois

**InterVarsity Press**
P.O. Box 1400 | Downers Grove, IL 60515-1426
ivpress.com | email@ivpress.com

©2024 by Paul Copan and Michael Martin Chester Reardon

All rights reserved. No part of this book may be reproduced in any form without written permission from InterVarsity Press.

InterVarsity Press® is the publishing division of InterVarsity Christian Fellowship/USA®. For more information, visit intervarsity.org.

Scripture quotations, unless otherwise noted, are from the New Revised Standard Version Bible, copyright © 1989 National Council of the Churches of Christ in the United States of America. Used by permission. All rights reserved worldwide.

The publisher cannot verify the accuracy or functionality of website URLs used in this book beyond the date of publication.

Cover design: David Fassett
Interior design: Daniel van Loon

Images: © Iana Kunitsa / Moment / Getty Images, © Kelly Cheng / Moment / Getty Images, © VartB / iStock / Getty Images Plus

ISBN 978-1-5140-1230-7 (hardcover) | ISBN 978-1-5140-0984-0 (paperback) | ISBN 978-1-5140-0985-7 (digital)

**Library of Congress Cataloging-in-Publication Data**
A catalog record for this book is available from the Library of Congress.

31  30  29  28  27  26  25  24   |   13  12  11  10  9  8  7  6  5  4  3  2  1

**From Paul:**

To my siblings Dan, Walter, Evelyn, Helen, Vic,

and Lil—with affection and love.

*Solang mein Jesus lebt*

*Und seine Kraft mich hebt,*

*Muß Furcht und Sorge von mir fliehn,*

*Mein Herz in Lieb erglühn.*

**From Michael:**

To Joyce, my fellow-heir of the grace of life (1 Pet 3:7).

# CONTENTS

Foreword by Michael J. Gorman — ix

Acknowledgments — xiii

Introduction by Paul Copan and Michael M. C. Reardon — xv

Abbreviations — xxvii

## PART 1—BIBLICAL FOUNDATIONS

1. Conformity to Divine Messiah in Paul — 3
   L. ANN JERVIS

2. The Church Is Christ — 16
   *The* Wirkungsgeschichte *of Interpreting Pauline Soteriology as Ecclesial Deification*
   MICHAEL M. C. REARDON

3. Deification Seen from Three Biblical Metaphors in Watchman Nee and Witness Lee with a Cognitive-Linguistic Interpretive Approach to Metaphors — 38
   JACOB CHENGWEI FENG

4. Deification and the Eschatological City — 63
   *Exegetical and Theological Connections in Early Christian Thought*
   NATHAN BETZ

5. Deification in Translation — 82
   *The Influence of Translation Philosophy on the Visibility of the Doctrine of Deification in Scripture*
   CHAO-CHUN LIU

## PART 2—PROTESTANT FOUNDATIONS

6. Deification or Christification? — 105
   *Martin Luther on Theosis*
   ALISTER E. MCGRATH

7. Deification in the Reformed Tradition from Zwingli to Vermigli — 123
   CARL MOSSER

| 8 | Jonathan Edwards, Theosis, and the Purpose of Creation<br>JAMES SALLADIN | 145 |
|---|---|---|
| 9 | John and Charles Wesley on Deification<br>MARK GORMAN | 166 |
| 10 | From *Bios* to *Zoe*<br>C. S. Lewis on the Doctrine of Deification<br>JAHDIEL PEREZ | 184 |
| 11 | Toward an Evangelical Doctrine of Deification<br>PAUL COPAN | 199 |

## PART 3—CONSTRUCTIVE INVESTIGATIONS *into the* DOCTRINE *of* DEIFICATION

| 12 | Deification as a Theological Foundation and Goal for Formational Theological Education<br>BRIAN SIU KIT CHIU | 219 |
|---|---|---|
| 13 | Sharing in the Life of God<br>Considering the Relationship Between Justification and Deification<br>BEN C. BLACKWELL | 242 |
| 14 | Justification as Union and Christ's Presence<br>A Lutheran Perspective<br>VELI-MATTI KÄRKKÄINEN | 268 |
| 15 | Deification and World Christianity<br>Hesychasm and "Calling upon the Name of the Lord"<br>SHU-CHEN HSU HSIUNG | 291 |
| 16 | Transhumanism as Active Effort of Technology Versus Deification as Active Reception of Grace<br>KIMBELL KORNU | 308 |

| List of Contributors | 331 |
|---|---|
| General Index | 337 |
| Scripture Index | 343 |

# FOREWORD

Michael J. Gorman

I AM HONORED AND GRATEFUL to have been invited to write the foreword to this important book. It is about a subject that has been near and dear to my academic and spiritual heart for quite some time, and I have attempted to make my own contributions to its study.

Perhaps the first thing to say about this volume is that it would have been unimaginable not that long ago. The (re)turn to deification, or, as some prefer, *theosis*—participation in the divine life that involves becoming like God, and specifically like Christ as the image of God—in theology and biblical studies has been in process for some time.[1] But what we have here is a set of new perspectives, all assembled in one place and issued by a somewhat unexpected publishing house, yet one I have enjoyed and respected for a long time.[2] These new perspectives entail the Christian traditions they represent, the subjects they explore, and the locations from which they are offered.

One of the distinguishing features of this volume is its focus on Protestantism, broadly understood (e.g., inclusive of Pentecostal/charismatic and nondenominational bodies). As a Protestant myself—a Methodist with Anabaptist leanings—I can only applaud this focus. At the same time, a remarkable aspect of the book is the sheer breadth of the contributors. There are established scholars whose appearance in such a book is completely expected as well as a few well-known academics whose presence may be a welcome surprise. Among the authors of these essays are also younger

---

[1] Terms related to *deification* and *theosis* include *divinization*, *Christification*, and *Christosis*. Some interpreters use some or all of these words interchangeably, while others differentiate carefully among some or all. The brief definition of *deification/theosis* I have used here is not intended to be comprehensive.

[2] Full disclosure: my first book was published by InterVarsity Press, and I am delighted to have had other associations with the press over the years.

scholars who are making their mark precisely on this topic or on other subjects that lead organically to the topic of deification.

These essays are not for the faint of heart; many are technical and demanding. Yet my ultimate hopes for them are four.

First, I hope these essays will continue the significant discussions about deification among biblical scholars, theologians, and ecclesial leaders in their own respective traditions so that the transforming work of God may be better understood and taught in conversation with more common approaches to the theological task. (Here I have in mind, for example, the common idiom of justification, sanctification, and glorification.)

Second, I hope these essays will enlarge the conversation about deification. For one thing, the volume could have a significant ecumenical impact, encouraging not only mutual respect but also mutual instruction and edification. This could happen both among Protestants and between Protestants and other Christians. In addition, the fresh topics addressed by some essays could open up new, interdisciplinary conversations with scholars and others whose primary interests lie elsewhere.

Third, I hope these essays will eventually, either directly or indirectly, affect seminarians and other theological students—the ecclesial influencers of tomorrow (and even today)—who can in turn broaden and deepen the lives of the communities and individuals in their care. In other words, I am looking for a trickle-down effect from these essays. Very few people in the pew, apart from Christians in the Orthodox traditions, have even heard of terms such as *deification* or *theosis*. But if the reality these terms represent is vital to Christian existence, then this situation of widespread unfamiliarity needs to change. This is not a change needed so that people can be theologically correct or proud of being in the know regarding some current theological fad. Rather, faithful Christians need to know about deification for their spiritual health and the health of their communities. They need to know that this topic is in no way a recent addition to the theological lexicon, a novelty in Christian spiritual experience, or a peculiar focus of some ecclesial outliers.

Which leads me to my fourth and final hope: that these essays will help to dispel what I call the fear of theosis. People rightly worry that the language of deification can sound like a transgression of the firm divide between Creator and creature—no matter how often that concern is addressed and the heretical conclusion shown to be erroneous. I remember one biblical scholar who said, "Humans, especially Americans, already think they are gods and don't need any encouragement in that direction." Fair enough. Good research and theology are needed on this topic. Hence the need for books such as this one.

Finally, I return to this set of essays as a unity, a volume, not merely a collection of individual papers. I am particularly pleased with the strong emphasis on the Holy Spirit throughout much of the book. To be sure, on this matter and others there are differences of perspective and interpretation among the contributors. But together they offer the Church, the churches, and interested others another reminder of the significance of an ancient topic, even as the various authors plow new ground on different theological fields.

# ACKNOWLEDGMENTS

*Paul:* Thanks to my friends at the Lanier Theological Library and Learning Centre at Yarnton Manor, Oxfordshire; they have shown remarkable generosity and hospitality to my wife, Jacqueline, and me during, among other times, the summer of 2023 and then my extended sabbatical in 2024 while I was a visiting scholar at Oriel College, University of Oxford. The quiet and beauty of Manor Farm, its community, and its proximity to Oxford greatly enriched my work on this book project. I am also grateful to Oriel College professors Mark Wynn and William Wood for extending to me the invitation to be a visiting fellow there. I am also indebted to Palm Beach Atlantic University for granting me another splendid sabbatical. Special thanks to my fine wife, Jacqueline, for her sweet friendship and unstinting support during this project and many others over the years.

*Michael:* I am thankful for Joyce—my best friend, lifelong companion, helpmate, and wife. Without her unending support throughout our marriage, especially during these past several years, my academic pursuits generally and this volume particularly could never have materialized. Thanks are also in order to our three children, my greatest joys in this life. May each of you grow in the Lord every day. I am also grateful to my mother, Vino—the first PhD in the family, who instilled a love of writing within me from a young age. And finally, thanks be to the One who does all things well: "For from him and through him and to him are all things. To him be the glory forever. Amen" (Rom 11:36).

*Paul and Michael:* We editors want to express our thanks to our IVP Academic editors Jon Boyd and Rebecca Carhart and other staff involved in this book project. They have been so very kind and professional, at times expending additional effort to bring this project to fruition. It has been a pleasure to work with them all.

# INTRODUCTION

PAUL COPAN AND MICHAEL M. C. REARDON

THE INSPIRATION FOR THIS VOLUME emerged from fellowship over meals with good friends beginning over a decade ago. These conversations led to gatherings at the annual meetings of the Evangelical Theological Society and Evangelical Philosophical Society. This led to copresentations at the Evangelical Theological Society in 2015 and 2016 by this book's coeditor, Paul Copan, and Chris Wilde of the "local churches" and Living Stream Ministry, which are associated with Watchman Nee and his successor Witness Lee—both proponents of the doctrine of deification, and whose theological outlook more closely resembles Paul's tradition (Protestantism) than it does Roman Catholicism or Eastern Orthodoxy.[1] The culmination of these collaborations was a four-paper session examining various portrayals of deification (or *theosis*) in 2022 and a three-year consultation further exploring the doctrine occurring in 2024–2026 at the Evangelical Theological Society.

Such fellowship, however, would not have always been welcome at the Evangelical Theological Society and like-minded groups. Prior to the Second World War, deification was somewhat of a "despised archaism" in the Christian West, especially in Protestant circles.[2] Viewed charitably, it was an eccentricity of Eastern Orthodoxy, but far more often it was portrayed as one of the remnants of a regrettable Hellenized trajectory in patristic Christianity.

This landscape shifted dramatically with the ascendancy of Tuomo Mannermaa's Finnish interpretation of Luther, a rereading of the mercurial monk

---

[1]Both Nee and Lee reject characterizing their ministry or themselves in line with historic traditions (Protestantism, Roman Catholicism, Eastern Orthodoxy, etc.) or denominationalism, and instead identify only as "Christians" or "believers." Care is taken here and elsewhere to acknowledge this preferred identification.

[2]For an excellent overview both of past Protestant distrust of the doctrine of deification and more recent interest in the doctrine, see Paul L. Gavrilyuk, "The Retrieval of Deification: How a Once-Despised Archaism Became an Ecumenical Desideratum," *ModTheo* 25, no. 4 (2009): 647-59.

that linked his doctrine of justification to themes of union, participation, and deification. Beyond causing a stir within Lutheranism, deification has since played a key role in Orthodox-Reformed dialogue, Baptist-Orthodox dialogue, and evangelical soteriologies that aspire to incorporate scriptural statements about participation in God and union with Christ that transcend purely forensic or juridical themes.[3] Additionally, scholars have demonstrated how themes of union and participation can be understood as deification—or at least, intrinsically linked to deification—in a host of significant Protestant thinkers such as John Calvin, Huldrych Zwingli, Peter Martyr Vermigli, Richard Hooker, John Owen, John and Charles Wesley, Jonathan Edwards, Herman Bavinck, C. S. Lewis, T. F. Torrance, Karl Barth, and Robert Jenson.[4]

Today deification is in vogue and does not appear to be going out of fashion any time soon. No fewer than ten collections of essays have been birthed by rapidly emerging interest in the doctrine: (1) *Theosis: Deification in Christian Theology*, Stephen Finlan and Vladmir Kharlamov (2006); (2) *Partakers of the Divine Nature: The History and Development of Deification in the Christian Traditions*, Michael L. Christensen and Jeffrey A. Wittung (2008); (3) *Theosis: Deification in Christian Theology*, vol. 2, Vladmir Kharlamov (2011); (4) *Called to Be Children of God: The Catholic Theology of Human Deification*, David Meconi and Carl E. Olson (2016); (5) *Visions of God and Ideas on Deification in Patristic Thought*, Mark Edwards and Elena Ene D-Vasilescu (2017); (6) *Theosis/Deification: Christian Doctrines of Divinization, East and West*, John Arblaster and Rob Faesen (2018); (7) *Mystical Doctrines of Deification: Case Studies in the Christian Tradition*, John Arblaster and Rob Faesen (2018); (8) *Deification in the Latin Patristic Tradition*, Jared Ortiz (2019); (9) *With All the Fullness of God: Deification in the Christian Tradition*, Jared Ortiz (2021); (10) *The Oxford Handbook of Deification*, Paul L. Gavrilyuk, Andrew Hofer, and Matthew Levering (2024).

---

[3] Carl Mosser, "Orthodox and Reformed Dialogue and the Ecumenical Recovery of Theosis," *EcRev* 73, no. 1 (2021): 131-51; Corneliu C. Simu, "Theosis and Baptist-Orthodox Discussions," *EcRev* 73, no. 1 (2021): 111-30; Robert V. Rakestraw, "Becoming Like God: An Evangelical Doctrine of Theosis," *JETS* 40, no. 2 (1997): 257-69.

[4] For a comprehensive bibliography of these investigations, see Michael Reardon, "Becoming God: Interpreting Pauline Soteriology as Deification," *CurBR* 22, no. 1 (2023): 84.

Introduction xvii

With a plethora of volumes exploring the doctrine already available, one might reasonably inquire why this collection of essays—at least the eleventh in two decades—is needed. To be clear, each of the above projects expands the sphere of research related to deification in promising ways. Notwithstanding this collective strength, nearly all the essays comprising the above volumes discuss the contours and content of deification in one of two ways: (1) as understood in Eastern Orthodox or Roman Catholic contexts or (2) in a manner primarily or completely subsumed under discussions of soteriology.

This volume extends beyond these delimited lines of inquiry. Several essays in this collection, whether explicitly or implicitly, offer tightly focused inquiries into Protestant conceptions of deification (e.g., Lutheran, Reformed, Baptist, Wesleyan, Pentecostal, evangelical). Perhaps even more uniquely, several of these essays contain constructive investigations into the doctrine of deification apart from its relationship to Christian salvation. Concerning this latter feature of the volume, readers will encounter chapters that discuss the fruitfulness of deification in theological education, the similarities and differences between Christian deification and secular transhumanism, the relationship between linguistic translation philosophy and the visibility of deification in Scripture, the presence of deification in theologies emerging from the Global South, how deification is embedded within various scriptural images (e.g., the Levitical grain offering, the body of Christ, and the new Jerusalem), the relationship between the doctrine and Christ's pre-incarnate existence, and so on. These novel and creative investigations, we believe and hope, positively contribute to the ever-growing body of literature about deification.

Part one of this volume is composed of five chapters that explore various scriptural foundations of deification. The first, L. Ann Jervis's "Conformity to Divine Messiah in Paul," expands the discussion of how deification is conceived of by Paul. According to Jervis, Paul is clear that believers are being conformed to Christ, not to God. Nonetheless, this is a form of deification, since for Paul, Christ is divine. Jervis suggests that two aspects of Jesus' identity, which have largely been undiscussed in relation to deification, are crucial to apprehending Paul's conception of who and what believers are being transformed into: (1) that for Paul, Jesus Christ is Messiah, God's saving agent; and (2) that Christ is a divine Messiah, which for Jervis entails that his messiahship was not limited to his earthly life but rather included both his exalted, pre-incarnate life and his eschatological life. This is what Jervis sees in Paul's writings: that believers are being conformed to the totality of this divine Messiah. Believers become, like Christ, those who are eternally obedient to God's saving purpose.

In the next essay, "The Church Is Christ: The *Wirkungsgeschichte* of Interpreting Pauline Soteriology as Ecclesial Deification," Michael M. C. Reardon takes a different approach to examining Paul's notion of deification. According to Reardon, Paul does not limit his notion of deification to the individual believer but rather includes and even prioritizes the corporate dimensions of this salvific transformation. In support of this claim, Reardon surveys nine Christian thinkers who interpret Paul's identification of the church as the body of Christ as referring to what he calls "ecclesial deification." The first six include some of the most significant theologians of the patristic era: Irenaeus of Lyons, Tertullian of Carthage, Origen of Alexandria, Athanasius of Alexandria, Hilary of Poitiers, and Augustine of Hippo. The last three are modern interpreters: Émile Mersch, John Zizioulas, and Witness Lee. Reardon demonstrates both that patristic thinkers consistently interpreted Paul's identification of the church as the body of Christ as referring to ecclesial deification and that this legacy has continued into the modern era by key Christian thinkers existing outside the modern guild of biblical studies.

The third essay, Jacob Chengwei Feng's "Deification Seen from Three Biblical Metaphors in Watchman Nee and Witness Lee with a Cognitive-Linguistic Interpretive Approach to Metaphors," employs cognitive-linguistic analysis to examine how the final interpreter surveyed in the previous essay, Witness Lee, and his better-known senior coworker, Watchman Nee, interpret the scriptural metaphors of grafting, the Levitical grain offering, and the new Jerusalem as deification. Feng's multidisciplinary endeavor demonstrates how both interpreters engage with Scripture in a manner consistent with patristic and postliberal exegesis—that is, with an eye toward utilizing typology and allegory as a means of creating a thick description of doctrinal commitments. Feng also discusses different metaphors for sin: as a burden, a debt, mortality, or, according to Nee and Lee, a shortage of God's glory. This latter connection to glory, Feng suggests, is a second means of arriving at a robust doctrine of deification in light of past studies that persuasively link the doctrine to the glory of God.

In the next chapter, "Deification and the Eschatological City: Exegetical and Theological Connections in Early Christian Thought," Nathan Betz traces the reception history of interpreting the new Jerusalem as a metaphor for deification. Betz's essay begins by surveying the intertwined relationship between Psalm 82—the most significant passage on deification for patristic interpreters—and Revelation 21–22 in the theological outlooks of Justin Martyr, Origen of Alexandria, Cyprian of Carthage, and a lesser-known group, the Naassaenes. He then locates the notions of the city of God, divine filiation, and *visio Dei* (vision of God)—the latter two being core commitments of nearly all historic conceptions of deification—in the writings of Justin Martyr and Irenaeus of Lyons. Betz later demonstrates how this nexus of theological themes was incorporated into the earliest surviving Greek commentaries on the book of Revelation, and he concludes his essay with an admonition for both theological educators and pastoral shepherds to take up these truths and, per the apostle Paul, "not shrink from declaring . . . the whole purpose of God" (Acts 20:27).

The fifth and final essay of part one, Chao-Chun Liu's "Deification in Translation: The Influence of Translation Philosophy on the Visibility of the Doctrine of Deification in Scripture," articulates how the theological outlook of Bible translators can affect the visibility of the doctrine of deification in Scripture throughout history. To demonstrate this claim, Chun Liu engages in a comparative case study of decisions made by the translation teams of the Chinese Union Version (or CUV, the most popular Chinese Bible for the past century) and the Chinese Recovery Version (or CRV, a more recent translation of the Nestle-Aland Greek text) in relation to verses dealing with three key concepts: union with Christ, eternal life, and spiritual growth. This study demonstrates that translators of the CUV, who were primarily drawn from twentieth-century Reformed and evangelical traditions, rendered verses in a manner that both aligned with their theological outlooks and made constitutive components of deification opaque to Chinese-speaking readers. This differs from decisions made by translators of the CRV, who were governed by a different theological outlook and thus rendered verses in a manner that increases the visibility of key themes related to deification for readers.

Part two turns its gaze from the scriptural foundations of deification to examine how the doctrine is incorporated into the intellectual topography of formative Protestant thinkers. Alister E. McGrath leads off this section by detailing how deification might properly describe aspects of the theology of the father of the Reformation, Martin Luther ("Deification or Christification? Martin Luther on Theosis"). McGrath begins by tracing the history of interpretation of Luther in Germany, the so-called German Old School approach, to underscore how strongly past interpreters sought to disassociate both Luther and Lutheran theology from any notion of theosis. Thereafter, he examines three ways by which Luther's use of the theme of theosis might be assessed: lexically (to what extent Luther employs theotic vocabulary), thematically (to what extent Luther incorporates the theme of deification), and doctrinally (whether Luther sees deification as a meta-doctrine that "governs or coordinates the Christian vision of reality"). McGrath ultimately takes what he calls a "cautious and critical approach," in which he proposes that *Christification* rather than theosis most accurately captures Luther's distinctive emphasis of the believer's transformation—especially in relation to her relationship with Christ's death and suffering—while still affirming the possible advantages and utility of reading Luther through the lens of theosis.

In the next chapter, "Deification in the Reformed Tradition from Zwingli to Vermigli," Carl Mosser builds on his previous work on deification to trace the presence of the doctrine in the first two generations of Reformed theologians. Readers may be surprised by the sheer volume and explicitness of deiform language in the writings of Huldrych Zwingli, Johannes Oecolampadius, Martin Bucer, John Calvin, and Peter Martyr Vermigli, not least because of the widespread (mis)conception that Reformed theology "has no room for a soteriology of deification." Mosser, however, does not limit his investigation only to how these thinkers conceived of the salvation of the elect. He further demonstrates that the Reformed churches of the sixteenth century affirmed the conclusions of the Sixth Ecumenical Council pertaining to the deification of Christ's human nature. Thus, Mosser avers, most of these Reformers "were in full agreement with consensual patristic teaching about deification as both a christological and soteriological doctrine."

The volume's eighth essay, James Salladin's "Jonathan Edwards, Theosis, and the Purpose of Creation," poses an important question: How might a recovery of theosis benefit a modern world where power is plentiful but finding meaning is increasingly rare? An answer to this question, Salladin suggests, is found in the writings of Jonathan Edwards, who posited that the purpose of creation was inextricably tied to the communication of God's fullness. For Edwards, this communication of divine fullness, at least in relation to the called saints, is actuated by a "real transformation" in which the nature of the souls of saints is changed through participation in the divine nature. Salladin's articulation of an Edwardsean notion of deification builds on his recent InterVarsity Press publication, *Jonathan Edwards and Deification: Reconciling Theosis and the Reformed Tradition*.

In the next chapter, "John and Charles Wesley on Deification," Mark Gorman extends a line of Methodist scholarship spanning decades that argues that the Wesley brothers, though not employing terms such as *theosis* or *divinization*, held to a notion of scriptural holiness that is participatory, transformational, and aligned with a particular understanding of deification. This notion of deification, per Bobby Rackley, (1) conceives of God desiring true union with humanity, (2) sees the telos of humanity as true Godlikeness, and (3) posits that redeemed humanity participates in the Godhead. In a careful examination of multiple hymns and sermons, Gorman argues that the relationship between perhaps the most famous Wesleyan doctrine, entire sanctification, and deification is, in his verbiage, "almost too obvious." After readers traverse Gorman's account of how the Wesley brothers conceived of humanity's capacity for God, the divine exchange, Christ's threefold office, and the role of the Holy Spirit in empowering believers to participate in the divine nature, it is likely that they will agree with Gorman's bold proposal.

The next essay, Jahdiel Perez's "From *Bios* to *Zoe*: C. S. Lewis on the Doctrine of Deification," turns from more traditional theologians to discuss how deification looms large in the writings of the acclaimed lay theologian and author. Perez begins by examining the meaning and implications of the deific process for Lewis, which, as the title suggests, is imagined in terms of transforming Bios (created and corporeal life) into Zoe, which is "eternal, spiritual, and the kind of life human beings can share with God." Next, he analyzes how Lewis employs the image of a Great Dance to describe both the mutual indwelling of Father, Son, and Spirit and the interaction between God and humanity. Third, Perez investigates whether Lewis conceives of the deific process in a methodological scientific sense or rather as a form of divine art. Last, he probes how Lewis conceives of divine make-believe, that is, the act of formational pretending as a means by which humans are deified.

Part two of the volume concludes with Paul Copan's chapter, "Toward an Evangelical Doctrine of Deification." Copan's essay may be considered to be a microcosm of this volume as a whole. He begins by tracing scriptural themes related to deification, such as humans being created in the *imago Dei*, humans being commissioned as God's priest-kings, and Jesus' identities as the second Adam (new creation) and true Israel (new exodus/covenant). Thereafter, Copan details his personal engagement with the doctrine of deification in the ministry of Watchman Nee and Witness Lee and surveys what he calls "a Protestant theosis tradition" in the writings of Martin Luther, John Calvin, Jonathan Edwards, the Wesley brothers, C. S. Lewis, and others. In line with his chapter's title, Copan waxes hopeful that deification may find its rightful place in the evangelical imagination as a theologically orthodox, biblically faithful, Protestant soteriological outlook.

While each of the above investigations contains fresh approaches to the doctrine of deification, and moreover several of them traverse multiple disciplines, part three of this volume is a collection of five essays that we felt are best characterized, per the volume's subtitle, as "constructive investigations into the doctrine of deification." The first of these essays, Brian Siu Kit Chiu's "Deification as a Theological Foundation and Goal for Formational Theological Education," contends that a robust retrieval of the doctrine of deification could positively affect evangelical theological education. Theological education, for Chiu, is a process of formation whereby students allow Christ to grow and mature within them. This trajectory, he suggests, is identical to patristic conceptions of deification. The first part of Chiu's essay identifies multiple distinctives of deification that he argues will revitalize evangelical theological education in both theory and praxis. The second half of his essay is a case study of a Bible training program associated with the ministry of Watchman Nee and Witness Lee that explicitly takes the actuation of deification in its attendees as one its formational goals.

In the next essay, "Sharing in the Life of God: Considering the Relationship Between Justification and Deification," Ben C. Blackwell takes an explicitly Protestant and participatory approach to examine the intersection of justification and life in Paul's theology. A Pauline view of justification, Blackwell argues, is centered on believers being made alive as a forensic reality. While John Calvin (and later Philipp Melanchthon) distinguishes justification from vivification, Blackwell shows that Martin Luther did not draw any such distinction, thus ensuring that his reorienting of more traditional accounts of justification was thoroughly situated within the Protestant tradition. Due to this nexus of doctrinal connections, Blackwell persuasively demonstrates that deification, which historically is also concerned with being made alive and sharing in God's life, is not incompatible with the forensic nature of justification but rather attends to aspects of the believer's experience on the same soteriological arc.

The next chapter, Veli-Matti Kärkkäinen's "Justification as Union and Christ's Presence: A Lutheran Perspective," similarly discusses Martin Luther and examines the relationship between justification and deification, albeit from a different angle from both McGrath and Blackwell. Kärkkäinen, who himself belongs to the Mannermaa school, takes up the aforementioned Finnish interpretation of Luther and pairs it with insights from both the Orthodox and Roman Catholic traditions to move toward a truly ecumenical understanding of Luther's theology of salvation. This understanding includes the relationship between justification, union with God, and Christ's presence in faith, all of which taken together approximate "materially what the ancient doctrine of theosis means to say." A real strength of this essay, however, is that it advances beyond other accounts of Luther's soteriology by drawing on resources from a trinitarian-pneumatological framework, which, per Kärkkäinen, are often overlooked by Protestants generally and Lutherans specifically.

In the next essay, "Deification and World Christianity: Hesychasm and 'Calling upon the Name of the Lord,'" Shu-chen Hsu Hsiung engages in a comparative exercise of praxes encouraged by fourteenth-century theologian Gregory Palamas and twentieth-century Chinese Christian Witness Lee. Both Palamas and Lee encouraged their followers to engage in prayer of the "Holy Name"—Palamas through hesychasm, which he is perhaps most famous for fiercely defending the orthodoxy of, and Lee through the practice of "calling upon the name of the Lord." Additionally, both thinkers place limitations on deification: for Palamas, human beings can participate in the divine energies but not the divine essence, whereas for Lee humans can become God in "life and nature but not in the Godhead." Hsu Hsiung highlights significant theological differences, however, undergirding what appear to be similar praxes. Whereas Palamas emphasizes the sanctifying effects of actual physical breathing during hesychastic prayer, Lee contends that the organ that breathes while calling upon the name of the Lord is the human spirit alone. Additionally, Hsu Hsiung notes that Palamas and the mystical tradition emphasize silence as a mark of holiness, whereas Lee promotes a spirituality of verbalization and activity.

The final chapter of the volume, Kimbell Kornu's "Transhumanism as Active Effort of Technology Versus Deification as Active Reception of Grace," brings deification into dialogue not with other Christian doctrines but rather the humanistically informed scientific movement known as Humanity+, or transhumanism. Kornu extends a line of inquiry advanced by a handful of scholars who have detected similarities between secular aspirations to escape human fragility through technological means and Christian hopes of salvation through actively receiving grace. Kornu's essay demonstrates at least three intriguing features. First, it illuminates a surprising connection regarding the active reception of a graced nature between seventh-century theologian Maximus the Confessor, one of the most highly cited resources on deification, and nineteenth-century French spiritualist Félix Ravaisson (despite the latter's lack in not accounting for suffering or Christ's role in this transformative process). Second, against other proposals advanced in recent years, Kornu concludes that transhumanism and Christian deification reflect fundamentally incompatible worldviews, as the former requires "muscular effort" to achieve auto-deification whereas the latter actively receives "the grace of God in prayer and in suffering." Last, due to the contrastive roles of moral agency in transhumanism and deification, Kornu argues that they function as "limit cases" for human agency and Christian spirituality.

In the pages that follow, we expect that readers will be both challenged and edified by what can only be described as a buffet of deification-related investigations. While a spectrum of responses to the content of the ensuing collection of essays may exist, these variegated contributions disallow one rejoinder from being spoken forevermore: that is, the notion that deification is not faithfully scriptural or profoundly evangelical. Indeed, our hope is that this volume is the first of many to explore the scriptural foundations of deification and the novel connections between the doctrine and countless other theological/philosophical outlooks, whether Christian or otherwise. Mikhail Bakhtin contends that "great works" speak beyond their temporal situatedness; they are understood in "great time"—that is, in eras beyond their writing—and with this increased understanding, readers of these great works are enabled to discover new semantic depth.[5] The Bible as the most significant narrative of the works of God and the Christian tradition, another sovereignly orchestrated divine work, continue to be a gold mine in which we may explore the unplumbed depths of the inexhaustible riches of God. May we do so. And in doing so, "with unveiled face beholding as in a mirror the glory of the Lord" may we be "transformed into the same image from glory to glory, even as from the Lord the Spirit" (2 Cor 3:18, ASV).

---

[5] See Mikhail M. Bakhtin, "Response to a Question from the *Novy Mir* Editorial Staff," in *Speech Genres and Other Late Essays*, ed. Caryl Emerson and Michael Holquist, trans. Vern W. McGee (Austin: University of Texas Press, 1986), 4-5.

# ABBREVIATIONS

**ANCIENT SOURCES**

| | |
|---|---|
| Cels. | Origen, *Contra Celsum* |
| Dial. | Justin Martyr, *Dialogus cum Tryphone* |
| Haer. | Irenaeus, *Adversus haereses* |
| Hom. Ezech. | Origen, *Homiliae in Ezechielem* |
| Inc. | Athanasius, *De incarnatione* |

**MODERN SOURCES**

| | |
|---|---|
| ACW | Ancient Christian Writers |
| ANF | *The Ante-Nicene Fathers: Translations of the Writings of the Fathers Down to A.D. 325.* Edited by Alexander Roberts and James Donaldson. 10 vols. 1885–1887 |
| BETL | Bibliotheca Ephemeridum Theologicarum Lovaniensium |
| BZNW | Beihefte zur Zeitschrift für die neutestamentliche Wissenschaft |
| CCNT | *The Conference Commentary on the New Testament* |
| CRV | Chinese Recovery Version |
| CurBR | *Currents in Biblical Research* |
| CUV | Chinese Union Version |
| CWWL | Witness Lee. *Collected Works of Witness Lee*. 138 vols. Anaheim, CA: Living Stream Ministry, 2020 |
| CWWN | Watchman Nee, *Collected Works of Watchman Nee*. 66 vols. Anaheim, CA: Living Stream Ministry, 1993 |
| EcRev | *The Ecumenical Review* |
| FC | Fathers of the Church |
| JETS | *Journal of the Evangelical Theological Society* |
| LW | *Luther's Works* [American edition]. 82 vols. planned. St. Louis: Concordia; Philadelphia: Fortress, 1955–1986, 2009 |
| ModTheo | *Modern Theology* |

| | |
|---|---|
| NPNF | *A Select Library of Nicene and Post-Nicene Fathers of the Christian Church*. Edited by Philip Schaff and Henry Wace. 28 vols. in 2 series. 1886–1889 |
| OECS | Oxford Early Christian Studies |
| PG | Patrologia Graeca [= *Patrologiae Cursus Completus: Series Graeca*]. Edited by Jacques-Paul Migne. 162 vols. Paris, 1857–1886 |
| SC | Sources Chrétiennes |
| *SJT* | *Scottish Journal of Theology* |
| WA | *D. Martin Luthers Werke: Kritische Gesamtausgabe*. 73 vols. Weimar: Hermann Böhlaus Nachfolger, 1883–2009 |
| WABR | *D. Martin Luthers Werke, Kritische Gesamtausgabe. Briefwechsel*. 18 vols. Weimar, 1930–1985 |
| WJE | Works of Jonathan Edwards. 26 vols. New Haven, CT: Yale University Press, 1957– |
| *WJW* | John Wesley. *The Works of John Wesley*. Nashville: Abingdon, 1975– |
| WUNT | Wissenschaftliche Untersuchungen zum Neuen Testament |

# PART 1

# BIBLICAL FOUNDATIONS

# CONFORMITY to DIVINE MESSIAH in PAUL

## L. Ann Jervis

INHERENT TO THE CONVERSATION about deification is the question: Into whom are the being-deified being deified? David Litwa rightly notes that *deification* etymologically means something like "God-making."[1] This raises the question of the character and identity of the deity into whom humans are made. This essay offers a perspective on deification in Paul by focusing on to whom it is that Paul thinks believers are transformed.

It is plain to me that Paul thinks that the faithful are in the process of being changed into the likeness of Christ. Paul says as much in Romans 8:29. Moreover, I regard Paul's prevalent union-with-Christ theme as chief among the ways Paul indicates his conviction that the faithful take on the life of Christ. As the apostle says in Galatians, "I have been crucified with Christ. It is no longer I who live, but Christ who lives in me" (Gal 2:20 ESV). Though connecting deification with Paul's union-with-Christ emphasis is certainly not a consensus view among Pauline scholars, I will not here argue for it.[2] Rather,

---

[1] David Litwa, *We Are Being Transformed: Deification in Paul's Soteriology* (Boston: de Gruyter, 2012), 6. Litwa summarizes well the evidence for treating Paul's soteriology as a form of deification (11-13).

[2] Recently, Teresa Morgan in particular has challenged the idea that Paul's "in Christ" theme has anything to do with participation in the person of Christ, let alone with deification. See Morgan, *Being "in Christ" in the Letters of Paul: Saved Through Christ and in His Hands* (Tübingen: Mohr Siebeck, 2020). On the other hand, see Albert Schweitzer and those influenced by him. Though not using the terminology of *deification*, Schweitzer speaks of those in union with Christ as "those who by transformation have taken on the resurrection mode of existence, which is thought of as eternal." See Schweitzer, *The Mysticism of Paul the Apostle*, trans. William Montgomery (Baltimore: Johns Hopkins University Press, 1998), 94.

my starting point is that Paul conceived of union with Christ as allowing for transformation into Christ, whom Paul understood to be the divine Son of God. To clarify: I take it that Paul regards Christ as divine, that the faithful are in the process of transformation from one degree of glory to another (that is, transformation into Christ's image [2 Cor 3:18]), and so it is appropriate to speak of conformity to Christ under the category of deification.

To talk about deification in Paul is, then, to raise the question of the identity of Christ. This question quickly becomes: To what aspect of Christ's life are believers conformed? Is conformity exclusively to Christ's incarnate life, or does it include conformity to his life prior to and subsequent to his incarnation? I suggest that since the apostle's understanding of Christ's life with God and so his divinity defines Paul's understanding of Christ's human life, we must take this into consideration when thinking about deification. It is Christ's divine, nonhuman existence that shapes the apostle's understanding of Christ's human life.[3] The obvious fact that Paul talks much less about the human Christ than about the risen and exalted Christ (and also about Christ prior to incarnation) underscores this. When we talk about deification in Paul—that is, becoming like Christ—we need to include, if not focus on, the Christ that Paul focuses on: the one who was in the form of God (Phil 2:6), who lives at God's right hand (Rom 8:34), and who is highly exalted (Phil 2:9).[4] That is, since Christ in Paul is primarily the being who lives with God, our understanding of who it is who believers are transformed into must take this into account. There has to my knowledge been little investigation of Christ's nonincarnate life in regard to deification. This is the focus of my essay.

I begin with the observation that, curious though it may be, Pauline interpreters regularly speak of deification in the same breath as assimilation to

---

[3] I work in this essay with only the undisputed letters. Consequently, I do not take into account a passage such as Col 2:9. (Gordon Fee's claim that Paul thinks Christ is divine in his incarnated life relies heavily on the disputed letters. See Fee, *Pauline Christology: An Exegetical-Theological Study* [Peabody, MA: Hendrickson, 2007], esp. 500-512.) It remains a matter of controversy what Paul means in the undisputed letters when he writes that Christ came in the likeness of human flesh or in the form of a servant. A passage such as Gal 4:4 demonstrates Paul's opacity: the apostle does not in any way make explicit that when God's Son is born of a woman the Son maintains his divinity, though that God's Son is able to redeem those under the law might imply that he does.

[4] Below I make observations on Phil 3:10-11.

Christ. This oddity rightly assumes that Paul thinks of Christ as divine but wrongly conveys the idea that Paul does not make a distinction between Christ and God.[5] We should, however, maintain clarity about the fact that for Paul the faithful are being deified into the likeness not of God the Father but of Jesus Christ, God's Son. The ancient world (both Jews and non-Jews) conceived there to be many deities inhabiting the cosmos.[6] I suggest that Paul thought of Jesus Christ as a divinity superior to all others, apart from God the Father.

As just mentioned, I contend that union with Christ, which allows for conformity to Christ, is for Paul much more expansive than conformity with Christ's earthly life. It involves, and essentially so, conformity to Christ's exalted life, life which includes all of Christ's time—Christ's time prior to his incarnation, the time of his incarnated life, and the time of his life post-resurrection.[7] To be noted is that when Paul describes conformity to aspects of Christ's earthly life, Christ's exalted life literally and conceptually surrounds Christ's incarnated life. The curious order in Philippians 3:10 perhaps demonstrates this most clearly. After Paul declares that he seeks to know Christ, the apostle states his longing to know the power of Christ's resurrection before describing his desire to share Christ's sufferings and to be conformed to Christ's death. Paul continues by expressing hope to attain resurrection from the dead.[8] Here we see that Paul wraps reference to conforming to aspects of Christ's incarnated life with references to Christ's exalted life.

Paul marries baptism with Christ's death to the possibility of walking in newness of life/resurrection life (Rom 6:3-4). The apostle describes the consequence of being crucified with Christ as Christ living in him (Gal 2:21). He then goes on to describe Christ (the Son of God) as the one who gave himself, that is, died (Gal 2:21). Since the one who died lives in Paul, again, crucifixion

---

[5] For instance, Michael Gorman's contribution to recognizing theosis (the term Gorman chooses for deification) in Paul focuses on conformity to Christ while claiming that for Paul "God has the same shape as Jesus." See Gorman, *Inhabiting the Cruciform God: Kenosis, Justification, and Theosis in Paul's Narrative Soteriology* (Grand Rapids, MI: Eerdmans, 2009), 34.

[6] See Paula Fredricksen, "How High Can Early High Christology Be?," in *Monotheism and Christology in Greco-Roman Antiquity*, ed. Matthew V. Novenson (Leiden: Brill, 2020), 292-319.

[7] See L. Ann Jervis, *Paul and Time: Life in the Temporality of Christ* (Grand Rapids, MI: Baker Academic, 2023).

[8] Does the curious εἰς τὴν ἐξανάστασιν (Phil 3:11) signal Paul's understanding that his resurrection will be derivative of Christ's?

is enveloped by life; conformity is not to Christ's earthly life except as that life is defined by Christ's resurrected and exalted (divine) life. Such is the dynamic also in Galatians 5:24-25: belonging to Christ means not only crucifying the flesh but living by the Spirit. Boasting in the cross of Lord Jesus Christ, through which the world is crucified to Paul and vice versa, means new creation (Gal 6:14-15). The cross—an event in Christ's earthly life—only means something in light of its power to introduce new creation. Conformity to Christ is more expansive than conformity to his earthly life.

In search of greater clarity about the character of Pauline deification, I will discuss two features of Christ's identity. These are features that, as far as I can tell, have not had much play in the conversation. I summarize these features here and expand on them shortly.

The first is that Paul understands the term *Christ* to mean "Messiah." While the apostle understood Messiah in light of Jesus crucified, risen, and exalted rather than within the boundaries of Jewish expectations, the fact of Paul's abundant use of the word Χριστός indicates that he, along with his fellow Jews, conceives of Messiah as God's saving agent.[9] Paul's choice to emphasize heavily that Jesus is Messiah, that is, God's redeemer, must be a significant factor in our understanding of the being into whom the faithful are transformed. As far as I can tell, this understanding is very rarely brought into conversation with the topic of deification in Paul.

The other feature of Christ's identity to which I draw attention is that, for the apostle, Jesus is a *divine* Messiah.[10] Paul conceived that though for a few decades Jesus Messiah had an earthly sojourn, Jesus Messiah lives with the eternal God. I propose that, for Paul, Jesus is Messiah not only when he is on

---

[9] As Peter Schäfer writes: "'Messianism' denotes the belief in a salvation figure (savior, redeemer) who terminates the present order and ushers in a new order of justice and blessing. Very often, but not always, the establishment of the new order is connected with the notion of the eschaton." See Schäfer, "Diversity and Interactions: Messiahs in Early Judaism," in *Toward the Millennium: Messianic Expectations from the Bible to Waco*, ed. Peter Schäfer and Mark R. Cohen (Leiden: Brill, 1998), 15. Matthew Novenson comments on the relatively rare occurrence of Χριστός in the literature of early Judaism compared with the extensive occurrence of Χριστός in Paul. See Novenson, *Christ Among the Messiahs: Christ Language in Paul and Messiah Language in Ancient Judaism* (Oxford: Oxford University Press, 2012), 2.

[10] See also Matthew Thiessen, who intriguingly writes that "believers in Jesus participate in [Messiah's] divinity even as they await the resurrection." Thiessen, *A Jewish Paul: The Messiah's Herald to the Gentiles* (Grand Rapids, MI: Baker Academic, 2023), 126.

earth but always. That is, both Christ's life prior to his incarnation and his exalted life are as Messiah. It is, then, not that Jesus is Messiah only during his human life and/or as an eschatological Messiah. Jesus is divine Messiah.

## THE DISTINCTION BETWEEN GOD AND CHRIST IN PAUL

My contention that Paul thinks that Christ is divine is not to say that the apostle thinks of Christ and God as one and the same. Rather, it seems abundantly clear that Paul thinks that though both are divine, there is a clear distinction between God and Christ. Paul's differentiation between God and Christ is clear, for instance, in 1 Corinthians 8:5-8, where, in the context of acknowledging that there are many so-called gods, Paul says that for "us" there is one God the Father and one Lord Jesus Christ. Clearly, Paul identifies both God and Jesus Christ as divine, in distinction from the so-called gods. However, while God and Christ share divinity, they are distinct from each other. God is the one from whom all things are and for whom "we" exist, whereas, though Christ also is the one through whom are all things, unlike God, it is through Christ that "we" are. Both are divine, and they are cocreators, but God is the divine being *unto* whom we are, whereas Christ is the one *through* whom we are. God is the one to whom we are to look exclusively, and so, in the patriarchal framework of Paul's day, he is designated Father. Christ, on the other hand, is the conduit allowing us to be what we should be/can be for God. Also to be noted is that Paul envisions Christ at the eschaton subjecting himself to God. This clarifies that there is a distinction between God and Christ (1 Cor 15:28). First Corinthians 3:23 summarizes it this way: "you are Christ's, and Christ is God's" (ESV).

Whether or not the customary term *deification* is the best label for Paul's conformity-to-Christ theme, for the sake of intellectual clarity it is important to recognize that Paul does not collapse the identities of God and Christ. It is to conformity with Christ (not God) that Paul beckons his hearers.[11]

To Paul's understanding of Christ we now turn more fully.

---

[11] This is one of the factors that distinguish the disputed from the undisputed letters; see Eph 5:1. Ben Blackwell's important contribution helpfully names this Pauline theme *Christosis*. See Blackwell, *Christosis: Engaging Paul's Soteriology with His Patristic Interpreters* (Grand Rapids, MI: Eerdmans, 2011).

## Christ as Messiah

I, along with some others, propose that the word Χριστός has messianic meaning for Paul.[12] This is not the standard understanding. Most Pauline scholars follow Wilhelm Bousset and many others who claim that Paul understands Χριστός simply to be Jesus' other name.[13] Andrew Chester is of this ilk, and his words may serve to summarize this viewpoint: "Paul uses Χριστός . . . almost entirely as a proper name . . . , not as a title as such."[14] This dismissal of messianic meaning for Christ extends, of course, to Paul's union-with-Christ theme.[15]

I concur with Matthew Novenson and Thomas Hewitt that Paul uses Χριστός messianically and does so in conversation with Scripture.[16] As Hewitt writes, "Paul was a participant in ancient Jewish messiah discourse."[17] Jews who took part in messianic discourse spoke about a savior who acted in obedience to God and for the sake of God's saving purposes. Likewise, Novenson considers that Paul means something messianic when using Χριστός. While Novenson's contribution does not extend to defining exactly what Messiah means for Paul, his claim, based on a wide survey of ancient texts, that Messiah means something honorific and refers to someone "who is and who should be in charge" is immensely helpful.[18]

I take it, then, that the word *Christ* signifies for Paul something important and essential about Jesus' identity: Jesus as Messiah is one who acts on God's behalf and has done something victorious, worthy of honor. He is the one who should reign. A significant factor in how Paul makes sense of Jesus is as the obedient Savior from God—the one who does God's saving will.

---

[12]See also Adela Yarbro Collins, who notes that *Christ* means "Messiah" for Paul. Adela Yarbro Collins and John J. Collins, *King and Messiah as Son of God: Divine, Human, and Angelic Messianic Figures in Biblical and Related Literature* (Grand Rapids, MI: Eerdmans, 2008), 122.

[13]Wilhelm Bousset, *Kyrios Christos: A History of the Belief in Christ from the Beginnings of Christianity to Irenaeus*, trans. John E. Steely (New York: Abingdon, 1970), 121.

[14]Andrew Chester, "Messianism, Mediators, and Pauline Christology," in *Messiah and Exaltation*, WUNT 207 (Tübingen: Mohr Siebeck, 2007), 382.

[15]J. Thomas Hewitt writes: "Modern interpreters of Paul have almost universally ignored the category 'messiah' when describing Paul's use of the phrase ἐν Χριστῷ even though Χριστός means 'messiah.'" Hewitt, *Messiah and Scripture: Paul's "In Christ" Idiom in Its Ancient Jewish Context*, WUNT 522 (Tübingen: Mohr Siebeck, 2020), 2.

[16]Novenson, *Christ Among the Messiahs*; Hewitt, *Messiah and Scripture*.

[17]Hewitt, *Messiah and Scripture*, 58.

[18]Matthew Novenson, *The Grammar of Messianism: An Ancient Jewish Political Idiom and Its Users* (Oxford: Oxford University Press, 2017), 272.

Paul, however, filled out the contours and content of *Christ* not with previous conceptions of Messiah but with his conceptions of Jesus himself. Consequently, in addition to agreeing with Novenson and Hewitt, I find myself sharing strange scholarly company with Nils Dahl, who is famous for his statement, "Paul's letters represent a strikingly advanced stage in the evolution that transformed *Christos* from a messianic designation to Jesus' second proper name." It is when Dahl states that "the messiahship of Jesus is essential to the inner coherence of [Paul's] Christology" that I am in hearty agreement. Dahl writes: "The messiahship of Jesus had for Paul himself a greater significance than emerges directly from the usage of the name 'Christ' in his epistles." Moreover, Dahl thinks that the apostle's convictions about the identity of Jesus are shaped primarily by the life of the earthly Jesus, which was one of "humiliation, obedience, and suffering."[19] As Dahl writes, "The title received its content from the person to whom it referred, more than from a preconceived notion of what the Messiah would be like."[20] With this also I agree, though, as I will emphasize, the person Paul understands Christ to be is not only the crucified but also the divine Messiah.

Before proceeding, it is important to take time to distinguish my understanding from that of another voice—N. T. Wright. To say that Wright's work emphasizes that for Paul Χριστός means Messiah would be a major understatement. Ever since his Oxford DPhil thesis, "The Messiah and the People of God" (1980), Wright's claim that *Christ* means "Messiah" for Paul has been an essential foundation of his voluminous output. Impressively, Wright takes into account the fact that Paul regularly uses the word *Christ* in prepositional phrases. According to Wright, the meaning of phrases that combine Christ with the prepositions ἐν, εἰς, σύν, and διά is that the Messiah is by definition incorporative: "The 'incorporative' thought . . . is best explained in terms of his belief that Jesus was Israel's Messiah."[21] Wright argues that Paul, on the basis of ideas about kingship in ancient Israel, understands the

---

[19]Nils Dahl, "The Messiahship of Jesus in Paul," in *Jesus the Christ: The Historical Origins of Christological Doctrine*, ed. Donald H. Juel (Minneapolis: Fortress, 1991), 18, 21, 19, italics original.
[20]Nils Dahl, "The Crucified Messiah and the Endangered Promises," in Dahl, *Jesus the Christ*, 65.
[21]N. T. Wright, *Paul and the Faithfulness of God*, Christian Origins and the Question of God 4 (London: SPCK, 2013), 825. See N. T. Wright, *The Climax of the Covenant: Christ and the Law in Pauline Theology* (Minneapolis: Fortress, 1991), 44.

meaning of *Messiah* as the representative of the whole people of God.[22] Wright claims that for Paul "*Jesus, as Messiah, has drawn together the identity and vocation of Israel upon himself.*"[23] Wright is to be commended not only for offering a reading of Χριστός that was (and is) very much against the scholarly grain but for recognizing that his reading had to make sense of the theme of union with Christ.

I agree with Wright that Paul understood Χριστός to mean "Messiah" and with his recognition that this opinion must make sense of the prepositional Christ phrases and with Paul's union-with-Christ theme in general. However, I do not agree that, for Paul, Jesus Messiah is the representative of Israel.[24] Apart from the problem that this leads inescapably to supersessionism (the church replaces Israel), this view rests on understanding messiahship as tied entirely to Jesus' earthly life (including his resurrection). Wright's Messiah is a historical person linked inextricably to the historical life of Israel and Israel's expectations. What Wright misses in my view is that, for Paul, Jesus' messiahship is not confined to his earthly and resurrected life. Only if this is missed can Wright make his famous claims that what Israel expected from God is what God did for Messiah as the representative of Israel, and that Messiah and election are of a piece so that the church is Messiah's, the people of the Messiah.[25] However, when we see that Paul thought that Jesus was the divine Messiah, Wright's claims no longer hold. To that we now turn.

## Messiah as Divine in Paul

There is a deep and widespread assumption that for Paul *Messiah* meant exclusively the human Jesus. As just mentioned, Wright assumes this. He describes Χριστός as "the same human being" as Jesus, "the man from

---

[22] It is to be noted that in *Paul and the Faithfulness of God*, Wright changes his mind, acknowledging about his use of texts from 2 Samuel that "I do not now think (as I once did) that these interesting biblical passages themselves constitute the explanation for [Paul's] usage" (830). Matthew Novenson and J. Thomas Hewitt rightly criticize Wright's understanding of the origin of Paul's "in Christ" theme. See Novenson and Hewitt, "Participationism and Messiah Christology in Paul," in *God and the Faithfulness of Paul: A Critical Examination of the Pauline Theology of N. T. Wright*, ed. Cristoph Heilig, J. Thomas Hewitt, and Michael F. Bird (Minneapolis: Fortress, 2017), 393-416, here 395-401.

[23] Wright, *Paul and the Faithfulness of God*, 825, italics original.

[24] Wright, *Climax of the Covenant*, 46.

[25] Wright, *Climax of the Covenant*, 47; *Paul and the Faithfulness of God*, 815, 833.

Nazareth, who died on the cross and rose again as a human being, and through whose human work, Paul believed Israel's God had achieved his long purposes."[26] Interestingly, in service of Dahl's apt claim that Paul does not conceive of Jesus as Messiah in light of a "previously fixed conception," Dahl assumes that Paul understands Messiah "from the person and work of Jesus Christ" and that "for Paul the earthly Jesus is the Christ."[27] That is, Dahl, unlike Wright, proposes that *Christ* for Paul was on the way to becoming a second name, yet he nevertheless shares with Wright the opinion that Paul identified Messiah with Jesus' human life.

I offer the view that Paul's understanding of Jesus Messiah included not only his human life but also his life as a divinity with God. That is, for Paul, Jesus' incarnation is the human manifestation of the divine Messiah.[28] There is not space to argue for this view in depth. However, there are two features of Paul's thought that I think validate it.

The first is that perhaps Paul's most explicit description of the nature of conformity to the incarnate Christ (Phil 3:10-11) is based on a claim that Jesus Christ was ἐν μορφῇ θεοῦ (Phil 2:6). Being in the form of God is not to be God. I hear this phrase aligning with what I noted earlier—Paul distinguishes between God and Jesus Christ. However, being in the form of God does indicate divinity.[29] April Deconick hears Paul well in this passage: Jesus comes from heaven as God's manifestation.[30] Jörg Frey's suggestion that Philippians 2:6-11 echoes "Greco-Roman concepts of the epiphany of gods who simply appear in human shape or undergo a metamorphosis which implies a mere temporal, and not real, change" hits the mark in terms of Philippians 2:6a.[31] There is, of course, a conversation to be had about whether this view accords with what Paul goes on to say about Christ emptying himself and taking the form of a servant. Since our focus is on what

---

[26]Wright, *Climax of the Covenant*, 46.
[27]Dahl, "Messiahship of Jesus in Paul," 17, 19.
[28]As noted above, it is unclear whether this entails for Paul that the incarnate Christ is at once both divine and human.
[29]So also Wright, "Jesus Christ Is Lord: Philippians 2:5-11," in Wright, *Climax of the Covenant*.
[30]April Deconick, "The One God Is No Simple Matter," in Novenson, *Monotheism and Christology*, 266.
[31]Jörg Frey, "Between Jewish Monotheism and Proto-trinitarian Relations: The Making and Character of Johannine Christology," in Novenson, *Monotheism and Christology*, 210.

Paul thought of Christ's life in addition to that of his human sojourn, I will not discuss whether Paul thought that when Christ poured himself out, he changed from being divine to being only and entirely human. I do, however, note that Romans 1:3 and Galatians 4:4 indicate that Paul thought that during his incarnated life, Jesus Christ was truly a human being.

While it is several paragraphs after the reference to ἐν μορφῇ θεοῦ (Phil 2:6) that Paul details aspects of conforming to aspects of the incarnate life of Christ (Phil 3:8-11), this latter passage should be understood in light of what Paul has declared: that the one to whom he would conform is in the form of God. It is further to be noted that Paul names that one as Christ Jesus (Phil 2:5). Wright, interestingly, ignores this fact, stating instead that Paul talks about "the one who was eternally 'equal with God,'" and the "pre-existent one."[32] Wright's stance here is most likely linked to his assumption that Paul understood Messiah to refer to the human Jesus. I suggest, however, that we take Paul's words straight up: it is "Christ Jesus" who is in the form of God.[33] Furthermore, Jesus Christ is highly exalted. Messiah, in other words, lives life both as a divinity with God and as a human. He is not only Messiah when living a human life.

The second feature of Paul's thought indicating that he considers the Messiah to be divine is that Messiah and Son of God are for the apostle the same being.[34] This is seen clearly in Romans 1:3-4, where the descendant of David (an obvious reference to a messiah) is God's Son. We might further note that the project of God's Son is to redeem (Gal 4:4)—a messianic task. Since Paul demonstrates that he thinks the Son of God is divine when he writes that God sent his Son (Gal 4:4; Rom 8:3), this is corroborative evidence that for the apostle Messiah (the same being as the Son) is divine.[35]

---

[32] Wright, *Climax of the Covenant*, 90.
[33] Thiessen comes close to this view (though not on the basis of Philippians; Thiessen uses 1 Cor 10 and Gal 4:4), stating, "the Messiah for Paul is a divine being of some sort even before his enfleshment as a human" (*Jewish Paul*, 114).
[34] Adela Yarbro Collins rightly states that for Paul "'son of God' is equivalent to 'messiah'" (Collins and Collins, *King and Messiah as Son of God*, 106).
[35] Fee opines that in Gal 4:4 Paul is speaking of "the eternal Son of God . . . and that Christ is himself divine," and that Rom 8:3 refers to "God's sending the eternal Son" (*Pauline Christology*, 213, 245). J. L. Martyn is more reticent. Gal 4:4 refers both to the Son's this-worldly and otherworldly character. However, Martyn seems to undercut this reticence when he speaks of the Son's sending as "an invasion of cosmic scope, reflecting the apocalyptic certainty that

It is, then, not only that Jesus Messiah, Son of God, is exalted after his work on earth is done. Rather, the human sojourn of Jesus Messiah was the earthly manifestation of the divine Jesus Messiah. This is a larger claim than that Paul thought of Jesus as existing with God prior to his incarnation.[36] Though Paul states only that God is eternal (Rom 1:20), I propose that Paul understands Jesus Messiah to be divine, which by implication means that he too is eternal.[37]

Wright wrote a fine and important article on Philippians 2:5-11, by which he convinced me that the rare word ἁρπαγμός in Philippians 2:6 indicates the attitude of taking advantage of a status. Wright contends that in this verse Paul is saying that Christ Jesus "did not regard his equality with God *as something to be used for his own advantage*." In other words, Christ Jesus was equal to God prior to his kenotic journey. I puzzle, however, over Wright's resistance to accepting Paul's own designation of the person who is equal to God prior to his kenosis. Wright speaks of "the pre-existent one . . . eternally 'equal with God.'" Yet, Paul says plainly that it is Christ Jesus who emptied himself. It is not an unidentified person who emptied himself and then, as Wright says, "*became* Jesus." Wright's resistance here may stem from his assumption that being the Messiah equals being a human. This is strongly indicated by Wright's declaration that "[Philippians 2] has nothing to do with the idea of a pre-existent *man* (hence, *a fortiori*, it does not refer either to a pre-existent *Messiah*)."[38]

However, in Philippians 2, Paul seems quite plainly to consider Messiah as living a divine life not only after his obedient death and exaltation but also prior to his incarnation, and living that pre-incarnation life not as an unidentified eternal being but as Messiah Jesus. We see something similar in 1 Corinthians 10:4, where Paul claims that Christ was the rock from which "our fathers" drank when they were with Moses in the wilderness.[39] At the

---

redemption has come from outside, changing the very world in which human beings live . . . in this sense the Son is a distinctly other-worldly figure who has his origin in God." Martyn, *Galatians* (New York: Doubleday, 1997), 408. Martyn's view that the Son's origin is in God would seem to accord with understanding the Son of God as divine.

[36]Thiessen hears Paul well: "God's son preexisted his birth" (*Jewish Paul*, 72). I am saying this and more.

[37]Chris Tilling rightly distinguishes between being preexistent and being eternal. See Tilling, *Paul's Divine Christology* (Tübingen: Mohr Siebeck, 2012), 37. My suggestion is that since Paul thinks Messiah is divine, it is not only that the Messiah preexisted but that he always exists.

[38]Wright, "Jesus Christ Is Lord: Philippians 2:5-11," 79, 90, 94, 96, italics original.

[39]Matthew Thiessen writes, "Paul's claim that the wilderness rock was Christ contains within it a surprisingly high christological implication: by claiming that the rock was Christ, Paul identifies

least this passage conveys that Paul understood Christ as present to and sustaining of Israel long before the human Jesus. Paul's description of the Messiah offering life-saving sustenance during Israel's wilderness wandering indicates that he thinks of Messiah as a divine being who existed at least as far back as the time of Moses.

Second Corinthians 8:9 names "our Lord Jesus Christ" as the one who, though he was rich, for our sake became poor. There may be a few assumptions on the part of readers that obstruct hearing what Paul says: that it was our Lord Jesus Messiah who though he was rich became poor. I have named one assumption in connection with Wright: that Messiah refers only to a human person. There are also the assumptions that the name *Jesus* refers to a human person and that for Jesus, "Lord" is a status that occurs only after exaltation. Though controversial, I hear Paul saying that it is Lord Jesus Christ who was rich, that is, lived with God, yet for our sakes became poor, that is, became incarnate.

Likewise, when Paul in Romans 1:3-4 identifies Jesus Christ our Lord as God's Son, I hear the apostle signifying that the divine Son of God is Jesus Christ our Lord. This strongly implies that there always is Jesus Christ our Lord. When the apostle says in 1 Corinthians 8:6 that there is one Lord Jesus Christ, through whom are all things and through whom we exist, I take Paul to be naming the Lord Jesus Christ as the eternal being who partnered with God in creation.

Paul, I propose, understood Jesus as the divine Messiah who, at a particular historical moment, was revealed in the flesh of a human person.[40]

## Conclusion

I offer here the idea that to affirm that Paul's thought of conformity to Christ as a form of deification is at once to explore who Paul thought Christ to be. I suggest that unless we think the apostle thought of Christ as divine, we cannot talk about deification in Paul, since the apostle only talks about

---

Christ with Israel's God. Just as ancient Israelites could envisage God becoming embodied in numerous objects (even at the same time), Paul envisages Christ becoming embodied in a rock." Thiessen, "'The Rock Was Christ': The Fluidity of Christ's Body in 1 Cor. 10.4," *Journal for the Study of the New Testament* 36 (2013): 121.

[40] As mentioned, I do not engage here with conversation about what Paul thought concerning the nature of the incarnate Christ—whether the human Christ was both fully human and divine to one degree or another. I do find it interesting that Paul does not allude to Jesus' miracles.

conformity to Christ, not to God. My exploration of Paul's identification of Jesus as Messiah and my contention that the apostle understood Messiah as divine (and almost certainly as eternal) invites further reflection. If this is correct, does it say that obedience to God's saving will is not only the fundamental and eternal character of Christ/Messiah but is also to be the fundamental shape of those joined to him? Even, perhaps, that the shape of eternal life is obedience to God?

Is Paul's stress on faith (understood as obedience [Rom 1:5]) the result of his conviction that Jesus is Messiah, the obedient one who does the will of God?[41] That is, does Paul understand faith itself as an enactment of conformity to Jesus Messiah? (Gal 3:26 might be read this way.) Does Paul think that those joined to Christ take on messianic roles? Is there a distinction between Christ's work when he was human Messiah and what is possible and/or expected of believers?[42] Perhaps the most difficult question is: When Paul speaks about believers' transformation from one degree of glory to another (2 Cor 3:18), is he talking about ontological transformation? If so, does this lead finally to there being no distinction between God and those joined to Christ?[43] (Does 1 Cor 15:28 imply that this is the case?) As always, deep study of Paul raises from the depths not only treasures but opportunities for new adventures for our minds and hearts.

With the lens of deification, asking what deity Paul thinks the faithful are made into puts our gaze right where Paul's is: on the divine Messiah Jesus, whose focus in turn is solely, completely, unalterably, and eternally on doing God's saving will.

---

[41] Paul's understanding of the faithfulness/obedience of Christ includes Christ's faithfulness in his life with God beyond his incarnate life. This will be incontrovertibly demonstrated at the eschaton, when Christ hands over the kingdom to God the Father and subjects himself to God (1 Cor 15:24-28). See Jervis, *Paul and Time*, 84-85.

[42] See my reflections on this in *Paul and Time*. In that book I also reflect on how the human experiences of suffering and physical death are transformed by living in Christ.

[43] There is important conversation about the degree or kind of ontological transformation Paul might be talking about. Litwa reviews various understandings, from metaphorical deification to becoming divine (*We Are Being Transformed*, 6-10). See also the unpublished dissertation by Michael Reardon, "'So Also Is the Christ': Ecclesial Deification in Pauline Soteriology" (PhD diss., Toronto School of Theology, 2023).

# THE CHURCH IS CHRIST

## The *Wirkungsgeschichte* of Interpreting Pauline Soteriology as Ecclesial Deification

### Michael M. C. Reardon

THE CONTENT AND TELOS of Pauline soteriology is perennially debated. Scholars contend whether Paul's notion of salvation is forensic or participatory, salvation-historical or apocalyptic, predicated on faith alone or inclusive of good works, sourced from the Greco-Roman milieu or Pharisaic Judaism, and so on. This chapter wades into this fraught discussion with yet another proposal, which in fact is not new but rather ancient—that is, a particular understanding of the doctrine of deification.

The notion that deification is synonymous with Christian salvation was near-universally affirmed by the early church, even to the point of providing a common foundation for conciliar pronouncements. For example, Athanasius of Alexandria, the foremost opponent of Arian Christology at Nicaea, used deification as a vehicle to advance his claims about the deity of the Son and of the Holy Spirit:

> But this would not have come to pass, had the Word been a creature.... For man had not been deified if joined to a creature, or unless the Son were very God.... And as we had not been delivered from sin and the curse, unless it had been by nature human flesh, which the Word put on (for we should have had nothing common with what was foreign), so also the man had not been deified, unless the Word who became flesh had been by nature from the Father and true and proper to Him. For therefore the union was of this kind, that He might

unite what is man by nature to Him who is in the nature of the Godhead, and his salvation and deification might be sure. (*Orationes contra Arianos* 2.21.70)[1]

If by participation in the Spirit, we become "partakers of divine nature," it would be insane to say that the Spirit belongs to created nature and not to God. For that is why those in whom he comes to dwell are those who are deified. And if he deifies there is no doubt that his nature is of God. (*Epistulae ad Serapionem* 1.25)[2]

Deification continued to be a core commitment of the Christian faith in the medieval and early Reformation eras. It increasingly fell out of fashion among hyperrational Protestants, however, who were formatively shaped by ideals of the burgeoning Enlightenment.[3]

Their dismissal of deification as a trite archaism or esoteric pagan doctrine became the default position of the academy for the ensuing three hundred years. It was only in the late twentieth century, due in part to Tuomo Mannermaa's Finnish interpretation of Luther, that deification experienced a renaissance of interest in the Protestant West. On the heels of Mannermaa, deification has played a formative role in Orthodox-Reformed dialogue, Baptist-Orthodox dialogue, and evangelical soteriologies that extend beyond purely forensic or juridical themes.[4] Additionally, scholars have reexamined how soteriological themes of union and participation relate to deification in a host of significant Protestant figures such as John Calvin, Huldrych Zwingli, Peter Martyr Vermigli, Richard Hooker, John Owen, John and Charles Wesley, Jonathan Edwards, Herman Bavinck, C. S. Lewis, T. F. Torrance, Karl Barth, and Robert Jenson.[5]

Notwithstanding this Protestant retrieval of deification, an intriguing bifurcation persists within the academy—biblical specialists are far more apprehensive to equate Paul's soteriology with deification than their theologian colleagues. Exceptions to this rule exist, such as Stephen Finlan, Michael

---

[1]*NPNF* 2/4:386-87, italics added.
[2]Quoted in Norman Russell, *The Doctrine of Deification in the Greek Patristic Tradition*, OECS (Oxford: Oxford University Press, 2004), 175.
[3]See Paul L. Gavrilyuk, "The Retrieval of Deification: How a Once Despised Archaism Became an Ecumenical Desideratum," *ModTheo* 25, no. 4 (2009): 647-59.
[4]Carl Mosser, "Orthodox and Reformed Dialogue and the Ecumenical Recovery of Theosis," *EcRev* 73, no. 1 (2021): 131-51; Corneliu C. Simu, "Theosis and Baptist-Orthodox Discussions," *EcRev* 73, no. 1 (2021): 111-30; Robert V. Rakestraw, "Becoming Like God: An Evangelical Doctrine of Theosis," *JETS* 40, no. 2 (1997): 257-69.
[5]For a comprehensive bibliography of these investigations, see Michael Reardon, "Becoming God: Interpreting Pauline Soteriology as Deification," *CurBR* 22, no. 1 (2023): 84.

Gorman, Ben Blackwell, M. David Litwa, L. Ann Jervis, Eduard Borysov, and David Burnett.[6] Yet, one shared shortcoming of recent investigations is an inordinate prioritization of individualistic aspects of Pauline deification. This emphasis is, in fact, a historical anomaly, as Christian thinkers outside the guild of biblical studies—whether patristic or modern, East or West—have most often understood Paul to be interested not primarily in individualistic deification but the corporate, *ecclesial* deification of believers.

A foundational text informing this claim is 1 Corinthians 12:12. Richard Hays notes that a curious turn of phrase—οὕτως καὶ ὁ Χριστός ("so also is Christ"), instead of what readers might reasonably expect, "so also is the church"—forces interpreters to consider whether Paul presses "beyond mere analogy to make an ontological equation of the church with Christ."[7] Broadly speaking, biblical specialists have dealt with Paul's identification of the church as Christ or the body of Christ in one of two ways: (1) as a metaphor, analogy, or skillful use of rhetoric to portray the unity of diverse believers (and particular to the rhetorical sense, a notion infused with political history that fosters concord among a populace); or (2) as a description of a real, ontological identity. While the consensus of the modern guild of biblical studies aligns with the former set of possibilities, this chapter surveys nine thinkers who interpret Paul's identification of the church as the body of Christ to be referring to a real, ontological identity, and even transformation. The first six include some of the most significant theologians of the patristic era: Irenaeus of Lyons, Tertullian of Carthage, Origen of Alexandria, Athanasius of Alexandria, Hilary of Poitiers, and Augustine of Hippo. The final three are modern interpreters: Émile Mersch, John Zizioulas, and Witness Lee.

This survey of Christian thinkers aims to demonstrate three realities: first, the early church not only affirmed deification generally but ecclesial deification specifically, as the content and telos of Christian salvation; second, the early church's conception of ecclesial deification was, at least in part, directly related to its interpretation of Paul's identification of the church as the body of Christ; and third, the legacy of interpreting Pauline soteriology

---

[6]For an overview of modern biblical scholars who interpret Pauline soteriology as deification, see Reardon, "Becoming God," 85-102.
[7]Richard B. Hays, *First Corinthians* (Louisville, KY: John Knox, 1997), 213.

and ecclesiology as ecclesial deification has continued into the modern era by Christian thinkers outside the guild of biblical studies.

## Methodology

In his magnum opus *Truth and Method*, Hans-Georg Gadamer persuasively illumines the dubious nature of "objective" exegesis. For Gadamer, all interpretation is formed and informed by the *Wirkungsgeschichte* (effective history) of a text—that is, by foregoing interpreters and interpretations, since past interpretation "determines in advance what seems to be worth inquiring about and what will appear as an object of investigation."[8] For our present concerns, we note that Pauline interpretation has been influenced by two interrelated developments: (1) the rise of higher criticism during the Enlightenment, and (2) a strict division between biblical studies and theology that occurred during the same time period.

Hans Jauss, a student of Gadamer, further proposed that "the meaning of a work . . . is extracted only during the process of its reception."[9] According to Robert Evans, this extraction process occurs "through successive engagements with generations of readers and their 'actualisations' of the potential meaning of the text." For Jauss, this process is necessary, as interpreters acquire an *Erwartungshorizont* (horizon of expectation), "which varies from one historical period to another: the same text can be valued in one period and rejected in another. Each generation (or 'audience') interacts with the text in terms of a different framework of expectations."[10] In view of our present concerns, the modern guild of biblical studies is guided by Enlightenment-based ideals, whereas both patristic interpreters and modern thinkers operating external to the guild are not beholden to the same exegetical strictures. Thus, these interpreters may assist in reshaping our horizons of expectation for the Pauline corpus and perhaps extract additional meaning from these writings.

Mikhail Bakhtin builds on Jauss's insights by arguing that "great works" speak beyond their temporal situatedness; they are understood in "great

---

[8]Hans-Georg Gadamer, *Truth and Method*, 2nd ed. (London: Continuum, 2004), 311.
[9]Hans Jauss, *Toward an Aesthetic of Reception*, trans. Timothy Bahti (Minneapolis: University of Minnesota Press, 1982), 59.
[10]Robert Evans, *Reception History, Tradition and Biblical Interpretation: Gadamer and Jauss in Current Practice* (London: Bloomsbury, 2014), 9-10.

time"—that is, in eras beyond their writing—and as interpreters successively engage great works, they discover new semantic depth.[11] Building on these collective insights, this chapter demonstrates how interpreters normally excluded from intra-guild discussions of Pauline soteriology engaged his corpus in a manner that, for those within the guild, unearths hidden semantic depth.

A final addendum: this chapter appeals to the broader concept of *Wirkungsgeschichte* as opposed to *Auslegungsgeschichte* (history of interpretation). While the latter is included in the former, the *Wirkungsgeschichte* of Paul's identification of the church as Christ or the body of Christ is not exhausted by interpreters' direct exegetical engagement with specific texts (e.g., 1 Cor 12; Rom 12).[12] This is because interpreters who discuss deification in relation to the body of Christ are discussing an ecclesial identity unique to the Pauline corpus (i.e., the notion of the church being identified as Christ or the body of Christ is only found in the fourteen letters comprising the traditional Pauline corpus) and thus are situated within the *Wirkungsgeschichte* of Pauline soteriology/ecclesiology.

## Patristic Interpreters

***Irenaeus of Lyons (AD 130–202).*** Irenaeus is best known as one of the first Christian apologists. His most important extant work, *Adversus haereses*, is both a refutation of Valentinian Gnosticism and a comprehensive presentation of his theology of ἀνακεφαλαίωσις ("recapitulation," lit. "heading up"; see *Haer.* 3.18.7; 5.14.2-3; 5.21.2). Though the totality of this outlook is complex, its fundamental core is discernably Pauline: the first Adam, by sinning against God, engendered humanity's downward anti-God trajectory. Thus, via the incarnation, Christ came as the last Adam, who by virtue of his human living, crucifixion, resurrection, and ascension reversed this trajectory, restored the *imago Dei* to humankind, sanctified humankind, and uplifted the capacity of humankind to participate in a deifying union with God.[13] This outlook is

---

[11]See Mikhail M. Bakhtin, "Response to a Question from the *Novy Mir* Editorial Staff," in *Speech Genres and Other Late Essays*, ed. Caryl Emerson and Michael Holquist, trans. Vern W. McGee (Austin: University of Texas Press, 1986), 4-5, quoted in Ben Blackwell, *Christosis: Engaging Paul's Soteriology with His Patristic Interpreters* (Grand Rapids, MI: Eerdmans, 2011), 19.
[12]Blackwell, *Christosis*, 19.
[13]Émile Mersch, *The Whole Christ: The Historical Development of the Doctrine of the Mystical Body in Scripture and Tradition* (Jackson, MI: Ex Fontibus, 2018), 230; Blackwell, *Christosis*, 42-43.

succinctly captured by his famed exchange formula: the Son of God became "what we are that He might bring us to be even what He is Himself" (*Haer.* 5. preface).[14] While this formula is often quoted in support of individualistic deification, Irenaeus explicitly situates it within the church's identity as the body of Christ:

> For it was for this end that the Word of God was made man, and He who was the Son of God became the Son of man, that man, having been taken into the Word, and receiving the adoption, might become the son of God. . . . As the Head rose from the dead, so also the remaining part of the body—of every man who is found in life—when the time is fulfilled of that condemnation which existed by reason of disobedience, may arise, blended together and strengthened through means of joints and bands by the increase of God, each of the members having its own proper and fit position in the body. For there are many mansions in the Father's house, inasmuch as there are also many members in the body. (*Haer.* 3.19.1, 3 [translation adjusted])

This passage states a surprising result of his posited divine-human exchange: humans become "sons of God" (plural) but that they become the "*son* of God" (singular). In other words, for Irenaeus, Christians are in a significant sense ontologically identified with and even *as* Christ himself. Moreover, he contends that Christ's recapitulatory salvation is actuated by Christ as the Head rising from the dead so that "the remaining part of the body" may partake of the immortality and incorruptibility that properly belongs to Christ alone. These partakers, per Irenaeus, are "blended together and strengthened by means of joints and bands by the increase of God" (Eph 4:16) and are properly fitted together as "members in the Body" (1 Cor 12:27; Rom 12:4-5). In sum, (Pauline) deification for Irenaeus is not primarily individualistic but rather fulfilled in and by the body of Christ—an outlook that may be rightly called ecclesial deification.

**Tertullian of Carthage (AD 160–220).** Like Irenaeus, Tertullian of Carthage was one of the earliest Christian apologists combating Gnostic influence in the ante-Nicene church. For Tertullian, the primary goal of Christ's incarnation was to actuate full reconciliation between humankind and God. This reconciliation, however, is predicated not on extrinsic obedience or mimesis.

---

[14]Translations of this work follow *ANF* vol. 1.

Rather, he contends that it is realized through humankind's participation in the divine nature: "Now, although Adam was by reason of his condition under law subject to death, yet was hope preserved to him by the Lord's saying, 'Behold, Adam is become as one of us;' that is, in consequence of the future taking of the man into the divine nature" (*Adversus Marcionem* 2.25).[15] Tertullian further contends that participation in the divine nature leads believers to "ultimately to stand forth to view, like Adam when summoned to hear from his Lord and Creator the words, 'Behold, the man is become as one of us!'" (*De Resurrectione Carnis* 63). In light of such statements, Mark Frisius rightly notes, "Tertullian's eschatological vision identifies the soul being reunited with the deified flesh, with the result being the deification of the whole human."[16]

Of greater import to the present discussion, however, is that Tertullian's notion of deification is robustly cast in corporate and ontological terms: "Why do you think these brothers to be anything other than yourself? . . . The church is Christ. When, then, you cast yourself at the brethren's knees, you are handling *Christ*, you are entreating *Christ*. In like manner, when they shed tears over you, it is *Christ* who suffers, *Christ* who prays the Father for mercy" (*De Poenitentia* 10). Here Tertullian builds on Paul's description of believers as "members one of another" to contend that emotions shared between believers are not predicated on human relationships but rather are constitutive of a divinely human experience. Indeed, for Tertullian it is *Christ himself* carrying out these actions between individual constituents of a corporate entity. This is because, per Tertullian, "the church *is* Christ."

**Origen of Alexandria (AD 185–254).** Origen of Alexandria is a towering figure in ante-Nicene Christianity. John McGuckin describes him as "undoubtedly the greatest genius the early church ever produced." He was a prolific writer, composing between two thousand and six thousand treatises during his ecclesiastical career.[17] While commentators rightly highlight his contemplative and ascetic impulses, it is noteworthy that Origen's notion of deification is articulated in explicitly ecclesial terms:

---

[15]Translations from Tertullian's works follow *ANF* vol. 3.
[16]Mark Frisius, "Sequestered in Christ: Deification in Tertullian," in *Deification in the Latin Patristic Tradition*, ed. Jared Ortiz (Washington, DC: Catholic University of America Press, 2019), 68.
[17]John Anthony McGuckin, ed., *The Westminster Handbook to Origen* (Louisville, KY: Westminster John Knox, 2004), 25.

> And the fact that the church is the aggregate of many souls and has received the pattern of its life from Christ may lead us to suppose that it has received that pattern not from the actual deity of the Word of God—and this obviously is far above those actions and dispositions in respect of which people ought to be given a pattern—but rather that it was the soul that he assumed and in which was the utmost perfection, that was the pattern displayed to people. It will then be the likeness of the same soul that he here calls "my neighbor," that the church—and this is the aggregate of those many souls that were formerly under Pharaoh's yoke and among his chariots and now are called the company of the Lord's horsemen—ought to bear. (*Commentarium in Canticum canticorum* 2.4)[18]

It is crucial to note that Origen does not consider believers' corporate submission and obedience to the pattern of Christ's life in an "I-Thou" relationship sufficient to fulfilling the church's mission. Rather, he argues that Christ himself is the animating factor—the soul—of the church as the body of Christ, and it is Christ in his headship who directs each member to be wholly united and identified with himself:

> But that we may win over to the reception of our views those who are willing to accept the inferences which flow from our doctrines, and to be benefited thereby, we say that the holy Scriptures declare the body of Christ, animated by the Son of God, to be the whole Church of God, and the members of this body—considered as a whole—to consist of those who are believers; since, as a soul vivifies and moves the body, which of itself has not the natural power of motion like a living being, so the Word, arousing and moving the whole body, the Church, to befitting action, awakens, moreover, each individual member belonging to the Church, so that they do nothing apart from the Word. (*Cels.* 6.48)[19]

A significant question remained for Origen when he conceived of the continuity between Christ and the church: Namely, how can a sinless, perfect Head and fallen, imperfect body exist as a single ontological identity?

In commenting on 1 Corinthians 15:28, Origen addresses this issue by proposing that the church is truly the body of Christ but nevertheless undergoing a perfective process:[20]

---

[18]Origen, *The Song of Songs, Commentary and Homilies*, trans. R. P. Lawson, ACW 26 (New York: Newman, 1957), 143.

[19]Trans. *ANF* vol. 4.

[20]1 Cor 15:28: "And when all things have been subjected to Him, then the Son Himself also will be subjected to Him who has subjected all things to Him, that God may be all in all" (Recovery Version).

> And as long as I am not subjected to the Father, neither is he said to be "subjected" to the Father. Not that he himself is in need of subjection before the Father but for me, in whom he has not yet completed his work, he is said not to be subjected, for, as we read, "we are the body of Christ and members in part." ... See that, although we are all said to be his body and members, he is said not to be "subjected" as long as there are some among us who have not yet been subjected by the perfect subjection. But when "he shall have completed" his "work" and brought his whole creation to the height of perfection, then he is said to be "subjected" in these whom he subjected to the Father. In these, "he finished the work that God had given him that God may be all in all." (*Homiliae in Leviticum* 7.2)[21]

In brief, Origen posits that since the individual Christ is sinless and perfect and has always been wholly subjected to the Father, Paul's statements pertaining to Christ's eschatological submission to the Father at the close of the present age are only intelligible when referencing imperfect believers, who both presently and progressively constitute Christ's ecclesial body.

**Athanasius of Alexandria (AD 296–373).** Like Irenaeus and Tertullian, Athanasius is renowned as a defender of the orthodox Christian faith. Known as *Athanasius contra mundum* ("Athanasius against the world") during his lifetime, he was a prominent figure in the fight against Arianism. For our purposes, however, he is highly significant due to using "the technical terms of deification much more frequently than any previous writer."[22] Additionally, he modified Irenaeus's exchange formula in robustly deiform language, stating that Christ "was made man that we might be made God" (*Inc.* 54.3).[23]

Less discussed by scholars, however, is the close relationship Athanasius posited between believers and their corporate identity as the body of Christ. For example, he proposed that Christ's humanity is, in fact, "the whole Church": "When Peter said: 'let the whole house of Israel know for certain that God hath made Him both Lord and Christ, even this Jesus who ye have crucified' (Acts 2:36), he was not speaking of the divinity, but he means that His humanity, which is the whole Church, was made Lord and Christ" (*Inc.* 21). Additionally, he contended that Christ's historical narrative becomes believers'

---

[21] Origen, *Homilies on Leviticus 1–16*, trans. Gary Wayne Barkley, FC 83 (Washington, DC: Catholic University of America Press, 1990), 135.
[22] Russell, *Doctrine of Deification*, 167.
[23] Trans. *NPNF* 2/4.

present reality by virtue of being incorporated into his body: "It is thus that men have received grace to be called gods and sons of God. First the Lord raised His own body from the dead and exalted it in His own person; then He raised up the members of His body, in order that as God He might bestow on them all the graces that He has received as man" (*Inc.* 12). Most strikingly, he extraordinarily softened nearly any distinction between the individual Jesus and the church by suggesting that Christ's vivification, sanctification, and exaltation of believers is *actually Christ vivifying, sanctifying, and exalting himself*:

> Therefore He gives life to Himself, He sanctifies Himself, He exalts Himself. Consequently when He says that the Father has sanctified Him, raised Him up and given Him a name which is above all names, and has given Him life, it is evident that the Father has done all this through Him. Through Him does God raise Him up, through Him God sanctifies Him, through Him does God glorify Him, and through Him does God give Him life. And when Jesus commends His spirit to the hands of His Father, He is commending Himself as man to God, in order thus to commend all men to God. (*Inc.* 12)

In view of such statements, Johann Adam Möhler rightly concludes that Athanasius "taught that Jesus Christ is interiorly united with the Church, and that in a sense He Himself is the church."[24]

**Hilary of Poitiers (AD 315–367).** The proposal that Christ *is* the church is articulated even more forcefully by Hilary of Poitiers, who in modern scholarship has been given the nickname "Athanasius of the West." Similar to his Greek namesake, Hilary rejected a straightforward distinction between Christ's individual and ecclesial/mystical body and instead understood the church to be "the extension of the Incarnation."[25] In *Tractatus super Psalmos*, his physicalistic conception of the church as the body of Christ is on full display: "He renews us unto a new life; He transforms us into a new man by placing us in the body of His flesh. For He is the Church; by the mystery of His body, He contains her wholly within Himself" (*Tractatus super Psalmos* 91.9).[26] A question remains, however: *How* does the church become Christ? For Hilary,

---

[24]Johann Adam Möhler, *Athanasius der Große und die Kirche seiner Zeit, besonders im Kampf mit dem Arianismus* (Mainz: Dei Florian Kupferberg, 1827), 122.
[25]Ellen Scully, *Physicalist Soteriology in Hilary of Poitiers* (Leiden: Brill, 2015), 273, 220.
[26]Quoted in Mersch, *Whole Christ*, 296.

the deification of believers takes place corporately by the reception of the sacraments—first actuated by baptism and thereafter sustained by the Eucharist:[27]

> For He says Himself, *My flesh is meat indeed, and My blood is drink indeed. He that eateth My flesh and drinketh My blood abideth in Me, and I in him*. As to the verity of the flesh and blood there is no room left for doubt. . . . I have dwelt upon these facts because the heretics falsely maintain that the union between Father and Son is one of will only, and make use of the example of our own union with God, as though we were united to the Son and through the Son to the Father by mere obedience and a devout will, and none of the natural verity of communion were vouchsafed us through the sacrament of the Body and Blood; although the glory of the Son bestowed upon us through the Son abiding in us after the flesh, while we are united in Him corporeally and inseparably, bids us preach the mystery of the true and natural unity. (*De Trinitate* 8.14-17)[28]

Hilary's notion that believers are united with Christ "corporeally and inseparably" so that their corporate deification results in the preaching of "the mystery of the true and natural unity" is incomprehensible apart from Paul's identification of the church as the body of Christ and even as Christ. Once more, we see how the semantic depth of Paul's writings may be examined and extracted by using patristic interpreters as hermeneutical lenses.

***Augustine of Hippo (AD 354–430).*** The final stop in our abbreviated, whirlwind tour of the patristic era is Augustine of Hippo. A towering figure in the Western tradition, Augustine's influence on numerous areas in theology and philosophy is beyond dispute. Despite past scholarship suggesting otherwise, recent investigations have persuasively demonstrated that deification not only exists in Augustine's intellectual topography but even is one of the core commitments of his theology.[29] Similar to Athanasius, Augustine used the doctrine of deification as a foundation for his affirmations of both

---

[27]Janet Sidaway, "Making Man Manifest: Deification in Hilary of Poitiers," in Ortiz, *Deification in the Latin Patristic Tradition*, 129.

[28]*NPNF* 2/9.

[29]Augustine Casiday, "St. Augustine on Deification: His Homily on Psalm 81," *Sobernost* 23 (2001): 23-44; Darren Sarisky, "Augustine and Participation: Some Reflections on His Exegesis of Romans," in *"In Christ" in Paul*, ed. Michael J. Thate, Kevin J. Vanhoozer, et al. (Tübingen: Mohr Siebeck, 2014), 357-74; portions of Ron Haflidson, "We Shall Be That Seventh Day: Deification in Augustine," in *Deification in the Latin Patristic Tradition*, ed. Jared Ortiz (Washington, DC: The Catholic University of America Press, 2019), 169-89. Also see my forthcoming article "'You Adore a God Who Makes You Gods': Augustine's Doctrine of Deification," *Horizons* (2024).

the deity of Christ and the deity of the Holy Spirit, and in further harmony with the Greek Doctor, reversed the latter's famed maxim—"for He was incarnate that we might be made God" (*Inc.* 54)—in his own axiom on deification: "In order to make gods of those who were merely human, one who was God made himself human" (Augustine, *Sermon* 192.1).[30]

For our purposes, the most striking aspect of Augustine's understanding of deification is its inextricable relationship to his ecclesiology. For Augustine, both the individual Christ as the Head and the church as the body of Christ form a single identity—that is, the *totus Christus* ("total/whole Christ"):

> Therefore, let us rejoice and give thanks, not only that we have been made Christians, but that we have been made Christ.... For if he is the head, we are the members—a whole man, he and we.... What does it mean, head and members? Christ and the Church. For we would proudly claim this for ourselves if he had not deigned to promise this who says through the same Apostle, "Now you are the body and members of Christ" (1 Cor. 12:27). (*In Johannis evangelium tractatus* 21.8)[31]

Per Johannes Quasten, the *totus Christus* is "the heart of Augustine's ecclesiology," and per Christopher Iacovetti, the interplay between these proposals results in "the *totus Christus* [being] the true and ultimate locus of all deification."[32]

Significantly, Augustine's notion of ecclesial deification moves in a more extraordinary direction than that of his predecessors. He contends that "the whole complete Christ, that is, Head and members," sometimes "speaks in the name of the Head alone" (*Enarrationes in Psalmos* 37).[33] In other words, Augustine's understanding of ecclesial deification entails that believers become God not only in their identity and expression but also in their function, insofar as their speaking is none other than the individual Christ's own words and thoughts.

---

[30]Augustine, *Sermons III/6 (184–229Z), The Works of Saint Augustine: A Translation for the 21st Century* (New York: New City Press, 1993).
[31]Augustine, *Tractates on the Gospel of John, 112–124; Tractates on the First Epistle of John*, FC (Washington, DC: Catholic University of America Press, 2014).
[32]Johannes Quasten, *Patrology* (New York: Newman, 1950), 4:447; Christopher Iacovetti, "Filioque, Theosis, and Ecclesia: Augustine in Dialogue with Modern Orthodox Theology," *Mod-Theo* 34, no. 1 (January 2018): 78.
[33]Quoted in Mersch, *Whole Christ*, 419.

***Summary of patristic thinkers.*** Significant diversity exists among patristic thinkers in the *Wirkungsgeschichte* of interpreting Paul's identification of the church as the body of Christ as ecclesial deification. Irenaeus embeds the corporate participation of believers in Christ in his doctrine of recapitulation, while Tertullian emphasizes the corporate, deifying results of *imitatio Christi*. Origen emphasizes the spiritual dimension of the body of Christ, going so far as to suggest that the submission of Christ to the Father in 1 Corinthians 15:28 is intelligible only when understood as referring to the progressive transformation of believers, while Athanasius proposes that Christ's vivification, sanctification, and exaltation of believers is actually Christ vivifying, sanctifying, and exalting himself. Hilary, the so-called Athanasius of the West, promotes a physicalist understanding of believers comprising the body of Christ, whereby their corporate identity is truly Christ's own flesh, while Augustine suggests that the ecclesial deification of believers causes the church to function as Christ, insofar as the church sometimes "speaks in the name of the Head alone." While these (and other) particularities exist between thinkers, the thread that holds them together is a unified presupposition that Paul's identification of the church as the body of Christ entails that believers possess a single ontological identity yet are being progressively transformed into the fullness of this identity—in brief, what we called ecclesial deification.

It is important to note that this interpretation of Paul is not unique to the church fathers mentioned above. I did not discuss the Cappadocian fathers, for example, of whom both Gregory of Nyssa (AD 335–395) and Gregory of Nazianzus (AD 329–390) affirm robust conceptions of ecclesial deification. Furthermore, I excluded other patristic thinkers—John Chrysostom, Cyril of Alexandria, Severian of Gabala, and others—who also link ecclesial deification to Paul's identification of the church as the body of Christ.

Moreover, it would make sense to trace the development of ecclesial deification through medieval, Reformation, and early modern time frames. There exists no dearth of material in this regard: interpreters ranging from Gregory the Great (AD 540–604) to Thomas Aquinas (AD 1225–1274), William of Saint-Thierry (AD 1075/1080–1148) to Pierre de Bérulle (AD 1575–1629), all advance various articulations of how the Pauline identification of the church as the body of Christ must be interpreted realistically, that is, as a deified identity united with and incorporated into Christ. For now, however, I set aside the desire for comprehensiveness and turn to discuss three twentieth-century interpreters: Émile Mersch, John Zizioulas, and Witness Lee. Although they represent divergent ecclesial outlooks, each affirms the crux of Augustine's *totus Christus*—that is, that ecclesial deification best apprehends Paul's identification of the church as the body of Christ and even as Christ.

## Modern Interpreters

***Émile Mersch (1890–1940).*** Though not well-known outside the academy, Mersch is a fascinating figure in Roman Catholicism who devoted his career to articulating a systematic theology centered on the mystical body of Christ. Concerning this aim, he states:

> To study all dogmas and all points of doctrine, and to show how they all lead eventually to the truth of the whole Christ, would be an endless task. Hence I have confined myself to the chief teachings. But all the rest converge toward these supreme summits. In showing how the doctrines treated lead to Christ, we show at the same time how everything else tends toward Him.[34]

A notable aspect of how Mersch relates ecclesial deification to the church's identity as the body of Christ is that it explicitly arises from his engagement with the Pauline corpus:

> The truth is precisely the truth of the whole Christ, of Christ God and man, head and body, is one. . . . This conception of Christian teaching is especially clear in St. Paul, the apostle whose ministry is best known. . . . He sums up his entire gospel in this teaching, just as Christ sums up everything in Himself. . . . The truth is that St. Paul sums up everything in the whole Christ, in Christ living in men and causing them to live in God, in Christ who dwells in God and causes men to dwell in God.[35]

Apart from his interpretation of Scripture, however, Mersch squarely situates his outlook within the Augustinian tradition by creatively expounding and extending what it means for the church to be the *totus Christus*. While

---

[34]Émile Mersch, *The Theology of the Mystical Body*, trans. Cyril Vollert (St. Louis: Herder, 1951), v.
[35]Mersch, *Theology of the Mystical Body*, 54-56.

Augustine contends that ecclesial deification allows the church to become God in function by speaking as Christ, Mersch further suggests that believers function as God by "giving and sending the Holy Spirit":

> As they are made fit by their adoption and divinization to be members of the Son who is God, they are made fit to be members of the Son who possesses the Spirit, by a possession of the Spirit and an indwelling of the Spirit which makes them "spiritual" in the strongest sense of the word. . . . When we consider [Christians] in this unity—and that is the only correct way of regarding them as they really are—we must acknowledge that they too give and send the Holy Spirit, by the fact that Christ their head gives and sends Him. Such, then, is the significance of the Holy Spirit for the mystical body. He is the power that brings it to birth and causes it to grow, the power the body possesses yet receives, the energy that invests for it, that rises up within it, and that can almost be said to emanate from it, since in Christ the force can be set in motion. Yet this power comes from on high, and is supremely free and all-powerful. These predicates assuredly differ, even to the point of contrast; but their union should not surprise us, for it is but the continuation of the union that is in the God-man.[36]

Beyond the deified believers' ability to give and send the Holy Spirit, this passage illumines other intriguing aspects of Mersch's ecclesial pneumatology: (1) the Spirit gives birth to the mystical body, (2) the Spirit imbues members with the strongest sense of spirituality, (3) the Spirit causes the mystical body to grow, and (4) the Spirit emanates from the mystical body.

Two final notes about Mersch's notion of ecclesial deification are necessary to accurately portray his conception of how this corporate transformation takes place. First, Mersch conceives of the church dichotomistically, with both a body and soul. The body is an "empirical, concrete, visible, tangible thing . . . a human institution, a human society" with "clearly defined members and its definite seat; it is the Church of Rome, as Jesus Christ was Jesus of Nazareth." The soul, which is interior and invisible, is "the factor that makes this society a living organism. . . . This factor can be nothing else than the grace which causes all these members to be living members of Christ, the divinizing grace that is infused into all by one and the same Christ."

---

[36]Mersch, *Theology of the Mystical Body*, 445-47.

While Mersch does suggest that those outside Rome may be participants in the mystical body in a limited sense, he nevertheless argues that "salvation is not found outside the Church, and that submission to the Roman Pontiff is necessary for the salvation of every human creature."[37]

Second, Mersch's notion of ecclesial deification is entirely sacramental. He argues that the sacred humanity of Christ is "the sacrament par excellence," being both "a sign and a cause of divinization and grace," and the visible church, as the continuation of Christ, "perpetuates the sacramental character of the sacred humanity as the sacrament par excellence." Due to this outlook, he devotes ample discussion to Rome's seven sacraments, describing them as variegated means of participating in God's deifying grace. Concerning baptism, Mersch quotes 1 Corinthians 12:12-13 and Galatians 3:27-28 in support of his claim that it "creates Christians," unites them "to Christ . . . to the Son, to God, to the Trinity." By virtue of incorporating them into Christ, baptism confers on them "divine adoption, grace, the supernatural life, and the indwelling of the whole Trinity." The sacraments of confirmation, penance, extreme unction, matrimony, and priestly orders are similarly understood to be means of divinizing grace. The Eucharist, however, is the most significant sacrament, as Mersch suggests that the Mass is the sacrifice of the mystical body insofar as the body is ontologically united with the Head. The Eucharist, per Mersch, "assimilates us to Christ," "perfects incorporation into Him," "transforms us into Him," and confers a grace of "divinization, divine adoption, and union with the whole Trinity." He thus concludes that the Eucharist perfects the "the permanence of our union with the Church, with Christ, and with grace," and for this reason may be considered the ultimate vehicle of ecclesial deification—or in his words, "the sacrament of the Church and the mystical body, the sacrament of the Christian and the Christian life."[38]

**John Zizioulas (1931–2023).** John Zizioulas was perhaps the most respected modern Orthodox theologian, at both the academic and popular levels. He served as the metropolitan of Pergamon of the Ecumenical Patriarchate of Constantinople since 1986 and was a leading figure in the

---

[37]Mersch, *Theology of the Mystical Body*, 482, 484, 507.
[38]Mersch, *Theology of the Mystical Body*, 548-49, 560-80, 585, 591.

ecumenical movement, having participated in dialogues with the Roman Catholic Church, Anglican Church, and the World Council of Churches in Geneva. Perhaps for this reason he subsumes Augustine's *totus Christus* in his ecclesiology, despite the latter's notoriety in the Greek East:

> The essence of Christianity and the Church should be sought in the very person of the Lord on which the Church was founded. . . . Accordingly, what is paramount in ecclesiology is not this or that doctrine, idea or value revealed by the Lord, but *the very person of Christ* and man's union with Him. In this way, the Church is described as Christ Himself, *the whole Christ* in Augustine's apt phrase, while ecclesiology ceases to be a separate chapter for theology and becomes an organic *chapter of Christology*. . . . The unity of the Church is seen, first and foremost, as a unity *in the person* of Christ, as *incorporation* into Him and His *increase* or *building-up*, the starting-point for studying the unity of the Church.[39]

One claim of this passage is particularly significant; for Zizioulas, ecclesiology is "an organic chapter of Christology." Even more strikingly, he subsumes both soteriology and the ontological identity of believers within his meta-doctrine of ecclesial deification:

> Christianity consequently is the proclamation to man that his nature can be "assumed" and hypostasized in a manner free from the ontological necessity of his biological hypostasis, which, as we have seen, leads to the tragedy of individualism and death. Thanks to Christ man can henceforth himself "subsist," can affirm his existence as personal not on the basis of the immutable laws of nature, but on the basis of a relationship with God which is identified with what Christ in freedom and love possesses as Son of God with the Father. This adoption of man by God, the identification of his hypostasis with the hypostasis of the Son of God, is the essence of baptism.[40]

The result of this hypostatic, baptismal identification with Christ is that participants are deified to really and truly "become Christ and the Church."[41] Thus, the "ontological significance" of baptism for a believer is that "identity

---

[39] John D. Zizioulas, *Eucharist, Bishop, Church: The Unity of the Church in the Divine Eucharist and the Bishop During the First Three Centuries* (Brookline, MA: Holy Cross Orthodox Press, 2001), 15-16, italics original.

[40] John D. Zizuoulas, *Being as Communion: Studies in Personhood and the Church* (Crestwood, NY: St. Vladimir's Seminary Press, 2007), 56.

[41] Zizioulas, *Eucharist, Bishop, Church*, 58.

is now rooted not in the relations provided by nature" (by their biological hypostasis) "but in the uncreated Father-Son relationship."[42]

While this claim may appear to prioritize individualistic transformation, we should take care to note the orientation of this existence: it is an "ecclesial hypostasis." In other words, the ontological transformation of believers can take place only in the church and as the church: "It is only *together* that all baptised members of the Church constitute the body that reveals Christ. The people (*laos*) created by baptism, laity and clergy together, are the revelation of the Son who is the truth of the new relationship of the world with God."[43] Baptism for Zizioulas is not a comprehensive, once-for-all act but rather the inauguration of one's ecclesial hypostasis. Once baptized, members of Christ are sustained by participation in the life of the church via the continual partaking of the Eucharist. On the ecclesial level, the church manifests all the members' eschatological destiny by virtue of this sacramental participation:

> The eucharist is the moment in the Church's life where the anticipation of the *eschata* takes place. The *anamnesis* of Christ is realized not as a mere re-enactment of a past event, but as an *anamnesis of the future*, as an eschatological event. In the eucharist the Church becomes a reflection of the eschatological community of Christ, the Messiah, an image of the Trinitarian life of God.[44]

To be sure, Zizioulas's eucharistic ecclesiology deserves a comprehensive, systematic treatment, which present space constraints disallow. He uses the Eucharist to strike a balance between the universalization and localization of the church, eschewing what he perceives as an overprioritization of the universal over the local (a Roman Catholic tendency) and the local over the universal (a Protestant tendency).[45] Moreover, he argues that the presence of the Eucharist is insufficient for ecclesial unity and transformation if not administrated by a bishop whose authority is established by apostolic succession, which in turn delimits his doctrine of ecclesial deification within institutional boundaries.[46]

---

[42]Zizuoulas, *Being as Communion*; John D. Zizioulas, *Communion and Otherness: Further Studies in Personhood and the Church* (London: T&T Clark, 2006), 109.
[43]John D. Zizioulas, *Lectures in Christian Dogmatics* (London: Bloomsbury Academic, 2008), 13.
[44]Zizioulas, *Being as Communion*, 254.
[45]Zizioulas, *Being as Communion*, 25.
[46]In fact, that the presence of the Eucharist is insufficient for ecclesial unity and transformation if not administrated by a bishop whose authority is established by apostolic succession is the primary argument forwarded by *Eucharist, Bishop, Church*. Zizioulas positions himself against

Still, while more could be said about Zizioulas's notion of ecclesial deification, the above discussion is adequate for our purposes.

**Witness Lee (1905–1997).** The final interpreter, Witness Lee, is likely the least familiar to readers, as he has no biography published in English. Born in 1905 in northern China, Lee was regenerated at nineteen and spent his early adult years meeting with the Brethren Assemblies (Benjamin Newton branch) before moving to Shanghai to work with Watchman Nee. By 1949 Lee, alongside his senior coworker Nee, established more than four hundred congregations in thirty provinces across China. Today an estimated 1.5–2 million Christians meet in churches directly established by the ministry of Nee and Lee, with millions more in underground Chinese churches formatively shaped by their teachings.[47]

Similar to foregoing interpreters, Lee interprets Paul's identification of the church as the body of Christ to mean that believers share a single corporate identity:

> [First Corinthians 12:12] says, "For even as the body is one and has many members, but all the members of the body being many, are one body, so also is Christ." "For" indicates that verse 12 is an explanation of verse 11. Verse 11 says that one Spirit operates all the various aspects of His manifestation, distributing them to many believers individually. This is just like our physical body being one and having many members. In Greek Christ in verse 12 is "the Christ," referring to the corporate Christ, composed of Christ Himself as the Head and the church as His Body with all the believers as its members. All the believers of Christ are organically united with Him and constituted with His life and element and have thus become His Body, an organism, to express Him. Hence, He is not only the Head, but also the Body. As our physical body has many members yet is one, so is this Christ.[48]

Although not explicit in this passage, Lee elsewhere proposes that the church's identity as the body of Christ exceeds the reality inherent to the physical world—the latter is reduced to a metaphor of the former:

---

purely eucharistic ecclesiologies by emphasizing the historic role of the bishop as the *alter Christus* and institutional means of unity during the first three centuries of the church.

[47]See Joseph R. Pitts of Pennsylvania, "Watchman Nee and Witness Lee," *Congressional Record* 160, no. 62 (April 29, 2014): E621-E622; Christopher Smith of New Jersey, "In Recognition of Watchman Nee," *Congressional Record* 155, no. 118 (July 31, 2009): E2110.

[48]Witness Lee, *Life-Study of First Corinthians* (Anaheim, CA: Living Stream Ministry, 1984), 520.

> When I was young, I was instructed that the term *the Body of Christ* was merely a metaphor signifying what the church is to Christ. I accepted this teaching at that time, but gradually, after many years, I found out that the Body of Christ is not a metaphor; it is a great reality in the universe. Rather, our physical body is a metaphor portraying the Body of Christ.[49]

Here is an important feature of Lee's outlook: Christ is the uniquely "real" person in existence.[50] By virtue of believers being incorporated into Christ, believers possess a corporate, ontological identity surpassing anything found in the physical universe—they become the corporate Christ.

For Lee, the formation of the corporate Christ is predicated on believers' ecclesial deification:

> God's New Testament economy is to make the believers God-men for the constitution of the Body of Christ so that the New Jerusalem may be consummated as the eternal enlargement and expression of the processed and consummated Triune God (Gal. 3:26; 4:7, 26, 31).... For us to be deified means that we are being constituted with the processed and consummated Triune God so that we may be made God in life and in nature to be His corporate expression for eternity (Rev. 21:11). The New Jerusalem is built by God's constituting Himself into man to make man the same as God in life, nature, and constitution so that God and man may become a corporate entity.[51]

It is noteworthy that Lee's notion of ecclesial deification differs from that of Mersch, Zizioulas, and a portion of patristic interpreters in two significant ways—both of which may make ecclesial deification more palatable for Protestant readers. First, he does not situate ecclesial deification within visible institutions, whether the Roman papacy, Eastern patriarchates, or denominational structures. Rather, he contends that any believer who inwardly experiences the growth of God contributes to the corporate growth of the

---

[49]*CWWL 1993* 1:484.
[50]Lee was an avid hymn writer. Consider the following stanza of one of his hymns:
   Christ is the one reality of all,
   Of Godhead and of man and all things else;
   No man without Him ever findeth God,
   Without Him man and everything is false.
Witness Lee, "Hymn 496," Hymns by Witness Lee and Watchman Nee, www.witness-lee-hymns.org/hymns/H0496.html.
[51]Witness Lee, *The Conclusion of the New Testament: Experiencing, Enjoying, and Expressing Christ*, vol. 3 *(Msgs. 382-436)* (Anaheim, CA: Living Stream Ministry, 2015), 4362.

body of Christ, regardless of whether that believer meets with a properly constituted ecclesial community. Second, he does not ground his notion of ecclesial deification in the sacraments—or, in his terminology, the visible symbols of baptism or the Lord's Table. He suggests, rather, that the church is deified by the spiritual realities these symbols significate. The cup, for Lee, typifies Christ's blood shed on the cross for the redemption of sins, which opens the way for believers to eat the Lord, while the bread typifies Christ presenting himself as food for believers to eat and enjoy in a daily, even moment-by-moment manner.[52] Lee posits that these spiritual realities— eating and drinking of the Lord in a daily manner through spiritual practices such as praying the words of Scripture, reading Scripture, or singing hymns—are the means by which deification occurs. Building on the common phrase "you are what you eat," he argues that transformation— defined as "an inward metabolic process in which a new and living element gradually discharges and replaces our old element (Rom. 12:2)"—primarily "takes place by eating, not by teaching."[53]

## Conclusion

At the outset of this chapter, I stated that the foregoing survey would demonstrate three realities: (1) ecclesial deification was a core commitment of the early church, (2) patristic thinkers regularly interpreted the Pauline identification of the church as the body of Christ as referring to ecclesial deification, and (3) the legacy of interpreting Paul's soteriology and ecclesiology as ecclesial deification has continued into the modern era by Christian thinkers external to the guild of biblical studies. Beyond highlighting the veracity of these claims, this chapter serves to expand the *Erwartungshorizont* of (largely Protestant) biblical specialists, which has historically neglected the possibility of Paul speaking about deification. Even in the midst of a recent surge of academic interest in the doctrine, this *Erwartungshorizont* delimited much of the discussion about the doctrine to its individualistic rather than its corporate/ecclesial contours. This survey may help to serve as a corrective within the aforementioned debates about Pauline soteriology.

---

[52] *CWWL (1963)* 4:309-14.
[53] *CWWL (1972)* 3:401-3.

This summation, however, only tells part of the story. Interpreting Paul through the lens of ecclesial deification incorporates and unifies numerous core elements of his theology. Beyond soteriology, the doctrine's very nomenclature, *ecclesial* deification, situates it within ecclesiology, and ecclesial *deification* within theology proper (i.e., the doctrine of God). Moreover, ecclesial deification in Paul is rooted in his identification of the church as the body of Christ and even as Christ. Thus, as Zizioulas beautifully articulated above, "Ecclesiology ceases to be a separate chapter for theology and becomes an organic *chapter of Christology*."[54] Ecclesial deification is also dependent on both Christ's incarnation and his resurrection: the former for its possibility, the latter for its actuality.

I also showed that the Spirit plays a crucial role in actuating the unity of believers as a single corporate identity, and thus ecclesial deification is robustly pneumatological. Further, we need only look at where ecclesial deification is most explicitly promoted in the Pauline corpus—for example, 1 Corinthians 12; Romans 12—to realize that Paul's paraenesis was not promulgated in a vacuum but rather was rooted in the church's corporate identity as the body of Christ and corporate transformation into the fullest expression of the body of Christ. Hence, we may rightly say that the doctrine of ecclesial deification ties together Pauline conceptions of theology proper, Christology, pneumatology, soteriology, ecclesiology, eschatology, and ethics.

In secularized appropriations of science there is an unending quest for a "theory of everything"—that is, "a hypothetical, singular, all-encompassing coherent framework of physics that fully explains and links together all physical aspects of the universe."[55] Within Pauline studies, scholars have been on a similar quest for a single theorem connecting and explaining all the elements of his theological outlook. Here I conclude by humbly proposing that ecclesial deification may be this holy grail, both unifying and articulating the totality of Paul's intellectual topography.

---

[54]Zizioulas, *Eucharist, Bishop, Church*, 15.
[55]Les Johnson, *A Traveler's Guide to the Stars* (Princeton, NJ: Princeton University Press, 2022), 197.

# DEIFICATION SEEN *from* THREE BIBLICAL METAPHORS *in* WATCHMAN NEE *and* WITNESS LEE *with a* COGNITIVE-LINGUISTIC INTERPRETIVE APPROACH *to* METAPHORS

### Jacob Chengwei Feng

Biblical and theological studies on deification have been gaining momentum in the past several decades.[1] In affirming and restating the Mannermaa school's ecumenical proposal based on its reinterpretation of Martin Luther, Veli-Matti Kärkkäinen insightfully exposes "a curious trinitarian deficit" and "the passive (or almost nonexistent) role of the Spirit" in most Protestant accounts of justification as opposed to the Eastern

---

[1] For some recent biblical studies on deification, see Michael J. Gorman, *Romans: A Theological and Pastoral Commentary* (Grand Rapids, MI: Eerdmans, 2022); Gorman, *Participating in Christ: Explorations in Paul's Theology and Spirituality* (Grand Rapids, MI: Baker Academic, 2019); Michael J. Thate, Kevin J. Vanhoozer, and Constantine R. Campbell, eds., *"In Christ" in Paul: Explorations in Paul's Theology of Union and Participation* (Grand Rapids, MI: Eerdmans, 2018); Ben C. Blackwell, *Christosis: Engaging Paul's Soteriology with His Patristic Interpreters* (Grand Rapids, MI: Eerdmans, 2016); Gorman, *Becoming the Gospel: Paul, Participation, and Mission* (Grand Rapids, MI: Eerdmans, 2015); M. David Litwa, *We Are Being Transformed: Deification in Paul's Soteriology*, BZNW 187 (Berlin: de Gruyter, 2012); Constantine R. Campbell, *Paul and Union with Christ: An Exegetical and Theological Study* (Grand Rapids, MI: Zondervan, 2012). For some recent theological studies on deification, see Jared Ortiz, ed., *With All the Fullness of God: Deification in Christian Tradition* (Lanham, MD: Lexington, 2021); John Arblaster and Rob Faesen, eds., *Theosis/Deification: Christian Doctrines of Divinization, East and West*, BETL 294 (Leuven: Peeters, 2018); Jordan Cooper, *Christification: A Lutheran Approach to Theosis* (Eugene, OR: Wipf & Stock, 2014); Alexander Chow, *Theosis, Sino-Christian Theology and the Second Chinese Enlightenment: Heaven and Humanity in Unity* (New York: Palgrave Macmillan, 2013); Norman Russell, *Fellow Workers with God: Orthodox Thinking on Theosis*, Foundations (Crestwood, NY: St. Vladimir's Seminary Press, 2009).

theology of deification.² Similarly, Frank Macchia observes that the Spirit's role is somewhat external in a typical Protestant conception of justification, which has nothing to do with the "substance of justification." Moreover, the Father "seems to be a relatively passive spectator who happily accepts Christ's advocacy" without having an active role to play.³ To make up for this trinitarian-pneumatological deficit, this chapter examines three biblical metaphors—grafting (Rom 11:17-24), grain offering (Lev 2:1-10), and new Jerusalem (Rev 3:12)—in order to recover the active roles of the Holy Spirit and the Father in justification in particular, and in deification in general.⁴

Since the inception of the revolution in cognitive science, founded on the axiom "human cognition is dependent upon embodied human experience," biblical scholars began using these tools in the 1990s.⁵ In his monograph *Without Metaphor, No Saving God: Theology After Cognitive Linguistics*, Robert Masson observes that compared to biblical scholars who "have begun to explore the implications of cognitive linguistics for interpreting the meaning and inferences of ancient texts, these resources have been given very little attention in theology and the philosophy of religion."⁶ Masson's keen insight applies particularly to the theology of deification. Therefore, this chapter identifies a lacuna, namely, a lack of theological exploration of cognitive analysis in the flourishing field of deification.⁷

---

²Veli-Matti Kärkkäinen, "Justification as Union and Christ's Presence: Deification in the Lutheran Tradition," in Ortiz, *With All the Fullness*, 69.
³Frank D. Macchia, *Justified in the Spirit: Creation, Redemption, and the Triune God*, Pentecostal Manifestos (Grand Rapids, MI: Eerdmans, 2010), 5, 39.
⁴Recent efforts along the same line led to my recent publication on highlighting the role of the Holy Spirit in deification. See Jacob Chengwei Feng, "Pneumasis/Pneumafication Based on Romans 8:1-17: Highlighting the Spirit's Role in Deification," *Religions* 14, no. 9 (2023): 1210, https://doi.org/10.3390/rel14091210.
⁵John Sanders, *Theology in the Flesh: How Embodiment and Culture Shape the Way We Think About Truth, Morality, and God* (Minneapolis: Fortress, 2016), 17-19. For a brief history and synopsis of the developing subfield of cognitive linguistics in biblical studies, see Bonnie Howe and Joel B. Green, eds., *Cognitive Linguistic Explorations in Biblical Studies* (Boston: de Gruyter, 2014), 1-6. Essays in the volume were collected from "the first six years of the Cognitive Linguistics in Biblical Interpretation section of the Society of Biblical Literature" (2006–2012). Also see Gary A. Anderson, *Sin: A History* (New Haven, CT: Yale University Press, 2009); Erik Konsmo, *The Pauline Metaphors of the Holy Spirit: The Intangible Spirit's Tangible Presence in the Life of the Christian* (New York: Peter Lang, 2010).
⁶Robert Masson, *Without Metaphor, No Saving God: Theology After Cognitive Linguistics*, Studies in Philosophical Theology 54 (Leuven: Peeters, 2014), 311.
⁷For example, Konsmo surveys Pauline spirit metaphors of re-creation, progression, and consummation. Nijay K. Gupta studies Paul's cultic metaphors. Both fail to capture Pauline spirit

The contribution of this chapter is threefold. First, it is an original attempt at applying the tools provided by cultural linguistics to biblical metaphors for an enriched understanding of deification. Second, the chapter identifies the three metaphors as valuable additions to the ninety-four metaphors for God discovered by May Therese DesCamp and Eve Sweetser.[8] Third, the chapter provides a fresh presentation of Watchman Nee's (Ni Tuosheng, 1903–1972) and Witness Lee's (Li Changshou, 1905–1997) understanding of deification as the telos of holiness as a viable addition to "receptive ecumenism."[9] While acknowledging the praiseworthiness of this ecumenical move by Jared Ortiz and his colleagues, this chapter intends to add other important voices from the Global South.

The chapter will begin by presenting the latest developments in studying metaphors in cognitive linguistics. Then I will follow the exemplary work of DesCamp and Sweetser and analyze the three biblical metaphors expounded by Nee and Lee in their understanding of deification. Finally, the chapter further identifies a tectonic mapping shift in the understanding of the nature of sin.

## METAPHORS, COGNITIVE LINGUISTICS, AND DEIFICATION

Sweetser and DesCamp argue that "both the Hebrew Bible and the Greek New Testament provide rich metaphoric repertoires for the understanding of the relationship between monotheistic humans and God."[10] However, there have been numerous approaches to interpreting metaphors, which can be traced as early as the pre-Aristotelian era.[11] After surveying the various

---

metaphors of deification. See Konsmo, *Pauline Metaphors*, 65-190; Gupta, *Worship That Makes Sense to Paul: A New Approach to the Theology and Ethics of Paul's Cultic Metaphors* (Berlin: de Gruyter, 2010).

[8]Mary Therese DesCamp and Eve E. Sweetser, "Metaphors for God: Why and How Do Our Choices Matter for Humans? The Application of Contemporary Cognitive Linguistics Research to the Debate on God and Metaphor," *Pastoral Psychology* 53, no. 3 (2005), https://doi.org/10.1007/s11089-004-0554-5.

[9]In Ortiz's edited volume, he brings together Catholic, Orthodox, Lutheran, Reformed, Anabaptist, Anglican, Baptist, and Wesleyan voices, and performs an exercise called "a receptive ecumenism," which is "not about debates or joint statements but about 'hospitality and an exchange of gifts.'" See Jared Ortiz, "Introduction," in Ortiz, *With All the Fullness*, 3-4.

[10]Eve Sweetser and Mary Therese DesCamp, "Motivating Biblical Metaphors for God: Refining the Cognitive Model," in Howe and Green, *Cognitive Linguistic Explorations*, 7.

[11]Konsmo surveys a handful of approaches to metaphor, including the pre-Aristotelian, Aristotelean, Hellenistic, Greco-Roman rhetorical, and modern approaches (including linguistic theories of metaphor and conceptual theories of metaphor such as the interaction theory, the

interpretations, Erik Konsmo argues that "the cognitive-linguistic interpretive approach to metaphor best embraces this reality" that "metaphors are conceptual at their root, but linguistically expressed."[12] For DesCamp and Sweetser, "cognitive linguistics considers metaphors to be substantive not figural: a matter of thinking rather than a matter of language."[13]

Regarding the application of cognitive linguistics to theology, Masson cautions his audience regarding "some of the more reductionist, expansive and speculative claims sometimes made by cognitive linguists." At the same time, Masson admits that the "key insights of cognitive linguistics are compatible with a more robust and less reductionist conception of God and theological reasoning than otherwise might seem the case."[14] Masson compares Mary Gerhart and Allan Melvin Russell's very different theory of metaphoric process to George Lakoff and Mark Johnson's and highlights the significant insights and limitations of both.[15] He introduces a broader

---

cognitive-linguistic theory, and conceptual theory of Kövecses). See Konsmo, *Pauline Metaphors*, 29-51.

[12] Konsmo, *Pauline Metaphors*, 52.

[13] DesCamp and Sweetser, "Metaphors for God," 226.

[14] Masson, *Without Metaphor*, 29.

[15] Mary Gerhart and Allan Melvin Russell, *Metaphoric Process: The Creation of Scientific and Religious Understanding* (Fort Worth: Texas Christian University Press, 1984); Mary Gerhart and Allan Melvin Russell, *New Maps for Old: Explorations in Science and Religion* (New York: Continuum, 2001). Masson points out the following differences between Lakoff/Johnson and Gerhart/Russell. First, Lakoff and Johnson construe cross-domain mapping as a directional mapping of a source domain to a target domain, which is at odds with Gerhart and Russell's conception of an equivalence of that is bidirectional and symmetric. Second, while Lakoff and Johnson's metaphor theory explains the creation of new meaning and worldviews, it is not clear whether their examples, or Gary Anderson's metaphorical shifts, meet the threshold, envisaged in Gerhart and Russell's theory, of high viewpoints that have a stereoscope and tectonic effect. A third difference in the investigated territory is indicated by Gerhart and Russell's concern to account for the rich symmetric equivalence and fundamental change of worldview intended in affirmations such as "Jesus is the Messiah" or "Jesus is divine." Cognitive linguistics might propose to explain the richness in meaning and bidirectionality in such cases as resulting from the combination of two separate but complementary cross-domain mappings. But this line of explanation still does not account for the clearly stronger symmetric equivalence intended by Christians who confess *not* that Jesus is Messiah-like or the Messiah Jesus-like, but that Jesus *is* the Messiah. Therefore, Lakoff and Johnson's metaphor theory does not appear to have an adequate way to account for a stronger symmetric equivalence, other than reducing it to univocal literalism. By insisting on one-way directionality, Lakoff and Johnson appear to preclude even the consideration of a bidirectional equivalence that is not literal and fundamentalist. Gerhart and Russell's theory, however, allows for the emergence of conceptualizations and inferences that, although rooted in prior and conventional source domains, also transcend those inputs. In his conclusion, Masson suggests that both theories offer crucial but partial accounts of that multidimensional topography. Fauconnier and Turner offer a higher viewpoint with which Gerhart and Russell's theory is preoccupied. See Masson, *Without Metaphor*, 59-94 (90-92 in particular).

conception of conceptual mapping elaborated more recently by Giles Fauconnier and Mark Turner, among others. Masson writes, "Notwithstanding the fundamental difference in the theoretical approach, Fauconnier and Turner's theory of conceptual mapping shares significant affinities with Gerhart and Russell's notion of metaphoric process," and "delivers promising resources within cognitive linguistics itself for articulating much more robust conceptions of God and theological reasoning."[16] Building on the contributions from cognitive linguistics' metaphor theory, Gerhart and Russell's conception of metaphoric process, and Fauconnier and Turner's conceptual integration theory, Masson argues that *"there is no saving God without conceptual mappings that are metaphorical (cross-domain) and that entail tectonic equivalence (or double-scope integration)."*[17]

Eastern theologians speak of deification not only as a metaphor but also as the reality of union with God.[18] Debates among the proponents of deification are centered on the different typologies of deification. For example, Norman Russell identifies various senses of deification in the ancient church and divides them initially into three categories (nominal, analogical, and metaphorical) and later into four categories (nominal, analogical, ethical, and realistic).[19] However, such an interpretation can no longer stand scrutiny based on the advances in metaphor research in the last decades.[20]

---

[16]Masson, *Without Metaphor*, 95-109. According to Masson, Fauconnier and Turner's theory of blending bridges and expands earlier metaphor theory in cognitive linguistics and Gerhart and Russell's work by broadening the notion and range of conceptual mapping. Blending accounts for both Lakoff and Johnson's directional cross-domain mapping and Gerhart and Russell's bi-directional equivalency. Moreover, it accounts for a continuum of cross-spatial mappings that more adequately reflect the complex and multidimensional topography of human cognition. See Masson, *Without Metaphor*, 57, 106.

[17]Masson, *Without Metaphor*, 111, italics original.

[18]Veli-Matti Kärkkäinen, *Spirit and Salvation: A Constructive Christian Theology for the Pluralistic World* (Grand Rapids, MI: Eerdmans, 2016), 319-20. See also Vladimir Lossky, *The Mystical Theology of the Eastern Church* (Crestwood, NY: St. Vladimir's Seminary Press, 1976), 67.

[19]Norman Russell, *The Doctrine of Deification in the Greek Patristic Tradition*, OECS (Oxford: Oxford University Press, 2004), 1, 9.

[20]Masson enumerates his hypotheses, the second of which is that *"there is often no direct isomorphism between the underlying cognitive processes entailed in our conceptualization of God and the surface products of this talk that we call literal, metaphorical, and analogical. In general, these surface expressions of cross-domain mappings and tectonic blends do not fit neatly into such common sense classifications or even more technical definitions of the tropes."* The third states that *"the distinction between literal and figurative is not helpful in characterizing metaphoric cross-domain mapping or the process of tectonic conceptual blending (equivalence). The processes and*

Since the biblical and theological concept of deification certainly is abstract, the remark of Friedrich Ungerer and Hans-Jörg Schmidt is undoubtedly relevant for the appreciation of deificational metaphors in Scripture: "We rely on models of the concrete world to conceptualize abstract phenomenon."[21]

Next, I analyze three biblical metaphors from the concrete world identified by Nee and Lee, who further integrate them into their doctrine of deification.

## Three Biblical Metaphors (Grafting, Grain Offering, and New Jerusalem), Conceptual Mappings, and Cognitive Blending

Nee did not use terms such as *deification* or *theosis* in his speaking and writing. However, one can easily find similar thoughts in the sixty-two volumes of *The Collected Works of Watchman Nee*. For instance, on September 1, 1948, Nee spoke of the significance of God's eternal life, the goal of which is "to bring God into man so that man may become lost in God. In this way, God and man, man and God, become perfectly one."[22] After a few brief mentions in passing of the matter of deification espoused by the early church fathers between 1984 and 1993, Lee began to speak unequivocally on deification on January 9, 1994: "God's intention is to make Himself one with man—to make Himself man so that man may become Him." Lee considers this teaching "the diamond in the Bible."[23]

In this section, based on Nee and Lee's findings, I analyze the metaphors for Christ and the Trinity related to deification: CHRIST IS CULTIVATED OLIVE

---

their expressions are cognitive. They are normal modes of conceptualization and inference. They can make genuine truth claims. They can be true or false." See Masson, *Without Metaphor*, 112, italics original.

[21]Friedrich Ungerer and Hans-Jörg Schmid, *An Introduction to Cognitive Linguistics* (London: Longman, 1996), 121. To Kallistos Ware, deification itself is a metaphor of salvation used in the Christian East, which describes the idea of union with God. Other similar terms and metaphors include transformation, participation, partaking, intermingling, elevation, interpretation, transmutation, commingling, assimilation, reintegration, and adoption. See Ware, *The Orthodox Way*, rev. ed. (Crestwood, NY: St. Vladimir's Seminary Press, 1995), 168. See further Georgios Mantzaridis, *The Deification of Man: St. Gregory Palamas and the Orthodox Traditions*, trans. Liadain Sherrar (Crestwood, NY: St. Vladimir's Seminary Press, 1984); Panayiotis Nellas, *Deification in Christ: Orthodox Perspectives on the Nature of the Human Person*, trans. Norman Russell (Crestwood, NY: St. Vladimir's Seminary Press, 1987).

[22]*CWWN* 55:47.

[23]*CWWL 1994–1997* 1:4. For instance, see *CWWL 1984* 3:499. For the record in 1990, see *CWWL 1990* 3:391; in 1991–1992, see *CWWL 1991–1992* 2:463; in 1993, see *CWWL 1993* 1:414.

TREE, CHRIST IS GRAIN OFFERING, and NEW JERUSALEM IS UNIVERSAL INCORPORATION.[24] The working assumption is that because there is so little literal illustration of how the Trinity operates together to achieve deification, we could learn what characteristics of the Trinity are essential to the Scripture writers by examining the metaphors they chose to describe the concept of deification.[25] Both in the case of very sparse mappings, such as grain offering and new Jerusalem, and in rich mappings, such as grafting, I assume that these metaphors, as all metaphors, highlight certain aspects of the Trinity in relation to deification.

I begin with the full diagram of each metaphor, followed by a table showing the source domain input and the resulting blend. In the table, the elements of the source domain input are on the left, and the elements of the resulting blend are on the right. The target domain input in every metaphor is Christ/the Trinity, with some undefined characteristics; humanity also appears in the target domain, along with a space for characteristics. The generic space will show an agent or an object with undefined characteristics, and occasionally an object or subject on which the agent acts, as well as that object's or subject's characteristics.[26]

***Grafting: Union between Christ and humanity in the life of God through the uniting bond of the Spirit (Romans 11:17-24).*** In his book *The Normal Christian Life*, Nee illustrates the process of grafting through his conversation with someone known for his skill in grafting. Nee asks: "But if a man can graft a branch of one tree into another, cannot God take of the life of His Son and, so to speak, graft it into us?" Nee's highly metaphoric and pictorial description highlights that the grafting of humanity takes place at the new birth, which is "the reception of a life which I did not possess before. It is not that my natural life has been changed at all; it is that another life, a life altogether new, altogether Divine, has become my life." This new birth happens during a Christian's regeneration and is publicly testified to through their baptism. However, for this new birth to be possible, "God has cut off the old creation by the Cross

---

[24]In cognitive metaphor research, the standardized notation for a cognitive metaphor is "TARGET DOMAIN IS SOURCE DOMAIN" in small caps. This convention will be used throughout the chapter.

[25]Adapted from DesCamp and Sweetser, "Metaphors for God," 226.

[26]Adapted from DesCamp and Sweetser, "Metaphors for God," 226.

of His Son in order to bring in a new creation in Christ by resurrection." For Nee, salvation is accomplished by God, who grafts the life of Christ into humanity so that through new birth, they can receive "another life, a life altogether new, altogether Divine" in order not to bear "miserably poor fruit" but "rich juicy fruit."[27] Expounding on 1 Corinthians 12:12, Nee states:

> Paul told the Corinthians, "For even as the body is one and has many members, yet all the members of the body, being many, are one body, so also is the Christ" (1 Cor. 12:12). Paul did not say, "So also are Christ and His church." Neither did he say, "So also are Christ and His people." Paul said, "So also is the Christ." In other words, the Head is Christ, the Body is Christ, and all the members are Christ. This is why he said that even as the body is one and has many members, yet all the members of the body, being many, are one body, so also is the Christ. This word shows us clearly that the Head, the Body, and all the members are Christ.[28]

For Lee, "grafting is one picture of this union between God and [humanity.]" In order for the branch to be grafted, both the branch and the tree "must be cut. Just binding them together will not join them organically. Both must be cut and then grafted together at the site of the cut. When the two wounds kiss each other, the graft can take place, and there will be the growth." Jesus was cut on the cross. A sinner experiences the cutting at the time of repentance, which is motivated by the Spirit's searching and enlightening.[29] In the grafting process, "the rich life will swallow up all the defects of the poor life and thus transform the poor life. In the same principle, when we are grafted into Christ, Christ swallows up our defects, but He does not eliminate our own life. On the contrary, . . . He uplifts our humanity."[30]

One aspect of Nee and Lee's vision of sin is that of defect, of falling short of God's glory in human life. As a result of such a defect, humanity cannot bear sweet, juicy fruit. Therefore, I propose the metaphors SIN IS SHORTAGE and CHRIST IS CULTIVATED OLIVE TREE.[31] As one can see from the figure 3.1,

---

[27]*CWWN* 33:64-65.
[28]*CWWN* 50:809.
[29]*CWWL 1979* 1:284, 287-88.
[30]Witness Lee, *Life-Study of Romans* (Anaheim, CA: Living Stream Ministry, 2001), 661-62.
[31]This metaphor is an addition to the fifty metaphors for God that DesCamp and Sweetser identify from the New Testament ("Metaphors for God," 226).

the generic space is extremely nonspecific.[32] The inputs represent two different mental spaces, or "sets of activated neuronal assemblies."[33] In this case, one of the inputs is a schematic of a cultivated olive tree, events that happen to the tree in the grafting process, the wild olive shoot, and their characteristics. The other input space is Christ. A more complex diagram based on double scope blends can be composed by considering the trinitarian involvement in this metaphor: the Father is the vine grower (Jn 15:1), and the Spirit is the uniting "bond of peace" (Eph 4:3) that binds Christ and humanity, and the sweet life sap that produces "the fruit of the Spirit" (Gal 5:22). But for the sake of simplicity, below I am presenting a simplified but full diagram of the metaphor CHRIST IS CULTIVATED OLIVE TREE (fig. 3.1) along with a table (3.1) for that metaphor.

**Table 3.1.** Christ as cultivated olive tree (Rom 11:17-24)

| Source Domain Entailments | Blend |
|---|---|
| *Root of the cultivated tree was cut off. | *Christ was cut on the cross. |
| *Root of the cultivated tree is grafted with the wild olive branches. | *Christ is grafted with humanity. |
| *Root of the cultivated tree supplies life sap to the wild olive branches. | *Christ supplies the Spirit to humanity. |
| *Wild olive branches are cut off from the original tree. | *Humanity is cut off from the old Adam. |
| *Wild olive branches are inserted into the cultivated olive tree. | *Humanity is inserted into Christ. |
| *Wild olive branches' shortages are swallowed up. | *Humanity's shortages are swallowed up. |
| *Wild olive branches used to bear sour olives but can now bear sweet ones. | *Humanity used to bear corruptible fruit but can now bear the eternal fruits of the Spirit. |

***Grain offering: Blending of Christ's divine nature and human nature as food for God and humanity (Leviticus 2:1-10).*** For Nee, the grain offering, or the meal offering, "is a type of the fineness of Christ's humanity on the earth." That such an offering contains no blood "signifies the living, good conduct, and virtue of the life of the Lord Jesus." The grain offering also

---

[32]The analysis follows the example of GOD IS A SHEPHERD. See DesCamp and Sweetser, "Metaphors for God," 218-20.

[33]Gilles Fauconnier and Mark Turner, *The Way We Think: Conceptual Blending and the Mind's Hidden Complexities* (New York: Basic Books, 2002), 40.

*Deification Seen from Three Biblical Metaphors ...*

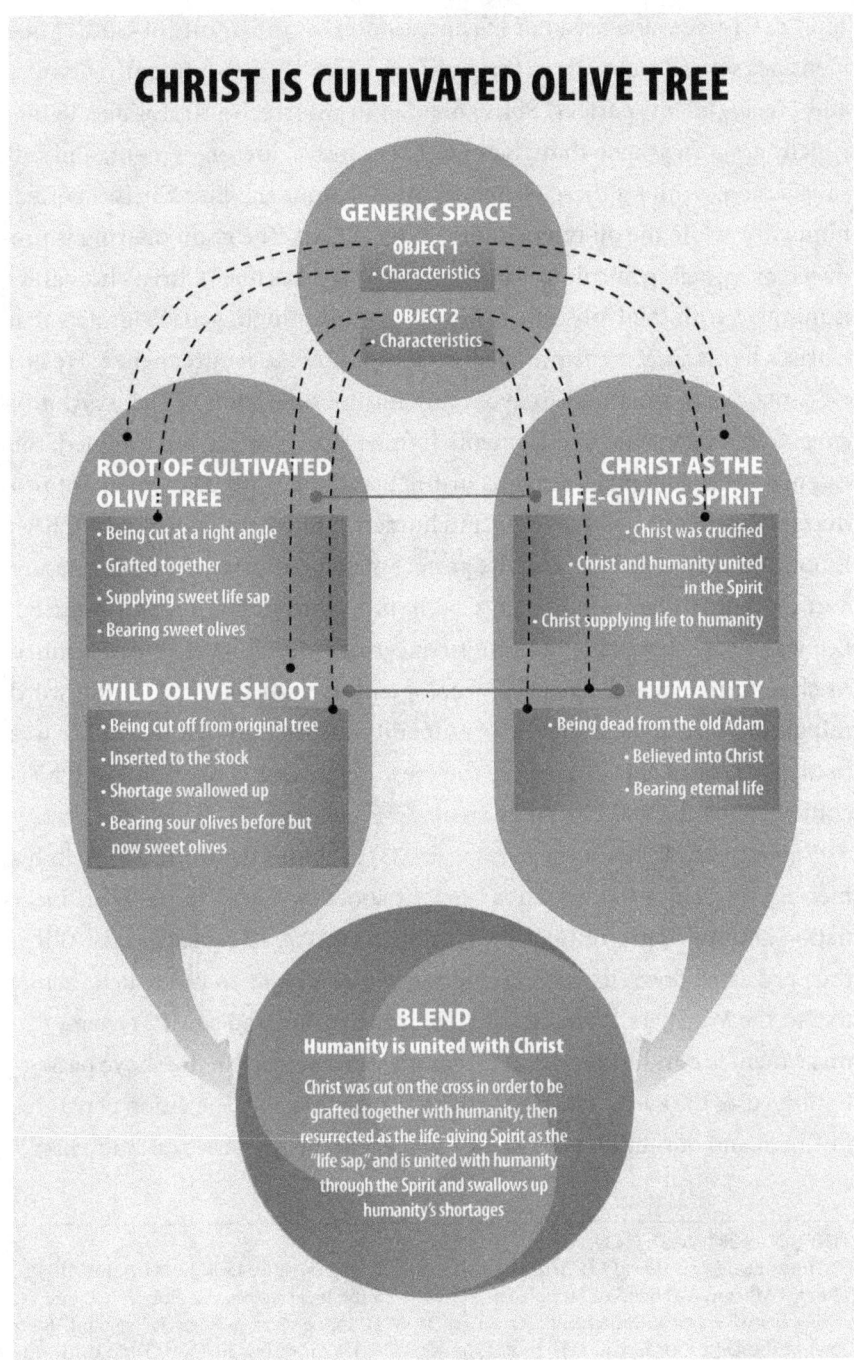

**Figure 3.1.** The full diagram of the metaphor CHRIST IS CULTIVATED OLIVE TREE

"typifies Christ as the bread of life and as food for the priests of God."[34] Lee identifies several elements in the grain offering: "Christ's humanity, divinity, and His excellent, perfect, Spirit-filled, and resurrection-saturated living," which "are a fragrance that gives God rest, peace, joy, enjoyment, and full satisfaction." Among these elements, the fine flour signifies Christ's perfect humanity, while the oil refers to the Spirit of God. The grain offering is produced by mingling fine flour with oil, which signifies that "Christ's humanity is mingled with the Holy Spirit (Mt 1:18b). This mingling also signifies that Christ's human nature is mingled with God's divine nature; hence, He is a God-man." Lee is careful to avoid any misinterpretation of the word *mingling*: "Although these two elements [of fine flour and oil] are mingled, the essence of each element remains distinct, and the third element is not produced." The mingling of divinity and humanity in Christ means that "Christ is both the complete God and the perfect man, possessing the divine nature and the human nature distinctly, without a third nature being produced." Lee was aware that some teachings concerning mingling were condemned in church history. As a result, "theologians did not dare to use the word mingle or to teach the mingling of humanity and divinity." However, Lee was bold to speak of this "based on the New Testament revelation [which] is confirmed by the Old Testament types."[35]

Interestingly, Ephrem the Syrian (d. 373) also uses the word *mingle* in his message on deification, which is brought about by Christ through his incarnation and the Spirit. In his *Hymn on the Faith, No. 10*, he exclaims: "When the Lord came down to earth, to mortals, / a new creation he created them, / like to the Watchers [the angels]. / He mingled fire and spirit in them, / to make them fire and spirit within."[36] For the word *mingled* in the above passage, Ephrem uses the Syriac term *mzag*, which describes both the union of natures in Christ and our union with him by grace and the mysteries (sacraments).[37]

---

[34]*CWWN* 58:284; 20:37; 5:439.
[35]Witness Lee, *Life-Study of Leviticus* (Anaheim, CA: Living Stream Ministry, 2001), 108, 111-13.
[36]Robert Murray, "A Hymn of St. Ephrem to Christ on the Incarnation, the Holy Spirit, and the Sacraments," *Eastern Churches Review* 3 (1970–1971): 143, quoted in Seely J. Beggiani, *Early Syriac Theology, with Special Reference to the Maronite Tradition*, rev. ed. (New York: University Press of America, 2014), 78.
[37]Murray, "Hymn of St. Ephrem," 147, quoted in Beggiani, *Early Syriac Theology*, 78.

Furthermore, God decrees that "what is left of the grain offering shall be for Aaron and his sons, a most holy part of the offerings by fire to the LORD" (Lev 2:3). For Lee, Aaron and his sons' partaking of the offering means the extension of the mingling to humanity. Paul was mingled with Christ, as he states, "It is no longer I who live, but it is Christ who lives in me" (Gal 2:20). The mingling takes place through eating (Jn 6:57) and the metabolic process of digesting and assimilation: "As our food, Christ strengthens us and energizes us."[38] As a result, humanity is transformed because "transformation is the issue of a metabolic process in which a new element, the element of Christ that we receive by eating Him, is assimilated into us to discharge and replace the old element of our natural being."[39] Below is a full diagram (fig. 3.2) of the metaphor CHRIST IS GRAIN OFFERING and a table (3.2) for that metaphor.

**Table 3.2.** Christ as grain offering (Lev 2:1-10)

| Source Domain Entailments | Blend |
|---|---|
| *Priests need constant nourishment by being mingled with the grain offering. | * Humanity needs spiritual nourishment by being mingled with Christ. |
| * Priests eat the grain offering. | * Humanity accepts and enjoys Christ in the way of spiritual assimilation. |
| * Priests assimilate the new elements of the grain offering and discharge old elements. | * Humanity assimilates the new elements of Christ's life and discharges the old elements of Adam. |
| * The grain offering is a mingled entity. | * Christ's human nature is mingled with divine nature. |
| * The grain offering gives life to the priests. | * Christ gives life to humanity. |

***New Jerusalem: Incorporation of God and humanity as already-not yet reality (Revelation 21:2).*** "The New Jerusalem is the masterpiece in the center of God's heart," declares Nee.[40] Nee and Lee take the new Jerusalem as an ultimate, consummating metaphor of deification.[41] For Nee, the new Jerusalem is the temple of God, the wife of the Lamb, the new humanity God

---

[38]Lee, *Life-Study of Leviticus*, 112, 126.
[39]*CWWL 1971* 3:363.
[40]*CWWN* 34:130.
[41]For an account of the early church fathers who took new Jerusalem as an important metaphor for deification, see Nathan Betz, "The New Jerusalem: A Metaphor for Deification in the Commentaries on Revelation by Oecumenius and Andrew of Caesarea," *Ephemerides Theologicae Lovanienses* 96, no. 1 (2022): 1-39.

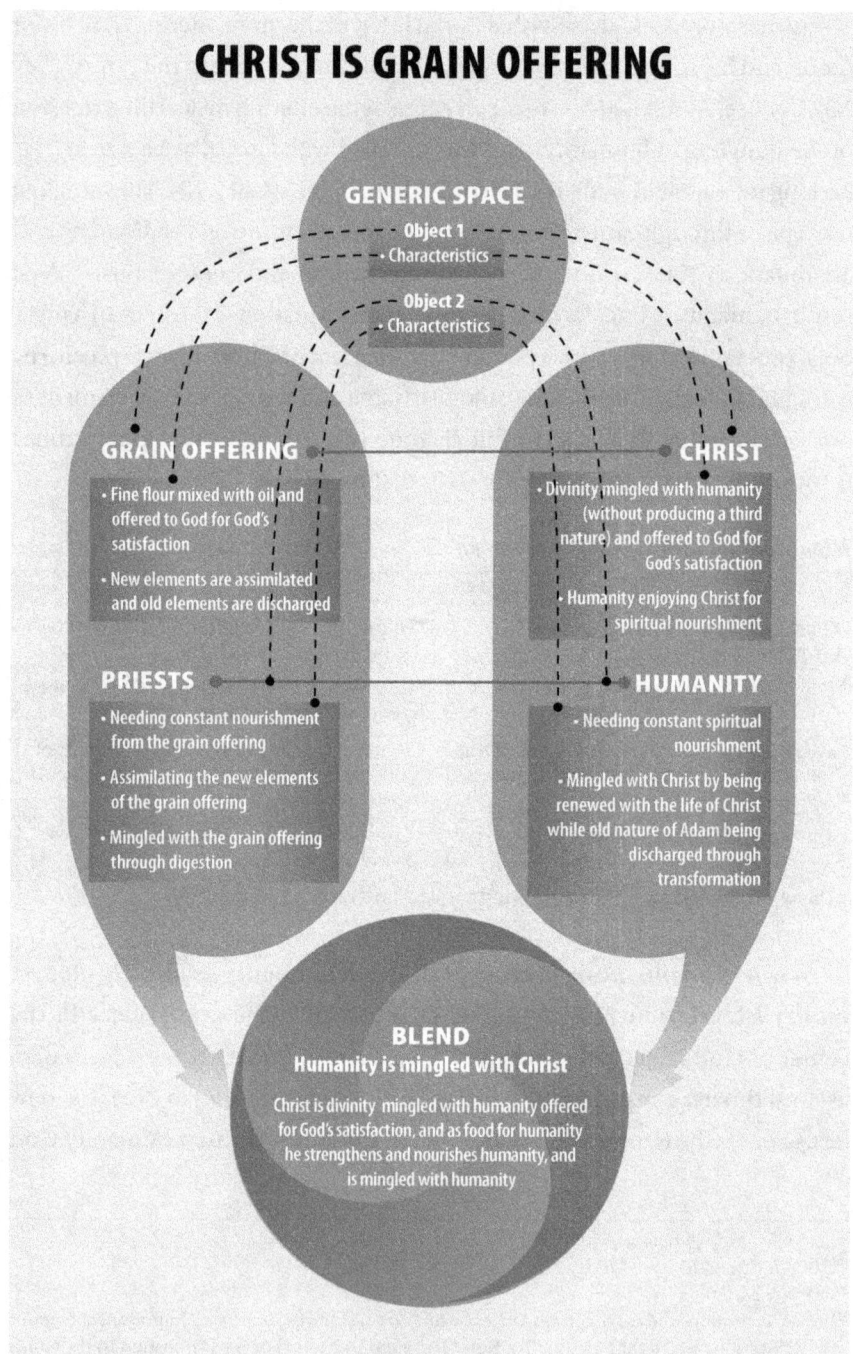

**Figure 3.2.** The full diagram of the metaphor CHRIST IS GRAIN OFFERING

has desired to obtain.[42] For Lee, "God in His Divine Trinity is an incorporation" "by coinhering mutually" and "by working together as one" (Jn 14:10). Christ incorporates believers into him in his resurrection and into the Father as a consequence of his incorporation with the Father (Jn 14:20). The Holy Spirit not only abides with the believers, dwells in them (Jn 14:16-17), but also beautifies and transforms them as the bride of Christ.[43] Lee suggests that the new Jerusalem is "the universal incorporation" of God and redeemed humanity as an issue of Christ's glorification, which can be presented in three aspects.[44]

The first aspect of the incorporation of God with regenerated believers is the house of God (Jn 14:2), typified by the temple (Jn 2:16-21). This Father's house "is built up by the constant visitation to the redeemed elect of the Father and the Son with the Spirit who indwells the regenerated elect to be the mutual dwelling place of the . . . Triune God and His redeemed elect." Second, the incorporation of God and the regenerated believers is the true vine (Jn 15:1), which "as a sign of the all-inclusive Christ is the organism" of the triune God. The branches "are the believers of Christ, who by nature were branches of the wild olive tree and have been grafted into the cultivated olive tree (Rom 11:17, 24) through their believing into Christ (Jn 3:15)." Through the fruit bearing of the believers as the branches by their faithful abiding in Christ, the true vine represents "the increase of the immeasurable Christ, the embodiment of the . . . Triune God" "for the glorification of the Father." The third aspect of the incorporation of God with regenerated believers is the child of the Spirit (Jn 16:13-16, 19-22). A new child, a new humanity, was created by Christ on the cross by abolishing in his flesh the law of the commandments in ordinances (Eph 2:15), was regenerated by the Father with the resurrected Christ (1 Pet 1:3; Rom 1:4), and is born by the Spirit in believers' spirits (Jn 3:6), consummating the body of Christ.[45] Below is a full diagram (fig. 3.3) of the metaphor NEW JERUSALEM IS UNIVERSAL INCORPORATION followed by a table (3.3) for that metaphor.

---

[42]*CWWN* 34:131, 146, 129.
[43]*CWWL 1994–1997* 5:334; Witness Lee, *Life-Study of Ephesians* (Anaheim, CA: Living Stream Ministry, 2001), 628, 801.
[44]*CWWL 1994–1997* 5:339, 331.
[45]*CWWL 1994–1997* 5:337, 345-46.

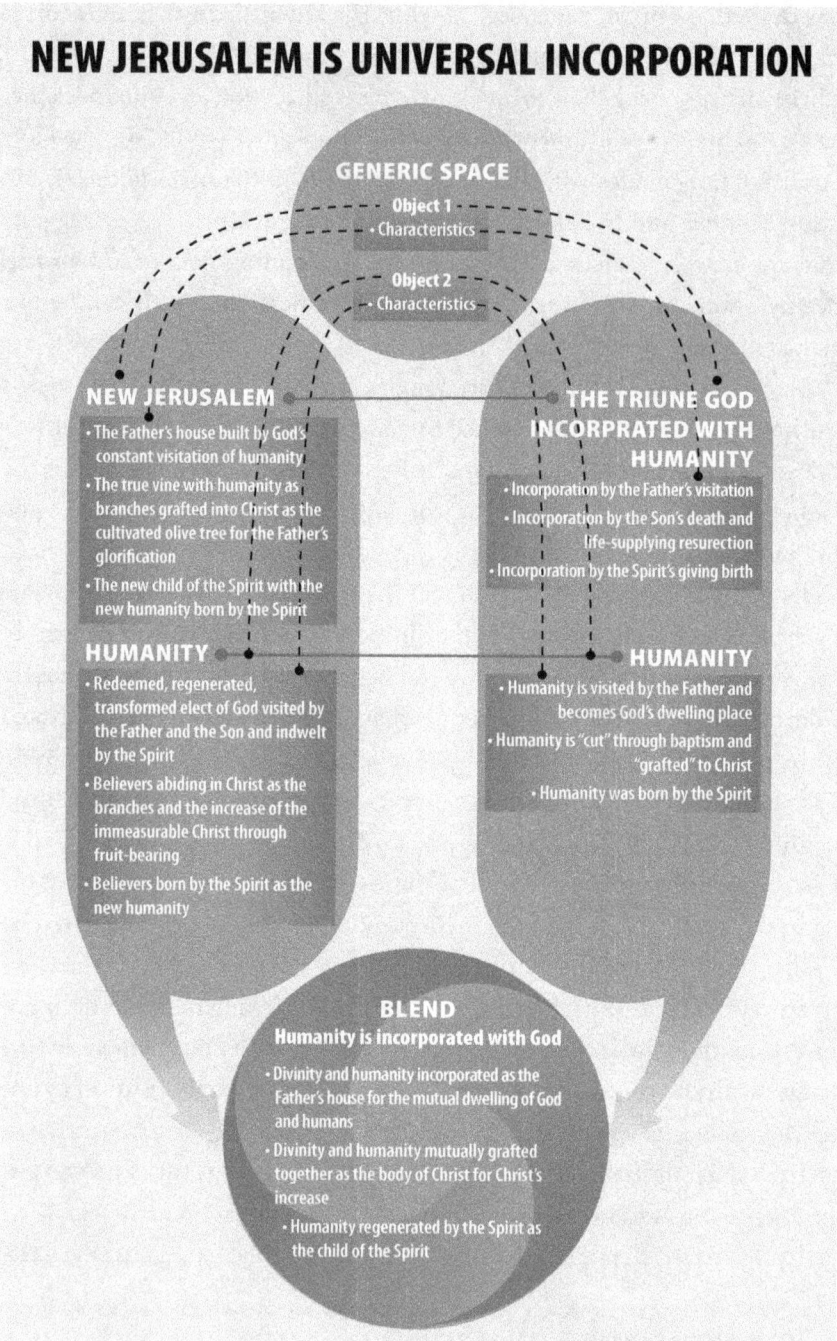

**Figure 3.3.** The full diagram of the metaphor NEW JERUSALEM IS UNIVERSAL INCORPORATION

**Table 3.3.** New Jerusalem as universal incorporation (Rev 21:2)

| Source Domain Entailments | Blend |
|---|---|
| *New Jerusalem is the Father's house as a result of the Father's visitation of humanity. | *Triune God and humanity are incorporated as the Father's house. |
| * New Jerusalem is the true vine, with Christ as the cultivated olive tree and humanity as branches for the increase of Christ. | *Triune God and humanity are incorporated as the body of Christ. |
| * New Jerusalem is the new child of the Spirit, with the Spirit giving birth to the new humanity. | *Triune God and humanity are incorporated as the new child of the Spirit. |
| *Humanity is visited by the Father as the dwelling place of God. | *Human and divine incorporation becomes the mutual dwelling place of humanity and divinity. |
| * Humanity was cut through baptism and is nourished by Christ as the body of Christ. | * Human and divine incorporation becomes the body of Christ with Christ as its head. |
| * Humanity was born by the Spirit. | *Human and divine incorporation becomes the new humanity renewed by the Spirit. |

***Summary.*** The three metaphors, CHRIST IS CULTIVATED OLIVE TREE, CHRIST IS GRAIN OFFERING, and NEW JERUSALEM IS UNIVERSAL INCORPORATION are metaphors for God in general and the God-human relationship in particular. The analysis of these metaphors is significant in that, first, they complement the ninety-four metaphors for God identified by DesCamp and Sweetser.[46] Second, the common characteristics resist the somewhat reductionistic classification of DesCamp and Sweetser, who identify seven "preferred" characteristics for God based on their study of the metaphors of God in the entire Scripture, namely, (1) protection, safety, sustenance; (2) mutual asymmetric relationship; (3) physical control; (4) change of state/essence; (5) authority; (6) destructive, power to punish; and (7) control.[47] I suggest adding another category titled deification to capture the union, mingling, and incorporation of God and humanity.

Third, contrary to the nontrinitarian nature of the findings of DesCamp and Sweetser, the three metaphors are thoroughly trinitarian in the understanding of Nee and Lee. The roles of the Father and the Holy Spirit are prominent in all three metaphors: In the CHRIST IS CULTIVATED OLIVE TREE metaphor, the Father is the vine grower, and the Spirit is the uniting bond of peace between Christ and humanity and the life sap that produces fruits

---

[46] DesCamp and Sweetser identify forty-four metaphors for God in the Hebrew Scripture and fifty in the New Testament ("Metaphors for God," 226-31).
[47] DesCamp and Sweetser, "Metaphors for God," 232.

of the Spirit. In the CHRIST IS GRAIN OFFERING metaphor, the Spirit is the oil that mingles with Christ's perfect humanity, which makes him the unique God-man and adds divinity into human beings to nourish their humanity. In the NEW JERUSALEM IS UNIVERSAL INCORPORATION metaphor, the Father and the Son with the Spirit, who indwells believers, visit humanity and make redeemed humans the Father's house. As the life sap of the true vine, the Spirit nourishes humanity as the branches for the Father's glorification. The Father regenerates believers, and the Spirit indwells them and gives birth to the new child and the new humanity, who constitute the body of Christ. The Father and the Spirit take on active roles in the theology of deification.

Fourth, the three biblical metaphors in the creative interpretation of Nee and Lee highlight their unique understanding of deification, which can be metaphorically unpacked as the union of God and humanity in the divine life, the mingling of the divine nature with the human nature, and the divine-human incorporation of the persons embodied in the new Jerusalem composed of deifying God and deified humanity.

Fifth, the analysis of these three metaphors confirms Masson's findings:

1. For Nee and Lee, the union, mingling, and incorporation between divinity and humanity represents a stronger symmetric equivalence, not being reducible to univocal literalism. Lakoff and Johnson's metaphor theory is inadequate in accounting for the theology of deification by "insisting on one-way directionality, [and appearing] to preclude even the consideration of the seismic emergence of new fields of meanings and logical entailments."[48]

2. Gerhart and Russell's theory allows for the emergence of conceptualizations and inferences that transcend the inputs that expose the limitation of Lakoff and Johnson's metaphor theory. Without escaping the constitutive role of the embodied mind, Gerhart and Russell's theory allows the reconfigured mappings to create the possibility for a revolutionary conception. For example, in the Greco-Roman world, people worshiped a multitude of gods. Even Caesar demanded to be worshiped. Therefore, by proclaiming that "Christ became human that humans might become divine," Athanasius and Jesus' early followers did make a revolutionary move (*Inc.* 54, 93).

---

[48] Masson, *Without Metaphor*, 91.

3. Fauconnier and Turner's theory of blending "bridges and expands earlier metaphor theory in cognitive linguistics and Gerhart and Russell's work by broadening the notion and range of conceptual mapping." Blending accounts for not only both Lakoff and Johnson's directional cross-domain mapping and Gerhart and Russell's bidirectional equivalence but also "a continuum of cross-spatial mappings that more adequately reflect the complex and multidimensional topography of human cognition," as illustrated in the broader understanding of conceptual space with a higher viewpoint provided by the three metaphors.[49]

Evidence of the emergence of different fields of meanings persists today in the difference between the statements "Christians are Christlike," "Christians are small christs," and "Christians are becoming God." I suggest that the Protestant fear of violating the Creator-creature difference can be overcome by adopting Lee's formulation based on the three metaphors: humanity can become God in God's life and nature but not in the Godhead.[50] These three biblical images are of salvific and deificational significance. Nee and Lee were not forced to use their formulation or to use it in the specific ways they did, Masson writes, "any more than Einstein was forced to use Riemann's geometry in this theory of relativity. For Gerhart and Russell, forcing an equivalence where none existed signifies a blending of inputs that is not a given but rather must be brought about by a creative process of cognitive integration." This chapter affirms Masson's eighth thesis, in that the truth and credibility of the conceptions and inferences cannot be determined apart from their tectonic mapping and that thick contextual interpretation of this mapping is absolutely critical.[51]

## Revolutionary Changes in Metaphoric Understanding of Sin

Gary Anderson makes a compelling argument that what Masson later calls a "tectonic metaphoric shift" occurred in Judaism at the beginning of the Second Temple era. This metaphorical shift had a revolutionary impact on

---

[49] Masson, *Without Metaphor*, 106.
[50] *CWWL 1993* 1:407.
[51] Masson, *Without Metaphor*, 113, 169.

the Jewish and Christian understandings of sin and salvation.[52] According to Anderson, in most of the Old Testament, sin is imagined as a weight borne on the shoulders of the sinner and the sinner's descendants. Forgiveness is having the weight carried away or lifted off. Anderson draws explicitly on Lakoff and Johnson's contention that when we conceptualize a more abstract target domain (in this case, sin) in terms of a more tangible source domain (bearing a physical weight), entailments of the target domain are mapped to the source domain, and he proposes a metaphor of SIN AS BURDEN. The first benefit in recognizing the ubiquity of this metaphor is that it helps explain biblical texts such as Leviticus 16:21-22 ("the weight of Israel's sins") and Genesis 4:13 ("the weight of my sin is too great for me to bear"). Anderson further identifies a metaphoric shift to SIN AS DEBT at the beginning of the Second Temple period, caused by the influence of Aramaic. In Aramaic, the standard word for "sin" has to do with debt, which was taken over in Rabbinic Hebrew and with it a new conception of sin. The linguistic revolution was so complete that the earlier idiom that spoke of sin as a weight "practically comes to an end in the rabbinic period."[53] Anderson provides a detailed analysis of the tectonic shift from the SIN AS BURDEN to SIN AS DEBT metaphor, and of the latter's role in the historical evolution of the metaphor of A TREASURY IN HEAVEN.[54]

Anderson argues that the ancient Jewish and Christian understanding of the practice of almsgiving motivated the medieval notion that acts of charity contribute to the heavenly treasury that counts against the immeasurable debt of our sins. Furthermore, a correct understanding of the logical entailments of the metaphor overcomes Luther's objection to the concept of a "treasury of merits" and a significant point of division between Protestants and Catholics. The heavenly treasury counts against the debt of sinfulness because "God has 'gamed' the system," not because of human merit. For Anderson, understanding the metaphors for sin also provides a new perspective for a more positive interpretation of St. Anselm's theory of satisfaction.[55] In the analysis of Masson, Anderson demonstrates the possibility of

---

[52] Anderson, *Sin*, 9. For Masson's comment, see *Without Metaphor*, 86.
[53] Anderson, *Sin*, 16-25, 6, 24-25, 8, 27-28.
[54] Anderson, *Sin*, 186-87, cited in Masson, *Without Metaphor*, 88.
[55] Anderson, *Sin*, 12, 190-99.

a robust, instructive, and nonreductive theological appropriation of cognitive linguistics' metaphor theory. Moreover, his detailed analysis of the metaphor for sin and forgiveness appears to demonstrate that cross-domain mapping of the sort envisioned by Lakoff and Johnson produced a "revolutionary change in thinking and worldview for Judaism and Christianity, and continues to have crucial interpretive significance."[56]

However, Anderson and Masson have neglected other equally revolutionary shifts in metaphors for sin and forgiveness. In the Eastern Orthodox view of salvation, sin is not viewed as guilt but as mortality.[57] One of the key texts quoted by the Orthodox theologians is 2 Peter 1:4, which speaks of becoming "partakers of the divine nature" and accentuates the key idea of release from the corruption and morality caused by the evil desires of the world.[58] Veli-Matti Kärkkäinen observes that justification is almost exclusively christologically loaded (whereas in sanctification the Spirit's role is more pronounced). A related issue has to do with the context of salvation: whereas Latin traditions have been dominated by legal, juridical, and forensic categories, Eastern theology understands the need for salvation in terms of deliverance from mortality and corruption.[59] Forgiveness is understood as part of the broad and general concept of deification, summarized by Irenaeus as the "Word of God, our Lord Jesus Christ who because of his limitless love became what we are in order to make us what even he himself is" (*Haer.* 5.preface). For Kärkkäinen, even though the comment made by Orthodox theologian Vladimir Lossky that theosis is "echoed by the fathers and the theologians of every age" may be an overstatement, it does reflect the general mindset of the fathers.[60]

In view of this significant development, I suggest that such a metaphoric shift of sin be labeled SIN AS MORTALITY. It is due to such a tectonic metaphor shift (to use Masson's terminology) that the Spirit's constitutive role

---

[56] Masson, *Without Metaphor*, 89.
[57] F. W. Norris, "Deification: Consensual and Cogent," *SJT* 49, no. 4 (1996): 422.
[58] Other texts include Ps 82:6 (quoted in Jn 10:34-36); Ex 34:30; 7:1; Mt 17:4; Jn 3:8; 14:21-23; 15:4-8, 17:21-23; 2 Cor 8:9; Heb 4:15; 1 Jn 3:2; 4:12. See Timothy Ware, *The Orthodox Church* (London: Penguin Books, 1997), 236-37, quoted in Kärkkäinen, *Spirit and Salvation*, 319.
[59] Kärkkäinen, *Spirit and Salvation*, 320.
[60] Lossky, *Mystical Theology*, 134; Kärkkäinen, *Spirit and Salvation*, 318. See further, for a profound statement by Bishop Kallistos of Diokleia, foreword to Mantzaridis, *Deification of Man*, 7.

in salvation is robustly presented. In other words, a trinitarian pneumatology drives the Eastern Christian theosis soteriology, in that participation in the triune God is made possible by the divine Spirit.[61] In contrast, in the West the Spirit's role is subservient to that of Christ.[62] Donald Fairbairn argues that whereas in later theology, especially in the Christian West, soteriology came to be linked predominantly with Christology, Eastern theology maintains a healthy balance between christological and pneumatological understandings of salvation.[63] Eastern theology even speaks of Christians as "christs," anointed ones.[64]

Another neglected theological framework that arrives at salvation as theosis via different a theological route is the theology of Watchman Nee and Witness Lee. Nee emphasizes that holiness is God's nature and God's character. God's discipline is not driven by temper for the purpose of punishment because "whoever thinks this way is altogether in the realm of the law and the courtroom." In speaking of salvation, Nee makes the distinction that "for Christ to become our holiness is one thing. For us to be sanctified is another thing." He elaborates, "Holiness is constituted through [God's] holiness, something constituted through [God's] scourging and daily, inner working. His discipline and operation are for the purpose of making us partakers of His holiness."[65] On top of the common understanding of sin as guilt, Nee also understands sin as "falling short of the glory of God" (Rom 3:23). He interprets it in contrast to the Western judicial understanding of sin: "If the Bible were to say that all have sinned because all have broken the Ten Commandments, there would be a difference between great sinners and small sinners, for some may have transgressed nine commandments, while others may have transgressed only one." Therefore, salvation is more than justification; it

---

[61]John Meyendorff, *Byzantine Theology: Historical Trends and Doctrinal Themes* (New York: Fordham University Press, 1974), 13. See, e.g., Athanasius, *Epistulae ad Serapionem* 1.15-33, esp. 1.22-24, 22-24. Quoted in Kärkkäinen, *Spirit and Salvation*, 320.

[62]Kärkkäinen, *Spirit and Salvation*, 320.

[63]Donald Fairbairn, "Salvation as Theosis: The Teaching of Eastern Orthodoxy," *Themelios* 23, no. 3 (1998): 42-43. Consider Irenaeus, *Haer.* 5.1.1; Pseudo-Macarius, *The Great Letter* 269-70. Quoted in Kärkkäinen, *Spirit and Salvation*, 320.

[64]Lossky, *Mystical Theology*, 174.

[65]*CWWN* 50:700.

is "God pulling a sinner from the mud of sin and taking him all the way to glory."[66]

Let me draw a few narrow conclusions here. First, Nee's soteriology is thoroughly trinitarian: God gives humanity his holiness as a gift so that they can partake of God's holiness through his discipline; Christ becomes the believers' holiness through his death on the cross; the Holy Spirit's daily and inner working constitutes God's holiness into humanity. Second, Nee understands that the Western view of sin as guilt is inadequate. I suggest that he complements it with one of the several aspects of sin he articulates, that is, a metaphor of SIN AS SHORTAGE OF GOD'S GLORY.

Lee continues Nee's theological vision. Following Augustine, "We are what we love," Lee poetically expresses his thought on deification as "if one loves dust, to dust he becomes; if one loves God, to God he becomes" in his translation of Albert Simpson's hymn.[67] For Lee, deification is summarized as "God became a man so that [humanity] can become God in the life and nature of God, but not in the Godhead."[68] This statement can be illustrated in strong trinitarian language:

> The life-giving Spirit as the consummation of the processed Triune God comes to regenerate, sanctify, renew, and transform the believers, to conform them to the image of the Son of God, and eventually to glorify them with the eternal glory of God that the Son of God may be the Firstborn among His many brothers, the many sons of God; thus, they become the many God-men to constitute the Body of Christ and consummately be enlarged and built up as the New Jerusalem.[69]

For Lee, Christ is the God-man who possesses both divinity (divine nature) and humanity (perfect human nature). Christians are therefore the "God-men" or "God-humans." Similar to Orthodox theologians, Lee pronounces that "through regeneration we are the same as Christ; we even are little 'Christs.'" Balancing between Christology and pneumatology, Lee speaks of "pneumatic Christ."[70] Nee and Lee's doctrine of deification is trinitarian in

---

[66] *CWWN* 28:49.
[67] Taiwan fuyin shufang [Taiwan gospel bookroom], *Shige* [Hymns] (Taipei: Taiwan fuyin shufang, 2011), 436-37.
[68] *CWWL 1994–1997* 1:402.
[69] *CWWL 1994–1997* 2:174.
[70] *CWWL 1994–1997* 1:407-8; 4:107-20.

general and pneumatological in particular: in the CHRIST IS CULTIVATED OLIVE TREE metaphor, the Holy Spirit is the life of the cultivated olive tree that "swallows up" the defective life of the wild olive tree; in the CHRIST IS GRAIN OFFERING metaphor, the Spirit is the oil that mingles the divinity and humanity; in the NEW JERUSALEM IS UNIVERSAL INCORPORATION metaphor, the Holy Spirit conforms believers to the image of Christ.

Following Fauconnier and Turner's "multiple-scope integration networks," it can be suggested that SIN AS MORTALITY or SIN AS SHORTAGE OF GOD'S GLORY, as a single-scope blend, would not have had a tectonic effect by itself. But when it is combined with the cross-domain mappings CHRIST IS CULTIVATED OLIVE TREE, CHRIST IS GRAIN OFFERING, and NEW JERUSALEM IS UNIVERSAL INCORPORATION, it contributes to the emergence of the more complex notion of THEOSIS IS GROWTH. In Christian contexts, multiple-scope networks motivated further complex blends, which affirm that humanity is saved so that God can gain corporate reproductions of Godself. If Anderson is correct, objections to the theology of deification may well have to do with a misinterpretation of the logic of these complex multiple-scope blends and their emergence in Scripture itself. Moreover, understanding the figurative logic of religious and theological language can make an essential contribution to understanding and helping to resolve contentious issues such as deification that still divide Christians.[71]

## Conclusion

In this chapter, I first presented the trends in the studies of metaphors and highlighted the advantages of the cognitive-linguistic interpretive approach to metaphor. Then I introduced Masson's critical evaluations of Lakoff and Johnson's metaphor theory, Gerhart and Russell's theory of metaphoric process, and Fauconnier and Turner's conceptual integration theory. Cognitive linguistics' accumulative insights over decades have shown that many past theories on metaphor, especially terms such as *literal*, *metaphorical*, and *analogical*, are no longer helpful. This observation shatters some existing theological understandings of deification and calls for fresh considerations.

---

[71]The reasoning is inspired by Masson (see *Without Metaphor*, 108-9).

Based on Nee and Lee's interpretation of three biblical metaphors, grafting, grain offering, and new Jerusalem, I identified the metaphors CHRIST IS CULTIVATED OLIVE TREE, CHRIST IS GRAIN OFFERING, and NEW JERUSALEM IS UNIVERSAL INCORPORATION. Following the exemplary work of DesCamp and Sweetser, I analyzed each metaphor and produced full diagrams and tables illustrating the conceptual blends to further the understanding of deification.

The results are groundbreaking: (1) three metaphors prove to be valuable additions to the list of the metaphors of God identified by DesCamp and Sweetser; (2) a valuable characteristic of God is identified beyond protection, mutual asymmetric relationship, physical control, change of state/essence, authority, and power to punish, namely, the power to deify humanity; (3) the metaphors make up for the "trinitarian deficit" in the Protestant theology of justification; (4) Masson's critical assessment of the three theories of cognitive linguistics is proven valid, in that Lakoff and Johnson's metaphor theory is inadequate, and the theories of Gerhart and Russell and of Fauconnier and Turner are instrumental to theological investigations that are metaphorical in nature; (5) Lee's formulation of deification, namely, God became a human so that humans can become God in the divine life and divine nature but not in the Godhead, can alleviate the Protestant concern with violating the Creator-creature divide.

After investigating the three metaphors and their implications for theologies of justification and deification, I analyzed the different metaphoric understandings of sin. Anderson's studies of a tectonic metaphoric shift from SIN AS BURDEN to SIN AS DEBT are highly innovative but incomplete due to his one-sided attention to the debates between the Catholic theologians and Luther. Both Anderson and Masson have neglected other equally revolutionary shifts in metaphors for sin and forgiveness. I then summarized the Eastern Orthodox understanding of sin as SIN AS MORTALITY, and Nee and Lee's as SIN AS SHORTAGE OF GOD'S GLORY. Both arrive at the doctrine of deification (albeit from different routes) and are revolutionary in changing worldviews on the God-human relationship.

If there is anything constructive—or perhaps novel—in this chapter, it is the original attempt at applying the cognitive-linguistic interpretive approach to the doctrine of deification. Nee and Lee's understanding of deification is a viable addition to the ecumenical presentation on such an important topic, which makes up the trinitarian and Spirit deficit in the Protestant account of the doctrine of justification. However, further in-depth application of the various analytical tools provided by cognitive linguistics to deification in particular, and constructive theology in general, is needed to fully realize the rich potential of the exciting developments in the field of cognitive linguistics.

# DEIFICATION *and the* ESCHATOLOGICAL CITY

## Exegetical and Theological Connections in Early Christian Thought

### Nathan Betz

In his peroration to the *Refutation of All Heresies*, the anonymous author, likely writing in Rome around the year 220, addresses his audience with a rousing statement concerning their divine destiny. In bracing language, he draws together two central items of Christian reflection: the eschaton, that is, the world's end, and the Christian telos or proper end unto which God created us:

> You will have an immortal and incorruptible body together with a soul, and you who lived on earth and knew the heavenly king will receive the kingdom of heaven. You will be a friend of God and coheir with Christ, no longer a slave to desires, sufferings, and diseases. For you have become a god [ἐπήγγελται θεός]! The sufferings you endured as a human being, these he gave because you are human. But whatever belongs to God, this God has promised to give when you, made immortal, become a god [ἐθεοποιήθης]. This is the meaning of "know yourself": when you recognize God your maker. For by knowing him, you who

---

This contribution is a significantly refocused development of several scattered lines of thought that appear in my monograph *City of Gods: The New Jerusalem of John's Revelation in Early Christianity*, Supplements to Vigiliae Christianae (Leiden: Brill, forthcoming), from which several paragraphs in this essay are adapted. This essay also contains important elements from papers that I delivered at the LERU Theology conference in Lund, Sweden (August, 2022), and the SHARI postdoctoral theology seminar (March, 2023). Deepest thanks to my colleagues for their thoughtful input as the elements of this contribution took shape.

are called are known by him. So then, do not be your own enemies, O human beings, or hesitate to reverse course. Christ is the God of all people, who commanded sin to be washed away from human beings, completing "the old human being" as new. He originally called the human being "the image," thereby showing through a model his affection for you. You have heard his holy commands, and after you become a good imitator of the Good, you will be honored by him as one like him. God is not poor; for his glory, he makes you also a god [καὶ σὲ θεὸν ποιήσας]! (*Refutatio omnium haeresium* 10.34.3-5)[1]

In this contribution, I will delve into the deep connection between eschaton and telos that this passage illuminates. In this quotation, it is expressed theologically (specifically in terms of the kingdom of heaven and humans as gods); what I wish to do in this chapter, however, is to look at this same connection from the perspective of early Christian biblical exegesis. Specifically, I will focus on how a number of influential early Christian authors saw a deep connection between deification on one hand, particularly as articulated by several biblical passages and images, and the rich portrayal of the new Jerusalem from Revelation 21–22 on the other. This essay is meant to reveal a rich network of scriptural, theological, and even geographical connections that emerges around two further expressions of the human telos and the last things—a network that will become increasingly apparent as this contribution unfolds.

The organization of this essay is simple. First, I will show how the intertwined early reception of two key scriptural passages—Psalm 82 and Revelation 21–22—demonstrates how closely linked the ideas of deification and the eschatological city are in early Christian theology. Second, I will point out how this early exegetical and theological connection is further seen through the early incorporation of two notions—divine filiation and the vision of God—into this nexus. Third, I will sketch how some of these passages and notions are received and developed within the earliest surviving Greek commentaries on the book of Revelation—specifically, those of Oecumenius and Andrew of Cappadocian Caesarea. I will conclude the essay with a reflection on the urgency of bringing this patristic line of thought to ordinary twenty-first-century Christians and those who minister to them.

---

[1] Text and translation: M. David Litwa, trans., *Refutation of All Heresies* (Atlanta: SBL Press, 2016), modified.

## Psalm 82 and Revelation 21: A Curious Connection in Ancient Christian Thought

In recent years, I have undertaken a prolonged study of the earliest Christian understandings and uses of Revelation's image of the new Jerusalem. During the first phase of this study, I was surprised to see that a consistent theological relationship between this extended passage and Psalm 82 existed in the minds of several key Christian authors of the second and third centuries. Psalm 82, of course, is the locus classicus of early patristic thought on the Christian doctrine of deification.[2] So consistently connected have I discovered these two passages to be that I have concluded that they must be considered part of a coherent intertextual tradition. Equally surprising to me was that this connection seemed to be present not only in Greek and Eastern authors, which are well-known for their use of the notion of deification, but also in second- and third-century Western and Latin sources. This section, then, presents soundings into where and how Psalm 82 and Revelation 21–22, or their themes at least, coincide in the patristic textual record. For ease, I reproduce here several key portions from each pericope. First, the verses from Psalm 82 (81 LXX) that early Christians tended to focus on in the present context: "God stood in a gathering of gods, but in their midst he discerningly judges gods.... I said, 'Gods you are, and sons of the Most High, but you all are dying like human beings, and like one of the rulers you fall'" (Ps 82:1, 6-7 NETS). From the very long new Jerusalem pericope of Revelation 21–22, I reproduce only the verses that are most pertinent to the present study:

> Then I saw a new heaven and a new earth.... And I saw the holy city, the new Jerusalem, coming down out of heaven from God, prepared as a bride adorned for her husband.... Those who conquer will inherit these things, and I will be their God, and they will be my sons.... And in the spirit he [the angel] carried

---

[2] The importance of Ps 82 to early Christian theologians is discussed in Carl Mosser, "The Earliest Patristic Interpretations of Psalm 82, Jewish Antecedents, and the Origin of Christian Deification," *Journal of Theological Studies* 56, no. 1 (April 2005): 30-74. General literature on the patristic articulations of deification has become increasingly rich with time; good entry points include Jules Gross, *The Divinization of the Christian According to the Greek Fathers*, trans. Paul Onica (Anaheim, CA: A&C, 2002); Norman Russell, *The Doctrine of Deification in the Greek Patristic Tradition* (Oxford: University Press, 2004); and Jared Ortiz, *With All the Fullness of God: Deification in Christian Tradition* (Lanham, MD: Lexington Books/Fortress Academic, 2021). A more exhaustive bibliography can be found in Paul L. Gavrilyuk, Andrew Hoffer, and Michael Levering, eds., *The Oxford Handbook of Deification* (Oxford: University Press, forthcoming).

> me away to a great, high mountain and showed me the holy city Jerusalem coming down out of heaven from God. It has the glory of God and a radiance like a very rare jewel, like jasper, clear as crystal.... The foundations of the wall of the city are adorned with every jewel.... The throne of God and of the Lamb will be in it, and his servants will worship him; they will see his face, and his name will be on their foreheads. (Rev 21:1-2, 7, 10-11, 19; 22:3-4, NRSV modified)

Several early Christian teachers linked these two texts. Here I will limit myself to three well-known representatives—Justin Martyr, Origen of Alexandria, Cyprian of Carthage—and one less-known but I hope illuminating representative—testimony from a little-known ancient Christian group called the Naassenes.

***Justin Martyr of Rome.*** If the ancient accounts are accurate, sometime likely in the mid-130s, Justin, a Samaritan Christian, dialogued with a Jewish interlocutor called Trypho in Ephesus, the city with which the author of Revelation was historically associated. Midway through the dialogue, Justin tells Trypho how, according to John's Revelation and prophetic literature of the Old Testament, he expects to dwell in a restored Jerusalem in the eschaton (*Dial.* 80.1–81.4), an existence that will be followed by a second phase of the eschatological Jerusalem, where the resurrected sons of God will enjoy eternal rest (*Dial.* 138.3). Justin strongly maintains that the recipients of the Old Testament promises, including the promises of a new Jerusalem, are to be granted not to the nonbelieving Jews but rather to those of any race—including the Jews—who are faithful to God. As Justin says to Trypho, "God did not address your land, but the people who are faithful to him, for whom he has prearranged a restful haven in Jerusalem" (*Dial.* 138.3).[3] It is those who believe in the gospel of Christ who are the true sons of God. "Gentlemen," Justin proclaims to his audience,

> Hear how the Holy Spirit says that this people are all sons of the Most High and that Christ himself shall be present in their assembly to pass judgment on every race. Here are his words as spoken through David, and as translated by you yourselves: "God stands in the assembly of gods; and in the midst he

---

[3]Text: E. J. Goodspeed, *Die ältesten Apologeten: Texte mit kurzen Einleitungen* (Göttingen, 1914), 90-265. Translation: Thomas B. Falls, *Justin Martyr: Dialogue with Trypho*, ed. Michael Slusser (Washington, DC: Catholic University of America Press, 2003).

judges gods. . . . I have said: You are gods, and all of you the sons of the Most High" [Ps 82:1, 6]. (*Dial.* 124.2)

These three passages (*Dial.* 81, 138, and 124), while not contiguous, fall very neatly on the dialogue's main theological trajectory: namely, that it is those who believe in Christ who are the inhabitants of the Jerusalem that John predicts and are the sons of God whom he, citing Psalm 82, identifies as gods. Put briefly, in Justin's mind, Revelation's new Jerusalem is populated by Psalm 82's gods.

**Naassene Christian discourse in the Refutation.** The *Refutation*, the conclusion of which I quoted at the outset of this essay, is the source for another juxtaposition of the idea of the heavenly Jerusalem with deification. It comes from what the anonymous author of the *Refutation* considers to be the earliest Gnostic Christian sect. While the author alleges that the source of the teaching was the serpent that misled Adam and Eve (*Refutatio omnium haeresium* 5.6.3), the members of the group itself, likely active in Alexandria at the end of the second century, viewed themselves as true Christians (*Ref.* 5.9.22), claiming that their doctrine was passed from Jesus' own brother, James the Just (*Ref.* 5.7.1).[4] A number of modern scholars have weighed the textual evidence and conclude that the Naassenes' claim to Christian identity is not far-fetched, considering it a movement that prized finding Christian or at least proto-Christian truths in preexisting Greco-Roman myth. According to R. P. Casey, the "structure of the Naassene Logos doctrine" was "very similar to one current at the time in orthodox Christianity."[5] Tuomas Rasimus considers the movement and its surviving texts to represent "a Christian attempt to explain pagan myths," and not, as scholars of the history-of-religions school have suggested, "a piece of secondarily Christianized pagan Gnosis."[6] According to David Litwa, whoever authored the surviving Naassene writings is "the only

---

[4] M. David Litwa, *The Naassenes: Exploring an Early Christian Identity* (London: Routledge, 2023), 5. For a presentation of the debate about the Naassene identity, see 2-5. On the provenance and historical milieu of the Naassene teaching, see 5-8.
[5] R. P. Casey, "Naassenes and Ophites," *Journal of Theological Studies* 27, no. 108 (1926): 374-87, here 374-75. Casey underscored the Naassenes' similarity to orthodox Christianity in important respects without conceding that the group was Christian.
[6] Tuomas Rasimus, *Paradise Reconsidered in Gnostic Mythmaking: Rethinking Sethianism in Light of the Ophite Evidence* (Leiden: Brill, 2009), 187-88. See a similar position in Maria Grazia Lancellotti, *The Naassenes: A Gnostic Identity Among Judaism, Christianity, Classical and Ancient Near Eastern Traditions* (Münster: Ugarit-Verlag, 2000), 10-29.

second-century Christian theologian who presented a theory about how to completely integrate Hellenic religion into the structure of Christian theology."[7]

Regardless of the Naassenes' specific Christian profile, the *Refutation*'s record of their doctrine demonstrates that Justin Martyr was part of a broader early-to-mid second-century Christian tendency to associate Psalm 82 and the heavenly Jerusalem. Consider the following passage, which contains Naassene reflection on the origins of humans and pagan gods according to a Homeric couplet:[8]

> "They went past the streams of Ocean and the Leucadian Rock / Past the gates of the Sun and the district of dreams" [Homer, *Odyssey* 24.9-10]. This, he says, refers to "Ocean, origin of gods and of human beings" [Homer, *Odyssey* 24.11-12]. It eternally turns in its ebb and flow, sometimes up, sometimes down. Now, he claims, when Ocean flows down, humans are generated, but when it flows up—to the wall, the palisade, the Leucadian Rock—gods are born.
>
> This is what is referred to in the scriptural verse: "I declared: 'You are gods and all of you children of the Most High'" [Ps 82:6]. *You are gods if you hurry to flee from Egypt and cross the Red Sea into the desert (that is, after you flee from the mixture below to "the Jerusalem above, mother of the living" [Gal 4:26].) But if you turn back to Egypt (that is, the mixture below), "You will die like human beings" [Ps 82:7].*
>
> All generation below, he says, is mortal, whereas that which is born above is immortal. For the spiritual one—not the fleshly—is "born from water alone and spirit" [Jn 3:3, 5]. But the one below is fleshly. This is what the scriptural verse refers to: "What is born from flesh is flesh, and what is born from spirit is spirit" [Jn 3:6]. This is their version of spiritual birth. (*Refutatio omnium haeresium* 5.7.38–40)[9]

While there is some question whether this passage is an entirely faithful reproduction of specific Naassene theological reasoning, there is little doubt that it represents their broad attempt to find Christian meaning within

---

[7]Litwa, *Naassenes*, 155-56. Litwa offers a persuasive case that the author surpassed even Clement of Alexandria, who repudiated his Hellene past while still drawing heavily from it. The author of the Naassene text feels no need to apologize; he simply appropriates.

[8]For a detailed discussion of Naassene theology, see Litwa, *Naassenes*.

[9]Text: Litwa, *Refutation of All Heresies*, 226, 228. Translation: Litwa, *Naassenes*, 21-22, which is a revision of Litwa's earlier translation (Litwa, *Refutation of All Heresies*, 227, 229). I have included here several lines from the earlier translation that are missing from the more recent one (set off by asterisks).

preexisting Greco-Roman mythology.[10] Noteworthy within it is the fact that the author here employs a presumably preexisting Christian way of reasoning. As the discussion of Justin above demonstrates, this line of reasoning draws a strong connection between the idea of humans as gods or sons of God and the idea of a heavenly Jerusalem. For the idea of humans as gods, the Naassene author quotes Psalm 82:6-7. For the notion of the heavenly Jerusalem, the author quotes Galatians 4:26, a verse whose distinguishing term "Jerusalem above" Irenaeus had already considered to be coextensive with the term "new Jerusalem" in Revelation 21 (*Haer.* 5.35.2). This theological connection between humans as gods and the heavenly kingdom, though without specific scriptural allusion, is of course affirmed again in the concluding lines of the *Refutation*, where the author, standing in the mainstream of early church tradition and writing in Rome early in the third century, ends his own presentation of what he considers to be "the true account" of Christian doctrine (10.4, reproduced above).

**Origen of Alexandria.** We now spring forward several decades to Caesarea Maritima in Syria in the 240s. It was then and there that the Alexandrian theologian Origen preached a series of sermons on the book of Ezekiel. In the thirteenth sermon, he discusses the fall of the prince of Tyre in Ezekiel 28. Origen's first point is to show that this prince is no man but rather the archangel Lucifer (*Hom. Ezech.* 13 2.1-2). This he indicates in part by relying on Psalm 82:6-7: "You are all gods and sons of the Most High; but you will die as men, and as one of the princes you will fall" (*Hom. Ezech.* 13 1.5).[11] The Prince of Tyre, Origen instructs his hearers, is one of these fallen angelic princes (1.5). The preacher then goes on to describe the fall of Lucifer in detail before dramatically turning the plot upside down and exhorting his hearers to reverse the fall of Lucifer in themselves. Instead of falling like Lucifer, we must ascend to heaven. "Arise, Jerusalem!" he exhorts, quoting Isaiah 51:17 (*Hom. Ezech.* 13 2.2). In this way, Origen goes on, we will fulfill the image and likeness of God in which we were created (*Hom. Ezech.* 3 2.7, quoting Gen 1:26).

---

[10]Litwa points out the difficulty of determining just how much of the Naassene material is brought over by the Refutor and how much is in fact the Refutor himself (*Naassenes*, 33-40).

[11]For the text of Jerome's Latin translation of Origen's now-lost Greek text, I use: Marcel Borret, ed., *Origène. Homélies sur Ézéchiel*, SC 352 (Paris: Cerf, 1989). Translation: Thomas P. Scheck, trans., *Origen: Homilies 1-14 on Ezekiel*, ACW 62 (New York: Newman, 2010).

More particularly to Ezekiel 28, it is in thus arising that we will array ourselves in the precious stones that once adorned the prefallen Lucifer and are destined to adorn Revelation's new Jerusalem (*Hom. Ezech.* 13.3.2). Indeed, Origen explains, it is by ornamenting ourselves with virtues that we "enter Jerusalem" by its twelve gates to enjoy the city's tree of life and the river of water of life (*Hom. Ezech.* 3 2.11; 4.2, alluding to Rev 21:12, 15; 22:1-2, 14). This Jerusalem, this "city of God," he says, is the church (*Hom. Ezech.* 13 2.10, 4.2). By beautifying ourselves with the "precious stones" of divine virtues, Origen strongly suggests, we become fully "like him" (*similes ei*; *Hom. Ezech.* 13 2.7, quoting 1 Jn 3:2) and attain the elevated position that God desires us to attain and indeed from which Lucifer fell (*Hom. Ezech.* 13 2.4, 7). If we hark back to the extended quotation of Psalm 82:6-7 in the beginning of the sermon, it is clear what it means to become "Jerusalem": it is to become like God, even to become gods and sons of the Most High (*Hom. Ezech.* 1.5).

Origen also makes this connection in *Contra Celsum*, which was likely written during the same period as the Ezekiel homilies.[12] At several points throughout the treatise, Origen develops the idea of the heavenly city and Revelation's new Jerusalem, doing so to such a degree that it should be considered an important motif within the work (e.g., *Cels.* 4.44; 5.42-43; 6.5, 23, 25; 7.28-31; 8.5, 74-75). As the Alexandrian develops the treatise's final argument and moves toward his concluding peroration, he underscores the benefit that Christians bring to the cities in which they reside. Psalm 82 features prominently:

> Christians do more good to their countries than the rest of mankind, since they educate the citizens and teach them to be devoted to God, the guardian of their city; and they take those who have lived good lives in the most insignificant cities up to a divine and heavenly city. To them it could be said: You were faithful in a very insignificant city; come also to the great city where "God stands in the congregation of the gods and judges between gods in the midst" [Ps 82:1], and numbers you even with them, if you no longer "die like a man" and do not "fall like one of the princes" [Ps 82:7]. (*Cels.* 8.74)[13]

---

[12]Henry Chadwick, *Origen: Contra Celsum* (Cambridge: Cambridge University Press, 1980), xiv.
[13]Text: Paul Koetschau, ed., *Origenes Werke I–II: Gegen Celsus*, Die griechischen christlichen Schriftsteller der ersten Jahrhunderte 3 (Leipzig: Hinrichs, 1899). Translation: Chadwick, *Origen: Contra Celsum*, modified.

Again, then, we see Origen theologically joining the ideas found in Psalm 82 and Revelation 21 in a context that emphasizes both believers' eschatological reward and their soteriological telos.[14]

**Cyprian of Carthage.** For Alexandrians, or even Greeks more broadly, to make this connection is perhaps not unexpected. But the same connection existed in the Latin West as well, specifically in Carthage, and is precisely the same decade that Origen was delivering his Ezekiel sermons and writing his tract against Celsus. Cyprian, who was a highly educated young man from the upper classes, converted to the faith in his thirty-fifth year. Thereupon he rapidly ascended to episcopal leadership during a time of great political and ecclesial unrest. While he is more recognized now for his pastoral abilities than for his activities as biblical exegete or academic theologian, he nevertheless collected three books of scriptural *testimonia* (lists of scriptural quotations compiled to prove a point) in order to address certain important theological topics of his time.[15] Book 2 of his *Testimonies* consists of thirty headings on christological topics. In section 6, he makes the argument "that Christ is God." After marching through several scriptural quotations, he quotes Revelation 21:6-7 in full and follows it first with *selecta* from Psalm 82, then further adduces Jesus' midrash of the same psalm in John 10. Cyprian's text for this entire string of verses reads as follows:

> Also in the Revelation [21:6-7]: "I am Alpha and Omega, the beginning and the end. I will give to him that is thirsty, of the fountain of living water freely. He that overcomes shall possess these things [i.e., the new Jerusalem with its blessings], and their inheritance; and I will be his God, and he shall be my son."
>
> Also in the eighty-first [LXX] Psalm: "God stood in the congregation of gods, and judging gods in the midst" [Ps 82:1]. And again in the same place: "I have said, You are gods; and you are all the children of the Highest: but you shall die like men" [Ps 82:6-7]. But if they who have been righteous, and have obeyed the divine precepts, may be called gods [*Quod si iusti qui fuerint et praeceptis diuinis obtemperauerint, dii dici possunt*], how much more is Christ, the Son of God, God!

---

[14]For a fuller treatment of Origen on Revelation's new Jerusalem, see Nathan Betz, "'The City Is the People': The New Jerusalem of Rev 21–22 in Origen," *Annali Di Storia Dell'Esegesi* 39, no. 2 (2022): 313-46.

[15]I adapt Litwa's pithy definition of *testimonia* from *Naassenes*, 3.

> Thus He Himself says in the Gospel according to John [10:34-38]: "Is it not written in the law, that I said, You are gods? If He called them gods to whom the word of God was given, and the Scripture cannot be relaxed, say to him whom the Father has sanctified and sent into the world, that you blaspheme because I said, I am the Son of God? But if I do not the works of my Father, believe me not; but if I do, and you will not believe me, believe the works, and know that the Father is in me, and I in him." (*Ad Quirinum testimonia adversus Judaeos* 2.6)[16]

The first thing to observe is that Cyprian concerns himself here not principally with the new Jerusalem, if even at all. Rather, he is using the divine status of the city's inhabitants as one of the propositions necessary for him to construct a syllogism to prove Christ's own deity. What is important to keep foremost in mind here, is that, to Cyprian, the discussion of gods in Psalm 82 and the discussion of the reward of the new Jerusalem in Revelation 21 are theologically linked. This is how: The text from Revelation identifies the inhabitants of the new Jerusalem as the sons of God: "I will be his God, and he shall be my son." Cyprian then proceeds to Psalm 82:1, 6-7, which together make plain that the term *son of God* is equivalent to the term *gods*. The first premise of the syllogism is now set—the sons of God are gods—and with it the syllogism's middle term, *gods*.

Cyprian now advances to establish the second proposition: that Christ is a son of God. This Christ does personally in his midrash of Psalm 82, which is recorded in John 10. For evidence of the claim to be a son of God, Christ points to his works, performed in obedience to his Father's words—works that demonstrate that the Father is in him, thus making him a son of God. And a son of God, as he has already established, of course, is a god. Therefore, Christ is a god. But the argument that Cyprian has set himself to defend is not merely that Christ is *a* god, *a* son of God, but rather more than that, that he is *God himself*. This point he makes thus: "If they who have been righteous, and have obeyed the divine precepts, may be called gods, how much more is Christ, the Son of God, God!" (*Quir.* 2.6).[17] So, while Cyprian is not here speaking of the new Jerusalem

---

[16]Text: Robert Weber and M. Bévenot, eds., *Cyprianus. Opera I: Ad Quirinum, Ad Fortunatum*, CCSL 3.3 (Turnhout: Brepols, 1972). Translation: *ANF* vol. 5, modified.

[17]For an exploration of Cyprian's appropriation of the idea of the doctrine of deification, see Benjamin Safranski, "After the Fashion of God: Deification in Cyprian," in *Deification in the Latin Patristic Tradition*, ed. Jared Ortiz (Washington, DC: Catholic University of America Press, 2019), 75-93, in which the author is under the impression that Cyprian nowhere discusses

(though he does elsewhere), in his mind, these two passages—Revelation 21 and Psalm 82, together with Christ's quotation and development of the latter in John 10—are deeply linked via Christology and, just below the surface, soteriology.

Thus does the testimony of Justin, Origen, Cyprian, and an unnamed Hellenic Christian source discussed in the *Refutation*—between them representing the wide-ranging regions of Asia Minor, Italy, Egypt, the Holy Land, and Northern Africa—amply demonstrate the early, broadly attested, widely accepted connection between Psalm 82 and Revelation 21–22 among some of the church's earliest and most influential authors both in the East and the West, and writing in both Greek and Latin.

## The City of God, the Sons of God, and the Vision of God: Expanding an Antique Nexus

In this same early period, and indeed sometimes in the same authors, we can observe two further notions that are sometimes woven into passages that link Jerusalem eschatology and deification teleology. I speak here of *divine sonship*, which we have already begun to see above, and of *the vision of God*. Both these notions, of course, had long been associated with deification in the Hebrew tradition and to an extent even within the pre-Christian Greek Hellenic tradition. Whatever their pre-Christian provenance, these images are neatly packaged together in the context of the new Jerusalem in Revelation 21–22, where God says of those who inherit the new Jerusalem, "I will be his God and he shall be my son" (Rev 21:7, NRSV modified), and where we are told that the saints "shall see his face" (Rev 22:4). There is neither space nor need for an exhaustive development of these two topoi; a focused study of these two authors—Justin and Irenaeus—will be sufficient to show how early patristic authors interwove these two additional images into the soteriological and eschatological visions in which the heavenly Jerusalem featured so prominently.

***Justin Martyr.*** I begin with Justin. As we have already seen, the notion of the sons of God is already present within Psalm 82, where the gods are identified as the "sons of the most high." Justin draws this out explicitly in *Dialogue* 124, already cited in part above, where he quotes the psalm in full on

---

Ps 82:6, a claim disproved both by this quotation and by Michael A. Fahey, *Cyprian and the Bible: A Study in Third-Century Exegesis* (Tübingen: Mohr Siebeck, 1971), 146.

the way to pointing out the particulars of the saints' reward when they fulfill God's purpose of being God's sons. Justin writes:

> When I noticed that my audience was perturbed because I had stated that we Christians are also children of God, I forestalled their objection by saying, "Gentlemen, hear how the Holy Spirit says that this people are all sons of the Most High and that Christ himself shall be present in their assembly to pass judgment on every race. [Justin here quotes Ps 82 in its entirety] ... My purpose ... is to prove to you that the Holy Spirit reprimands men, who were created like God [θεῷ ὁμοίως], free from pain and death, provided they obeyed his precepts, and were deemed worthy by him to be called his sons, and yet, like Adam and Eve, brought death upon themselves, hold whatever interpretation of the psalm you please. It has been shown that they were considered worthy to become gods [θεοὶ γενέσθαι], and to have the capability of becoming sons of the Most High, yet each is to be judged and convicted, as were Adam and Eve. (*Dial.* 124.1, 4)

As we have already seen above, Justin connects the idea of divine sonship with the new Jerusalem by identifying its resurrected inhabitants, via a quotation of Luke 20:36, as "sons of God" (*Dial.* 81.4).

What then of Justin's understanding and use of the vision of God? According to the *Dialogue*, the idea of the vision of God was central to Justin's conversion in the first place. Immediately preceding his conversion, he reports, he engaged in a prolonged conversation on the topic with a Christian philosopher. Taking Plato as a starting point—likely the ideas in *Republic* 7.533d and *Sophist* 254a—they discuss what sort of soul is worthy of seeing (ὁράω) God (*Dial.* 3–5). Justin recounts his Christian interlocutor's summary of this discussion thus, taking care to highlight both the salvific and the eschatological context of *visio Dei*:

> The souls of the devout dwell in a better place, whereas the souls of the unjust and the evil abide in a worse place, and there they await the judgment day. Those, therefore, who are deemed worthy to see God will never perish, but the others will be subjected to punishment as long as God allows them to exist and as long as he wants them to be punished. (*Dial.* 5.3)[18]

---

[18]Verbs of seeing and perception in relation to seeing God, while appearing throughout the passage, are frequently left implicit. Thomas Falls rightfully supplies the thought of seeing in his translation of this particular passage based on the extended context of the dialogue leading to this point of summary.

It is immediately apparent how this image was contemplated by Justin as part of a unified eschatological vision that he presents in the passages of the *Dialogue* highlighted above in connection with Psalm 82 and Revelation 21. Viewed as a whole, then, Justin's theology of the end contains these four elements in close theological configuration: the new Jerusalem, believers in Christ as sons of God, their status as gods, and their final, unperishing vision of God.

**Irenaeus of Lyons.** Irenaeus also connects the idea of the sons of God with deification and the heavenly Jerusalem. As Jacques Fantino notes, adoption as sons of God is one of the five different "tonalities" in which Irenaeus expresses the economy of God.[19] Indeed, in the new Jerusalem the divine filiation of human beings realizes its fullest degree. There they, having been originally created to be sons of God and having become "sons of the Most High" by receiving the grace of adoption (*Haer.* 3.6.1), become full-grown and achieve the glorious liberty of the sons of God (*Haer.* 5.36.3; cf. 5.32.1).[20] The heavenly Jerusalem is therefore the endpoint of a process that extends throughout human history, beginning with humanity's creation as God's children and consummating at their glorification as God's mature sons.

This process of becoming God's mature sons we can see repeatedly and in detail throughout books 4–5. The process begins with our creation as natural sons of God (*Haer.* 4.51.2). Due to Adam's and our own disobedience, however, we were disinherited as God's sons. This did not, however, nullify our status as natural sons of God (4.51.3-4). Through obeying God through the gospel and living a virtuous life, Irenaeus makes clear, our status as God's sons may be recovered, so that our status and our nature correspond, and we may advance to become mature or perfected sons, in which status we then inherit his gift of immortality: "But when they should be converted and come to repentance, and cease from evil, they should have power to become

---

[19] For his development of these five tonalities, see Jaques Fantino, *La théologie d'Irénée: lecture des écritures en réponse à l'exégèse gnostique: une approche trinitaire* (Paris: Cerf, 1994), 207-18.

[20] For the text of *Adversus haereses*, I use François Sagnard, ed., *Irénée de Lyon: Contre les hérésies. Livre III: texte latin, fragments grecs*, SC 34 (Paris: Cerf, 1952); Adelin Rousseau, Bertrand Hemmerdinger, Louis Doutreleau, and Charles Mercier, eds., *Irénée de Lyon: Contre les hérésies, Livre IV, tome I: edition critique d'après les versions arménienne et latine*, SC 100* (Paris: Cerf, 1965); Adelin Rousseau, Louis Doutreleau, and Charles Mercier, eds., *Irénée de Lyons. Contre les hérésies. Livre V: édition critique d'après les versions arménienne et latine*, SC 152-53 (Paris: Cerf, 1969). Translation: *ANF* vol. 1. A rich study of Irenaeus's understanding and use of Ps 82 is found in Mosser, "Earliest Patristic Interpretations," 41-54.

the sons of God, and to receive the inheritance of immortality which is given by Him" (*Haer.* 4.51.3). It is precisely in this matured or perfected state that we as sons of God truly become gods:

> We have not been made gods from the beginning, but at first merely men, then at length gods [*dii*]. . . . He declares, "I have said, Ye are gods; and ye are all sons of the Highest" [Ps 82:6–7]. . . . For after His great kindness He graciously conferred good [upon us], and made men like to Himself, [that is] in their own power; while at the same time by His prescience He knew the infirmity of human beings, and the consequences which would flow from it; but through [His] love and [His] power, He shall overcome the substance of created nature. For it was necessary, at first, that nature should be exhibited; then, after that, that what was mortal should be conquered and swallowed up by immortality, and the corruptible by incorruptibility, and that man should be made after the image and likeness of God, having received the knowledge of good and evil. (*Haer.* 4.38.4)

Irenaeus also connects the notions of maturation as God's sons and deification with the sons' attainment of the *visio Dei*:

> Now it was necessary that man should in the first instance be created; and having been created, should receive growth; and having received growth, should be strengthened; and having been strengthened, should abound; and having abounded, should recover [from the disease of sin]; and having recovered, should be glorified; and being glorified, should see his Lord [*videre suum Dominum*]. For God is He who is yet to be seen, and the beholding of God [*visio Dei*] is productive of immortality, but immortality renders one nigh unto God [*vero proximum facit esse Deo*]. (*Haer.* 4.38.3)

Irenaeus beautifully brings together all these ideas—the new Jerusalem, divine filiation, deification, and the vision of God—in the final sections of book 5 (especially sections 32 and 35-36). However, it is still in book 4 where he, whether explicitly or implicitly, draws together the ideas most compactly and lucidly:

> When [the law] is read by the Christians, it is a treasure, hid indeed in a field, but brought to light by the cross of Christ, and explained, both enriching the understanding of men, and showing forth the wisdom of God and declaring His dispensations with regard to man, and forming the kingdom of Christ beforehand, and preaching by anticipation the inheritance of the holy Jerusalem, and proclaiming beforehand that the man who loves God shall arrive

at such excellency as even to see God [*videat Deum*], and hear His word, and from the hearing of His discourse be glorified to such an extent, that others cannot behold the glory of his countenance [*tantum glorificabitur, uti reliqui non possint intendere in faciem gloriae ejus*]. (*Haer.* 4.26.1)

Space precludes exploration of this conjunction of ideas in other important pre-Nicene authors. This limited study, however, begins to reveal the degree to which the early exegetical and theological connection between Psalm 82 and deification on one hand with Revelation 21 and the heavenly Jerusalem on the other hand is further developed with the additional notions of divine sonship and the vision of God.

## Reception in the Greek Patristic Commentaries on Revelation: Oecumenius and Andrew

This nexus of Scriptures and theological ideas was received deep into the eschatological and soteriological tradition of the Christian church, not least in its exegesis of Revelation. The two earliest surviving Greek commentaries on the book of Revelation—penned by Oecumenius and Andrew of Cappadocian Caesarea respectively, both dating to around the turn to the seventh century—present the new Jerusalem as a metaphor or sign of the final end of God's creation and Christian salvation. As I have pointed at elsewhere, given that they draw so heavily on their Alexandrian and Cappadocian forebears as well as on the likes of Dionysius the Areopagite (himself the first Christian author to set forth a surviving definition of theosis [*Ecclesiastical Hierarchy* 1.3]), it is natural that these two commentators would incorporate the language and theology of deification in their vision of the end.[21] For the purposes of this section, the connection between deification and the new Jerusalem is simply assumed: it is instead on their connection of the new Jerusalem with the vision-of-God and sons-of-God motifs that I will focus here.

Oecumenius, author of the first surviving Greek commentary on Revelation (ca. 590), writes that it is in the new Jerusalem that "the saints shall worship him with a worship that is not burdensome, but a worship of pleasure and spiritual joy." This sort of exalted worship in fact will derive

---

[21]See Nathan Betz, "The New Jerusalem: A Metaphor for Deification in the Commentaries on Revelation by Oecumenius and Andrew of Caesarea," *Ephemerides Theologicae Lovanienses* 96, no. 1 (2020): 1-39.

from what the worshipers see. This, however, only as much as they are able—an idea central to the thought of Dionysius, the influence of which on Oecumenius's commentary is well attested: "This [worship] will result from their beholding his face, for he says, 'they shall see his face' [Rev 22:4]; they shall see him insofar as he is accessible to human nature" (Oecumenius, *Comm. Apoc.* 12.7.8-9).[22] It is precisely there, in the new Jerusalem, where "God is present with the saints in a way sharing his life with them," where he "is seen by them face to face, insofar as he may be approached" (*Comm. Apoc.* 12.3.16).

A similar colocation of topoi is present also in Andrew of Cappadocian Caesarea, author of the most influential Greek patristic commentary on Revelation (ca. 614). For Andrew, the vision of God and the new Jerusalem are just two metaphors that image the saints' deified end. Now liberated from evil powers, the saints, having entered the new Jerusalem, have authority through Christ "to delight in beholding him" (*Comm. Apoc.* 24.71 [text 259]), seeing him, as Dionysius taught, not in riddles but face to face, even as the apostles saw him on the Mount of Transfiguration (*Comm. Apoc.* 23.68 [text 253], alluding to Dionysius, *Divine Names* 1.4).[23] As I have elsewhere noted, through their virtue, it becomes possible for the saints "to behold with the clear eye of the soul the divine glory in heaven," although "not its very essence" but rather "the divine manifestation" made possible through "images of divine concessions" (*Comm. Apoc.* 24.72 [text 263]).

And who are these beholders of this blessed and divine vision? Oecumenius: it is the sons of God, heirs of God, fellow heirs of Christ, brothers and friends and children of Christ—those who reign with him and are glorified together with him (*Commentary on the Apocalypse* 5.5.3). Andrew likewise: "The victor . . . <in> the war against the invisible demons" will obtain the blessings of the new Jerusalem "by becoming a son of God, and delighting in the blessings of the Father" (*Commentary on the Apocalypse* 22.66 [text 236]).

---

[22]Text: Marc de Groote, *Oecvmenii Commentarivs in Apocalypsin* (Leuven: Peeters, 1999). Translation: John N. Suggit, trans., *Oecumenius: Commentary on the Apocalypse* (Washington, DC: Catholic University of America Press, 2006). On Dionysius's influence on Oecumenius's commentary, see de Groote, *Oecvmenii Commentarivs in Apocalypsin*, 336-37.

[23]Text: Josef Schmid, ed., *Studien zur Geschichte des griechischen Apokalypse-Textes: Der Apokalypse-Kommentar des Andreas von Kaisareia*, vol. 1 (München: Zink, 1955). Translation: Eugenia Constantinou, trans., *Andrew of Caesarea: Commentary on the Apocalypse* (Washington, DC: Catholic University of America Press, 2011).

While self-conscious faithfulness to tradition is a common trait among post-Nicene Christian theologians, the consistency with which Oecumenius and Andrew carry through the very earliest Greek conceptions of the new Jerusalem is nevertheless remarkable, providing as they do a case study of the patristic impulse to join the eschaton and believers' divinely ordained telos via a common set of metaphors.

## Concluding Reflections: What Does This Mean for Us?

Thus far, I have attempted to point out how connected in early Christian teaching were the ideas of the eschatological heavenly Jerusalem on the one hand and the divinely instituted telos of Christian deification on the other. I did this first by demonstrating the intimate connection that Justin, Origen, Cyprian, and other early Christians saw between Psalm 82 and Revelation 21–22, and the ideas they contain. I then pointed out how the topoi of the city of God, the vision of God, and the sons of God formed a theological nexus that Justin and Irenaeus developed. Following that, I briefly sketched out how this cluster of theological ideas is received in the earliest surviving full commentaries on the book of Revelation. Now, in this concluding section, I turn to reflect on the urgency of bringing the patristic inheritance concerning the Christian telos and the eschaton to ordinary believers in our own time. In order to do this, I want to draw out what I view as an important implication of how this juxtaposition of Scriptures and ideas occurs in these ancient Christian texts.

Here Origen leads the way. It is a matter of historical fact that the works of Origen that we have just investigated were delivered specifically to largely lay audiences. The first work, *Against Celsus*, was written to a literate Christian, and perhaps even non-Christian, audience—readers who, even if they had faith, were not so strong in it that they needed no strengthening on its basics. The Christian part of his audience were educated Christians who lived daily lives in a broadly pagan population and did not take Christian instruction for granted. Perhaps his target audience was even students such as he taught as his school in Antioch, where he instructed the likes of Gregory of Pontus—promising young men who were as culturally literate as they were spiritually ignorant. Likewise, Origen's Ezekiel sermons were delivered to an audience of laypersons in a context of common Christian gatherings for worship. These assemblies were open to all comers—not just bright, young men from leading families but anyone in good standing in the body of Christ, many of them likely illiterate. *These* were the people who would have constituted the audiences to whom Origen delivered these intricate developments of Scripture on themes of eschatology and high mystical soteriology. Whoever they were, these men and women had far less theological education than the average reader of this essay.

To get a sense of how Origen addressed a mixed congregation concerning the mysteries of Psalm 82, let us observe how he starts a late sermon on Psalm 81 LXX (82).[24] Speaking to a gathering of Christians—several sermons earlier he had addressed them as "catechumens"! (*Hom. Psa.* 76 [LXX] 5)—Origen begins his sermon by articulating the telos of the Christian life and the divine economy:

> The goal [σκοπός] for a disciple is to become like the teacher, and the *telos* of a slave is to become like the lord. . . . And the teacher aims for this, that he may, to the extent that he can, make the disciples like him. . . . But our teacher, Christ Jesus, is a god, and if it is sufficient for the disciple that he become like the teacher, the *telos* of the disciple is to become a christ from Christ and a god from a god. (*Hom. Psa.* 81 LXX 1)

He continues: "This gathering, when we genuinely are gathered, . . . is not a gathering of human beings, but a gathering of gods; the devil can do nothing; but God visits, and he visits standing in the midst of the gathering of gods. Therefore, it is said, 'God stood in the gathering of gods' [Ps 82:1]" (*Hom. Psa.* 81 LXX 1). Why or how Origen could or would have done this he outlines in a passage of *Against Celsus*. It is nothing short of their basic responsibility that Christian ministers lead everyone—not merely the intellectually advanced—to be mingled with Christ and united with God:

> It is both necessary and right for [Christians] to be leaders and to be concerned about all men, both those who are within the Church, that they may live better every day, and those who appear to be outside it, that they may

---

[24] Text for the "new" Psalms homilies: Lorenzo Perrone, Marina Molin Pradel, Emanuela Prinzivalli, and Antonio Cacciari, eds., *Origen: Die neuen Psalmenhomilien: Eine kritische Edition des Codex monacensis graecus 314*, Origenes Werke 13 (Berlin: de Gruyter, 2015). Translation: Joseph Wilson Trigg, trans., *Origen. Homilies on the Psalms: Codex Monacensis Graecus 314* (Washington, DC: Catholic University of America Press, 2020), with modifications.

become familiar with the sacred words and acts of worship; and that, offering a true worship to God in this way and instructing as many as possible, those they teach may become mingled [ἀνακραθῶσι] with the Word of God and the divine law, and so be united [ἑνωθῶσι] to the supreme God through the Son of God, the Logos, Wisdom, Truth, and Justice, who unites [ἑνοῦντος] to Him every one who has been persuaded to live according to God's will in all things. (*Cels.* 8.75)

Origen's pedagogical program, it seems, was that Christ instructs us to be gods so that we, now deified, can in turn teach others to be gods.

The record is clear: at least in his later years of preaching, Origen felt free to preach mystical realities to his audience, even when it was composed of the catechumens and spiritually underdeveloped. He urged them to become the new Jerusalem, and he talked about this in terms of becoming gods. The Alexandrian preacher was not content to leave his hearers on the earth—he wanted to elevate their minds, inflame their spirits, and inspire their actions. He did this actively, and considering the long influence of his mystical teaching within his own lifetime and long beyond it, he did so with profound effect. As Gregory the Theologian, a well-known collector of Origen's writing proclaimed in his second homily to his humble congregation in Nazianzus, the greatest responsibility of the Christian minister is nothing short of "becoming God and making others God"—καὶ τὸ μεῖζον εἰπεῖν, Θεὸν ἐσομενον, καὶ θεοποιήσοντα (*Or.* 2.73).[25]

In light of the historical record, I conclude with a final question. What if those of us charged with the ministry of the Word, the training of Christian ministers, and the feeding of God's flock took Origen, Justin, Cyprian, Irenaeus, and Gregory Nazianzen as our patterns? What if, as we found in the anonymous quotation that began this essay, we announced *this* as the gospel to "all people"? What if, like the apostle Paul himself, we did "not shrink from declaring . . . the whole purpose of God" (Acts 20:27)? The audience, if we listen carefully, is there—waiting, pleading, deserving, and above all hungry. May we all be found prepared to answer our Lord's injunction when he sides with the sheep (Lk 9:13) and enjoins us to answer their cry.

---

[25]Dionysius develops this idea in his *Ecclesiastical Hierarchy* 1.1, 3-5.

# DEIFICATION *in* TRANSLATION

## THE INFLUENCE OF TRANSLATION PHILOSOPHY ON THE VISIBILITY OF THE DOCTRINE OF DEIFICATION IN SCRIPTURE

### Chao-Chun Liu

WHILE THE ANCIENT CHRISTIAN doctrine of deification has enjoyed a renaissance of scholarly interest in recent decades, one crucial field has yet to be investigated for a fuller understanding of how this doctrine has coursed through the last two millennia of Christian history: that of Bible translation. This gap in scholarship on deification is not insignificant, for it is now almost universally recognized by Bible translation scholars that translating the Bible is essentially a theological task, that is, it is inevitably influenced by the theology or theological beliefs of the translators.[1] That being the case, it can be reasonably deduced or at least hypothesized that translators who believe in deification are likely to translate the Bible in a way that makes the doctrine of deification in Scripture more visible than those who do not. Related to this hypothesis are many other questions, such as: What is the

---

[1] See, e.g., Daniel C. Arichea, "Taking Theology Seriously in the Translation Task," *The Bible Translator* 33, no. 3 (1982): 309-16; all the articles in *The Bible Translator* 53, no. 3 (2002); Piotr Blumczynski, *Doctrine in Translation: The Doctrine of the Trinity and Modern English Versions of the New Testament* (Łask: Oficyna Wydawnicza Leksem, 2006); Chao-Chun Liu, "Theology in Translation," *Journal of Language, Culture, and Religion* 3, no. 1 (2022): 1-26; Liu, "Towards a Theoretical Framework for a Systematic Study of Theological Influence in Bible Translation," *Journal of Translation* 18, no. 1 (2022): 67-93; Liu, "The Influence of the Translators' Theology on Bible Translation: A Comparative Study of the Chinese Union Version and the Chinese Recovery Version of the New Testament" (PhD diss., Durham University, 2023).

relationship between the doctrine of deification and Bible translation? Did the former influence the latter or vice versa? How has the doctrine of deification been reflected in Bible translation in different periods and places in history? How have Bible translators contributed to the reception—positively or negatively—of the doctrine of deification, even determining its fate through their Bible translations? All of these are neither simple nor unimportant questions, especially to historians of Christianity, theologians, and Bible translation scholars.

As an introductory investigation on this subject, this chapter will take as a case study the still most famous and popular Chinese Bible version among Chinese Christians today since its publication in 1919—the Chinese Union Version (CUV)—for examination in comparison with other Chinese Bible translations. The goal of the comparison is to see how different translation philosophies held by the translators might have affected the visibility of the doctrine of deification in Scripture. Through this case study, this chapter hopes to shed some initial light on the importance of this new line of investigation and thereby inspire more scholarly inquiries into this hitherto largely neglected subject.

At the outset, an explanation of the term *translation philosophy* as used in this chapter is in order. *Translation philosophy* in this chapter refers to the set of beliefs and criteria embraced by the translators as to how translation in general or a certain translation project in particular should be done. As such, it can be defined as "a whole system of interlocking components" that functions as an overall guide to a Bible translation project.[2] Related to the usage of this term, I have suggested recently that, when it comes to Bible translation, the translator's theology likely plays one of the most important roles, if not the most important role, in guiding the translation.[3] However, the term *translation philosophy* is adopted here instead of *translator's theology* because it is a broader and more inclusive term that includes the translator's theology but may also include nontheological components, such as financial constraints or social, literary, and linguistic norms, which

---

[2]Leland Ryken, *Understanding English Bible Translation: The Case for an Essentially Literal Approach* (Wheaton, IL: Crossway, 2009), 14.
[3]Liu, "Theology in Translation," 8-11; Liu, "Influence of the Translators' Theology," 311-16.

separately or collectively may all affect a translation project in a certain way. Meanwhile, since the purpose of this chapter is to investigate the relationship between the doctrine of deification and Bible translation, it is the translator's theology as a main component of the translator's translation philosophy and its influence on the translation that will be the main focus of inquiry.[4]

The following sections will first present a brief overview of the doctrine of deification in the thought of the CUV's translators and their translation philosophy, followed by a comparative analysis of the CUV's translation of some key Bible verses related to the doctrine of deification. The conclusion will summarize the findings of this analysis and provide suggestions for future studies along the same line.

## Deification in the Thought of the Translators of the CUV and Their Translation Philosophy

The translators of the CUV, in addition to belonging to the larger tradition called evangelicalism, were mostly of the Reformed tradition. The Reformed tradition played a prominent role in Protestant mission in China from the beginning of the nineteenth century until the early part of the twentieth century.[5] Thus, our case study will begin by a brief overview of the relationship of the doctrine of deification and the Reformed tradition.

Although some scholars in recent decades have argued for a more prominent role of deification in the theology of some early Reformers, including John Calvin, it is generally recognized that in the Reformed tradition, deification—granted that it was somewhat prominent in the thought of some early Reformers—"receded into the background" soon after that generation.[6] A study of existing material written by and about the main translators of the CUV and *The Conference Commentary on the New Testament*

---

[4]It should be noted that the term *translator's theology* is not limited to the personal theological beliefs of the translator(s) and may also include the theological tradition or standards according to which the translator(s) carry out a translation task.
[5]Liu, "Influence of the Translators' Theology," 84-99. Also see Alexander Chow, *Chinese Public Theology* (Oxford: Oxford University Press, 2018), 97-98.
[6]Carl Mosser, "The Gospel's End and Our Highest Good: Deification in the Reformed Tradition," in *With All the Fullness of God: Deification in Christian Tradition*, ed. Jared Ortiz (Lanham, MD: Lexington Books, 2021), 83. See also Mosser, "The Greatest Possible Blessing: Calvin and Deification," *SJT* 55, no. 1 (2002): 36-57.

*Deification in Translation*

(*CCNT*), which more or less represents the general theological consensus of these translators as well as their fellow missionaries, confirms this, for it shows that deification features very little, if any, in their theological vision and language.⁷

The overall theological convictions of the CUV's translators could be summarized as follows: God created Adam in his own image and intended for him to rule for God (Gen 1:26), but Adam by his disobedience to God fell and brought sin and death into the human race (Rom 5:12). Thus the human race became fallen and alienated from God, is enslaved by Satan, sin, and death, and needs salvation. Then at the fullness of the time God sent his only begotten Son, Jesus Christ, to be born as a man on the earth (Gal 4:4) to die a vicarious death on the cross to accomplish redemption for humankind (1 Cor 15:3). He rose after three days, went to heaven to sit at the right hand of God, and sent down the Holy Spirit to lead people (God's elect) to believe in Christ and to be with them always (Acts 2:33; Jn 14:16). By believing in Christ and accepting him as Savior (and being baptized), people become Christians, who are justified by God and adopted to be his children and who have the promise of eternal life (Jn 3:16) and may live a new life sanctified by the Holy Spirit (Rom 6:4; 1 Pet 1:2). Christians should join a local church to be taught and edified, and the primary commission of the church as well as Christians is to evangelize the world (Mt 28:19). Such an evangelization of the world will establish God's kingdom on earth and usher in Christ's second coming, after which all Christians will enjoy eternal bliss in heaven with God, and non-Christians will suffer eternal perdition in the lake of fire (Rev 20–22).⁸

---

⁷The main translators of the CUV were Calvin W. Mateer, Chauncey Goodrich, Frederick W. Baller, and Spencer Lewis (see Liu, "Influence of the Translators' Theology," 91-92). For the CCNT, see William Muirhead, et al., *The Conference Commentary of the New Testament* (Shanghai: American Presbyterian Mission Press, 1898/1907). This was commissioned by the same General Missionary Conference of 1890 that commissioned the CUV. The theology presented in this commentary should represent the theological consensus of the Protestant missionaries in China, at least on the conservative side, during the time when the CUV was in the making, because this commentary, like the CUV, was intended to be a union commentary, i.e., to be a standard Bible commentary to be used by Christians throughout China at the time. See Samuel Isett Woodbridge, "The Conference Commentary," *The Chinese Recorder and Missionary Journal* 29 (1898): 355.

⁸For more details, see Liu, "Influence of the Translators' Theology," 91-99.

Generally speaking, the above is the theological conviction of the CUV's translators as well as of most of their fellow missionaries. Such a theological conviction does not employ the concept and language of deification and does not allow much room for them either. Although many more nuances and differing doctrinal details could be added, such as those concerning the so-called five points of Calvinism and the different understandings of sanctification and eschatology, it suffices our purpose to keep this overall theological conviction in view when examining how this theological vision as the main component of these translators' translation philosophy might have affected the visibility of the doctrine of deification in their translation of the CUV, in comparison with other Chinese Bible translations. Other main defining features of the CUV's background include evangelicalism, ecumenism, simplification, and indigenization, which I discuss in detail elsewhere.[9] These other features can be considered part of the translators' translation philosophy, which means that the CUV was mainly designed as an evangelical tool to introduce Christianity to the Chinese, as an ecumenical effort that would produce one standard Bible version for all Protestant Christians in China at the time, and with an emphasis on simplification and indigenization for easy understanding and acceptance among the Chinese. All these elements will be taken into account in the following section.

## A Comparative Analysis of the CUV's Translation of Some Key Bible Verses Related to the Doctrine of Deification

This section will be a comparative analysis of the CUV's translation focused on Bible verses related to three key theological concepts that are central to a doctrine of deification: union with Christ, eternal life, and spiritual growth. Since a comparison of the CUV with all existing Chinese Bible translations shows that, in terms of the visibility of the doctrine of deification, the contrast between the CUV and the Chinese Recovery Version (CRV) is the most evident, the following discussion will focus on a comparison between these two versions.[10]

---

[9]Liu, "Influence of the Translators' Theology," 76-91; see appendix 1, 24-26, for minor features.

[10]Witness Lee, ed., *Xinyue Shengjing Huifuben* [The New Testament Recovery Version], Chinese ed. (Taipei: Taiwan Gospel Book Room, 1987). The contrast being most evident between the CUV and the CRV is unsurprising, because the CRV's main translator and editor, Witness Lee,

## Union with Christ: *In* and *Into*

ἐν *("in")*. The first set of Bible verses deal with the translation of the Greek word ἐν when it is commonly translated by English Bible translators as "in" to denote the spiritual union believers have with Christ and the Holy Spirit, often expressed respectively as "in Christ (Jesus)" and "in the (Holy) Spirit" or other similar expressions throughout the New Testament. As the doctrine of deification is closely related to the biblical concept that, by faith and baptism, believers have entered into a spiritual (mystical) union with Christ through the Spirit to participate in what he has and has accomplished, including the divine nature (2 Pet 1:4), the CUV's renderings of these terms certainly concern the visibility of the doctrine of deification in Scripture.[11]

A survey of the CUV's renderings of ἐν Χριστῷ ("in Christ") and ἐν πνεύματι ("in the Spirit") throughout the New Testament finds a very interesting, sharp contrast: while the CUV almost always translates the former as *zai jidu li* ("in Christ"), it only translates the latter twice as *zai shengling li* ("in the Holy Spirit"), in Romans 14:17 and Jude 20; but in all other occurrences, the term is always translated *not* as "in the (Holy) Spirit" but variously as *bei shengling gandong* ("moved by the Holy Spirit," as in Rom 9:1), *yong shengling* ("with the Holy Spirit," as in Mk 1:8), *jiezhe shengling* ("by or through the Holy Spirit," as in 1 Cor 6:11), or otherwise.[12] While not all the verses where these various renderings of the CUV occur are related to the

---

was the Chinese minister who emphasized and wrote about deification the most in his ministry among all Chinese ministers and theologians. For Lee's teachings on deification, see *CWWL 1994-1997*. For a detailed study of the CRV, see Liu, "Influence of the Translators' Theology," 100-319.

[11] See Lewis B. Smedes, "Being in Christ," in *Major Themes in the Reformed Tradition*, ed. Donald K. McKim (Grand Rapids, MI: Eerdmans, 1992), 147-150, 153.

[12] Moreover, when the word πνεῦμα ("spirit") is commonly understood as referring to part of the human constitution, it is also most often translated as *xin* ("heart," as in Mt 5:3) or other words that denote either the heart or soul in Chinese, which reflects the translators' dichotomous view of the human constitution. See Chao-Chun Liu, "Discipled by the West?—The Influence of the Theology of Protestant Missionaries in China on Chinese Christianity Through the Translation of the Chinese Union Version of the Bible," *Religions* 12, no. 4 (2021): 250. Throughout this chapter, all Chinese characters will be presented in transliteration, followed by English translation. Those who are interested in reading the Chinese characters should have no difficulty finding them because all discussions of Chinese characters in this chapter are clearly referenced to and quoted from a Bible verse, and both the CUV and the CRV are easily accessible online. For the same reason, the Chinese texts of the CUV and the CRV will also not be included in all the tables presented to enhance readability to the main target readers of this publication.

doctrine of deification, thirty-one of them are related.[13] For illustration, two are shown in table 5.1.

**Table 5.1.** Examples of CUV translations of ἐν πνεύματι

| Verses | Greek | ESV | Comments on the CUV |
|---|---|---|---|
| Rom 8:9 | Ὑμεῖς δὲ οὐκ ἐστὲ ἐν σαρκὶ ἀλλὰ ἐν πνεύματι, εἴπερ πνεῦμα θεοῦ οἰκεῖ ἐν ὑμῖν. εἰ δέ τις πνεῦμα Χριστοῦ οὐκ ἔχει, οὗτος οὐκ ἔστιν αὐτοῦ. | You, however, are not in the flesh but in the Spirit, if in fact the Spirit of God dwells in you. Anyone who does not have the Spirit of Christ does not belong to him. | The CUV translates ἐν πνεύματι ("in the Spirit") here as *shu shengling* ("belong to the Holy Spirit"). |
| Rom 9:1 | Ἀλήθειαν λέγω ἐν Χριστῷ, οὐ ψεύδομαι, συνμαρτυρούσης μοι τῆς συνειδήσεώς μου ἐν πνεύματι ἁγίῳ, | I am speaking the truth in Christ—I am not lying; my conscience bears me witness in the Holy Spirit | The CUV translates ἐν Πνεύματι Ἁγίῳ ("in the Holy Spirit") here as *bei shengling gandong* ("moved by the Holy Spirit"). |

Like the two cases presented above, a survey of the thirty-one verses listed in the footnote shows that in these cases the CUV always translates ἐν πνεύματι with expressions other than *zai ling li* ("in Spirit"), in sharp contrast to how it almost always translates ἐν Χριστῷ as *zai jidu li* ("in Christ"). As a result, the biblical revelation that believers may live and act "in the Spirit," who represents and even is the resurrected Christ, is hidden from view.[14] Instead, the Holy Spirit is depicted as an agent but not as a realm, as the resurrected and pneumatic Christ, into whom believers have entered by faith and baptism.[15] Therefore, if deification is understood as believers participating in the divine nature by entering into a spiritual union with Christ to live and move in Christ as the Spirit, this vision of deification cannot be seen from these numerous Bible verses that speak of the believers being "in the Spirit."

---

[13]Mk 1:8; Lk 10:21; Jn 1:33; Acts 1:5; 11:16; 19:21; 20:22; Rom 8:9, 15; 9:1; 15:16; 1 Cor 6:11; 12:3, 9, 13; 14:2; 2 Cor 2:13; 12:18; Eph 2:18, 22; 3:5; 4:23; 5:18; 6:18; Col 1:8; 2:5; 1 Pet 4:6; Rev 1:10; 4:2; 17:3; 21:10.

[14]According to 1 Cor 15:45 and 2 Cor 3:17, and the biblical revelation that the triune God—the Father, the Son, and the Spirit—is one and cannot be divided. See James D. G. Dunn, *The Christ and the Spirit*, vol. 2, *Pneumatology* (Grand Rapids, MI: Eerdmans, 1997), 79, 117.

[15]Whether this agent is personal or impersonal is not specified by these renderings of the CUV.

Of course, the Greek word ἐν, depending on the context, can be translated in a variety of ways, and the point I am making here is not that ἐν πνεύματι in the New Testament can only be translated as "in the Spirit." The point I am making here is simply that the CUV's translators, by deciding to translate all instances of ἐν Χριστῷ as "in Christ" but nearly all instances of ἐν πνεύματι not as "in the Spirit," have affected the visibility of at least one possible way of understanding deification in Scripture, as explained above. Now, is there a correlation between this translational decision and the theological background of the CUV's translators? Yes. The Reformed theological tradition is known for its emphasis on the concept of believers being "in Christ" as their union with Christ, and this is reflected in the CUV's decision to translate nearly all instances of ἐν Χριστῷ as "in Christ."[16] But as Robert Letham recognizes, the Reformed tradition's vision of believers' union with Christ or salvation is more Christocentric than pneumatocentric, and this may be one reason for the CUV's way of rendering ἐν πνεύματι.[17] Other reasons may be the relatively late development of pneumatology in Protestantism and the tradition of English Bible translations, among others, but a further discussion of these possible reasons will need to be left for a future study.[18]

Besides also almost always translating ἐν Χριστῷ as *zai jidu li* ("in Christ"), the CRV, in sharp contrast with the CUV, almost always translates ἐν πνεύματι as "in the Spirit," thus highlighting the belief that the believers today can practically live and abide in the Spirit as the pneumatic Christ.[19] A careful study of the theology of the translators of the CRV reveals the strong connection between the translators' theology (as a main component of their translation philosophy) and their translational decision regarding ἐν πνεύματι.[20] The CRV's translators indeed hold a doctrine of deification

---

[16]See Lewis B. Smedes, "Being in Christ," in McKim, *Major Themes in the Reformed Tradition*, 142-54; and Robert Letham, *Union with Christ: In Scripture, History, and Theology* (Phillipsburg: P&R, 2011), 102-28.

[17]See Letham, *Union with Christ*, 102-3; also see Robert Letham, *Through Western Eyes: Eastern Orthodoxy, a Reformed Perspective* (Fearn, UK: Mentor, 2007), 253-54.

[18]Among English Bible translations, the CUV was influenced the most by the KJV and the RV, which also do not always translate ἐν πνεύματι as "in the (Holy) Spirit."

[19]Except in 1 Thess 1:5 and Lk 1:17.

[20]Liu, "Influence of the Translators' Theology," 99-119.

that hinges on and emphasizes believers' being in the Spirit experientially, as the CRV's footnote on Romans 8:9 reads:

> This chapter unveils to us how the Triune God—the Father (v. 15), the Son (vv. 3, 29, 32), and the Spirit (vv. 9, 11, 13-14, 16, 23, 26)—dispenses Himself as life (vv. 2, 6, 10, 11) into us, the tripartite men—spirit, soul, and body—to make us His sons (vv. 14-15, 17, 19, 23, 29) for the constituting of the Body of Christ (Rom. 12:4-5)…. If we allow the Spirit of the Triune God to make His home in us, that is, to settle Himself in us with adequate room, then in our experience we are in the spirit and are no longer in the flesh. If we are so, the Triune God as the Spirit will be able to spread from our spirit (v. 10) into our soul, represented by our mind (v. 6), and eventually He will even give life to our mortal body (v. 11).[21]

In the note above, "the spirit" is rendered in the lowercase in the phrase "in the spirit" in the English version of the CRV because the CRV's translators believe that human beings are composed of spirit, soul, and body, and it is in the regenerated spirit of the believers that Christ as the Spirit dwells.[22] Therefore, according to the theology of the CRV's translators, to live and walk in Christ as the Spirit is to live and walk in one's regenerated spirit, because the divine Spirit and the human spirit have become one spirit, as the following notes on Romans 8:9-10 explain:

> Our being of Christ depends on His Spirit. If there were no Spirit of Christ, or if Christ were not the Spirit, there would be no way for us to be joined to Him and to belong to Him. However, Christ is the Spirit (2 Cor. 3:17), and He is in our spirit (2 Tim. 4:22) and is one spirit with us (1 Cor. 6:17)…. Our spirit has not only been regenerated and made living; it has become life [Rom 8:10]. When we believed in Christ, He as the divine Spirit of life came into our spirit and mingled Himself with it; the two spirits thereby have become one spirit (1 Cor. 6:17).

εἰς *("into")*. Another closely related translational contrast between the CUV and the CRV can be seen in their different ways of translating the preposition εἰς when it is modifying verbs meaning "believing" or "being

---

[21] All the footnotes of the CRV in this chapter are quoted from *The New Testament: Recovery Version*, rev. ed. (Anaheim, CA: Living Stream Ministry, 1991). The CRV and its English edition share the same footnotes. All the footnotes in the CRV were composed by Witness Lee, the main translator of the CRV, as indicated in both the Chinese and English editions of *The Recovery Version of the New Testament*. Also see Liu, "Influence of the Translators' Theology," appendix 3.

[22] That humans are composed of spirit, soul, and body is based on 1 Thess 5:23; Heb 4:12; Jn 3:6; 4:24; Rom 1:9; 8:16; 1 Cor 2:11-15; Tim 4:22; Jude 19; etc.

*Deification in Translation*

baptized." In these instances, similar to the previous case, whereas the CUV always renders εἰς in a way that means something other than "into," the CRV always renders it as "into," as shown in the example of John 3:16 in table 5.2.

**Table 5.2.** John 3:16

| Original Greek | My Translation | Comments on the CUV and the CRV |
|---|---|---|
| Οὕτως γὰρ ἠγάπησεν ὁ θεὸς τὸν κόσμον, ὥστε τὸν υἱὸν τὸν μονογενῆ ἔδωκεν, ἵνα πᾶς ὁ πιστεύων εἰς αὐτὸν μὴ ἀπόληται ἀλλ" ἔχῃ ζωὴν αἰώνιον. | For God so loved the world that he gave the only begotten Son so that everyone believing into him should not perish but should have eternal life. | The CUV translates the phrase πιστεύων εἰς (lit., "believing into") as *xin* ("believe"), but the CRV as *xinru* ("believe into"). |

The CUV's translators omit the Greek preposition εἰς, apparently because they do not consider the preposition important enough to retain. Retaining it would also create a phrase that did not exist in the Chinese language at the time. Thus, most likely for both theological and linguistic reasons, they translate πιστεύων εἰς αὐτὸν (literally, "believing into him") simply as *xinta* ("believing him"), which certainly sounds more idiomatic and matches the translation's evangelistic preference for more idiomatic expression. However, the CRV's translators see great significance in this preposition and give the following note on John 3:16: "Believing into the Lord is not the same as believing Him ([John] 6:30). To believe Him is to believe that He is true and real, but to believe into Him is to receive Him and be united with Him as one. The former is to acknowledge a fact objectively; the latter is to receive a life subjectively." Thus, by emphasizing *into*, the CRV's emphasis on the spiritual union between Christ and believers, an essential component of a doctrine of deification, is conveyed. This translational difference caused by theological difference occurs throughout their translations of the whole New Testament.[23]

This same translational difference can also be observed in verses related to baptism, such as Matthew 28:19, where the CUV translates βαπτίζοντες αὐτοὺς εἰς τὸ ὄνομα ("baptizing them into the name") as *feng . . . ming gei tamen shixi* ("washing them under the authority of the name"), but the CRV as *jiang tamen*

---

[23]See Mt 18:6; Mk 9:42; Jn 1:12; 2:11, 23; 3:15-16, 18, 36; 4:39; 6:29, 35, 40; 7:5, 31, 38-39, 48; 8:30; 9:35-36; 10:42; 11:25-26, 45, 48; 12:11, 36-37, 42, 44, 46; 14:1, 12; 16:9; 17:20; Acts 10:43; 14:23; 19:4; 20:21; 24:24; 26:18; Rom 10:14; Gal 2:16; Phil 1:29; Col 2:5; 1 Pet 1:8, 21; 1 Jn 5:10, 13.

*jingru . . . de mingli* ("baptizing them into the name"). Similar to the case of John 3:16, the CRV's translators understand εἰς here quite differently from the CUV's translators, as the CRV's note on this verse reads: "*Into* indicates union, as in Rom. 6:3 and Gal. 3:27. The same Greek word is used in Acts 8:16; 19:5; and 1 Cor. 1:13, 15. To baptize people into the name of the Triune God is to bring them into spiritual and mystical union with Him." The CRV again is clearly emphasizing the spiritual and mystical union between believers and the triune God.

Therefore, in these verses concerning εἰς as in "believing into" and "baptizing into," the CUV's deemphasis and the CRV's emphasis on believers entering into a union with Christ or the triune God can be seen as another example of translation philosophy affecting the visibility of the doctrine of deification in Scripture. These translators' different understandings of believers' union with the triune God function as part of their translation philosophies governing their translations of these verses.

### Eternal Life

This section concerns examples of different understandings between the CUV's and the CRV's translators concerning what the terms ζωή ("life") and ζωὴν αἰώνιον ("eternal life") mean as a gift promised by God to believers in the New Testament. To the CUV's translators, whose understanding of God's overall plan for humankind can be summarized as God's saving his chosen people from eternal perdition to eternal bliss in heaven, life or eternal life that is promised to believers in the New Testament primarily means eternal bliss in heaven in the future, that is, an everlasting and joyful state of existence granted to believers after they have finished their present life on earth.[24] While individual missionaries might differ in their personal beliefs regarding certain details of the meaning of eternal life and eternal bliss, generally speaking, the above is largely the gospel presented to the Chinese in the nineteenth century and early twentieth century, as can be observed throughout the notes in the *CCNT* and contemporary missionary literature.

For example, the note on eternal life in John 3:16 in the *CCNT* reads: "Eternal life is to receive God's grace to enjoy eternal bliss; this verse is the most precious word in the Bible. . . . We all should rely on [Christ], to escape eternal

---

[24]See Liu, "Influence of the Translators' Theology," 91–99.

suffering and enjoy eternal bliss."²⁵ Protestant missionaries who were influenced by the contemporary holiness movement or other similar contemporary or historical strands of Christian thought might have believed that the eternal life promised by God was the new life, even the divine life, already obtained by them in Christ through faith, and as such was a life that they could experience in their present daily life. However, for the most part eternal life was understood among Protestant missionaries and Chinese Christians in China at the time as a promised blessing to be obtained in the future, as an everlasting state of existence, as something different or separate from God himself. Such an understanding is perhaps especially prevalent among those associated with the Reformed tradition—the main theological background of the CUV's leading translators—because of the tradition's emphasis on the majesty of God, the depravity of human beings, the great gulf between God and humanity, and understanding God's salvation primarily in judicial terms.²⁶

In contrast, in the theology of the CRV's translators, because of their understanding of God's overall plan (economy) for humankind—as to dispense himself in his divine Trinity into believers to be their divine life in order to produce the church as the body of Christ to be his eternal corporate expression—the life or eternal life promised by God to believers is understood not as *something* given by God but as *God himself* dispensed into believers upon their believing and continually hereafter through their living and abiding in spiritual union with Christ. Therefore, not only is eternal life something present and available for believers to experience and enjoy, but even more it is a present, living person, God himself embodied in Christ and realized as the Spirit dispensed into and indwelling believers (see Rom 8:10; 2 Cor 13:5; Gal 2:20; 4:19).²⁷ This difference between the CUV and the CRV is reflected in their translations of Matthew 7:14 (table 5.3).

---

²⁵All the notes from the *CCNT* quoted in this chapter are my translation from the Chinese.

²⁶In the Westminster Confession of Faith, the classic confession of the Reformed tradition, eternal life is mentioned only four times, and everlasting life two times, and there is no mention of divine life. In all these instances, eternal life and everlasting life are described as something promised or given by God, to be received in the future, not as something already possessed in the present, and definitely not as God himself.

²⁷Because of this understanding, the divine life was a crucial emphasis in Watchman Nee's and Witness Lee's ministry, and throughout their ministry they emphasized that there are three different Greek words for the word *life* in the New Testament: βίος, ψυχή, and ζωή, which refer to the physical life, psychological life, and the divine life, respectively. See footnote on Rom 5:17 in the CRV.

**Table 5.3.** Matthew 7:14

| Original Greek | My Translation | Comments on the CUV and the CRV |
|---|---|---|
| ὅτι στενὴ ἡ πύλη καὶ τεθλιμμένη ἡ ὁδὸς ἡ ἀπάγουσα εἰς τὴν ζωήν, καὶ ὀλίγοι εἰσὶν οἱ εὑρίσκοντες αὐτήν. | For narrow is the gate and compressed is the way that leads to life and few are those who find it. | The CUV translates ζωή ("life") as *yongsheng* ("eternal life"), but the CRV as *shengming* ("life"). |

As table 5.3 shows, the CUV adds *eternal* to *life*, most likely because the CUV's translators understand *life* here to mean "eternal bliss" in heaven in the future, and also because *yongsheng* ("eternal life") was already a popular term in Chinese religious traditions, including Daoism, generally referring also to a state of eternal bliss, so it satisfied their evangelistic concern for understandability, recalling the CUV's key components of evangelicalism and indigenization mentioned earlier. Since the CRV's translators emphasized that this life given to believers through faith is simply the triune God himself and is not merely a state of eternal existence in the future, which is how *yongsheng* ("eternal life") was (and still is) commonly understood among the Chinese, the CRV's translators usually translate ζωή in the New Testament simply as *shengming* ("life") without adding the word *eternal*. In fact, the CRV's translators try to avoid the popular futuristic notion of *yongsheng* ("eternal life") so much that this term is never used in the CRV, in contrast to its sixty-four appearances in the CUV. When the original text is ζωὴν αἰώνιον ("eternal life"), they always use the longer expression *yongyuan de shengming* ("eternal life") to translate it, most likely to avoid the unwanted associations of *yongsheng*. By adopting this longer expression, which emphasizes life as a substance, the emphasis is shifted from an everlasting state of existence to a kind of life that is eternal and divine in nature and that actually refers to the life of God, being simply Christ himself (Jn 1:4; 11:25; 14:6; 1 Jn 5:12). Hence, the different understandings of the life or eternal life promised by God to believers in the New Testament clearly functioned as part of the translation philosophies governing the two versions' translations of Matthew 7:14.

A related example can be seen in Romans 5:10, as shown in table 5.4.

*Deification in Translation*

**Table 5.4.** Romans 5:10

| Original Greek | My Translation | Comments on the CUV and the CRV |
|---|---|---|
| εἰ γὰρ ἐχθροὶ ὄντες κατηλλάγημεν τῷ Θεῷ διὰ τοῦ θανάτου τοῦ Υἱοῦ αὐτοῦ, πολλῷ μᾶλλον καταλλαγέντες σωθησόμεθα ἐν τῇ ζωῇ αὐτοῦ· | For if we, being enemies, were reconciled to God through the death of his Son, much more shall we, having been reconciled, be saved in his life. | The CUV translates σωθησόμεθα ἐν τῇ ζωῇ αὐτοῦ ("we shall be saved in His life") as *women . . . yao yin tade sheng dejiuliao* ("we shall be saved because of His being alive"), but the CRV as *women . . . yao zai tade Shengmingli dejiuliao* ("we shall be saved in His life"). |

The difference here lies in what it means to "be saved in His life." According to the note in the *CCNT* on this verse, the CUV's translators likely understood it to mean to be saved because of Christ's resurrection, that is, because he is alive. This interpretation, however, does not indicate or necessitate a union between believers and Christ. In contrast, the CRV's note on this verse reads:

> To be saved in Christ's life is to be saved in Christ Himself as life. He dwells in us, and we are organically one with Him. By the *growth* of *His life* in us, we will enjoy His full salvation to the uttermost. Redemption, justification, and reconciliation are for the purpose of bringing us into *union* with Christ so that He can save us in His life unto *glorification* ([Rom] 8:30). (emphasis added)

So, to the CRV's translators, "to be saved in His life" is to be saved by being in Christ himself as the divine life. It is not merely to be saved because Christ is alive, as the CUV's translators seem to understand it. Also, it is significant how the crucial elements of God's overall plan according to the CRV's translators—which can be summarized as union, divine life, growth, and deification (of which glorification is the last step)—are all alluded to by this note in the CRV.[28] Therefore, we can say that these translators' different understandings of these four elements functioned as parts of their translation philosophies governing their translations of these verses.

---

[28] For more on these four elements, see Liu, "Influence of the Translators' Theology," 228-48.

## Spiritual Growth

This section concerns examples showing the different understandings between the CUV's and the CRV's translators concerning believers' spiritual growth in the New Testament. The first example of this is Romans 6:5 (table 5.5).

**Table 5.5.** Romans 6:5

| Original Greek | My Translation | Comments on the CUV and the CRV |
|---|---|---|
| εἰ γὰρ σύμφυτοι γεγόναμεν τῷ ὁμοιώματι τοῦ θανάτου αὐτοῦ, ἀλλὰ καὶ τῆς ἀναστάσεως ἐσόμεθα· | For if we have become united in the likeness of his death, certainly we will also be in the likeness of his resurrection. | The CUV translates σύμφυτοι ("united with, grown together") as *lianhe* ("joined or united"), but the CRV as *lianhe shengzhang* ("united and grow [or grow together in union]"). |

According to the note in the *CCNT* on this verse, here the CUV's translators might understand this verse as saying that since believers are joined to or united with Christ in his death through baptism, they will also be joined to or united with Christ in the future when they are physically resurrected from death. In other words, to the CUV's translators, believers' being united with Christ in his resurrection is a future matter. But this is very different from what the CRV's translators understand, as the note on this verse says specifically that "in the likeness of His resurrection" here "does not refer to a future, objective resurrection but to the present process of *growth*.... We are *growing* into His resurrection" (emphasis added). For the CRV's translators, believers' union with Christ in his death and resurrection as described in this verse is a present matter, and it is in this present union that the believers may grow spiritually, as another note on this verse says:

> This [word σύμφυτοι, "united with, grown together"] denotes an organic union in which growth takes place, so that one partakes of the life and characteristics of the other. In the organic union with Christ, whatever Christ passed through has become our history. His death and resurrection are now ours because we are in Him and are organically joined to Him. This is grafting ([Rom] 11:24). Such a grafting (1) discharges all our negative elements, (2) resurrects our God-created faculties, (3) uplifts our faculties, (4) enriches our faculties, and (5) saturates our entire being to transform us.

This note shows that in the CRV's translators' understanding, union and growth are inseparable: it is in the union that growth (as the increase of the divine life in the believers) takes place. This explains why the CRV's translators translate σύμφυτοι here as *lianhe shengzhang* ("united and grow [or grow together in union]"), not just *lianhe* ("joined or united"). In contrast, since the CUV's translators most likely understand "life" or "eternal life" promised by God as a future gift to be obtained only after Christ's second coming, they probably believe neither in the current possession of the divine life nor in the growth of this divine life. Therefore, for them, to translate σύμφυτοι here as *lianhe* ("joined or united with") is sufficient. In this case the different understandings of union, the divine life, and growth can all be seen as parts of the translation philosophies resulting in the translational difference.

**Table 5.6.** Romans 8:29

| Original Greek | My Translation | Comments on the CUV and the CRV |
|---|---|---|
| ὅτι οὓς προέγνω, καὶ προώρισεν συμμόρφους τῆς εἰκόνος τοῦ υἱοῦ αὐτοῦ, εἰς τὸ εἶναι αὐτὸν πρωτότοκον ἐν πολλοῖς ἀδελφοῖς· | For those whom he foreknew, he also predestined to be conformed to the image of his Son, for him to be the firstborn among many brothers. | The CUV translates συμμόρφους ("conformed to") as *xiaofa* ("imitate, follow the example of, learn from"), but the CRV as *mocheng* ("conformed to"). |

The case addressed in table 5.6 deals with the concept of conformation, which can be considered part of the process of spiritual growth. The CUV, most likely out of its evangelistic concern for understandability and idiomatic expression, chooses the very common Chinese phrase *xiaofa* ("imitate, follow the example of") to render συμμόρφους ("conformed to"). According to the note in the *CCNT* on this verse, this also seems to have been the common understanding of the term *conformed* in this verse among the missionaries at the time. But the CRV's translators, who often emphasized that believers should not imitate Jesus outwardly but allow him to grow in them as the divine life and thereby transform them from within, translate this term quite literally and explain in a footnote on Romans 8:29:

> Conformation is the end result of transformation. It includes the changing of our inward essence and nature, and it also includes the changing of our

outward form, that we may match the glorified image of Christ, the God-man. He is the prototype and we are the mass production. Both the inward and the outward changes in us, the product, are the result of the operation of the law of the Spirit of life (v. 2) in our being.

Here the CRV's translators' understanding of God's economy—as the growth of the divine life (by God's continual dispensing of himself into believers), resulting in transformation and conformation, which equals deification and "Christification"—can be clearly seen. Whereas the CUV renders this verse as saying that believers are to *xiaofa* ("imitate") Christ's likeness, which can be done by teachings and doctrines, in line with the emphasis on doctrine in the Reformed tradition, the CRV renders it as saying that believers are to be conformed to Christ's image, which can be done only by the continual dispensing of God himself into believers as the divine life and by the growth of this life in believers, resulting in their transformation and conformation.

The following four verses shed more light on the different understandings between the two versions' translators regarding spiritual growth (table 5.7).

**Table 5.7.** Ephesians 4:15

| Original Greek | My Translation | Comments on the CUV and the CRV |
|---|---|---|
| ἀληθεύοντες δὲ ἐν ἀγάπῃ αὐξήσωμεν εἰς αὐτὸν τὰ πάντα, ὅς ἐστιν ἡ κεφαλή, Χριστός, | But speaking the truth in love, we should grow up into him in all things, who is the Head, Christ. | The CUV translates αὐξήσωμεν εἰς αὐτὸν ("we should grow up into Him") as *zhangjin, lianyu ta* ("progress, joined to Him"), but the CRV as *zhangdaota . . . limian* ("grow up into Him"). |

The CUV, most likely for evangelistic reasons, translates this phrase in a way that is easier to understand or sounds more idiomatic to the Chinese. The note in the *CCNT* interprets this verse as meaning that the believers should learn from or imitate Jesus as their model (see the case discussed in table 5.6). Translating αὐξάνω ("grow [up]") as "progress" or "making progress" shows that the CUV's translators do not interpret *grow* here as a kind of organic growth by the increase of the divine life in believers (as the CRV's translators understand it), but more as a kind of progress or improvement of character and behavior, which certainly fits the Chinese

*Deification in Translation* 99

mindset, as it resembles Confucius's moral teachings. In contrast, the CRV translates this phrase "grow up into Him" and gives this note for this verse: "To be no longer little children (v. 14), we need to grow up into Christ. This is, to have Christ increase in us in all things until we attain to a full-grown man (v. 13)." The note further says, "*Head* here indicates that our growth in life by the increase of Christ should be the growth of the members in the Body under the Head." These notes show again the CRV's translators' emphasis on the growth of the divine life in believers and on such a growth being the growth of the members in the body of Christ, for the building up of the church as the body of Christ.

**Table 5.8.** Ephesians 4:18

| Original Greek | My Translation | Comments on the CUV and the CRV |
|---|---|---|
| ἐσκοτωμένοι τῇ διανοίᾳ ὄντες, ἀπηλλοτριωμένοι τῆς ζωῆς τοῦ θεοῦ, διὰ τὴν ἄγνοιαν τὴν οὖσαν ἐν αὐτοῖς, διὰ τὴν πώρωσιν τῆς καρδίας αὐτῶν, | Being darkened in the understanding, being alienated from the life of God, because of the ignorance in them, because of the hardness of their heart. | The CUV translates τῆς ζωῆς τοῦ θεοῦ ("the life of God") as *shen suo ci de shengming* ("the life given by God"), but the CRV as *shen de shengming* ("the life of God"). |

This case is very significant because Ephesians 4:18 is the only verse in the entire Bible that contains the phrase τῆς ζωῆς τοῦ Θεοῦ ("the life of God"). According to the note in the *CCNT*, the CUV's translators most likely understand "the life of God" here as meaning "the eternal life given by God" to believers, which reflects their understanding of what God's overall plan for humankind is. They most likely do not believe that the eternal life given by God is the life of God, and they most likely also think that it would be too difficult for the Chinese to understand what "the life of God" means, so they translate "the life of God" as "the life given by God." But the CRV's translators, who emphasize Christ himself as the divine life of God and that believers, by receiving Christ into them, have received the life of God, choose to translate this phrase literally. The note on this verse reads:

> This [life] is the uncreated, eternal life of God, which man did not have at the time of creation. After being created, man with the created human life was

placed before the tree of life (Gen. 2:8-9) that he might receive the uncreated divine life. But man fell into the vanity of his mind and became darkened in his understanding. Now, in such a fallen condition man is unable to touch the life of God until he repents (has his mind turned to God) and believes in the Lord Jesus to receive God's eternal life (Acts 11:18; John 3:16).

Here the translational difference is clearly influenced by the translators' different understandings of what "the life of God" means, which function as part of their translation philosophies governing their translations.

This difference is likewise reflected in Colossians 1:10 (table 5.9).

**Table 5.9.** Colossians 1:10

| Col 1:10 | My Translation | Comments on the CUV and the CRV |
|---|---|---|
| περιπατῆσαι ἀξίως τοῦ κυρίου εἰς πᾶσαν ἀρεσκείαν, ἐν παντὶ ἔργῳ ἀγαθῷ καρποφοροῦντες καὶ αὐξανόμενοι τῇ ἐπιγνώσει τοῦ θεοῦ, | To walk worthily of the Lord, pleasing (him) in all things, in every good work bringing forth fruit and growing in (or by) the knowledge of God | The CUV translates αὐξανόμενοι τῇ ἐπιγνώσει τοῦ θεοῦ ("growing in [or by] the knowledge of God") as *jianjiandi duo zhidao shen* ("increase gradually in the knowledge of God"), but the CRV as *jiezhe renshi shen er zhangda* ("growing by the knowledge of God"). |

The difference here may reflect the contrasting emphases in the Reformed tradition versus in the theology of the CRV's translators. As the Reformed tradition generally emphasizes the knowledge of correct doctrines, the CUV, like the KJV, the RV, and the Peking Version, renders αὐξάνω ("grow") here as an increase of the knowledge of God. But the CRV's translators, who emphasize the importance of the growth of the divine life in believers over the learning of doctrines, translated the phrase "as growing by the knowledge of God." They state in the note on this verse that the knowledge spoken of here is not "knowledge in letters in the mind but the living knowledge of God in spirit, by means of which we grow in life." Thus, the CUV's emphasis is on increase of the knowledge of God, but the CRV's emphasis is on growth in life by the knowledge of God.

A similar contrast can be observed in Colossians 2:19 (table 5.10).

*Deification in Translation*

**Table 5.10.** Colossians 2:19

| Original Greek | My Translation | Comments on the CUV and the CRV |
|---|---|---|
| καὶ οὐ κρατῶν τὴν κεφαλήν, ἐξ οὗ πᾶν τὸ σῶμα διὰ τῶν ἁφῶν καὶ συνδέσμων ἐπιχορηγούμενον καὶ συμβιβαζόμενον αὔξει τὴν αὔξησιν τοῦ θεοῦ. | And not holding fast to the head, from whom all the body, by the joints and ligaments being supplied and knit together, increases (or grows) with the increase (growth) of God. | The CUV translates αὔξει τὴν αὔξησιν τοῦ θεοῦ ("increase [or grow] with the increase [or growth] of God") as *jiu yin shen dade zhangjing* ("have great progress because of God"), but the CRV as *yi shen de zengzhang er zhangda* ("grow with the growth of God"). |

According to the note in the *CCNT* on this verse, the missionaries at the time might have understood the increase or growth here as gaining more grace and knowledge of Christ, as spoken of in 2 Peter 3:18. Thus, the CUV's translators interpret "the increase of God" as "the progress because of God." But the CRV's translators, who emphasize the growth of God himself as the divine life in believers, translate this phrase literally as "grow with the growth of God." The CRV note on this verse reads:

> Growing is a matter of life, which is God Himself. As the Body of Christ, the church should not be deprived of Christ, who is the embodiment of God as the source of life. By holding Christ, the church grows with the growth of God, with the increase of God as life.... The growth of the Body depends on the growth of God, the increase of God's element, in the Body.

The belief of the CRV's translators that God's overall plan (economy) is to dispense himself as the divine life into his chosen people is again seen as the theological norm governing the CRV's translators' interpretation and translation of the phrase αὔξει τὴν αὔξησιν τοῦ θεοῦ in this verse. In contrast, the CUV's rendering is also seen as governed by its translators' understanding of salvation and emphases on the learning of doctrines and the progress of character and behavior, which are typical of the Reformed tradition.

## Conclusion

The analysis in the preceding section shows that the main theological tradition of the CUV's translators, namely, the Reformed tradition, and by way of contrast the theology of the CRV's translators, clearly functioned as a main component of their translation philosophies in guiding their translational decisions in the verses examined above, which makes the doctrine of deification either more or less visible in their translations, depending on how *deification* is defined. While questions concerning the influence on Chinese Christianity of such differences between the two Bible versions are beyond the scope of this chapter, I can point out that Chinese Christianity today, as a whole, is still mostly unfamiliar with and often unreceptive to the Christian doctrine of deification, and the CUV, with its immense influence on Chinese Christianity since 1919 until today, has likely played an important role in this phenomenon.[29]

The findings of this chapter suggest that this new way of investigating the doctrine of deification is valuable and may shed light on the history of transmission and reception of the doctrine. Similar studies can and should be done on major Bible versions in different languages around the world, from ancient times to the present, followed by studies on how these various Bible versions have affected the transmission and reception of the doctrine of deification. Of course, other doctrines or topics can become the subjects of such studies as well, and there is almost no limit as to the topics that can be studied in this way. Therefore it may not be too much an exaggeration to suggest that this new line of inquiry has the potential of becoming an entire new field of interdisciplinary study, perhaps under the name "theological Bible translation studies," combining Bible translation studies, theology, and church history, to shed new light on the complex and interrelated natures and history of these subjects.

---

[29]Chinese Christianity's unfamiliarity with and unreceptivity to the Christian doctrine of deification is evidenced by the generally critical reception of the CRV and particularly of Lee's teaching on deification among Chinese Christians. For a similar phenomenon in the English-speaking world, see "Responses to Criticism," Contending for the Faith, https://contendingforthefaith.org/en/responses-to-criticism/ (accessed January 3, 2024).

PART 2

PROTESTANT
FOUNDATIONS

# DEIFICATION or CHRISTIFICATION?

## Martin Luther on Theosis

### Alister E. McGrath

In a sermon preached on Christmas Day 1514, Martin Luther set out what he then regarded as a core element of the Christian proclamation of the incarnation: "God becomes man so that man may become God."[1] We become "partakers of the divine nature, when we receive the word and adhere to it by faith."[2] Luther here echoes a familiar theme in early Christian theology, particularly associated with Irenaeus of Lyons and Athanasius of Alexandria. For Irenaeus, the Son of God "became what we are in order to make us what he is" (*Haer.* 5.preface).[3]

Nothing in the sermon suggests that Luther considered himself to be saying anything new or controversial. He was simply unfolding the inner logic of the Western framing of the economy of salvation in a conventional

---

[1] WA 1:28.27-28: "ideo Deus fit homo, ut homo fiat Deus." For the background to Luther's sermons of this early period, especially their theological grounding in the prologue to John's Gospel (Jn 1:1-18), see Roland M. Lehmann, *Reformation auf der Kanzel: Luther als Reiseprediger* (Tübingen: Mohr Siebeck, 2021), 55-67.

[2] WA 1:28.34-36. "Divinae consortes naturae, quando assumimus verbum et per fidem adhaeremus." Luther here alludes to the Vulgate text of 2 Pet 1:4, "per haec efficiamini divinae consortes naturae." For the exegetical issues relating to this text, see James Starr, "Does 2 Peter 1:4 Speak of Deification?," in *Partakers of the Divine Nature: The History and Development of Deification in the Christian Traditions*, ed. Michael J. Christensen and Jeffery A. Wittung (Grand Rapids, MI: Baker, 2008), 81-92.

[3] For discussion, see Ben C. Blackwell, *Christosis: Pauline Soteriology in Light of Deification in Irenaeus and Cyril of Alexandria* (Tübingen: Mohr Siebeck, 2011), 36-70.

manner, including an affirmation that believers somehow share in the divine nature as a result of faith—a theme already familiar to his audience due to Augustine of Hippo's declaration that "in order to make gods of those who were merely human, one who was God made himself human" (*Sermo* 192.1).[4]

So, does this referencing of 2 Peter 1:4 indicate an early interest on Luther's part in the theology of theosis, before his distinctive theology of justification began to emerge? The evidence is not supportive of this possibility but rather suggests that Luther saw this biblical verse as adding to the conceptual and imaginative richness of the Christian understanding of salvation, and as an appropriate means of connecting the incarnation of the Son of God and the restoration and redemption of human nature.[5] Luther's sermon weaves this verse, along with others, into an incarnational vision of reality—an appropriate topic for a Christmas Day sermon.

Yet, in recent decades it has been suggested that Luther's understanding of salvation should be framed not simply in terms of *justification* but also as *deification*. This suggestion initially caused considerable surprise due to the prevailing assumption that Luther's characteristic emphasis on justification negated or precluded the recognition of theosis as a significant aspect of his thought and subsequently of Lutheran theology. Most Lutheran theologians in the recent past seem to have regarded Eastern Orthodoxy as placing an unhelpful emphasis on this model of salvation while neglecting the significance of the theme of justification by faith, so central to Luther's concerns as well as to the Pauline articulation of the nature of salvation and the structure of salvation history. As might be expected, such a suggestion caused discussion and debate that have been helpful in clarifying what is distinct about both Luther and Lutheranism. In this chapter, I will reflect on the contours of Luther's vision of salvation and consider how this is illuminated by these new perspectives.

---

[4]Migne Patrologia Latina 38.1012. "Deos facturus qui homines erant, homo factus est, qui deus erat." For a good discussion of this theme in Augustine, see David Vincent Meconi, SJ, *The One Christ: St. Augustine's Theology of Deification* (Washington, DC: Catholic University of America Press, 2013), xi-xx.

[5]For the general theme of the theological interconnection and correlation of New Testament images of salvation, see Alister E. McGrath, *The Nature of Christian Doctrine: Its Origins, Development, and Function* (Oxford: Oxford University Press, 2024), 137-63.

*Deification or Christification?* 107

Yet before considering Luther's views on theosis, it is important to reflect on the factors that shaped how both Luther and the notion of deification have been assessed and interpreted within German Lutheranism, as well as note some difficulties in achieving a consensus about what the term *theosis* actually designates. Why was there such surprise, perhaps even astonishment, at this new interpretation of Luther? To understand this, we need to reflect on this history of interpretation of Luther within Germany.

## INTERPRETING LUTHER'S DOCTRINE OF JUSTIFICATION: SOME HISTORICAL PERSPECTIVES

Martin Luther is widely regarded as a defining presence and influence on the emergence of Protestantism, functioning as a continuing theological resource and inspiration to (and far beyond) the German Lutheran theological community. Following the general disillusionment arising from the trauma of the Great War (1914–1918) with the dominant trends of German Protestant theology that emerged during the Wilhelmine period, Karl Holl and others urged a return to the *fons et origo* of Protestant theology in the writings of Luther as a corrective to earlier failures and a resource for postwar renewal and consolidation.[6] Although this movement found its greatest support in Germany during the 1920s, it was also significant in parts of Scandinavia, particularly Sweden and Denmark.[7]

This pragmatic recognition of the significance of Luther represented a confluence of historical, cultural, and theological concerns, often reflecting critically important assumptions about what constituted the core of Luther's theological program and its ongoing significance for the church and the

---

[6]Karl Holl, *Gesammelte Aufsätze zur Kirchengeschichte: Luther* (Tübingen: Mohr Siebeck, 1921). See also Christian Albrecht, "Zwischen Kriegstheologie und Krisentheologie: Zur Lutherrezeption im Reformationsjubiläum 1917," in *Luther zwischen den Kulturen: Zeitgenossenschaft—Weltwirkung*, ed. Hans Medick and Peer Schmidt (Göttingen: Vandenhoeck & Ruprecht, 2004), 482-99; Heinrich Assel, *Der andere Aufbruch: Die Lutherrenaissance—Ursprünge, Aporien und Wege: Karl Holl, Emanuel Hirsch, Rudolf Hermann (1910–1935)* (Göttingen: Vandenhoeck & Ruprecht, 1994); James M. Stayer, *Martin Luther, German Saviour: German Evangelical Theological Factions and the Interpretation of Luther, 1917–1933* (Montreal: McGill-Queen's University Press, 2000).

[7]Dietz Lange, "Eine andere Luther-Renaissance," in *Luthers Erben: Studien zur Rezeptionsgeschichte der reformatorischen Theologie Luthers*, ed. Notger Slenczka and Walter Sparn (Tübingen: Mohr Siebeck, 2005), 245-74. The rise of Nazism in the 1930s led to Swedish Lutherans (such as Anders Nygren) distancing themselves from this interpretation of Luther.

academy. The distinctively German tradition of Luther interpretation that began to emerge in the later sixteenth century in the aftermath of the Osiandrist controversy created a fixed perception within late nineteenth- and early twentieth-century German Luther scholarship that Luther developed an essentially juridical or forensic understanding of justification, which conceptualized the Christian life primarily as a new ethical or juridical relation between God and a human being, affirming "the absolute priority of imputation and its exclusive sway in justification," and eschewing any notion of salvation as deification.[8]

This filter of normative assumptions shaped preconceptions of Luther's views, especially within Germany. But how did they emerge? And how reliable are they? Recent scholarship emphasizes how doctrines often function as communal demarcators, offering a way of distinguishing communities that might otherwise appear similar.[9] The historical evidence suggests the existence of diversity within early evangelical communities during the 1520s and early 1530s concerning how *reformation* was to be defined theologically, particularly in relation to the role of the doctrine of justification by faith, which quickly became a demarcator between evangelical communities and the Catholic Church.[10] There was a clear need to find a controlling narrative that could bring unity and coherence to this diverse movement. The Osiandrist controversy of the 1550s is significant for several reasons, not least in that it led to a communal clarification of the nature of justification that framed this concept forensically rather than ontologically—in other words, in terms of a changed human status in the sight of God rather than a transformed human nature—and determined that this was the authentic and authoritative interpretation of Luther on this matter.[11]

---

[8]Kurt E. Marquart, "Luther and Theosis," *Concordia Theological Quarterly* 64 (2000): 182-205, here 204.
[9]McGrath, *Nature of Christian Doctrine*, 70-73.
[10]See, e.g., Berndt Hamm, "Was ist reformatorische Rechtfertigungslehre?," *Zeitschrift für Theologie und Kirche* 83 (1986): 1-38; Alister E. McGrath, *Iustitia Dei: A History of the Christian Doctrine of Justification*, 4th ed. (Cambridge: Cambridge University Press, 2020), 187-92.
[11]See the detailed study of Timothy J. Wengert, *Defending Faith: Lutheran Responses to Andreas Osiander's Doctrine of Justification, 1551-1559* (Tübingen: Mohr Siebeck, 2012). Wengert's discussion of how Luther was treated as a theological authority in this debate (242-316) is of particular importance to the present study.

The outcome of this debate was to establish that Lutheranism came to define itself by rejecting Osiander's account of the role of the righteousness of Christ in justification, affirming instead Melanchthon's concept of forensic justification as normative for both the confessional identity of Lutheranism and the authorized interpretation of Luther's statements on this matter.[12] Recent studies rightly raise questions about whether Osiander's opponents really understood his position. While this is an important issue, my concern is to note how this controversy created a perception that both Luther and Lutheranism were committed to, even characterized by, a forensic or transactional understanding of justification. This, in turn, made it inconceivable to think that Luther's doctrine of justification might have transformational aspects.

This position hardened during the late nineteenth century, particularly through the influence of Adolf von Harnack (1851–1930).[13] For Harnack, early Christian writers such as Irenaeus syncretized Greek philosophical ideas with their accounts of the gospel, leading to the formulation of "dogmas"—a "work of the Greek spirit on the soil of the Gospel."[14] In his critical account of early Christian doctrinal development, Harnack argues that the "Hellenization" of Christianity led to its corruption and decline, and identified Luther as a theologian who resisted such a development, enabling the recovery of the authentic ethos of early Christianity.[15]

While Harnack was severely critical of the emergence of dogma as a direct consequence of this distorting influence of Hellenism, he singled out the notion of deification (apotheosis) as a particularly disturbing example of

---

[12]See, e.g., Anna Briskina, *Philipp Melanchthon und Andreas Osiander im Ringen um die Rechtfertigungslehre* (Frankfurt am Main: Peter Lang, 2005); Olli-Pekka Vainio, *Justification and Participation in Christ: The Development of the Lutheran Doctrine of Justification from Luther to the Formula of Concord (1580)* (Leiden: Brill, 2008), 95-118.

[13]Peter Grove, "Adolf von Harnack and Karl Holl on Luther at the Origins of Modernity," in *Lutherrenaissance Past and Present*, ed. Christine Helmer and Bo Kristian Holm (Göttingen: Vandenhoeck & Ruprecht, 2015) 106-24.

[14]William V. Rowe, "Adolf von Harnack and the Concept of Hellenization," in *Hellenization Revisited: Shaping a Christian Response with the Greco-Roman World*, ed. Wendy Helleman (Lanham, MD: University Press of America, 1994), 69-98.

[15]For an influential contemporary account of Harnack's position, see Walter Glawe, *Die Hellenisierung des Christentums in der Geschichte der Theologie von Luther bis auf die Gegenwart* (Berlin: Trowitzsch und Sohn, 1912). For critiques of Harnack's position at this point, see Aloys Grillmeier, *Hellenisierung-Judaisierung des Christentums als Deuteprinzipien der Geschichte des kirchlichen Dogmas* (Freiburg: Herder, 1975); Paul L. Gavrilyuk, *The Suffering of the Impassible God: The Dialectics of Patristic Thought* (Oxford: Oxford University Press, 2004).

such pagan distortions of the Christian gospel. Harnack saw this as an essentially pagan notion, evident in the deification of Greek heroes such as Herakles and Orpheus.[16] To think of salvation in terms of deification represented a deplorable form of syncretism between Christianity and "Oriental cults."[17] As Fergus Kerr remarks, Harnack was outraged at this development: "One need only track the references to deification in the index to Harnack's great work to see how angry the theme makes him."[18]

Understanding salvation as deification, Harnack argued, was a luminous example of the assimilation of Christianity to alien forms of thought, an improper and degrading attempt to make Christianity intelligible and attractive to pagan audiences through the doctrine of "the deifying of the human race through the incarnation of the Son of God." This, Harnack argues, is not an authentically Christian view but is rather "the idea of salvation which was taught in the ancient mysteries."[19] It is essential, Harnack argues, to reverse this destructive development.

For Harnack, Luther was a towering German figure, whose achievement lay in his recovery of an authentic vision of Christianity that stripped away the accretions of a discredited Hellenism. It was about the recovery of inner freedom and the potential for self-actualization, and the removal of ecclesiastical authority from properly secular domains of existence.[20] Harnack thus accentuated Luther's greatness as a religious and culture figure while at the same time holding up the idea of deification as a pagan distortion of Christianity. After Harnack, it seemed utterly implausible to associate Luther with deification. They seemed to belong to different universes.

These reflections on the "German Old School approach" help us understand two points.[21] First, they cast light on why the suggestion that Luther's

---

[16]David Aune, "Heracles and Christ: Heracles Imagery in the Christology of Early Christianity," in *Greeks, Romans, and Christians*, ed. David L. Balch, Everett Ferguson, and Wayne Meeks (Minneapolis: Fortress, 1990), 3-19.

[17]Adolf von Harnack, *History of Dogma* (Edinburgh: Williams & Norgate, 1894–1899), 1:117-71.

[18]Fergus Kerr, *After Aquinas: Versions of Thomism* (Oxford: Blackwell, 2002), 155.

[19]Harnack, *History of Dogma* 2:10-11.

[20]Adolf von Harnack, *Martin Luther und die Grundlegung der Reformation* (Berlin: Wiedmannsche Buchhandlung, 1917), 63-64.

[21]I borrow this term from Veli-Matti Kärkkäinen, "Salvation as Justification and Theosis: The Contribution of the New Finnish Luther Interpretation to Our Ecumenical Future," *Dialog: A Journal of Theology* 45, no. 1 (2006): 74-82, here 75. Kärkkäinen here highlights the tendency of

doctrine of justification might enfold some notion of deification met so much initial resistance. Second, they help us to understand the importance of the Finnish interpretation of Luther, which originated *from outside a German context* and hence was not shaped by the same set of expectations and norms that seem to have blinded earlier German Luther scholarship to the transformational aspects of Luther's account of justification and to their wider significance.[22]

Yet this historical analysis points to a further issue of relevance to any attempt to explore the role of deification in general and not necessarily in specific relation to Luther himself—the relatively recent collapse of scholarly confidence in Harnack's negative account of deification.[23] The cumulative impact of these critical historical studies has been twofold; first, a disarming of Western theological suspicion about the soteriological category of deification, and second, an appreciation of how this concept seems to have featured *implicitly* in Western reflection about the nature of salvation and might therefore be open to further development.[24] There is a growing realization

---

certain Finnish writers—such as those represented in the collected volume of essays *Union with Christ: The New Finnish Interpretation of Luther*, ed. Carl E. Braaten and Robert W. Jenson (Grand Rapids, MI: Eerdmans, 1998)—to engage selectively with a German tradition of Luther interpretation held to originate with nineteenth-century philosopher Hermann Lotze. For the difficulties that this raises, see the critical review of these essays by Timothy J. Wengert, *Theology Today* 56, no. 3 (1999): 432-34. Other concerns may also be noted, such as those raised by William Schumacher, *Who Do I Say That You Are? Anthropology and the Theology of Theosis in the Finnish School of Tuomo Mannermaa* (Eugene, OR: Wipf & Stock, 2010).

[22]For a good introduction to the Finnish interpretation of Luther, see Olli-Pekka Vainio, ed., *Engaging Luther: A (New) Theological Assessment* (Eugene, OR: Wipf & Stock, 2010). See also Tuomo Mannermaa, *Christ Present in Faith: Luther's View of Justification* (Minneapolis: Fortress, 2005); Veli-Matti Kärkkäinen, "'Drinking from the Same Wells with Orthodox and Catholics': Insights from the Finnish Interpretation of Luther's Theology," *Currents in Theology and Mission* 34, no. 2 (2007): 85-96.

[23]For the history of this development, see Paul L. Gavrilyuk, "The Retrieval of Deification: How a Once-Despised Archaism Became an Ecumenical Desideratum," *ModTheo* 25, no. 4 (2009): 647-59. For some good examples of the historical studies that have contributed to this development, see Norman Russell, *The Doctrine of Deification in the Greek Patristic Tradition* (Oxford: Oxford University Press, 2004); David Vincent Merconi, "The Consummation of the Christian Promise: Recent Studies on Deification," *New Blackfriars* 87, no. 1007 (2006): 3-12; Christensen and Wittung, *Partakers of the Divine Nature*.

[24]For some recent reflections on this theme, see Georg Kretschmar, "Die Rezeption der orthodoxen Vergöttlichungslehre in der protestantischen Theologie," in *Luther und Theosis: Vergöttlichung als Thema der abendländischen Theologie*, ed. Simo Peura and Antti Rauniom (Helsinki: Martin-Luther Verlag, 1990), 61-80. The growing receptivity toward the category of deification within the evangelical theological community is a good indication of this trend: see the critical

that while Western theologians such as Aquinas generally do not *explicitly* use the language or conceptualities of deification, the notion can be argued to be implicit at many points in his writings.[25] Might this be true of Luther as well?

## Luther and Theosis: Criteria for Assessment

The term *theosis* is contested, open to multiple interpretations, thus making any attempt to determine Luther's position vulnerable to definitional uncertainty. Understandings of deification have changed over time and have adapted in response to changes in the theological landscape.[26] There is a need for some degree of clarity in defining how we are to understand theosis and correlate this with its various articulations in Eastern and Western Christian theology. Gösta Hallonsten, for example, makes the important point that Eastern Christian theology understood deification as a comprehensive doctrine enfolding the entire economy of salvation, including creation and incarnation.[27] In speaking of deification in other contexts, such as Western theology, Hallonsten suggests that it is more appropriate to use terms such as the *theme, motif,* or *concept* of deification, partly to indicate that this refers to a *part* or *aspect* rather than the *totality* of Luther's theological perspective.

In what follows, I will extend Hallonsten's helpful framework of assessment and offer three criteria by which Luther's use of the theme of theosis might be assessed: lexical (to what extent does Luther use the *vocabulary* of deification?); thematic (to what extent can the *theme* of deification be found in Luther's writings?); and doctrinal (does Luther see deification as a "comprehensive doctrine" or *master concept* that governs or coordinates the Christian vision of reality?).

---

yet reflective studies of Daniel B. Clendenin, "Partakers of Divinity: The Orthodox Doctrine of Theosis," *JETS* 37, no. 3 (1994): 365-79; Myk Habets, "Reforming Theosis," in *Theosis: Deification in Christian Theology*, ed. Stephen Finlan and Vladimir Kharlamov (Eugene, OR: Wipf & Stock, 2006), 146-67; R. Lucas Stamps, "Baptizing Theosis: Sketching an Evangelical Account," *Perichoresis* 18, no. 1 (2020): 99-115.

[25]A good example is Thomas Aquinas. See Anna Williams, *The Ground of Union* (Oxford: Oxford University Press, 1999), 158-59.

[26]Daniel A. Keating, "Typologies of Deification," *International Journal of Systematic Theology* 17, no. 3 (2015): 267-83.

[27]Gösta Hallonsten, "Theosis in Recent Research: A Renewal of Interest and a Need for Clarity," in Christensen and Wittung, *Partakers of the Divine Nature*, 281-93.

***Lexical criterion: Luther's use of the vocabulary of deification.*** One of the defining characteristics of the Protestant Reformation, unquestionably reflecting the personal influence of Luther himself, is a decisive shift in both the conceptualities and the vocabulary of the Christian theological tradition.[28] Up to this point, the Western theological tradition, while finding the category of justification useful in exploring questions such as the relation of Abrahamic and Christian faith, had developed its thinking about how humanity was reconciled to God primarily in terms of "salvation by grace" (Eph 2:8). During the sixteenth century, however, Protestant and Catholic writers came to reconceive and reformulate the rich Christian vocabulary of salvation primarily—if not exclusively—in terms of the Pauline term *justification*.[29] For a relatively short yet theologically significant period, the reconciliation of humanity was discussed within the entire Western theological tradition primarily in terms of "justification by faith" (Rom 5:1).[30]

Luther's works are saturated with the vocabulary of justification and related concepts, such as the righteousness of God (*iustitia Dei*). Yet Luther rarely uses the vocabulary of *deification*, which occurs about thirty times in his writings; given the considerable extent of Luther's writings, this relatively sparse use of the specific terminology of deification is significant and suggestive.[31] There is no evidence that Luther saw the vocabulary of deification as being of critical, strategic, or pedagogical importance. While later interpretations of Luther may consider the concept of theosis to be implicit within (or at least consistent with) Luther's theological vision, it seems that Luther did not choose to make this explicit in terms of the vocabulary he deployed to articulate that vision. Those who argue otherwise tend to infer the importance of theosis, reflecting the absence of its explicit vocabulary. So, how important is this theme for Luther?

---

[28]Hamm, "Was ist reformatorische Rechtfertigungslehre?"; Gunther Wenz, *Versöhnung: Soteriologische Fallstudien* (Göttingen: Vandenhoeck & Ruprecht, 2015), 295-317; McGrath, *Iustitia Dei*, 332.
[29]Vittorio Subilia, *La giustificazione per fede* (Brescia: Paideia Editrice, 1976), 117-27.
[30]Thomas Söding, "Der Skopos der paulinischen Rechtfertigungslehre," *Zeitschrift für Theologie und Kirche* 97, no. 4 (December 2000): 404-33.
[31]I here follow Simo Peura, "Vergöttlichungsgedanke in Luthers Theologie 1518–1519," in *Thesaurus Lutheri: Auf der Suche nach neuen Paradigmen der Luther*, ed. Tuomo Mannermaa et al. (Helsinki: Luther Agricola Society, 1987), 171-84, esp. 171-72.

***A thematic criterion: Luther's use of the motif of deification.*** It is often suggested that the theme of deification is implicit at several points in Luther's theological exposition of soteriological issues. Luther offers definitions or descriptions of salvation at many points in his writings of the 1520s, providing a form of theological mapping of its core component or elements. For example, consider this statement from his *Greater Catechism* (1529): "To be saved, as we know, is nothing other than to be delivered from sin, death, and the devil, and to enter into the kingdom of Christ, and to live with Him forever" (XIV).[32] Yet there is no reference to theosis or cognate terms here, or in many other pedagogical passages in which one might expect it to occur if Luther considered theosis to be an integral and significant aspect of salvation. The silence of these pedagogical tools on the issue of deification—which is never explicitly mentioned, either as an important theme or as an article of faith—is of considerable significance in relation to the topic of this chapter, and must be given due weight.

It might be suggested that the notion of deification is *implicit* within Luther's theology. Surely Luther's explicit references to the believer's union with Christ implies the believer's union with *God*, in that Christ is God? The theological logic of such suggestions can be summarized thus: the presence of Christ in the believer amounts to a participation in the triune God because Christ *is* God.

Yet this conclusion is problematic and is better reframed in terms of a trinitarian understanding of the economy of salvation.[33] As Christoph Schwöbel points out, Luther's concept of the Trinity undergirds and coordinates the core Reformation affirmations—*solus Christus, sola gratia, sola fide,* and *sola Scriptura*—all of which "are based on the understanding of the Trinitarian self-giving," allowing the distinctive roles of Christ and the Holy Spirit to be identified and respected on the one hand, and correlated and coordinated on the other.[34]

---

[32]A good account of Luther's understanding of salvation can be found in Georg Kretschmar, "Das Heilsverständnis Luthers im Rahmen von Patristik und Scholastik," *Cristianesimo nella storia* 14 (1993): 221-62.

[33]For Luther's doctrine of the Trinity, see Pekka Kärkkäinen, *Luthers trinitarische Theologie des Heiligen Geistes* (Mainz: Philipp von Zabern, 2005).

[34]Christoph Schwöbel, "Einfach Gott: Trinitätstheologie am Anfang des 21. Jahrhunderts," *Neue Zeitschrift für Systematische Theologie und Religionsphilosophie* 62 (2020): 519-41, esp. 531-40.

***A doctrinal criterion: Does Luther see deification as a master doctrine?***
One of the most significant aspects of Luther's later theology is his increasing emphasis on the "article of justification" as a master doctrine. Ernst Wolf rightly argues that Luther insists that the *articulus iustificationis* defines the "centre and limits of Reformation theology"; Reinhard Schwarz prefers to speak of it as function as the "cornerstone" of both Christian theology and the Christian community.[35] While Luther himself did not formulate the slogan that the doctrine of justification is "the article by which the church stands or falls (*articulus stantis et cadentis ecclesiae*)," this idea is clearly present in his writings.[36]

Luther's magisterial account of the doctrine of justification is significant for two reasons. First, it makes it clear that Luther's explicit theological formulations are to be seen as emerging from and converging on the doctrine of justification, which is seen as articulating the heart of the Christian faith. Second, even if we can discern elements of an understanding of theosis in aspects of Luther's theology, these need to be seen as subordinate to the doctrine of justification. If Luther's explicit statements about the role of the article of justification are to be given their due weight, it seems that Luther attached an importance to this doctrine that is comparable to that now attached to the notion of deification in contemporary articulations of Orthodox theology.

In this section, I have identified three criteria that I consider to be appropriate for adjudicating whether deification plays a significant role in Luther's theology. My conclusion is that while the *theme* of deification may be discerned beneath the surface of Luther's explicit theological statements, this is not explicitly articulated nor treated as pedagogically important. This does not, I must emphasize, invalidate or diminish the importance of scholarly exploration of deification as a heuristic lens

---

[35]Ernst Wolf, "Die Rechtfertigungslehre als Mitte und Grenze reformatorischer Theologie," in *Peregrinatio II: Studien zur reformatorischen Theologie, zum Kirchenrecht und zur Sozialethik* (Munich: Kaiser, 1965), 11-21; Reinhard Schwarz, "Luthers Rechtfertigungslehre als Eckstein der christlichen Theologie und Kirche," *Zeitschrift für Theologie und Kirche* 10 (1998): 14-46.
[36]Theodor Mahlmann, "Zur Geschichte der Formel 'Articulus stantis et cadentis ecclesiae,'" *Lutherische Theologie und Kirche* 17 (1993): 187-94. For example, see WA 40/3:352.3: "quia isto articulo stante stat Ecclesia, ruente ruit Ecclesia."

through which to view Luther's theology or explore his potential relevance for ecumenical dialogues with Orthodox theologians. Every theologian possesses a depth that is open to scholarly interrogation and exploration, which often reveals or suggests hidden levels of meaning that can be profitably engaged. My point is that deification is not a significant surface issue for Luther, even if it may be helpful to explore whether it plays a covert role in his thought.

In the following section I will consider some of the leading themes of Luther's thought and how these inform our reflections on the place of theosis in his vision of the Christian faith.

## LUTHER AND THEOSIS: AN ANALYSIS

Luther's theological journey as a Reformer took place over 1513–1519, during which he engaged a series of theological questions, including the meaning of the Pauline term "righteousness of God."[37] During this period, Luther forged his theology in direct engagement with biblical texts in lecture courses delivered in the Faculty of Theology at the University of Wittenberg.[38] The two most important such series of lectures were his commentaries on the Psalter (1513–1515) and on Paul's letter to the Romans (1515–1516). In both these series of lectures, Luther interprets justification as a transformative process of becoming: *fieri est iustificatio*.[39] Yet neither of these works shows much overt engagement with the theme of deification, which often has to be read into, rather than out of, the texts.

In his Romans lectures, Luther follows Augustine in treating justification as a restorative or healing process, in which human nature is healed of its infirmities. This is made clear in Luther's analogy of a patient recovering

---

[37]For an account of Luther's theological realignments during this formative period, see Alister E. McGrath, *Luther's Theology of the Cross: Martin Luther's Theological Breakthrough*, 2nd ed. (Oxford: Blackwell, 2011). On the specific issue of deification at this stage in Luther's development, see Simo Peura, *Mehr als ein Mensch? Die Vergöttlichung als Thema der Theologie Martin Luthers von 1513–1519* (Stuttgart: Steiner, 1994). Peura's basic argument is that Luther here articulates a theology of effective justification, which should be understood ontologically as the indwelling of Christ.

[38]Oswald Bayer, "Luther as an Interpreter of Holy Scripture," in *The Cambridge Companion to Martin Luther*, ed. Donald McKim (New York: Cambridge University Press, 2003), 73-85.

[39]WA 56:442.3. For Augustine's earlier use of medical analogies for salvation, see Thomas F. Martin, "Paul the Patient: *Christus Medicus* and the 'Stimulus Carnis' (2 Cor. 12:7): A Consideration of Augustine's Medicinal Christology," *Augustinian Studies* 32, no. 2 (2001): 219-56.

from illness, which is borrowed from Augustine. Christ is both the physician and the medicine that bring about the process of healing.

> It is like someone who is ill, who trusts the doctor who promises a certain recovery and in the meantime obeys the doctor's instructions. . . . Now this person who is ill, is he healthy? In fact, he is a man who is both ill and healthy at the same time [*immo aegrotus simul et sanus*]. As a matter of fact, he is ill; but he is healthy on account of the certain promise of the doctor, whom he trusts and who reckons him as healthy already, because he is sure that he will cure him. . . . And so he is totally healthy in hope, but is a sinner in fact [*sanus perfecte est in spe, in re autem peccator*].[40]

Although Luther is finding his way toward his new understanding of the righteousness of God, this remains framed within a transformative understanding of Christian existence.

Yet Luther is careful to insist that believers cannot be said to *possess* divine righteousness or to have any intrinsic qualities that might be thought to merit or justify their acceptance in the sight of God. The righteousness of Christ is indeed reckoned to believers—but this remains an external righteousness, shielding or clothing the believer, rather than being part of their person. While the righteousness of believers is and will remain extrinsic to them, Christ is nonetheless really present within believers, effecting their renovation and regeneration.[41] In 1520, Luther explored the nature and consequences of a believer's union with Christ using an analogy that has attracted wide attention. The relation of Christ and the believer is analogous to that of a husband and wife. This cultural analogy is clearly dependent on certain contemporary German conventions relating to marriage, such as the core assumption that the wife takes on the social status of her husband, and Luther's views on prostitution as a devaluation of the identity and calling of women.[42] Luther sets out this analogy as follows:

> Faith does not merely mean that the soul realizes that the divine word is full of all grace, free and holy; it also unites the soul with Christ [*voreynigt auch*

---

[40] WA 56:272.3-21.
[41] WA 56:279.22: "Ideo recte dixi, quod extrinsecum nobis est omne bonum nostrum, quod est Christus."
[42] For the context, see Lyndal Roper, *The Holy Household: Women and Morals in Reformation Augsburg* (Oxford: Oxford University Press, 1991), 89-131.

*die seele mit Christo*], as a bride is united with her bridegroom. From such a marriage, as St Paul says (Ephesians 5:31-2), it follows that Christ and the soul become one body, so that they hold all things in common, whether for better or worse. This means that what Christ possesses belongs to the believing soul; and what the soul possesses, belongs to Christ. Thus Christ possesses all good things and holiness; these now belong to the soul. The soul possesses lots of vices and sin; these now belong to Christ. Here we have a happy exchange [*froelich wechtzel*]! . . . Christ, the rich, noble, and holy bridegroom, takes in marriage this poor, contemptible, and sinful little prostitute [*das arm vorachte boetzes huerlein*], takes away all her evil, and bestows all his goodness upon her![43]

This important passage is indicative of Luther's capacity to communicate theology effectively and accessibly. For our purposes in this study, I will focus on two of its aspects.

1. The union that Luther explores in this analogy is primarily relational and has no discernible ontological consequences or implications. Christ is embraced, enfolded, and by faith within the human soul, leading to the transformation of the human soul. The analogy is robustly christological, with no obvious link with the soteriological category of theosis.

2. Luther uses this analogy to communicate the theological plausibility of the transfer of human sin to Christ, and Christ's righteousness and holiness to believers. The analogy is not intended to demonstrate the reality of the union between Christ and the believer but to affirm and illuminate two soteriological consequences of this union—namely, Christ bearing our sin and bestowing his righteousness on us, and the transformation of human status in the sight of God, paralleling the marriage of a "rich, noble, and holy bridegroom" to a "sinful little prostitute." Neither of these two benefits is articulated using the concepts or vocabulary of theosis, although they could be argued to be consistent with it. In his later writings, Luther continues to emphasize the importance of taking hold of, apprehending, or grasping Christ through faith, which secures the new status and identity of Christian believers.

---

[43]WA 7:25.26–26.9.

So what are the benefits of taking hold of Christ? What understanding of salvation does Luther articulate? In his Galatians commentary of 1535, Luther declares that "faith takes hold of Christ in such a way that Christ is the object of faith, or rather, so to speak, is present in this faith itself [*in ipsa fide Christus adest*]."[44] Luther is not speaking of deification here but rather of what might best be described as Christification—a process of being conformed to Christ and his righteousness.[45] Yet Luther concludes his reflection by insisting that we cannot adequately articulate the manner of Christ's presence within the believer, even though we can identify the benefits that this brings: "So faith justifies because it takes hold of and possesses this treasure, the present Christ. But the mode in which he is present is not conceivable."[46]

This point is reaffirmed in a 1541 joint letter with Johann Bugenhagen, in which Luther makes it clear that the ultimate basis of the righteousness of Christians in the sight of God is the presence of Christ within them. "Thus says God: Your heart is holy because of my Son, who dwells there through faith."[47] Luther here proposes God as the evaluating *observer*, and Christ as the internal agent of human transformation and the basis of acceptance.

Luther also proposes Christ as a model of the redeemed life, in effect embodying and enacting an evangelical mode of living. There is an interesting parallel between Luther's christological focus on issues of ethics and spirituality and Gregory of Nyssa's reframing of the quest to be like God in terms of the imitation of Christ.[48] The classic philosophical question of what it means to act in a Godlike manner could be refocused on how Christ acted.[49]

---

[44]See the important discussion at WA 40/1:228.28–229.30. For commentary, see Vainio, *Justification and Participation in Christ*, 19-27.

[45]*Christification* is the suggestion of Panayiotis Nellas, *Deification in Christ: Orthodox Perspectives on the Nature of the Human Person* (Crestwood, NY: St. Vladimir's Seminary Press, 1997), 115-59. More recently, see Peter Bouteneff, "Christ and Salvation," in *The Cambridge Companion to Orthodox Christian Theology*, ed. Mary Cunningham and Elizabeth Theokritoff (Cambridge: Cambridge University Press, 2008), 93-106, esp. 104.

[46]"Iustificat ergo fides, quia apprehendit et possidet istum thesaurum, scilicet Christum praesentem. Sed quo modo praesens sit, non est cogitabile."

[47]WABR 9:408.60-61.

[48]Shigeki Tsuchihashi, "The Likeness to God and the Imitation of Christ: The Transformation of the Platonic Tradition in Gregory of Nyssa," in *Christians Shaping Identity from the Roman Empire to Byzantium*, ed. G. D. Dunn and W. Mayer (Leiden: Brill, 2015), 100-116.

[49]For the classic philosophical question of what it means to act in a godlike manner in Plato, see David T. Runia, "The Theme of 'Becoming Like God' in Plato's Republic," in *Dialogues on Plato's Politeia (Republic)*, ed. N. Notomi and L. Brisson (Sankt Augustin: Akademia, 2013), 288-93.

## Forensic Justification? Luther and Melanchthon in the 1530s

During the 1530s, Luther's Wittenberg colleague Philipp Melanchthon developed a forensic or declarative approach to justification. Luther had laid the groundwork for such an approach in the late 1510s, arguing that justification was to be seen as the enfolding of the believer in the "alien righteousness [*iustitia aliena*] of Christ." Yet at this time, Luther tended to see this as a protective external shield or garment, which enabled the believer to grow in faith and holiness.

Melanchthon took this idea in a somewhat different direction, arguing that justification is to be understood *forensically*, as the declaration that the believer is righteous on account of the alien righteousness of Christ.[50] Justification thus comes to be understood primarily as "pronouncing righteous."[51] Although Luther was not opposed to this theological move, his own thought remained focused on the indwelling Christ as the agent of transformation.[52] This, in the view of many scholars, allowed the declarative and transformative aspects of justification to be held together, anticipating John Calvin's idea of the "double grace" of justification and sanctification, grounded in the believer's union with Christ.[53]

It could be argued that incorporating the notion of theosis into a Lutheran account of justification would counter the limitations of its impersonal, transactionalist, or declaratory emphases. Yet Luther's own account of justification is not vulnerable to such criticisms, in that his clear emphasis on the believer's transformative union with Christ is capable of accommodating both declaratory and effective accounts of justification, providing a

---

[50] *Apologia*, art. 4, para. 305; *Die Bekenntnisschriften der Evangelisch-Lutherischen Kirche: Vollständige Neuedition* (Göttingen: Vandenhoeck & Ruprecht, 2014), 219.43-45.

[51] *Apologia*, art. 4, para. 252; *Die Bekenntnisschriften der Evangelisch-Lutherischen Kirche*, 209.32-34.

[52] See the important study of Sibylle Rolf, *Zum Herzen sprechen: Eine Studie zum imputativen Aspekt in Martin Luthers Rechtfertigungslehre und zu seinen Konsequenzen für die Predigt des Evangeliums* (Leipzig: Evangelische Verlagsanstalt, 2008).

[53] J. V. Fesko, *Beyond Calvin: Union with Christ and Justification in Early Modern Reformed Theology (1517-1700)* (Göttingen: Vandenhoeck & Ruprecht, 2012), 13-52. On this theological move allowing for the declarative and transformative aspects of justification to be held together, see the discussion in Mark Mattes, "Luther on Justification as Forensic and Effective," in *The Oxford Handbook of Martin Luther's Theology*, ed. Robert Kolb, Irene Dingel, and L'ubomír Batka (Oxford: Oxford University Press, 2014), 264-73.

theological bridge between them. Although many would argue that Calvin's more rigorous analysis of the grounds and consequences of the believer's union with Christ provides a more satisfactory intellectual foundation for the correlation of the declarative and affective aspects of justification, Luther's account, particularly in his later writings, is perfectly adequate to secure this connection.

## Conclusion

In his important study of theosis in Pauline soteriology, Ben Blackwell suggests that exploring Paul's ideas through the lens of deification may help us to "read Paul in a way that draws out and connects aspects of his theology that Western readers have routinely missed or underplayed."[54] This chapter has offered a critical but constructive account of the place of theosis in the theology of Martin Luther. I have aimed both to explain the initial resistance to exploration of this question, partly as a consequence of the influence of older accounts of Luther's theology, and to set out an assessment of his own position on this question. The publication of the Weimar edition of Luther's works and a growing awareness of the complexity of early modern intellectual history has created space for exploration of alternative or expansionary accounts of Luther's vision of the Christian life, including the question whether he implicitly articulates some form of theosis.

While I have taken a cautious and critical approach to some recent trends in the field, such as the Finnish interpretation of Luther, I am clear that these represent important research programs that have opened up new ways of reading traditional texts for critical evaluation within the scholarly community. The evidence that Luther explicitly or implicitly incorporates the theme of theosis in his writings is suggestive, I believe, though ultimately not totally persuasive. Yet reading Luther afresh using this lens has certainly, in my own case, led me to reconsider aspects of Luther's theology that I and other readers might hitherto "have routinely missed or underplayed." My own view is that the term *Christification* more accurately captures Luther's

---

[54]Blackwell, *Christosis*, 3. Blackwell points to several studies that have opened up exploration of this theme within the New Testament, including Michael J. Gorman, "Romans: The First Christian Treatise on Theosis," *Journal of Theological Interpretation* 5 (2011): 13-34.

distinctive emphasis, particularly in relation to his incorporation of death and suffering into his theology of the Christian life. While there is a clear and illuminating link between *deification* and *Christification*, they differ in their emphasis and capacity to correlate the life of faith with the life of Christ—a key theme in Luther's theology in general and his theology of the cross in particular.[55]

It remains important to further explore and clarify what advantages result from reading Luther through the lens of theosis. Luther may not explicitly articulate this notion, but exploring the theological substructure of his writings may illuminate other aspects of his thought in helpful ways. This chapter has tentatively opened up some lines of exploration; there is much more, however, remaining to be discovered in Luther's writings.

---

[55]See, e.g., McGrath, *Luther's Theology of the Cross*, 148-81.

# DEIFICATION *in the* REFORMED TRADITION *from* ZWINGLI *to* VERMIGLI

CARL MOSSER

IN POPULAR DISCOURSE, DEIFICATION is associated with mystical, esoteric, and pagan notions that suggest human beings can merge into the being of God or become deities. That is unfortunate. *Deification* or *divinization* is one of the earliest entries in the Christian theological lexicon. In the second century, patristic writers began to use the evocative Greek word θεοποίησις to succinctly refer to the biblical vision of final salvation as participation in divine immortality, incorruption, glory, and sonship.[1] Later patristic writers introduced the word *theosis* to additionally convey the idea that salvation includes intimate union with God. Latin translators rendered both terms as *deificatio*. Patristic writers were careful to employ a variety of formulations and analogies to safeguard the Creator-creature distinction. In an orthodox Christian context, *deification* refers to the transformation

---

[1] Etymologically, θεοποίησις refers to making gods. Patristic writers did not, however, think Christians would become deities or merge into God. From the classical period onward, the word θεός ("god") could refer to a deity *or* express qualities associated with the divine such as immortality, glory, incorruptibility, blessedness, and sublimity. Thus, it was natural for Greek-speaking Christians to understand the New Testament promises associated with the resurrection to mean that Christians will be made "gods." Synonymous parallelism between "sons of the Most High" and "gods" in Ps 82:6 facilitated this equation. Patristic writers, building on earlier Jewish interpretations, saw the declaration in this verse fulfilled in the adoption of Christians as sons of God as taught by the apostle Paul. See further Carl Mosser, "The Earliest Patristic Interpretations of Psalm 82, Jewish Antecedents, and the Origin of Christian Deification," *Journal of Theological Studies* 56, no. 1 (2005): 30-74.

believers will undergo in the resurrection when they are saturated with divine life by virtue of union with Christ, the full indwelling of the Spirit, and vision of God.[2] Christians across many theological and liturgical traditions report episodes in which they experience extraordinary foretastes of these eschatological blessings.

Liberal Protestant histories of dogma written in the nineteenth century convinced generations of scholars that the fundamental difference between the Christian East and West lies in two mutually exclusive visions of salvation rather than politics, cultural differences, or traditional disputes about the *filioque*, papal supremacy, purgatory, and so forth. They claimed the Eastern tradition understands salvation in terms of immortality and deification, while the West understands it as reconciliation and justification. In the twentieth century, Eastern Orthodox theologians appropriated this claim and made it central to their description of Orthodoxy's theological identity. As a result of this consensus, deification was long treated as a distinctively Greek patristic and Eastern Orthodox doctrine foreign to the churches of the Reformation.

Jaroslav Pelikan already disputed this portrait in the early 1960s. While formulations of salvation as deification are more frequent in the Eastern tradition, he countered, "Western theology and spirituality spoke in such language also; so, for that matter, did the Reformers and other Protestant divines."[3] This chapter will illustrate the truth of Pelikan's counterclaim in relation to the Reformed tradition. We will first see that Huldrych Zwingli, Johannes Oecolampadius, and Martin Bucer—three key founders of the Reformed tradition—affirmed patristic and medieval teaching about deification. Focus will then shift to deification in the thought of second-generation Reformers who further shaped and deepened the Reformed tradition, with particular focus on John Calvin and Peter Martyr Vermigli. Not only do

---

[2]I borrow the metaphor of saturation from James T. Turner Jr., "The Mind of the Spirit in the Resurrected Human: A Mereological Model of Mental Saturation," *Philosophia Christi* 21, no. 2 (2019): 167-86. For an overview of several ways Christians affirm deifying union with God while firmly upholding the Creator-creature distinction, see Carl Mosser, "Deification and Union with God," in *T&T Clark Handbook of Analytic Theology*, ed. James M. Arcadi and James T. Turner Jr. (London: T&T Clark, 2021), 271-78.

[3]Jaroslav Pelikan, *The Light of the World: A Basic Image in Early Christian Thought* (New York: Harper & Brothers, 1962), 82.

their writings describe ultimate salvation in terms of deification; they attest that sixteenth-century Reformed churches officially embraced deification as a christological doctrine as well.

## Deification in Reformers of the First Generation

The Reformed tradition emerged as a distinct expression of catholic Christianity out of the reforming work of Huldrych Zwingli in Zurich. Zwingli started down the path toward reform when he was persuaded by his teacher Thomas Wyttenbach and by Erasmus of Rotterdam that Scripture and the church fathers are the most reliable theological sources rather than the medieval scholastic theologians. When he began his career as a Reformer, Zwingli was familiar with patristic and later teaching about deification. Zwingli embedded deification within the Reformed tradition's earliest theological expositions.

One of Zwingli's first patristic acquisitions was Jacques Lefèvre d'Étaples's Latin translation of John of Damascus, *De Fide Orthodoxa* (1507), an important compendium of Greek patristic theology. His personal copy contains approximately one thousand underlines, marginalia, and other traces of careful study written before July 1519, showing that Zwingli "worked his way through this collection of dogmatic writings with great intensity."[4] The doctrine of deification plays an important role in Damascene's theology and "colors his treatment of many other issues."[5] That caught Zwingli's attention. The first time the word *deificatio* appeared, Zwingli wrote a long comment in the margin. The annotation is difficult to read, but Zwingli seems to contrast God, who deifies, and believers, who are deified. Zwingli later underlined Damascene's point that deification is not transformation into the divine substance as well as statements about the deification of Christ's flesh and will.[6]

It is possible Zwingli encountered deification in works by Irenaeus, Athanasius, and the Cappadocian fathers that he owned. We cannot be certain

---

[4]Urs B. Leu and Sandra Weidmann, *Huldrych Zwingli's Private Library* (Leiden: Brill, 2019), 58.
[5]Maurice Fred Himmerich, "Deification in John of Damascus" (PhD diss., Marquette University, 1985), iii.
[6]See Zwingli's copy of *Theologia Damasceni*, trans. Jacques Lefèvre d'Étaples (Paris: Stephanus, 1507), 16r, 34v, 73r, 73v; see also 93v and 94r. High-quality photographs can be read online. See *Theologia Damasceni*, e-rara, www.e-rara.ch/zuz/content/titleinfo/17482862 (accessed February 18, 2024). I am grateful to Urs Leu for kind assistance deciphering Zwingli's handwriting.

because his copies contain few markings, but Zwingli did not always mark books that he is known to have read or consulted. His copy of Cyril of Alexandria's commentary on John, however, is intermittently underlined throughout. Cyril's commentary is notably permeated by the doctrine of deification even though it does not rely on technical terminology to express the idea.[7] A later form of the doctrine is also found in works by Florentine philosopher Giovanni Pico della Mirandola, which Zwingli read and with which he was known to be sympathetic.[8]

Zwingli wrote the earliest formal statement of Reformed theology for the First Zurich Disputation in 1523, the Sixty-Seven Articles. In comparison with Luther's more famous Ninety-Five Theses, the Sixty-Seven Articles express a more fully formed Protestant theology. Article VIII expresses Zwingli's commitment to catholicity. So, one should not be surprised when article XIII affirms a vision of salvation consonant with patristic and medieval teaching about deification: "Where this (the head) is hearkened to one learns clearly and plainly the will of God, and man is attracted by his spirit to him and changed into him [*in inn verwandlet*]."[9] Zwingli published an exposition of the articles that clarifies his intent. Alluding to 2 Corinthians 3:18, he says, "That a person is drawn to God by God's Spirit and deified, becomes quite clear from scripture."[10] "Deified" is the modern translator's attempt to capture the sense of Zwingli's German *in got verwandlet* ("transformed/changed into God"). The Reformer elaborates: "One must be drawn to God and deified [*in inn verwandlet*] so that we might be fully emptied, cleaned and able to deny ourselves, no longer trusting in our own mind, heart and works but putting all our confidence in God our sole

---

[7]This is illustrated by the sheer number of passages from the commentary discussed in Daniel A. Keating, *The Appropriation of Divine Life in Cyril of Alexandria* (Oxford: Oxford University Press, 2004).

[8]Oswald Myconius, Zwingli's friend and first biographer, mentions the Reformer's approval of Mirandola's propositions. See Henry Bennet, *A Famous and Godly History, Contaynyng the Lyues and Actes of Three Renowmed Reformers of the Christian Church* (London: John Awdelay, 1561), 84.

[9]Samuel Macauley Jackson, ed., *Selected Works of Huldreich Zwingli (1484–1531), the Reformer of German Switzerland* (Philadelphia: University of Pennsylvania Press, 1901), 112. Zwingli's sixteenth-century Swiss German does not follow the spelling and style conventions of modern standard German. The same applies to quotations from Meister Eckhart below.

[10]Huldrych Zwingli, *The Defense of the Reformed Faith*, vol. 1 of *Huldrych Zwingli Writings*, ed. E. J. Furcha (Allison Park, PA: Pickwick, 1984), 57.

hope to which we cling. For thus we are being transformed into God [*in gott verwandlet*].¹¹ Because God wills to bring about this transformation in human beings, Zwingli says Christians should be diligent to ensure the gospel of Christ is preached everywhere (article XIV).

Zwingli's *Commentary on True and False Religion* (1525) has been described as the "first full vision" of Zwingli's new form of Christianity and "earliest truly comprehensive treatise on Protestant theology."¹² In it, Zwingli says God—as the supreme good—is kind and bountiful. He desires "the profit of those to whom he gives with only this one thing in view. For he desires to impart himself freely." The apex of human perfection is described as transformative union with the Spirit of God. The Spirit draws "the wretched spirit of man to itself, to unite and to bind it to itself, and wholly to transform it into itself [*ac prorsus in se transformare*]." When God discloses himself to a starving soul, it "leaps for joy, and daily grows and increases in strength more and more, being transformed into the form of God [*formam Dei transformatur*] until it develops into the perfect man."¹³

Though familiar with patristic terminology, Zwingli prefers to talk about deification in terms of transformation into God. He does not intend to suggest believers lose their identity in God's being or otherwise compromise the distinction between Creator and creature. Even so, his language is bold. In 1329, Pope John XXII issued a bull condemning seventeen statements by Meister Eckhart.¹⁴ Zwingli's language is very similar to three of the condemned statements that appear in one of Eckhart's sermons.¹⁵ The first one says, "We are transformed completely into God [*alzemâle transformieret in got*] and changed [*verwandelt*] into him." Twice more Eckhardt refers to believers being transformed into God using the phrases *wirde ich verwandelt*

---

¹¹Zwingli, *Defense of the Reformed Faith*, 57.
¹²Bruce Gordon, *Zwingli: God's Armed Prophet* (New Haven, CT: Yale University Press, 2021), 163; see also 147 and William Walker Rockwell, preface to *The Latin Works of Huldreich Zwingli*, ed. Clarence Nevin Heller (Philadelphia: Heidelberg, 1929), 3:iii.
¹³Zwingli, *Latin Works*, 70, 208, adjusted.
¹⁴"Errors of Ekhart on the Relation of the World and Man," in *Compendium of Creeds, Definitions, and Declarations on Matters of Faith and Morals*, 43rd ed., ed. Heinrich Denzinger (San Francisco: Ignatius, 2012), DS 950-80 (pp. 297-300).
¹⁵Meister Eckhart, "Sermon 65," in *Deutsche Mystiker des vierzehnten Jarhunderts: Meister Eckhart*, ed. Franz Pfeiffer (Leipzig: G. J. Göschen, 1857), 202-6; English translation: Maurice O'C. Walshe, *The Complete Mystical Works of Meister Eckhart* (New York: Crossroad, 2009), 328-33.

*in in* and *warden wir in got verwandelt*.[16] Matthew of Aquasparta, Henry of Ghent, Bonaventure, Thomas Aquinas, John Gerson, Nicholas of Cusa, and other medieval writers employed similar language. Whether Zwingli picked up this way of describing salvation's goal from one of these writers or elsewhere, Zurich's Reformer describes a vision of redemption that affirms deification in continuity with medieval Latin theology.

At the Marburg Colloquy (1529), the Reformed churches of Switzerland and southern Germany were represented by Zwingli, Caspar Hedio, Johannes Oecolampadius, and Martin Bucer. The writings of these first-generation Reformed theologians reflect the influence of Greek patristic teaching about salvation as deification. For example, in his sermons on 1 John, Oecolampadius says, "Christ became man, that we might become sons of God," and "We are through adoption what Christ is by nature."[17] These statements are variations on the patristic exchange formula, a common way to express deification without recourse to quasi-technical vocabulary. Salvation is also described as participation in the light that is God, which illumines the believer out of darkness and restores the image of God within.[18] Participation in God is a common synonym for deification in patristic texts. The Reformer of Basel was a well-known translator of the Greek fathers; so it is unsurprising that he would use such formulations. In his commentary on Romans, Oecolampadius states, "Whoever clings to the creature becomes vain, but whoever clings to the Lord becomes divine [*divinus fit*]."[19] He cites a classic deification prooftext in support: "Whoever clings to the Lord is one spirit [with Him]" (1 Cor 6:17). Erik Lundeen describes this as "rather blunt and unguarded use of the language of divinization."[20] While it may sound that way to modern

---

[16]Eckhart, *Deutsche Mystiker*, 205-6.

[17]Johannes Oecolampadius, *In Epistolam Ioannis Apostoli Catholicam primam, Ioannis Oecolampadii Demegoriae, hoc est, Homiliae una & XX* (Basel: Andreas Cratandrum, 1524), 19r, 85r-85v, as translated in Erik Lundeen, "Preaching Justification in the Early Reformation: The 1523 Advent Sermons of Johannes Oecolampadius on 1 John," *Archiv für Reformationsgeschichte / Archive for Reformation History* 112 (2021): 108.

[18]Oecolampadius, *In Epistolam Ioannis*, 14v, 27v, 49r; Lundeen, "Preaching Justification," 109.

[19]Johannes Oecolampadius, *In Epistolam B. Pauli Apost. ad Rhomanos Adnotationes* (Basel: Andreas Cratander, 1525), 16r, as translated in Lundeen, "Preaching Justification," 109.

[20]Lundeen, "Preaching Justification," 109.

readers, Strasbourg's Reformer, Martin Bucer, spoke about deification much more forthrightly.

In 1523, Bucer published a lovely book on why we should not live for ourselves but for others instead. Readers are repeatedly told that true faith manifests itself in seeking the well-being of your neighbor over your own well-being. Bucer says this principle should guide the way government officials and ministers exercise their offices as well as guide parents advising children about what profession to enter. Christians should consider themselves nothing, following the example of Christ. At the same time, they must also consider themselves blessed, though "now only in hope, since we shall receive God's eternal inheritance only on the day in which we shall with Christ appear in the glory of God and be like God (Colossians 3:3-4; I John 3:2)."[21] We should imitate God during this life in how we love our neighbors because God promises to share his glory with us and make us like himself. The incarnation, justifying faith, good works, and deification come together in the final sentence of the book: "The divine Word brings faith; faith brings love; love brings good deeds as its fruits—after which God gives us the eternal inheritance, a wholly divine and blessed life."[22] The divine Word, in short, came to give us a wholly divine life. In the Tetrapolitan Confession (1530), Bucer says this should motivate us now to "show ourselves to others as gods—i.e. true children of God—by love striving for their advantage so far as we are able" (article IV).[23]

Bucer affirms deification more overtly in his commentary on St. John's Gospel (1528). In concert with patristic teaching, deification is identified as the ultimate purpose of the incarnation. Explaining the reason "the Word became flesh" (Jn 1:14), Bucer says, "The Father wanted to make gods out of men" (*voluit nanque Pater ex hominibus deos facere*). He refers to this as the "deification of the elect" (*deificationem electorum*). Believers should piously contemplate the way the Word humbled himself to bring us to this divine destiny

---

[21] Martin Bucer, *Instruction in Christian Love [1523]*, trans. Paul Traugott Fuhrmann (Richmond, VA: John Knox, 1952), 44-45.
[22] Bucer, *Instruction in Christian Love*, 52.
[23] See further Carl Mosser, "The Gospel's End and Our Highest Good: Deification in the Reformed Tradition," in *With All the Fullness of God: Deification in Christian Tradition*, ed. Jared Ortiz (Lanham, MD: Lexington Books/Fortress Academic, 2021), 90.

(*sortis divinae*) and serve their neighbors in response.[24] Bucer made substantial cuts in the third edition of the commentary (1536) but did not remove this language. Nor was it removed from a posthumous edition published in Geneva in 1553. Bucer's language is as bold as anything encountered in the church fathers, but it did not spark controversy or elicit critique. Why? Sixteenth-century theologians were well-acquainted with patristic literature, so they knew what this language meant within the parameters of creedal orthodoxy.

## DEIFICATION IN REFORMERS OF THE SECOND GENERATION

John Calvin was a second-generation Reformer who "inherited the Reformed tradition forged in Zurich, Basel, and Strasbourg, and his great contribution was to draw it together compendiously and to deepen its furrows."[25] This is evident in his teaching about redemption's final ends. Calvin affirmed deification in the same ways that the Reformers of Zurich, Basel, and Strasbourg did. He also went beyond them in his eucharistic theology and the way he vividly described union with God as the ultimate goal of salvation.

Like Zwingli, Calvin unapologetically speaks of transformation into God. Near the beginning of the second edition of the *Institutes* (1539), he added a passage that indicates Plato rightly understood "the highest good of the soul is likeness to God, where, when the soul has grasped the knowledge of God, it is wholly transformed into him [*in ipsum tota transformatur*]" (*Inst.* 1.3.3, corrected).[26] In 1543, Calvin revised the preface to Pierre Robert Olivétan's translation of the New Testament. A new paragraph poses the following rhetorical question: "What more would we ask for, as spiritual doctrine for our souls, than to know God, to be transformed into him, and to have his glorious image imprinted in us, so that we may partake of his righteousness, to become heirs of his Kingdom and to possess it in the end in full?"[27] The parallelism with medieval formulations and Zwingli is obvious in both the

---

[24]Irena Backus, ed., *Martini Buceri Opera Latina*, vol. 2, *Enarratio in Evangelion Iohannis (1528, 1530, 1536)* (Leiden: Brill, 1988), 44.

[25]Gordon, *Zwingli*, 7.

[26]Unless noted otherwise, quotations from the *Institutes* follow John Calvin, *Institutes of the Christian Religion*, ed. John T. McNeill, trans. Ford Lewis Battles (Louisville, KY: Westminster John Knox, 1960).

[27]John Calvin, *Calvin: Commentaries*, trans. Joseph Haroutunian (Philadelphia: Westminster, 1958), 70, adjusted.

French and Latin version of the preface (French: *transformez in luy*; Latin: *in ipsum transformemur*).

Like Oecolampadius, Calvin made use of the patristic exchange formula.[28] Here is one of several examples found in the first edition of the *Institutes* (1536): "Christ, the true son, has been given to us as our brother by Him in order that what belongs to him by nature may become ours by benefit of adoption."[29] A variant found in Calvin's first catechism (1538) bears even greater resemblance to patristic precursors: "Indeed, he put on our flesh in order that having become Son of Man he might make us sons of God with him; having received our poverty in himself, he might transfer his wealth to us; having submitted to our weakness, he might strengthen us by his power; having accepted our mortality, he might give us immortality; having descended to earth, he might raise us to heaven."[30] The most famous example of the exchange formula in Calvin's corpus is also one of the most beautiful found anywhere in the Christian tradition. In the final edition of the *Institutes* (1559), while discussing the Lord's Supper, Calvin says that in partaking of the sacrament we "have a witness of our growth into one body with Christ such that whatever is his may be called ours." Geneva's Reformer then elaborates:

> This is the wonderful exchange which, out of his measureless benevolence, he has made with us; that, becoming Son of man with us, he has made us sons of God with him; that, by his descent to earth, he has prepared an ascent to heaven for us; that, by taking on our mortality, he has conferred his immortality upon us; that, accepting our weakness, he has strengthened us by his power; that, receiving our poverty unto himself, he has transferred his wealth to us; that, taking the weight of our iniquity upon himself (which oppressed us), he has clothed us with his righteousness. (*Inst.* 4.17.2)

Calvin returns to the exchange motif a few paragraphs later. This time he specifies that Christ was given to make us partakers of divine life:

---

[28] The exchange formula structures Calvin's entire theology of atonement. See Carl Mosser, "Graced Exchange and Vision of God in Calvin's Atonement Theology," *Reformed Theological Review* 82, no. 1 (2023): 48-74.

[29] John Calvin, *Institutes of the Christian Religion, 1536 Edition*, rev. ed., trans. Ford Lewis Battles (Grand Rapids, MI: Eerdmans, 1986), 76.

[30] I. John Hesselink, *Calvin's First Catechism: A Commentary* (Louisville, KY: Westminster John Knox, 1997), 23.

Rather, he had been given as such to us by the Father and showed himself as such when, being made a sharer in our human mortality, he made us partakers in his divine immortality; when, offering himself as a sacrifice, he bore our curse in himself to imbue us with his blessing; when, by his death, he swallowed up and annihilated death; and when, in his resurrection, he raised up this corruptible flesh of ours, which he had put on, to glory and incorruption. (*Inst.* 4.17.4)

Like Bucer, Calvin expressly describes redemption in terms of deification. Commenting on 2 Peter 1:4 in 1551, he says, "We should notice that it is the purpose of the Gospel to make us sooner or later like God; indeed it is, so to speak, a kind of deification."[31] The older translation conveys the verbal idea of Calvin's Latin more adequately: "Let us then mark, that the end of the gospel is, to render us eventually conformable to God, and, if we may so speak [*ut ita loquamur*], to deify us [*quasi deificari*]."[32] His immediately preceding comments link deification with the faithful being clothed with God's glory, endowed with his power, and restored in his glorious image, and God himself being possessed in such a way that what is his becomes theirs by grace.

Calvin was well-acquainted with heterodox notions of divinization promoted by the ancient Manicheans, a contemporary sect known as the Libertines, and individuals such as Michael Servetus and Andreas Osiander. Therefore, he is careful to distinguish the kind of deification he finds in 2 Peter 1:4 from alternatives. He first insists the word *nature* does not denote God's essence but kind. What the apostles were concerned to teach is that "when we have put off all the vices of the flesh we shall be partakers of divine immortality and the glory of blessedness, and thus we shall be in a way one with God so far as our capacity allows." Therefore, this verse does not mean "we cross over into God's nature so that His nature absorbs ours," as some fanatics assert. The distinction between Creator and creature is inviolable. Calvin once again recognizes genuine similarity with Plato's teaching that the highest human good is conformity to God (see *Theaetetus* 176b). Plato,

---

[31] John Calvin, *The Epistle of Paul the Apostle to the Hebrews and the First and Second Epistles of St Peter*, trans. William B. Johnston (Grand Rapids, MI: Eerdmans, 1963), 330.

[32] John Calvin, *Commentaries on the Catholic Epistles*, trans. John Owen (Edinburgh: Calvin Translation Society, 1855), 371.

however, was "wrapped up in the fog of errors, and afterwards he slipped away into his own invented ideas."[33]

While Calvin affirmed deification in the same ways Zwingli, Oecolampadius, and Bucer did, he also expressed the idea in other ways. Especially important to Calvin was the notion that Christ's flesh was made life-giving, a teaching he took from Cyril of Alexandria. According to Cyril, the humanity assumed by the Word of God was endowed with immortal life, glory, and incorruption as well as the ability to communicate divine life to those who partake of him.[34] Christ communicates his life-giving flesh to believers by means of the Eucharist and Holy Spirit. Calvin similarly teaches that Christ's flesh was "endowed with immortality" and is "pervaded with fullness of life to be transmitted to us." Christ "quickens our very flesh in which he abides, that by partaking of him we may be fed unto immortality" for the purpose of being "made one in body, spirit, and soul with him." The Spirit serves as the bond of this union like "a channel through which all that Christ himself is and has is conveyed to us." Deification comes especially in view when Calvin says the life-giving flesh of Christ "is like a rich and inexhaustible fountain that pours into us the life springing forth from the Godhead [*divinitate*] into itself" (*Inst.* 4.17.9, 12).

Calvin frequently says that divine, celestial, and heavenly life or immortality is communicated to believers. This life is not divine merely because God is its source. In what sense, then? Calvin leaves no room for doubt when he explains what it means to be "alienated from the life of God" (Eph 4:18). God, he observes, is the source of three kinds of life in this world: animal life, which we have in common with brute beasts; the human life we possess as children of Adam; and supernatural life that is obtained by the faithful alone. Each kind of life can be called "the life of God" since they all come from God. The regeneration believers experience, however, is "the life of God" in the highest sense "because then does God properly live in us, and we enjoy His life, when he governs us by His Spirit."[35]

---

[33] Calvin, *Epistle of Paul the Apostle to the Hebrews*, 330-31; see also *Inst.* 3.25.2.
[34] See Keating, *Appropriation of Divine Life*, 44-46, 69-74, 202-3.
[35] John Calvin, *The Epistles of Paul the Apostle to the Galatians, Ephesians, Philippians and Colossians*, trans. T. H. L. Parker (Grand Rapids, MI: Eerdmans, 1965), 187.

According to Bruce McCormack, had Calvin been more willing to address ontological questions, he "might have realized that he could not reasonably affirm Cyril's rhetoric on the life-giving character of Christ's 'body' without accepting Cyril's soteriology of divinization."[36] Calvin, however, did not inherit a Reformed tradition infected by the prejudice against deification that nineteenth-century historians of dogma bequeathed modern Protestant theology. Calvin affirmed Cyril's rhetoric about the life-giving flesh of Christ *because* he accepted Cyril's soteriology of divinization. When Calvin says the end of the gospel is "to deify us," he explains what that means in terms of partaking of divine immortality, partaking of the glory of blessedness, conformity or likeness to God, and being made "one with God so far as our capacity allows."[37] That is an apt summary of common patristic teaching. It also comports with the definition of deification offered by an anonymous sixth-century author who wrote under the name of Dionysius the Areopagite: "deification [*theosis*] is likeness to God and union with him so far as possible" (*Ecclesiastical Hierarchy* 1.3).[38]

Calvin's commentary on 2 Peter 1:4 finds parallels in passages that speak in terms of union with God rather than deification. For example, in one place he says, "It is the end of the Gospel to be united with God." In another we are told, "The highest human good is therefore simply union with God. We attain it when we are brought into conformity with His likeness."[39] Union with God is one of the primary ways the concept of deification is expressed within late patristic and medieval theology. These parallels show that Calvin could also mention union with God as a synonym for deification. Once that is recognized, it becomes evident that Calvin held a robust soteriology of deification from the beginning of his career.

The oddly titled book *Psychopannychia* was Calvin's earliest theological work. The first draft was completed in 1534. On the advice of Wolfgang

---

[36]Bruce L. McCormack, "What's at Stake in Current Debates over Justification?," in *Justification: What's at Stake in the Current Debates*, ed. Mark Husbands and Daniel J. Treier (Downers Grove, IL: InterVarsity Press, 2004), 104-5.
[37]Calvin, *Epistle of Paul the Apostle to the Hebrews*, 330.
[38]PG 3:376a.
[39]John Calvin, *The Gospel According to St John 11–21 and The First Epistle of John*, trans. T. H. L. Parker (Grand Rapids, MI: Eerdmans, 1959), 247; Calvin, *Epistle of Paul the Apostle to the Hebrews*, 48; see also 47.

Capito and Martin Bucer, the young Reformer refrained from publishing it at that time. A revised edition was eventually released in 1542. *Psychopannychia* critiques the idea of soul sleep between death and the resurrection as well as the idea that the soul is not a substance distinct from the body. In an evocative passage, Calvin depicts a robust vision of deifying union with God as uncontested catholic teaching.

> For it is admitted by all, that perfection of blessedness or glory nowhere exists except in perfect union with God. Hither we all tend, hither we hasten, hither all the Scriptures and the divine promises send us.... That kingdom, to the possession of which we are called, and which is elsewhere denominated "salvation," and "reward," and "glory," is nothing else than that union with God by which they are fully in God, are filled by God, in their turn cleave to God, completely possess God—in short, are "one with God."[40]

Calvin again describes a deifying union with God as universal Christian teaching in his *Treatise Against the Anabaptists* (1544):

> There is no one who does not concur that the perfection of our beatitude consists in our being perfectly united with God. It is the goal toward which all the promises of God point us. For what was formerly said to Abraham is equally addressed to us: that God is our highest reward (Gen. 15:1). Hence the end of our beatitude, of our glory and salvation, is to belong wholly to God, to possess Him, and for Him to be wholly in us.[41]

Modern scholars commonly treat deification and justification as mutually exclusive visions of redemption. That, however, is to commit a simple category error. Justification is concerned with how sinners are reconciled to God and receive forgiveness in the present. Deification is "a kind of summary term that expresses all that God intends for us in Christ through the Spirit."[42] It is concerned with the divine life, glory, and holiness with which the forgiven sinner will be fully endowed in the resurrection. Calvin's teaching illustrates how justification and deification can relate to each other in a properly ordered soteriology.

---

[40] John Calvin, *Psychopannychia*, in *Calvin's Tracts Relating to the Reformation*, trans. Henry Beveridge (Edinburgh: Calvin Translation Society, 1851), 3:463-64.

[41] John Calvin, *Treatises Against the Anabaptists and Against the Libertines*, trans. Benjamin Wirt Farley (Grand Rapids, MI: Baker, 1982), 146-47.

[42] Daniel A. Keating, *Deification and Grace* (Naples, FL: Sapientia, 2007), 7.

"The union of our soul with God is the true and only life," Calvin says, but "outside Christ we are altogether dead, because sin, the cause of death, reigns in us." Sin and death make union with God impossible without help from outside ourselves. "The highest human good is to be united with God who is the fountain of life and of all good things. It is their own unworthiness that keeps everyone from approaching Him, and it is therefore the proper office of the Mediator to help us here, and to stretch out His hand to lead us to heaven." Justification grounded in the obedience and satisfaction of Christ makes union with God possible. "The union of God with us is true and real salvation; but no one can be united to God without righteousness, and there is found in us no righteousness; hence God himself freely imputes it to us; and as we are justified freely, so our salvation is said to be gratuitous."[43]

A few scholars allege that Calvin's Christology lacks the ontological ground needed for a soteriology of deification.[44] They observe that the patristic doctrine turns on the idea that Christ's humanity was gifted or deified by its union with divinity. The Sixth Ecumenical Council (i.e., Third Council of Constantinople) formalized this fundamental christological claim in AD 681: "Just as his most holy and immaculate flesh, animated by his soul, has not been destroyed by being divinized but remains in its own state and kind, so also his human will has not been destroyed by being divinized. It has rather been preserved."[45] Through union with Christ, human beings can become partakers of the divine nature and experience deification without merging into the essence of God or becoming deities. However, McCormack writes, "For the Reformed, the human nature of Christ could not undergo 'divinization' in the sense of participating in *any* of the divine attributes

---

[43]Calvin, *Epistles of Paul the Apostle to the Galatians*, 139; Calvin, *Epistle of Paul the Apostle to the Hebrews*, 101; John Calvin, *Commentaries on the Twelve Minor Prophets: Habakkuk, Zephaniah, Haggai*, trans. John Owen (Edinburgh: Calvin Translation Society, 1848), 83.

[44]Jonathan Slater, "Salvation as Participation in the Humanity of the Mediator in Calvin's *Institutes of the Christian Religion*: A Reply to Carl Mosser," *SJT* 58, no. 1 (2005): 39-58; Bruce L. McCormack, "Union with Christ in Calvin's Theology: Grounds for a Divinization Theory?," in *Tributes to John Calvin*, ed. David W. Hall (Phillipsburg, NJ: P&R, 2010), 504-29; Sung W. Park, "The Question of Deification in the Theology of John Calvin," *Verbum et Ecclesia* 38 (2017): 1-5; Andrew Snyder, "John Calvin and the Holy Spirit: Pneumatological Union with Christ," in *The Holy Spirit and the Reformation Legacy*, ed. Mark J. Cartledge and Mark A. Jumper (Eugene, OR: Pickwick, 2020), 129-44.

[45]Denzinger, *Compendium*, DS 556 (p. 194).

without ceasing to be human." McCormack refers to this as the "originating impulse in Reformed Christology."[46]

The allegation under consideration rests on a misunderstanding of Calvin's disagreement with the Lutheran notion that Christ's humanity was specifically made omnipresent or multi-locatable in the hypostatic union. Geneva's Reformer does not object to patristic teaching about the deification of Christ's humanity and nowhere says Christ's humanity would cease to be human if it participated in *any* divine attribute whatsoever. To the contrary, in the *Psychopannychia* he clearly states: "Jesus Christ is Son of God and man, that which he is by nature as God is he also by grace as man, that thus we may all receive of his fulness, and grace for grace."[47] The mature Calvin continued to ascribe numerous supernatural gifts enjoyed by Christ's humanity. These include divine immortality, incorruption, and glory as well as prerogatives the Son of God held prior to the incarnation by virtue of his divinity such as the power to remit sin, raise to life, judge the living and the dead, and bestow salvation (*Inst.* 2.14.3). He even goes so far as to say the very *majesty* of God resides in the humanity of Christ by virtue of his exaltation—a significant claim in the context of debate with Lutheran teaching (*Inst.* 2.17.6).

Calvin's complaint against the Lutherans is that they ascribe *all* the divine attributes to Christ's humanity in the absence of scriptural warrant, leading to metaphysical absurdities that, he insists, entail that the exalted Christ does not possess a genuine human nature. Calvin was quite clear about this in his final summary of the debate in 1563: "I reject only absurd things which appear to be either unworthy of Christ's heavenly majesty, or incompatible with the reality of his human nature" (*Inst.* 4.17.32).

Peter Martyr Vermigli is another influential second-generation Reformer who affirmed patristic teaching about deification. Vermigli and Calvin "were as closely joined in mind and judgment as were any other pair of theologians in sixteenth-century Europe" and inseparable on the fundamental issues related to the person and work of Christ.[48] Vermigli, though, tends to express

---

[46]Bruce L. McCormack, *The Humility of the Eternal Son: Reformed Kenoticism and the Repair of Chalcedon* (Cambridge: Cambridge University Press, 2021), 249-50.

[47]Calvin, *Psychopannychia*, 437.

[48]Marvin W. Anderson, "Peter Martyr, Reformed Theologian (1542–1562): His Letters to Heinrich Bullinger and John Calvin," *Sixteenth Century Journal* 4, no. 1 (1973): 63-64.

their shared convictions with greater theological precision and nuance. This reflects the fact that Vermigli was trained as a theologian whereas Calvin's training was in law.

In 1544, Vermigli published an exposition of the Apostles' Creed that affirms the doctrine of deification of Christ's humanity in terms of gifts with which it was endowed, just as Calvin does. Vermigli also identifies the deification of believers as the purpose of the incarnation:

> There is no need for me to discuss at length just how far the qualities and gifts of Christ's humanity exceeded the endowments granted Adam. Nor . . . those magnificent and glorious manifestations that revealed his divine majesty and angelic nature. Let me instead focus on what may be most useful for our consideration. Everyone reborn in Christ ought to contemplate the great love God has shown towards us. He did not loathe our nature, dirty and filthy because of sin, but instead purified it and clothed himself with it, so that we might share in his divine nature.[49]

The notion of Christ's deified humanity fully accords with the formal creedal commitments of the early Reformed churches. In 1549, Heinrich Bullinger published the first volume of the *Decades*, a work of dogmatics presented in the form of learned sermons. As Zwingli's successor in Zurich, Bullinger was widely regarded as the de facto leader of the Reformed churches. For this reason, the *Decades* was more influential in the sixteenth century than Calvin's *Institutes*. Bullinger prefaces the work with an essay on creeds and councils of the early church, in which he indicates that Reformed churches are committed to the teaching of the first six ecumenical councils. The fifth and sixth councils, he adds, determined nothing "but what is to be found in the first four councils."[50] While Bullinger objected to Lutheran teaching and heterodox claims about the deification of Christ's humanity, by implication he accepted the teaching of the Sixth Ecumenical Council quoted above.[51]

---

[49]Peter Martyr Vermigli, *Early Writings: Creed, Scripture, Church*, ed. Joseph C. McLelland (Kirksville, MO: Sixteenth Century Essays & Studies, 1994), 37; see also 38, 44, 75-76. Additional deification themes in Vermigli's exposition are discussed in Mosser, "Gospel's End and Our Highest Good," 91-93.

[50]Heinrich Bullinger, "Of the Four General Synods or Councils," in *The Decades of Henry Bullinger, 1-2*, ed. Thomas Harding (Cambridge: Cambridge University Press, 1849), 14.

[51]A cursory reading of Bullinger's Second Helvetic Confession might lead one to think otherwise: "For neither do we think or teach that the body of Christ ceased to be a true body after his glorification, or was deified, and deified in such a way that it laid aside its properties as regards body

In 1560, the ministers of Zurich were asked to address a controversy within the Reformed churches of Poland about Francesco Stancaro's claim that Christ is our mediator only according to his humanity. Having previously written to the Polish nobles about this a few years earlier, Vermigli was commissioned to write the response.[52] A year later he wrote a second letter in the name of Zurich's ministers to address further developments in the controversy.[53] "There can be no doubt," Donnelly surmises, "that he coordinated both letters with Heinrich Bullinger."[54] Vermigli's letters argue that Christ is mediator according to both natures and rebut Stancaro's insinuation that the common Reformed position somehow leads to heresy. Along the way, he reiterates Bullinger's affirmation of the first six ecumenical councils but with additional specificity relevant to our topic. He also indicates that Zurich's ministers examined the teaching of the councils by the standard of Scripture, something Calvin exhorted should be done (*Inst.* 4.9.8):[55]

> We swear that our churches embrace unanimously and with a firm consensus the three creeds, namely the Nicene, apostle's [sic], and Athanasian creeds, and on this one basis—that without doubt they agree very beautifully with the divine letters. We likewise accept the Councils of Nicaea, Constantinople, first Ephesus, and Chalcedon, as well as the fifth and sixth councils in what they decreed about the blessed Trinity, the incarnation of God's Son, and the redemption of the human race obtained through him, because we have found nothing is defined or established there which is not taught by the divinely inspired Scriptures.[56]

---

and soul, and changed entirely into a divine nature and began to be merely one substance" (article XI). However, if one attends to the specific positions rejected in this passage, it is evident that Bullinger has Lutheran teaching and heterodox notions in view, not the patristic doctrine.

[52]Vermigli's personal letter to the Polish nobles is letter 126 in Peter Martyr Vermigli, *Life, Letters, and Sermons*, ed. and trans. Joseph Patrick Donnelly (Kirksville, MO: Sixteenth Century Essays & Studies, 1999), 142-52.

[53]Vermigli's correspondence on behalf of the Zurich ministers consists of letters 247 and 267 in *Life, Letters, and Sermons*, 178-83, 198-220.

[54]Donnelly in Vermigli, *Life, Letters, and Sermons*, 198n272.

[55]Calvin goes on to similarly say, "We willingly embrace and reverence as holy the early councils, such as those of Nicaea, Constantinople, Ephesus I, Chalcedon, and the like, which were concerned with refuting errors—in so far as they relate to the teachings of the faith. For they contain nothing but the pure and genuine exposition of Scripture." This material was added to the *Institutes* in 1543. There is no reason to doubt that Calvin included the Sixth Ecumenical Council under the phrase "and the like."

[56]Vermigli, *Life, Letters, and Sermons*, 202.

A lengthy paragraph paraphrases and approvingly quotes from John of Damascus's elaboration on the teaching of the Sixth Ecumenical Council. The most relevant quotation says the theandric operation of the Son "was the act of God made man, that is, of God humanized. Even his human operation was divine, that is, was divinized and in no way cut off from the divine operation."[57] In the preceding paragraph, Vermigli says, "Since he is joined with us by nature, our nature is joined to the divine substance in him, and in this way we communicate in the divine nature."[58] Vermigli's letters were published together as an official christological statement of the Zurich church "so that everywhere all may see what we think about adoring the Trinity and about the saving mystery of the incarnation as against all strange doctrines."[59] The mother church of the Reformed tradition could not more clearly express its view that a properly Reformed Christology includes the deification of Christ's humanity. The driving impulse of early Reformed Christology was to uphold the ecumenical judgments of the early church.

In coordinated action with the Zurich church, Calvin also addressed the Stancaro controversy in two letters signed by the ministers of Geneva that were subsequently published as a statement of their christological position.[60] Like Vermigli, Calvin insists that Christ is mediator according to both natures. That is what allows "the life which was otherwise hidden in God" to flow from Christ into us. Christ judges the world, has life in himself, and overcomes death and the devil according to his human nature even though these powers "cannot be properly attributed to human nature." Divinity was required to do everything necessary to discharge Christ's priestly mediation,

---

[57] Vermigli, *Life, Letters, and Sermons*, 216. See also John of Damascus, *De Fide Orthodoxa* 3.19 (chap. 63 in the Greek division of the book).

[58] Vermigli, *Life, Letters, and Sermons*, 215.

[59] *Epistolae duae, ad ecclesias Polonicas, Jesu Christi Evangelium amplexas, scriptae a Tigurinae ecclesiae ministris, de negotio Stancariano, et mediatore dei et hominum Jesu Christo, an hic secundum humanam naturam duntaxat, an secundum utranque mediator sit* (Zurich: Froschauer, 1561). Donnelly translates the preface from which the quotation comes in Vermigli, *Life, Letters, and Sermons*, 198n271.

[60] John Calvin, *Responsum ad fratres Polonos, quomodo Christus sit Mediator, ad refutandum Stancari errorem* (Geneva: Conrad Badius, 1561). Joseph Tylenda translates the first letter in "Christ the Mediator: Calvin Versus Stancaro," *Calvin Theological Journal* 8, no. 1 (1973): 11-16, and the second letter in "The Controversy on Christ the Mediator: Calvin's Second Reply to Stancaro," *Calvin Theological Journal* 8, no. 2 (1973): 146-57.

proving that "Christ is the Son of God in respect to both natures."[61] In Calvin's idiolect, that is equivalent to saying Christ's humanity was divinized.[62] For what purpose? "It is the proper function of the mediator to unite us to God." "What is the goal of our adoption which we attain through him," Calvin asks, "if it is not, as Peter declares, finally to be partakers of the divine nature (2 Pet. 1:4)?" Furthermore, "The grace of adoption depends on this, that he transfers to us what he naturally possesses."[63]

Vermigli's *Dialogue on the Two Natures in Christ* was published the same year that the Zurich and Geneva churches published their refutations of Stancaro. The *Dialogue* was written in response to Lutheran theologian Johannes Brenz. Vermigli reiterates that the Reformed churches are committed to the christological and soteriological teachings of the three creeds and first six ecumenical councils.[64] He also directly addresses how one should and should not understand the deification of Christ's humanity. Brenz appealed to the patristic fired-iron analogy as it appears in Basil of Caesarea to support his distinctive Lutheran Christology. Vermigli turned the tables on Brenz by showing that the analogy actually supports the Reformed position.

"I don't deny what Basil has rightly said, namely that the divine nature distributes to the humanity of Christ its faculties," Vermigli says, but "not all of them but only those which do not go beyond its capacity. It does not give the humanity power to be immense or to be uncreated or to be everywhere." All the same, "beyond question it gives the human nature glory and happiness as well as the power of performing miracles and sanctifying and other similar powers. I am not unhappy with the comparison with iron since it is beautiful and fits elegantly the matter under discussion."[65]

Vermigli redirects the analogy against Brenz with the observation that fire does not communicate all of its qualities to the iron. For example, the iron

---

[61] Tylenda, "Christ the Mediator," 13-14.
[62] "I contend that he is called 'Son of God' by virtue of his deity and eternal essence. For it is just as appropriate to refer to the fact that he is called 'son of God' to his divine nature, as it is to refer to the fact that he called 'Son of man' to his human nature" (*Inst.* 2.14.6; see also 2.14.7-8).
[63] Tylenda, "Controversy on Christ the Mediator," 148-49; see also 153.
[64] Peter Martyr Vermigli, *Dialogue on the Two Natures in Christ*, ed. and trans. John Patrick Donnelly (Kirksville, MO: Thomas Jefferson University Press, 1995), 23.
[65] Vermigli, *Dialogue on the Two Natures*, 76.

does not become lightweight or ascend upward like a flame. Furthermore, the direction of communication is a one-way street. Iron does not communicate solidity, blackness, weight, or anything else to the fire. In like manner, Christ's divinity communicates attributes to his humanity but not all divine attributes. His human nature does not communicate any properties to the divine nature, much less passibility, as Brenz taught. "Just so the Lord's flesh also becomes a partaker in the Godhead without transferring its own weakness to the Godhead."[66] Vermigli's mature Christology was fully committed to the ontological ground needed for a soteriology of deification.

In 1554 or 1555, Theodore Beza sent Vermigli a letter from Lausanne that inquired about the Italian Reformer's understanding of our communion with Christ. Vermigli replied in March 1555. Vermigli also sent a letter to Calvin in which he elaborated on his position and solicited the Frenchman's judgment on the topic. Anyone familiar with patristic soteriology will recognize that what Vermigli describes is a full-bodied soteriological doctrine of deification along patristic lines, even though he does not use the word.

Vermigli's letter to Beza distinguishes three senses of union with Christ. At one pole is "the conjunction of nature." Every human being is joined to Christ in this sense just as they are to one another because Christ partook of our common human nature (see Heb 2:14). At the other pole is "the conjunction of similarity," in which believers "are restored in all respects and are made holy and just, and *are adorned with divine properties* and claim for ourselves the gift of immortality and of eternal glory from the gifts of God."[67] In this state, we will no longer be weak, sin-ridden, corrupt, or sick in our soul. Instead, "we are clothed in Christ's flesh, we are watered by his blood, we live and move in the soul of Christ." This does not happen because we will somehow discard our human nature but because Christ assumed our nature when he was born of the Virgin.[68] Vermigli presupposes the patristic teaching that human nature has been transformed in principle by the incarnation and is realized in individual human beings who are joined to Christ.

---

[66] Vermigli, *Dialogue on the Two Natures*, 77.
[67] Vermigli's letter to Beza is no. 114 in *Life, Letters, and Sermons*, 134-37 (here 135, emphasis added).
[68] Vermigli, *Life, Letters, and Sermons*, 136.

Between these poles lies a middle "conjunction of union" whereby in the present "we draw the Spirit, heavenly life, and all *the properties and powers of God* and of Christ." The sacraments strengthen and increase this conjunction, and "by faith we are lifted up from the level of nature so that we are joined to Christ even as members are joined to their head." From Christ "the immortal and heavenly head . . . various gifts, heavenly benefits, and *divine properties flow down to us*." This is not a physical union in which "the very substance of Christ's body and blood is really mixed in with the substances of the body and blood of each one of us." Rather, this is "a secret and mystical communion" whereby "we are joined with Christ's body and blood by a marvelous and intimate association, even though our substances remain unmixed in both parts." Beza's letter is lost; so we do not know what he said on the topic, but Vermigli concludes, "Between the two of us there is little or no difference in opinion."[69]

Vermigli's letter to Calvin observes that Christians disagree about "the communion we have with the Body of Christ and the substance of His nature."[70] He again states his view that there are three distinct senses of union with Christ. Using slightly different terminology, he refers to the two poles of union as our "natural" union with Christ and union "effected by the Spirit of Christ, by which we are from our very generation renewed into the fashion of His glory." In this latter union, we "have not only the remission of sins and reconciliation with God (wherein consists true and solid method of justification), but, further, receive the renovating influence of the Spirit whereby our bodies also, our flesh, and blood, and nature, are made capable of immortality, and become every day more conformable to Christ [*Christiformia*]." The fount and origin of this "celestial and spiritual likeness" is the middle or "secret communion whereby we are said to be grafted into Him." It is from the middle union that "the latter one is perfected as long as we live on earth."[71] Calvin's letter in reply describes his similar understanding of the second and third species of union with Christ and informs Vermigli, "We entirely agree in sentiment."[72]

---

[69] Vermigli, *Life, Letters, and Sermons*, 136-37, emphasis added.
[70] Most of Vermigli's letter and Calvin's reply are translated in George Corenelius Gorham, *Gleanings of a Few Scattered Ears* (London: Bell and Daldy, 1857), 340-52 (here 342).
[71] Vermigli in Gorham, *Gleanings*, 342-43.
[72] Calvin in Gorham, *Gleanings*, 352.

## Conclusion

Jaroslav Pelikan was correct: the Protestant Reformers did indeed speak about salvation in terms of deification. The concept is attested in the writings of the first-generation Reformers Huldrych Zwingli, Johannes Oecolampadius, and Martin Bucer as well as those of second-generation Reformers such as John Calvin and Peter Martyr Vermigli. According to patristic teaching, Christ possessed both a divine and human nature united in his person. The union of natures did not lead either one to lose its distinctive properties or merge into the other. It did, however, cause Christ's humanity to participate in certain divine attributes and prerogatives. This was the first step toward bringing about the deification of human beings who are drawn by the Holy Spirit into union with Christ. Modern scholars sometimes claim Reformed theology has no room for a soteriology of deification because the Reformers supposedly rejected the idea that Christ's humanity was deified. However, we have seen that this claim represents a serious misunderstanding of early Reformed Christology. Using different ways of expression, Calvin and Vermigli both affirmed the deification of Christ's humanity. More importantly, by the mid-sixteenth century the Reformed churches were officially committed to the teachings of the Sixth Ecumenical Council, where the idea is clearly taught. There is, therefore, no reason to doubt that by the middle of the sixteenth century, the leading theologians of the Reformed tradition were in full agreement with consensual patristic teaching about deification as both a christological and soteriological doctrine.

# JONATHAN EDWARDS, THEOSIS, and the PURPOSE of CREATION

## James Salladin

"Modernity is a deal," writes Yuval Noah Harari. "Humans agree to give up meaning in exchange for power." It is a striking statement; and in a strange (ironic?) twist, this exchange is connected to a godless form of divinization. Harari anticipates that humanity, as it gains power without meaning, will "upgrade *Homo Sapiens* into *Homo deus*."[1] The odd paring of meaninglessness and a sort of divinization goes back (at least) to Frederick Nietzsche. His parable of the Madman is famous for proclaiming the death of God. But what is less noticed is the Madman's prophecy of humanity's divinization. The Madman cries out in (ambiguous but) astonished wonder at the power of humanity to kill God. "We are all his murderers! But how have we done it? How were we able to drink up the sea? Who gave us the sponge to wipe away the whole horizon? What did we do when we loosened this earth from its sun?" But then the parable shifts from the murder of God to humanity's need to replace God, to *become* gods: "Shall we not ourselves have to become Gods, merely to seem worthy of it? There never was a greater event, and on account of it, all who are born after us belong to a higher history than any history hitherto!" Nietzsche's deicide yields a kind of divinization, and this shift breaks us into a new and "higher history."[2]

---

[1] Yuval Noah Harari, *Homo Deus: A Brief History of Tomorrow* (New York: HarperCollins, 2017), 200, 46.
[2] Friedrich Nietzsche, *Complete Works of Friedrich Nietzsche* (Hastings, UK: Delphi Classics, 2015), 1705.

But this higher history remains void of meaning. It is a history "without aim." If we are to become gods in this story, it is only by discovering that "this world is the Will to Power—and nothing else! And even ye yourselves are this will to power—and nothing besides!"[3]

It appears we can grasp for divinity—at least a parody of it—while suppressing a need for meaning. The question is, Will this path make us gods or monsters?

Meaninglessness, or at least a *sense* of meaninglessness, is a peculiarly modern experience. It is something of a side effect of what Charles Taylor calls the "buffered identity." Modernity gives us a sense that we can relate to this world more or less exclusively in the naturalistic, horizontal framework. On the one hand, this gives us a sense of invulnerability—at least we are not concerned about interference from the spiritual world. On the other hand, it can also mean we no longer know how to access any kind of significance beyond us. If we feel somewhat safer, we also feel less significant, and therefore (ironically) less existentially secure.[4] Yet this shift did more than make us feel less secure; it also alienated us from an older vision of theosis. Taylor points out that the early deists leveraged natural causality to edit God (largely) from view, but at the same time they overlooked the central role *communion with God* had previously held in making sense of the world. Classical Christianity disrupted ancient paganism by positing a personal God, and insisting on the corresponding idea that humanity was made *for communion* (κοινωνία) *with this God*.[5] This was the purpose that animated the Christian life with meaning.[6] But deism turned God from a Father to a clockmaker, editing communion out of our story, and so drained meaning from modern life. Meaning and theosis were always deeply related.

But deists were not the only voice; there was a minority report. Jonathan Edwards spent his life reflecting on, writing about, and wrestling with the question of teleology. What was God's purpose, his *end*, in creating the

---

[3]Nietzsche, *Complete Works of Friedrich Nietzsche*, 3745.
[4]Charles Taylor, *A Secular Age* (Cambridge, MA: Belknap, 2007), 303.
[5]Taylor, *Secular Age*, 278-80.
[6]Taylor writes, "God's intervention in history, and in particular the Incarnation, was intended to transform us, through making us partakers of the communion which God already is and lives. It was meant to effect our 'deification' (theiosis)" (*Secular Age*, 278).

world? Edwards's answer reclaims the idea that his deist contemporaries failed to see. God's purpose for the world is communion (κοινωνία) with himself. As Edwards writes:

> Christ who is a divine person, by taking on him our nature, descends from the infinite distance and height above us, and is brought nigh to us. . . . And, on the other hand, we, by being in Christ a divine person, do as it were ascend up to God. . . . Christ has brought it to pass, that those that the Father has given him, should be brought into the household of God; that he, and his Father, and his people, should be as it were one society, one family; that the church should be as it were admitted into the society of the blessed Trinity.[7]

Edwards believed that this was God's purpose in creating the universe. He often uses more technical language: God created the world in order to communicate his own divine fullness. I will argue that when this technical language is decoded it amounts this claim: theosis is God's purpose for the world.

Edwards's minority report helps the church remember its teleological birthright, and it also teaches us that a recovery of theosis doctrine is no theological novelty, nor even only a robust vision for individual soteriology. It is a word of hope to a world destitute of meaning.[8]

This chapter will survey key elements of his vision by addressing four questions:

1. How does Edwards discern creation's end?
2. To what extent is creation's end embedded in nature itself?
3. How is creation's end achieved through Christ and the Spirit?
4. How does creation's end elevate created nature?

## How Does Edwards Discern Creation's End?

The thing that made Edwards so different from the deists of his day is the same thing that drove him toward a vision of theosis. Deists and their successors began with the natural world, and if they wanted to know something of God, they extrapolated from the clock to the clockmaker. Of course, their interest was not typically in God per se but in the system of this natural

---
[7]WJE 19:593-94.
[8]Norman Russell argues that theosis is an attempt to answer the question, "Why were we born?" See Russell, "Why Does *Theosis* Fascinate Western Christians?," *Sobornost* 34, no. 1 (2012): 5, 15.

world. They were leaning from transcendence toward imminence; and that meant that any consideration of teleology would focus on imminent and natural ends, not supernatural ones. The deists did not start this move, nor did they complete it, but they did hasten it.[9]

Edwards was the opposite. It was not that he undervalued the natural world—he followed Enlightenment thought and he was a keen observer of nature.[10] But when he came to consider *creation's end*, he refused to begin with *creation itself*. Rather, he began with God—and that move made all the difference. I mentioned above that Charles Taylor identifies the Christian centering of a personal God as the defining break with ancient paganism. He goes on to argue that this centering of a personal God, and more specifically the centering of the Holy Trinity, launched early Christianity toward a vision of theosis.[11] Edwards, whether intentionally or coincidently, follows those well-worn tracks.

You can watch Edwards follow those tracks in his formidable dissertation *Concerning the End for Which God Created the World* (*The End of Creation* for short). Composed in fragments over the course of his life and only published after his death, the work takes aim at the question implied in the title: *What was God's ultimate end in creating the world?* It is an ambitious question, and Edwards addresses it from multiple angles.[12] But he strikes a theme early on that he maintains throughout: God must be his own highest aim in the creation of the world: "It is reasonable to suppose that [God] had respect to *himself as* his last and highest end in this work; because he is worthy in himself to be so, being infinitely the greatest and best of beings." No one should be surprised to find Edwards affirming that God's glory is God's highest aim. But very quickly Edwards argues that the glory God sought for himself is also something in which creation may participate. The end that

---

[9] Simon Oliver, commenting on radical orthodoxy and Henri De Lubac, points to the much older notion of pure nature as a key step on the way to secularity. See Oliver, "Henri De Lubac and Radical Orthodoxy," in *T&T Clark Companion to Henri de Lubac*, ed. Jordon Hillebert (New York: Bloomsbury, 2017), 399-400.
[10] See, e.g., Edwards's famous "Spider Letter," WJE 6:163-69.
[11] Taylor, *Secular Age*, 278-79.
[12] Edwards addresses this question from the vantage point of both reason (philosophical focus) and revelation (exegetical focus). My focus will be on the first, but it is key to note that Edwards justifies his philosophical account with exegesis. See the second chapter in WJE 8:466-536.

moved God to create must be "attainable by creation."[13] This is a pregnant little phrase. It suggests that God and creation are aimed at the same thing, that there is a teleological link between the two. Put differently, creation's ultimate end must be supernatural, beyond itself. This does not (yet) require a vision of theosis, but he is setting the table for it.

The question is: How might God's glory be attainable by creation? A key clue comes when Edwards argues God's glory should be seen and known by beings other than himself.[14] Not only should they be seen and known, but it is right that his glory be *delighted in*. Only other beings, in some ways like God himself, are capable of seeing and delighting in God's displayed perfections.[15] God's glory displayed is God's aim in creating; God's creatures seeing (knowing) and delighting in this glory is how creation may attain to this glory. God's end in creation and creation's end in God are coming together.

Edwards binds them more forcefully together by introducing a key category and by making a key assertion. The key category is the concept of fullness. Fullness is central to Edwards's thought, and it runs through his entire corpus (as it will run through this chapter). For the moment, it refers (at least) to the communicable perfections of God—Edwards sometimes uses the term *internal glory* as a near synonym. "There is an infinite fullness of all possible good in God, a fullness of every perfection, of all excellency and beauty, and of infinite happiness. And . . . this fullness is capable of communication or emanation *ad extra*." *Capable of communication*: that means it can be shared with the creature, and the creature can see it (know it) and delight in that vision. This is central to Edwards's idea of creation's end and humanity's participation in the divine life. But alongside this key category (fullness—with its near synonym *internal glory*), Edwards adds a key assertion about God: God has a disposition, an inclination, to communicate this divine fullness, and this disposition is "a perfection of his nature." Thus, it is not only that God is full of perfection but that part of his perfection is a disposition to share his perfections with beings capable of seeing (knowing) and delighting in them. This sets the stage for

---

[13]WJE 8:421.
[14]"Glorious attributes," WJE 8:429.
[15]WJE 8:431-32. See WJE 8:529: Humans must have understanding and will to receive and return the divine attributes. This is an aspect of the image of God.

Edwards to roll out his fundamental understanding of creation's end: "a disposition in God, as an original property of his nature, to an emanation of his own infinite fullness, was what excited him to create the world; and so that the emanation itself was aimed at by him as a last end of the creation."[16]

There is a lot going on here, so it is helpful to pause and consolidate. Edwards begins his exploration of teleology with the personal God of the Bible and Christian tradition. God seeks his own glory as his highest end in all things, including God's decision to create the world.[17] And inside God's glory, so to speak, as an aspect of that glory, God bears a disposition to communicate or emanate his glory to other beings, so that they can see it (know it) and delight in it. Edwards typically uses the notion of fullness when speaking about this communication of divine glory. Thus we can ask: What is God's end in creating the world? Answer: to communicate his divine fullness to creatures designed to receive it and return it.[18]

But what does it mean that creatures are *designed* to receive the divine fullness? And why would God's communicating his divine fullness to creatures be a way of God seeking his own glory?

In order to answer the first question, we have to grasp how God glorifies himself *internally* and then how this sets the stage for glorifying himself *outwardly*. Edwards states, "God is glorified *within himself* these two ways: (1) by appearing or being manifested to himself in his own perfect idea, or, in his Son, who is the brightness of his glory; (2) by enjoying and delighting in himself, by flowing forth in infinite love and delight towards himself, or, in his Holy Spirit."[19] Notice how central God's self-knowledge and self-delight is within this framework. Indeed, God's self-knowledge is the divine Son, and God's self-delight is the Holy Spirit. Edwards's trinitarianism integrates this idea of God's internal glory.

Watch now how Edwards matches this internal self-glorification to his communication to human beings: "So God glorifies himself towards the creatures also two ways: (1) by appearing to them, being manifested to their

---

[16] WJE 8:513, 515, 521, 527-32, 432-35.
[17] See WJE 8:527 for how God's glory maps to the communication of divine fullness.
[18] WJE 8:531.
[19] Emphasis added. See Miscellanies 448, WJE 13:495.

understandings; (2) in communicating himself to their hearts, and in their rejoicing and delighting in, and enjoying the manifestations which he makes of himself." Humanity is structured, designed, with understanding and will ("hearts" in the quote above). They constitute the divine image in humanity, and they equip humanity to receive the communications of God's internal glory, or his divine fullness.[20]

It also explains why Edwards thinks that God seeking his own glory (on the one hand) and God communicating the divine fullness to creatures (on the other) are two aspects of one reality. When God communicates his divine fullness to the creature, he loves it because it is his own glory in outward expression: "because he infinitely values his own glory, consisting in the knowledge of himself, love to himself, and complacence and joy in himself; he therefore valued the image, communication or participation of these, in the creature."[21] The union between God and the creature (who receives divine fullness) is so close that when God loves the graced creature, God is loving himself at the same time.

That is a bold idea, and Edwards defends it with another bold assertion: graced creatures (those who receive the divine fullness) will go on receiving this fullness and growing in nearer union with God to all eternity. As this union increases, so will the happiness of the graced creature: "As the happiness will be increasing to eternity, the union will become more and more strict and perfect; nearer and more like to that between God the Father and the Son; who are so united, that their interest is perfectly one."[22]

This perpetual growth in union with God means two key things. First, while the graced creatures and God will forever grow nearer in union, there will never be a moment when they are perfectly one. This protects the Creator-creature distinction. But the second thing to see emphasizes the astonishing vision of union Edwards held. According to Edwards, God sees this eternal progress toward union in one united vision. God looks at the whole infinite duration of increasing nearness as being equivalent to an infinite union with himself. As Edwards says, when eternal progress toward

---

[20]Miscellanies 448, WJE 13:495; 8:529.
[21]WJE 8:532.
[22]WJE 8:533-34.

union with God is in view, "the creature must be looked upon as united to God in an infinite strictness."[23]

It is a remarkable vision. Edwards began looking back into eternity past to discern God's motive in creating. Edwards ends by looking into eternity future and seeing eternal progression toward unity between the Creator and the creature. In between Edwards sees God communicating himself in the economy in a manner consistent with God's imminent self-glorification. And throughout it all Edwards maintains an unflinching focus on God. God is more key to understanding creation's end than creation itself is.

> The emanation or communication of the divine fullness . . . has relation indeed both to God and the creature: but it has relation to God as its fountain, as it is an emanation from God; and as the communication itself, or thing communicated, is something divine, something of God, something of his internal fullness; as the water in the stream is something of the fountain; and as the beams are of the sun. . . . In the creature's knowing, esteeming, loving, rejoicing in, and praising God, the glory of God is both exhibited and acknowledged; his fullness is received and returned. Here is both an *emanation* and *remanation*. The refulgence shines upon and into the creature, and is reflected back to the luminary. The beams of glory come from God, and are something of God, and are refunded back again to their original. So that the whole is *of God*, and *in* God, and *to* God; and God is the beginning, middle and end in this affair.[24]

Edwards does not use the term *theosis*. He does not need to. By centering the classical doctrine of God and affirming that God's own glory must be God's aim in creating, and then by affirming that creation is capable of receiving and returning this glory, he has set the stage for created participation in divine life. When he then argues that this is creation's end, he makes this participation the central story of created existence.[25]

---

[23]WJE 8:534.
[24]WJE 8:531.
[25]Andrew Louth argues that Eastern Orthodox theology sees theosis as the fulfillment not only of redemption but of creation as well. Edwards displays a Western approach to seeing theosis as the fulfillment of both redemption and creation. See Andrew Louth, "The Place of *Theosis* in Orthodox Theology," in *Partakers of the Divine Nature: The History and Development of Deification in the Christian Traditions*, ed. Michael J. Christensen and Jeffery A. Wittung (Grand Rapids, MI: Baker Academic, 2008), 34-35.

## To What Extent Is Creation's End Embedded in Nature Itself?

If creation's end is to receive and return the divine fullness, then we should ask: To what extent is this divine fullness already embedded in created nature itself? Is the communication of the divine fullness given *in the act* of creation, or is the communication subsequent to the act of creation? This is a question about the relation between nature and grace.[26] It is not a vain curiosity.

If the divine fullness is given, in some measure, in the act of creation, then it will have implications for how we discover the divine fullness, how we pursue our teleological fulfillment. If the divine fullness is embedded in created nature, then we may perhaps begin by *looking at nature* in order to discover the divine fullness. Such epistemic priority for nature would fit well with the early modern Enlightenment project. Alternatively, it might turn theosis from a real transformation into a process of discovering a divinity already nested within.[27]

The idea that divinity (in some measure or of some type) is already nested in nature has a robust pedigree. Platonists, in their many versions, did not always distinguish the created from the uncreated in the robust way monotheism demands. Divinity had to do with being and reality. The more real a thing was, the more divine it was.[28] Humanity bore something of the divine intrinsically, and the telos of life was to grow up into likeness to God by looking within and discovering the aspect of humanity (rational soul) capable of that journey.[29] Christianity's monotheism established a clear distinction between the Creator and the creature. Yet there was always a stream

---

[26] Edwards defines special grace as a communication or participation in the divine fullness. See Jonathan Edwards, "True Grace Is Divine (1738)," in *Jonathan Edwards: Spiritual Writings*, ed. Kyle C. Strobel, Adriaan C. Neele, and Kenneth P. Minkema, Classics of Western Spirituality (New York: Paulist Press, 2019), 350-62.

[27] Both Gavrilyuk and Martin Wisse caution (in different ways) about a stream of participatory metaphysics in which the divine is somehow, perhaps in small measure, already present in the natural. See Paul Gavrilyuk, "The Retrieval of Deification: How a Once-Despised Archaism Became an Ecumenical Desideratum," *ModTheo* 25, no. 4 (2009): 651; Maarten Wisse, *Trinitarian Theology Beyond Participation*, ed. Ian A. McFarland, John Webster, and Ivor Davidson, T&T Clark Studies in Systematic Theology (London: T&T Clark, 2011), 305.

[28] See Norman Russell, *The Doctrine of Deification in the Greek Patristic Tradition*, OECS (Oxford: Oxford University Press, 2006), 35.

[29] Russell, *Doctrine of Deification*, 39. "We are already gods in our true, higher selves. We do not need to *become* gods but simply to realize what we are" (41).

of Christian Platonism that retained some idea that the seed of theosis is embedded in nature. The Cambridge Platonists loomed large in Edwards's intellectual world, and they spoke of rationality as the "candle of the Lord." This was a kind of "deiform seed" implanted from creation that could be nurtured toward greater deiformity.[30] This deiform seed may be insufficient of itself (it needs grace), but the basic capability is in place.[31] Does Edwards fit into this line of thought?

At first glance we might imagine the answer is yes. If God created the world in order to emanate (or communicate) his divine fullness (as we have seen above), then perhaps we should expect that emanation to be part of the act of creating. *Emanation* is a strong word, and it is easy to read it in a Platonic frame. Additionally, Edwards maintains a very strong notion of natural dependence on God. He argues that all created substance is "nothing but the Deity acting in that particular manner . . . he thinks fit. So that, speaking most strictly, there is no proper substance but God himself." He also believed that God created the world in a continual stream of activity.[32] If all substance is God's activity, and God's activity of creation is continuous, and if God's end in the creating activity is to emanate the divine fullness, then why not conclude that this divine fullness is nested in nature?

However, despite all this, when we read the rest of Edwards's corpus, we find he specifically rejected the idea that the divine fullness is nested in nature per se. The divine fullness is the fulfillment of created nature but not its content.

In *The End of Creation* Edwards speaks of God creating the world in order to *communicate the divine fullness*. Elsewhere, Edwards uses this same terminology as a technical description for special grace: "Grace is a communication

---

[30]Charles Taliaferro and Alison J. Teply, "Introduction to Cambridge Platonism," in *Cambridge Platonist Spirituality*, ed. Charles Taliaferro and Alison J. Teply (New York: Paulist Press, 2004), 14-15.

[31]"Platonist anthropology, even as corrected by the Greek fathers, in order to deal with the dynamic aspect of Christianity, sees in man a being capable from the very beginning of reaching the highest degree of spiritual life, union with God, although unable to reach it by his own efforts." Charles Moeller and G. Philips, *The Theology of Grace and the Oecumenical Movement*, trans. A. Wilson (London: Mowbray, 1961), 39.

[32]WJE 6:215; Miscellanies 125.a, WJE 13:288. See also Miscellanies 18, WJE 13:210; Miscellanies 346, WJE 13:418; also Oliver D. Crisp, *Jonathan Edwards on God and Creation* (Oxford: Oxford University Press, 2012), 9.

or a participation of God's own fullness or of his good, a partaking of his riches, his own treasure, a partaking in some sort of his own bounty and happiness." This grace he is speaking about is what he calls true or *special* grace.[33] In his *Treatise on Grace*, Edwards takes great pains to distinguish special grace from common grace—they "differ, not only in degree, but in nature and in kind."[34] Edwards could speak of created nature *without* the divine fullness. When he does, he describes created nature as a vessel, a cup, designed to be filled with the divine fullness, but which has no fullness *in itself*.[35]

All this indicates that the divine fullness, which is the fulfillment of all creation, is not nested in created nature, but rather it is a properly supernatural gift from the outside. Edwards is emphatic: "Grace . . . in the creature is undoubtedly something divine and supernatural. . . . It is super-human. . . . It is something above all created nature. 'Tis natural to none but God. 'Tis something higher than the whole universe, yea higher than heaven itself. It is . . . something divine, something of God who is infinitely above both heaven and earth."[36]

But what of Edwards's idea of natural dependence on God? Did he not hold a strong view of the natural world's participation in God for being? How does his vision of natural participation relate to his view of special grace and divine fullness? I argue elsewhere that Edwards employed two complementary approaches to participation.[37] This is not new in the tradition. Origen and Athanasius, among others, spoke of an aspect of participation that undergirds the natural world, and another that undergirds the dynamic of saving grace.[38] Edwards follows this broad approach. He views all things as depending on God for their being. This is a strong view of

---

[33]Edwards, "True Grace Is Divine (1738)," 353-54.
[34]See the title of chap. 1: WJE 8:153.
[35]See "Notes on Scripture" 448, WJE 15:530.
[36]Edwards, "True Grace Is Divine (1738)," 359.
[37]James Salladin, "Nature and Grace: Two Participations in the Thought of Jonathan Edwards," *International Journal of Systematic Theology* 18, no. 3 (2016): 290-303. See also Salladin, *Jonathan Edwards and Deification: Reconciling Theosis and the Reformed Tradition* (Downers Grove, IL: IVP Academic, 2022), 65-95.
[38]See Russell, *Doctrine of Deification*. For Origen's twofold participation, see 148-49; for Athanasius's, see 186-87; for Cyril of Alexandria's, see 191. For an example from the English tradition, see Richard Hooker, *The Lawes of Ecclesiastical Polity*, ed. John Keble (Oxford: Clarendon, 1888), 2:247-49.

participatory metaphysics that I call "common participation." But this common participation is not load-bearing for his view of special grace. Common participation is a gift of being, of substance, but not of the divine fullness. Divine fullness comes with another gift, the gift of what I call "special participation." This is the emanation Edwards describes in *The End of Creation*.[39] It is not a gift of being or substance but rather a gift of supernatural, uncreated, divine love or fullness.[40]

What role does such a sharp distinction between created nature and divine grace play within Edwards's theology? At least two answers stand out: it preserves a bold vision of sinful depravity and at the same time a bold vision of transforming gratuity.

Sinful depravity, for Edwards, is the inevitable consequence of created nature on its own, without divine grace filling it. He lived in an age that was vigorously rejecting the traditional Reformed vision of depravity. Among the many objections was this: to affirm sinful depravity implied that God was the author of evil in the sense that he *implanted* evil dispositions within the human heart.[41] But Edwards rejected the underlying premise. God did not implant any such evil within the human heart. Evil is not the fruit of a positive principle infused within humanity at all. What then explains evil? Edwards answers by distinguishing nature from grace, though he uses different terms. He distinguishes *mere human nature* from *the divine nature*; *natural principles* from *supernatural principles*. In the beginning God created humanity to experience a union between their human nature and the divine nature. The fall meant that the divine nature was withdrawn, leaving mere human nature on its own. In that moment, as "light ceases in a room . . . when the candle is withdrawn . . . thus man was left in a state of darkness."[42]

---

[39]While *emanation* can be used in a Platonic manner, it was also used by Reformed tradition to describe special grace. See John Owen, *Communion with God: Of Communion with God the Father, Son, and Holy Ghost, Each Person Distinctly, in Love, Grace, and Consolation; or, The Saints' Fellowship with the Father, Son, and Holy Ghost Unfolded* (Oxford: Benediction Classics, 2017), 1.2, p. 10.

[40]"That principle in the soul of the saints, which is the grand Christian virtue, and which is the soul and essence and summary comprehension of all grace, is a principle of divine love" (WJE 21:166).

[41]WJE 3:380.

[42]WJE 3:382.

Why did mere human nature, left by itself, result in this darkness? "The inferior principles of self-love and natural appetite, which were given only to serve, being alone, and left to themselves, of course became reigning principles; having no superior principles to regulate or control them, they became absolute masters of the heart."[43] Before the fall, the divine nature (or grace or the divine fullness) kept the self-orientation of human nature in proper boundaries. But without the divine nature, humanity turns inward, and depravity follows. Does this imply that human nature, or created nature generally, is somehow intrinsically evil? No. It rather highlights that created nature, specifically human nature, is intrinsically designed for fulfillment in union with the divine nature. As a cup is meant to be filled and will never achieve its end without that filling, so human nature is meant to be filled with the divine.[44]

But the distinction between nature and grace also amplifies a vision of transforming gratuity. Norman Russell points out that so long as Platonism saw a continuity in essence between the divine and human, no technical deification was possible. Only when the divine and human are essentially distinct can a deifying transformation be possible.[45] All classical Christian views of deification posit a difference in essence between the uncreated and the created. Yet even within this framework, when nature already has something of deifying grace embedded within it, it calls into question whether the telos is really theosis, the transformation "from one degree of glory to another" (2 Cor 3:18), or whether it reduces to self-realization.[46] One might ask: Does the spirituality look within to find something of the divine, or does the spirituality look beyond its own nature for its transformation? Edwards warns against the former and insists on the latter. He directs our gaze away from ourselves and outward to find a gratuitous God. He does not aim to evacuate grace from nature but to make space for a true transforming encounter with the uncreated Other.

---

[43] WJE 3:382.
[44] Edwards compares created nature without divine filling as an empty cup or vessel, a capacity in need of filling (see WJE 15:530).
[45] Russell, *Doctrine of Deification*, 43.
[46] Russell views radical orthodoxy's approach to theosis as more Neoplatonic than Greek or patristic ("Why Does *Theosis* Fascinate Western Christians?," 9-10).

## How Is Creation's End Achieved Through Christ and the Spirit?

So what is the nature of this encounter with the uncreated Other? We have seen that created nature does not bear the divine fullness within itself. At the same time, humanity is designed to receive it. But theosis requires us to consider the other side of the dynamic. That is, we must consider not only how created nature may partake in God but, crucially, how God can become his own gift to creation. We saw earlier that God's self-knowledge and God's self-delight flow outward to the humans' understanding and will. But this leaves a great deal unsaid. What of the incarnation? What of the gift of the Spirit? Classical Christianity argued that it was through the economic missions of the Son and the Spirit that God may be his own gift to creation.[47] Edwards followed the same line to argue that the divine fullness is christologically mediated and pneumatological in content.

In the middle of Edwards's *The End of Creation* he makes a christological claim that remains intriguingly underdeveloped. Edwards reasons that whatever end Jesus sought in his mission must be decisive for understanding God's last end in creation. Yet there Edwards leaves the question open—what is Christ's aim?[48] We might add: Does Christ's aim have anything to do with the divine fullness? Insight comes in Edwards's private reflections in his Miscellanies notebooks. In Miscellanies 487 Edwards takes up the question of Christology, and there we find he follows an exegetical through line that unites the divine fullness, Christology, and grace in the saints.[49]

The through line begins with the apostle Paul's fullness theology in Colossians: God's *fullness* dwelt in Christ bodily (Col 2:9).[50] Edwards takes this observation and concludes that Christ bears this divine fullness to an immeasurable extent.[51] However, he adds that Christ does not bear this divine

---

[47]Khaled Anatolios helpfully surveys the soteriological import of the early church's christological controversies. See Anatolios, *Deification Through the Cross: An Eastern Christian Theology of Salvation* (Grand Rapids, MI: Eerdmans, 2020), 167-226.

[48]Paul Ramsey remarks that Edwards's thought seems inexplicably undeveloped (WJE 8:474n1).

[49]Miscellanies 487, WJE 13:528-29.

[50]This does not refer to Christ's sharing the divine essence. See Edwards's explicit distinction between the divine essence and the divine fullness in WJE 2:203.

[51]This is based on the KJV's translation of Jn 3:34: "For God giveth not the Spirit by measure unto him" (Miscellanies 487, WJE 13:528-29).

fullness only for himself.[52] He notes John 1:16, "And from his fullness we have all received, grace upon grace," and argues that Christ's immeasurable quantity of divine fullness is the source from which grace pours out to believers.[53] Finally, the through line returns to Paul in Ephesians 3:19, where he prays "that you may be filled with all the fullness of God." The fullness Paul prays for—Edwards concludes—is the same fullness that Christ bears without measure. Finally, this gift of divine fullness, which flows from Christ to the saints, explains the inner content of the claim of 2 Peter 1:4 that the saints are "partakers of the divine nature."[54] The divine fullness, which is the fulfillment of creation's end and the center of theosis, is through Christ alone. The aim of Christ's incarnate mission is the same as God's aim in creating the world: to communicate the divine fullness. Yet the question remains: What is the content of this christological fullness?

Edwards felt his tradition undervalued the Holy Spirit. It was traditional to say something like: the Father planned redemption, the Son is the price of redemption, and the Spirit *applies* salvation. But Edwards thought that line of thinking presented the Spirit with less glory than the Father and the Son, and he wanted to redress that inequality. His solution was to say that, yes, the Father plans salvation, and, yes, the Son is the price of salvation, but the Holy Spirit is the *good purchased* in the exchange.[55] The Father gave the Son in order to give the Holy Spirit.

How does this relate to the divine fullness? The Holy Spirit, the good purchased in salvation, *is* the divine fullness.[56] "The Holy Spirit is the sum

---

[52] See the argument in "Sermon 180. John 1:16," In *Sermon Series II, 1729–1731*, WJE Online vol. 45.
[53] Some of Edwards's Reformed predecessors viewed the divine fullness in Colossians as *incommunicable*. See Francis Turretin, *Institutes of Elenctic Theology*, ed. James T. Dennison Jr., trans. George Musgrave Giger (Phillipsburg, NJ: P&R, 1994), 2:231; John Owen, *The Works of John Owen*, ed. William H. Goold (Edinburgh: Banner of Truth Trust, 1976), 2:231.
[54] Some may be concerned that Edwards's view suggests a Nestorianism, where the difference between Christ and the saints is merely the extent of grace rather than the kind of union with the divine. Edwards avoids this by embracing the grammar of classical Chalcedonian Christology. For more, see Salladin, *Jonathan Edwards and Deification*, 198-214.
[55] WJE 21:190-91.
[56] In *The End of Creation* Edwards states the divine fullness is the communication of both God's understanding (his self-knowledge) and God's will (his happiness or self-delight). In *Treatise on Grace*, he argues the divine fullness is the Holy Spirit. These are not contradictory. God's self-knowledge is the divine Son. God's self-delight is the Holy Spirit. In grace, the communication of the Holy Spirit is always mediated christologically, which implies some knowledge of Christ. This knowledge of Christ is the communication to the understanding. The delight in Christ is

of all good. 'Tis the fullness of God. The holiness and happiness of the Godhead consists in it; and in the communion or partaking of it consists all the true loveliness and happiness of the creature."[57]

This is a crucial moment in Edwards's theology. God is the center of Edwards's soteriology. That is true not only because God is the *agent* of salvation but because God is the *gift* of salvation. Not only is God the gift of *salvation*, but God is the gift that fulfils *creation's* purpose.

But Edwards moves further. The Holy Spirit, God's own fullness, operates within the saint in a manner that replicates the Spirit's operation within the imminent Trinity.

Edwards followed Augustine's exegesis to conclude that the Holy Spirit is the love between the Father and the Son.[58] The Spirit acts as the Father's love to the Son and the Son's love to the Father. This shared love is a κοινωνία, a communion, between the Father and the Son wherein they enjoy "intimacy and differentiation."[59]

In the gift of grace, the Spirit replicates an answerable activity between Christ and the saint. Christ loves the saint(s) by the Spirit, and the saint(s) loves Christ back by the Spirit.[60] The result is a shared κοινωνία in the Spirit where Christ and the saint(s) enjoy intimacy and differentiation. Notice the closeness between the dynamic of the Spirit *ad intra* and the dynamic of the Spirit between Christ and the saint(s): "[There is] an image of the eternal Trinity; wherein Christ is the everlasting father, and believers are his seed, and the Holy Spirit, or Comforter, is the third person in Christ, being his delight and love flowing out towards the church. In believers the Spirit and delight of God, being communicated unto them, flows out toward the Lord Jesus Christ."[61] This is the concrete and personal expression of what remained

---

the communication to the will. Edwards can abbreviate and call the Spirit the divine fullness because the gift of the Spirit presupposes communication to the understanding. See WJE 8:528; 21:188; see also Salladin, *Jonathan Edwards and Deification*, 37-41.

[57] WJE 21:188.

[58] WJE 21:121. Compare to Augustine's argument in *The Trinity* 15.5.31.

[59] I take the phrase "intimacy and differentiation" from Julie Canlis's helpful analysis in *Calvin's Ladder: A Spiritual Theology of Ascent and Ascension* (Grand Rapids, MI: Eerdmans, 2010), 13.

[60] I say *answerable* because it is not identical (it is economic and not imminent), but it is real (it is a finite repetition of the Spirit's work *ad intra*).

[61] Miscellanies 104, WJE 13:273-74.

abstract in *The End of Creation*. There Edwards stated that God's end in creating was to display his internal glory, his divine fullness, to the understandings and wills of created beings. Now we can see that God fulfills that aim through the mediation of Christ and the gift of the Spirit. God communicates his Spirit to the saint, establishing a bond with Christ. This bond facilitates the communication of God's self-knowledge to the understanding, because Christ is God's self-knowledge.[62] But it is not only a communication to the understanding but also to the will, because the Spirit is God's self-delight.[63] The Spirit acting in the will is the saint's delight in God. Thus God's self-glorification flows toward the creation through the missions of the Son and the Spirit. "So that the whole is *of God*, and *in* God, and *to* God; and God is the beginning, middle and end in this affair."[64]

## How Does Creation's End Elevate Created Nature?

But in all Edwards's God-centeredness, does *creation* fall out of view? I argued earlier that Edwards sharply distinguishes created nature from divine fullness so that he can explain depravity and make space for a transforming encounter with the divine Other. How does this encounter effect a real change, a real transformation, in created nature?[65] Further, the communication of divine fullness is God's aim in creating all things, but the divine fullness itself is communicated only to the saints.[66] What about the rest of creation? How is all creation fulfilled through a gift that is so narrow in scope?

It turns out Edwards is bold in asserting the real transformation in the saints. In his *The Religious Affections*, he writes, "The soul of a saint receives light from the Sun of Righteousness, in such a manner, that its nature is changed, and it becomes properly a luminous thing: not only does the sun shine in the saints, but they also become little suns, partaking of the nature of the fountain of their light." *Not only does the sun shine . . . but they become little suns.* The created nature (in the saints) is not merely passive, but there

---

[62] WJE 21:116-17.
[63] WJE 21:121.
[64] WJE 8:531.
[65] See Davison's helpful caution that real theosis, while relational, is also ontological. Andrew Davison, *Participation in God: A Study in Christian Doctrine and Metaphysics* (Cambridge: Cambridge University Press, 2019), 297.
[66] Miscellanies 332, WJE 13:410.

is also an active return toward God. As we saw above, grace is an *emanation*, but there is also what Edwards calls a remanation.[67] It is in this remanation that the saints shine forth.

The model and the source for this shining forth is the humanity of the incarnate Christ. The divine Son's glory "shines in the human excellencies of Christ." Notice that it is the humanity of Jesus that displays the glory of divinity. Edwards believed that all created nature was designed to display the glory of God's Son. "The beauties of nature are really emanations, or shadows, of the excellencies of the Son of God." Yet while all nature reflects the Son, the human soul is uniquely fitted for this display. This happens in the incarnation when the humanity of Jesus displays the divine Son's excellencies perfectly. Christ is the model for how humanity may display God, and Christ is also the source. When God communicates the divine fullness and joins saints to Christ, then Christ's excellencies shine through the saints' humanity, though in an imperfect manner. "We see far the most proper image of the beauty of Christ, when we see beauty in the human soul."[68] This beauty, the beauty of Christ stamped on the saints by virtue of their union with him, is the light that shines, the reality that makes the saint's soul "a luminous thing." Thus in the incarnation the divine Son reaches down to humanity in order to elevate humanity to share in the divine.

As we saw before, Edwards states:

> Christ who is a divine person, by taking on him our nature, descends from the infinite distance and height above us, and is brought nigh to us.... And, on the other hand, we, by being in Christ a divine person, do as it were ascend up to God.... Christ has brought it to pass, that those that the Father has given him, should be brought into the household of God; that he, and his Father, and his people, should be as it were one society, one family; that the church should be as it were admitted into the society of the blessed Trinity.[69]

---

[67]WJE 2:343; 8:531.
[68]WJE 19:590; Miscellanies 108, WJE 13:279; Miscellanies 487, WJE 13:528; Miscellanies 108, WJE 13:280. The context makes clear that the beauty of the human soul Edwards refers to is the beauty derived from grace. Edwards points to the fall as the reason why so little of the graces of Christ's excellencies remain in the human soul, and to the future state when they will be restored. Thus it is the beauty of saving grace (special participation) that most fully displays the excellencies of Christ.
[69]WJE 19:593-94.

Is it possible for created nature to bear a greater elevation? Edwards muses that holiness is "almost too high a beauty for any creatures to be adorned with; it makes the soul a little, sweet and delightful image of the blessed Jehovah."[70] That reflection came early in his life, and he spent the rest of his life trying to work out precisely in what way the saint becomes like God.[71] In the end, the elevation of created nature is so high, so profound, that the saint partakes of the trinitarian life itself.

But what of the rest of creation? How is the rest of the natural world gathered up in God's grand purpose to communicate the divine fullness?

The answer to that question requires us to change the camera angle and imaginatively enter the psychology of the saints. Keep in mind that God's attributes, his glory, his beauty, his excellencies, must be seen and delighted in by the saints in order for creation to achieve its purpose. When God communicates the divine fullness to the saints, the saints begin to see God's excellencies, but not only through a direct contemplation of God. They also see God indirectly, through God's works in creation and providence. They see the natural world displaying God; they see the history of God's work in providence and redemption displaying God; they see God's glory shining through the entirety of God's world. For the one who partakes of grace, Edwards argues:

> There is a world of new objects that is discovered, a spiritual world, a great variety of beautiful and glorious objects that were till now altogether hidden. And there is a light that shines from outward objects that before did not; the visible world has a light shining in it that before was not seen. There is a light shines from God's works of creation and providence. The face of the earth, the fields and trees, they have a spiritual light shining from them that discovers the glory of the Creator. And the sun, moon, and stars shine with a new kind of light, even spiritual light. The sun shone bright with outward light before, but it shines brighter now with discoveries of the glory of its Creator. Though this spiritual light indeed is but dim here, and often interrupted, a true saint can see this light from the Word of God or the works of God at all times.[72]

---

[70]Miscellanies a, WJE 13:163.
[71]That reflection is the first of his Miscellanies entries, which he would write throughout his life (WJE 13:163).
[72]WJE 17:323.

This means that the whole of created nature is bound up in God's purpose to communicate the divine fullness. While the communication itself is strictly to the saints, the rest of creation is required to make God's beauty visible. The saints will look at the natural created world and see something of Christ, and they will also look at history, the narrative of God's work of redemption, and see him as well. The saints will never tire of delighting in Christ displayed in this story. "There is wonderfulness and glory enough in it to keep the souls of saints and angels forever in admiration and rapture."[73]

This experience of seeing God all through creation was central to Edwards's own spirituality. "God's excellency . . . seemed to appear in everything; in the sun, moon and stars; in the clouds, and blue sky; in the grass, flowers, trees; in the water, and all nature; which used greatly to fix my mind." He kept a notebook for recording "Images of Divine Things" and meditated on how nearly anything could point to Jesus. Indeed, the "silkworm is a remarkable type of Christ" for Edwards.[74]

And so all creation is gathered up into God's great telos, his great purpose in creating. God created in order to communicate his divine fullness. This required creating beings capable of knowing him and delighting in him, and it demanded that the Son become human in order to elevate the saints to share in his excellencies. Those elevated by this grace *know* and *delight* in the divine glory by contemplating God reflected in the whole of the created universe. Nothing is left out.[75]

## Conclusion

What gift might a recovery of theosis theology bear for the present world? We are awash with power; we are gasping for meaning. This is not trivial. Great power in a world "without aim," is erratic, explosive, destructive and dangerous.[76] Some will argue this is an unavoidable reality. Many conclude that Nietzsche is right: God is dead, and his murder leaves a gaping power

---

[73]WJE 17:324.
[74]WJE 16:794; 11:100. See Edwards's notebook titled "Image of Divine Things," WJE 11:50-130.
[75]How would hell factor into this vision? See Miscellanies 279, WJE 13:379; also Miscellanies 288, WJE 13:381. For a sermon on how the damned fulfill their purpose in creation, see WJE 46, sermon 210 on Prov 16:4. For the saints' joy in God's glory through viewing inanimate creation, see WJE 17:323.
[76]Nietzsche, *Complete Works of Friedrich Nietzsche*, 3744-45.

vacuum. Perhaps we can all agree that there is something deep within humanity that drives us, compels us, to fill this void, this vacuum, this emptiness. Is this drive (only) the will-to-power? Maybe all our attempts to upgrade from *Homo sapiens* to *Homo deus*, all our attempts to defy nature and transcend our humanity, all our politicking is really just a mass power grab and "nothing besides."[77] Is this our divinization? Is this our higher history? If it is, "Do we not stray, as through infinite nothingness? Does not empty space breathe upon us? Has it not become colder? Does not night come on continually, darker and darker?"[78]

Or might there be another vision? Jonathan Edwards spent his life asking the question: For what end was the world made? He offered a countertestimony in the middle of an age eager if not to murder at least to decenter God. His vision presses a question for us. What if Nietzsche was right (in a way)? What if it is true that we must become divine, but not for the reason he thought? What if we must become divine, not because there is an absence of God in this world but because there is a designed emptiness of God within us? Yes (an Edwardsean might say), this emptiness, left unfilled, will center the self and act as a will-to-power. But what if there is *something else besides*? What if it is a clue to our ultimate end? What if we discovered not only that the serpent lied when he offered divinization through autonomy but also that God had planned a better theosis for the saints from the very beginning (Rom 8:29)? What if we discovered that the same doctrine of God, Father, Son, and Holy Spirit, that led Christianity out of paganism remains the unexpected but perfect fulfillment of our world's deepest purpose? What if the fullness we seek is found in the Christ we have forsaken? For "from his fullness we have all received, grace upon grace" (Jn 1:16). Receiving this fullness, we may find ourselves looking out on a world, previously colder and darker, but now "a light shines from God's works . . . the earth, the fields and trees . . . the sun, moon, and stars shine with a new kind of light, even a spiritual light."[79]

---

[77]Nietzsche, *Complete Works of Friedrich Nietzsche*, 3745; Harari, *Homo Deus*, 46.
[78]Nietzsche, *Complete Works of Friedrich Nietzsche*, 1705.
[79]WJE 17:323.

# JOHN *and* CHARLES WESLEY *on* DEIFICATION

## Mark Gorman

WHEN EIGHTEENTH-CENTURY ANGLICAN CLERGYMEN brothers John and Charles Wesley set out to "reform the nation, and especially the Church," their stated goal was neither to improve shortcomings in the doctrines of the Church of England nor to revise the church's liturgy. Both Wesleys warmly embraced the church's fundamental teachings, and both were fervent in the daily and weekly worship practices of the Book of Common Prayer. Their focus instead was "to spread scriptural holiness over the land."[1] The Wesleys' diagnosis of the church in their day was that while many people who subscribed to its doctrines and attended to its liturgy, there were far fewer who were genuinely Christian by bearing the marks of "holiness of heart and life." Thus, in their late thirties and early forties, Charles and John joined forces with like-minded friends and colleagues and began the work that became the early Methodist movement.

Though dramatic moments such as the night John's heart was "strangely warmed" in a May 1738 Aldersgate Street meeting provided some of the inspiration for the Wesleys' Methodist reform movement (Charles had a similar experience around the same time), the foundation for their work had been laid from the earliest days of their youth. Susanna Wesley, their mother, raised and educated them at home, giving them ample instruction in the

---

[1] John Wesley, "The 'Large' Minutes," §4, *WJW* 10:845, reports that the Methodists understood that their purpose was "to reform the nation, and in particular the Church, to spread scriptural holiness over the land."

Christian faith and holding them to a high standard of personal devotion. They both attended Oxford University, where their studies included readings from the ancient church and where their personal lives eventually centered on strict living, Bible study, and sharing in the Lord's Supper. Their turbulent travels in the North American colonies frustrated their hopes of sharing the gospel with Native Americans but also introduced them to the Moravians, a Pietist branch of Lutheranism.

All of these proved influential on John and Charles, and on early Methodism, as they sought to teach and form practitioners of scriptural holiness. For indeed, even if John and Charles did not set out to revise the Church of England's liturgy or doctrines, there was a need to lead people into a good understanding of this "scriptural holiness" and to form them in the ways of "holiness of heart and life."[2] Methodism under the Wesleys had, if not new or different doctrines, distinctive doctrinal emphases, such as the universal availability of grace and salvation, and the possibility for all believers of what they called Christian perfection. Early Methodism also had distinctive practices, such as field preaching and a system of small groups called bands and classes, in addition to its emphasis on the means of grace, which included activities such as prayer, searching the Scriptures, and receiving Holy Communion.

In this chapter I examine the place deification had as the Wesleys taught and formed their contemporaries in scriptural holiness. *Deification* was not a term used by either John or Charles, nor did they employ similar terms such as *divinization* or *theosis*.[3] Nevertheless, what the Wesleys believed and taught about scriptural holiness, from their understanding of creation to their expectation of entire sanctification, evinces a participatory and transformational notion of the work of God. In his dissertation on this very topic, Bobby Rackley identifies "three theological axes which must be firmly established" in order to associate a theologian or theological perspective with deification: "1) an **understanding of God** as desiring true union with

---

[2]While noting different emphases of Charles and John Wesley, John R. Tyson insists, "The Wesleys were united in their concern for 'vital piety' and 'scriptural holiness.'" Tyson, *Charles Wesley on Sanctification: A Biographical and Theological Study* (Grand Rapids, MI: Francis Asbury, 1986), 308.
[3]I will use the terms *deification* and *divinization* interchangeably in this chapter but, unless citing the work of another author, will treat *theosis* as a technical term belonging to the theological tradition of Eastern Orthodoxy.

humanity; 2) a **theological anthropology** which sees the telos of humanity as true Godlikeness; and 3) a **soteriological thrust** that points to redeemed humanity as participating in the Godhead."[4] Rackley affirms that all three are present in the Wesleys' writings. In so doing, Rackley follows a long line of Methodist scholarship that spans decades. I begin by tracing this trajectory and then turn to the Wesleys' own thought, placing their approach to deification within the context of what they taught as Christian perfection while emphasizing its scriptural basis and its theocentric perspective.

## SCRIPTURAL HOLINESS AND WESLEYAN DEIFICATION

Early interest in examining the place of deification in the Wesleys' work was sparked by a timely renewal of Wesley studies and scholarship during a period of flourishing international ecumenism in the mid-twentieth century. It was perhaps natural, if not inevitable, that Methodist scholars engaged in positive dialogue with Eastern Orthodox theologians would reread their own tradition in light of that dialogue. That appears to have been the case with Albert Outler, a church historian and ecumenist who became a towering figure in Wesley studies. In the late 1960s Outler argued that the Wesleys' theology could best be understood in the company of Eastern Orthodox theologians. Outler's influence was such that his contention sparked decades of essays, dissertations, and monographs comparing John or Charles to figures such as Irenaeus of Lyons, Ephrem the Syrian, or Symeon the New Theologian—and not just by Methodist or Wesleyan scholars but also by Orthodox scholars and even publications from Orthodox printing houses.[5]

There have been some objections to this trajectory in Wesley studies. Some scholars have argued that reading the Wesleys as Orthodox, or Orthodox in all but name, ignores their historical context and necessarily downplays Protestant or Western/Latin themes that are also prominent in the writings of both John

---

[4]Bobby Lynn Rackley, "Recovery of the Divine Nature: Wesleyan Soteriology and *Theosis* Calmly Considered" (ThD diss., Duke University Divinity School, 2020), 5, emphasis original.

[5]See the fruitful conversations across the following volumes: S. T. Kimbrough Jr., ed., *Orthodox and Wesleyan Spirituality* (Crestwood, NY: St. Vladimir's Seminary Press, 2002); Kimbrough, ed., *Orthodox and Wesleyan Scriptural Understanding and Practice* (Crestwood, NY: St. Vladimir's Seminary Press, 2006); Kimbrough, *Orthodox and Wesleyan Ecclesiology* (Crestwood, NY: St. Vladimir's Seminary Press, 2007).

and Charles.[6] Others have objected to the East/West schematization as a legacy of historical studies that fail to do justice to the complexities of Christian thought across geographical bounds.[7] The most damaging objections, however, have come from historians Ted Campbell and Richard Heitzenrater. Campbell shows that John Wesley may have had only a cursory familiarity with many Eastern Orthodox texts and that he often excised sections of those texts that could be considered most typically Orthodox in their theology.[8] Heitzenrater, building on Campbell's work, has further demonstrated the difficulties of tracing any direct references to Orthodox sources in John's writings.[9]

Thankfully, in the decades since Outler proposed this path for Wesley studies, increased interest in the topic of deification broadened how scholars understand the concept. Though acknowledging that there are particular ways of understanding divinization (or theosis) in Eastern Orthodoxy that differ from Roman Catholicism or Protestantism, these scholars have argued both that deification can be found in typically Western theologians such as Augustine of Hippo or Thomas Aquinas and also that divinization is ultimately a scriptural doctrine. This outlook stands in contrast with past interpreters who argued that deification solely reflected the influence of Platonic or neo-Platonic philosophy.[10] This is fortuitous for understanding John and Charles Wesley, because while some may question whether the Wesleys had much in common with Eastern Orthodoxy, no one would deny that the Wesleys understood themselves to be teaching and proclaiming what Scripture itself teaches.[11]

---

[6]See, e.g., Kenneth J. Collins, *The Theology of John Wesley: Holy Love and the Shape of Grace* (Nashville: Abingdon, 2007).

[7]See Edgardo A. Colón-Emeric, *Wesley, Aquinas and Christian Perfection: An Ecumenical Dialogue* (Waco, TX: Baylor University Press, 2009). See also the fine note on this very point in a foreword by Peter Bouteneff to S. T. Kimbrough Jr., *Partakers of the Life Divine: Participation in the Divine Nature in the Writings of Charles Wesley* (Eugene, OR: Cascade Books, 2016).

[8]Ted A. Campbell, *John Wesley and Christian Antiquity: Religious Vision and Cultural Change* (Nashville: Kingswood Books, 1991).

[9]Richard P. Heitzenrater, "John Wesley's Reading of and References to the Early Church Fathers," in Kimbrough, *Orthodox and Wesleyan Spirituality*, 25-32.

[10]To offer but a brief and thoroughly incomplete list of publications in this area: A. N. Williams, *The Ground of Union: Deification in Aquinas and Palamas* (New York: Oxford University Press, 1999); Michael J. Gorman, *Inhabiting the Cruciform God: Kenosis, Justification, and Theosis in Paul's Narrative Spirituality* (Grand Rapids, MI: Eerdmans, 2009); Paul M. Collins, *Partaking in Divine Nature: Deification and Communion* (London: T&T Clark International, 2010).

[11]See Randy L. Maddox, *Responsible Grace: John Wesley's Practical Theology* (Nashville: Kingswood Books, 1994); John R. Tyson, *Assist Me to Proclaim: The Life and Hymns of Charles Wesley* (Grand Rapids, MI: Eerdmans, 2007).

Indeed, not only did the Wesleys seek to spread scriptural holiness through the Methodist movement; they championed scriptural Christianity more broadly. Scriptural Christianity, for the Wesleys, was their appeal for an orthodox faith that was embodied in the holy fellowship of men and women united by Christ. Though they believed scriptural Christianity transcended particular traditions within the church, this belief did not temper their passion or rhetoric.[12] They railed against what they saw as the insufficient practice of the Christian faith among their contemporaries, against having "the form of religion without the power."[13] That power, which they argued was promised in Scripture and available to all, was the power of God to transform a person from a life of sin into a life of holiness.

That transformation reached its culmination in what the Wesleys called Christian perfection, or entire sanctification. Despite the potentially jarring name for this essential teaching, in the Wesleys' hands Christian perfection was a carefully nuanced concept. It was also a concept over which John and Charles had some disagreement. For example, there was a question regarding whether the gift of entire sanctification could occur during this life and be lived out over a long period of time, as John believed, or whether it preceded death by a short time, as Charles thought.[14] We should not, however, overemphasize these fraternal differences. The Wesleys were united in their understanding of Christian perfection as the culmination of God's work of grace and salvation in an individual; as a gift available to all Christians, not just a select few, in this life and not just in the life of the world to come; and as the perfect, holy love of God and neighbor. They further agreed that Christian perfection, as John says, "is again and again mentioned in Scripture."[15] Christian perfection does not mean, in this life, the perfection of angels, nor does it mean,

---

[12]See, e.g., John Wesley, "A Letter to a Roman Catholic," *WJW* 14:163-75. D. Stephen Long, "The Non-Catholicity of a Catholic Spirit," in *Embodying Wesley's Catholic Spirit*, ed. Daniel Castelo (Eugene, OR: Pickwick, 2017), 62, 64, helps us to understand John Wesley's catholic spirit by insisting, "Wesley offers a theological *ressourcement* within catholic Christianity," and adds that "a 'catholic spirit' does not characterize a single sermon or idea in Wesley but his corpus, including his reflections on law, sacraments, philosophy, doctrine, and virtues."

[13]John Wesley, "Thoughts upon Methodism," §1, *WJW* 9:527.

[14]See the discussion in Julie A. Lunn, *The Theology of Sanctification and Resignation in Charles Wesley's Hymns* (London: Routledge, 2019), 18-21.

[15]John Wesley, *A Plain Account of Christian Perfection*, ed. Randy L. Maddox and Paul W. Chilcote (Kansas City, MO: Beacon Hill, 2015), §26, 155.

either in this life or in the life of the world to come, perfection equal to God's; rather, it is holiness to the fullest extent possible in humanity.[16]

The relationship of deification to Christian perfection is almost too obvious. The Wesleys took their scriptural cues on the topic from two key texts: Matthew 5:48, in which Jesus commands his disciples, "Be ye therefore perfect, even as your Father which is in heaven is perfect" (KJV), and 2 Peter 1:4, in which Peter proclaims that by the power and promises of God Christians "might be partakers of the divine nature" (KJV). Concerning the command in Matthew, Charles writes, "Thus, thus may I the prize pursue, / And all th' appointed paths pass thro' / To perfect poverty: / Thus let me, Lord, thyself attain, / And give thee up thine own again, / Forever lost in thee."[17] Interpreting the Petrine epistle, John paraphrases the comment as "being renewed in the image of God, and having communion with him, so as to dwell in God and God in you."[18] Christian perfection means attaining the Lord and a mutual indwelling with God, becoming so thoroughly united with God (deified, we might say) as to be forever lost in God.

The Wesleys taught a recognizably Protestant way of salvation, beginning with a person's conviction of sin leading to repentance, followed by justification by faith, sanctification by faith bearing fruit in good works, and finally glorification. Both John and Charles connected perfection with sanctification rather than justification: distinct yet also inseparable, since for them sanctification began in the moment of justification. Combined with how straightforwardly deification relates to Christian perfection, this may lead us mistakenly to associate deification entirely with Wesleyan sanctification. The logic of Christian perfection, however, extends far beyond sanctification for both John and Charles, and is entirely involved in how they conceived

---

[16]"But what is perfection?" John Wesley asks in his sermon "The Scripture Way of Salvation." "The word has various senses: here it means perfect love. It is love excluding sin; love filling the heart, taking up the whole capacity of the soul. It is love 'rejoicing evermore, praying without ceasing, in everything giving thanks.'" See Wesley, Sermon 43, "The Scripture Way of Salvation," 1.9, *WJW* 2:160.

[17]Charles Wesley, *Short Hymns on Select Passages of the Holy Scriptures*, vol. 2 (Bristol: Farley, 1762), #54, stanza 3. All hymns cited in this chapter can be found on the website for the Center for Studies in the Wesleyan Tradition of Duke Divinity School, https://divinity.duke.edu/initiatives/cswt.

[18]John Wesley, *Explanatory Notes upon the New Testament* (London: Epworth, 1976), 890.

of and taught about everything from the doctrine of creation to the work of Christ, the work of the Holy Spirit, and the hoped-for new creation. Thus, as we shall see, deification for the Wesleys is comprehensive and not at all narrowly conceived.

## Created for Divine Holiness

The divine work of Christian perfection belongs to a broader theological anthropology whose foundation is the Wesleyan understanding of humanity's creation in the image and likeness of God. The Wesleys affirmed that God created humans with a *capax dei*, a capacity for God, not as a right or as something held intrinsically apart from God but rather as God's preeminent gift. In an early sermon predating his Aldersgate transformation, John linked this gift with the human faculties of intellect, will, and freedom. In his description of these faculties, John treated them not merely as analogous to God's own characteristics but as truly divine: an intellect with "a comprehension . . . to take in at once almost an infinity of objects"; a will that meant "man was what God is, Love"; and a freedom such that "he was the sole lord and sovereign judge of his own actions."[19] In this sermon, John directly connected salvation in Jesus Christ to the restoration of these human faculties, which have been damaged by humanity's turn to sin and death.

John Wesley did not publish this sermon in his lifetime: perhaps it veered too sharply toward the enthusiastic and high estimation of humanity's state before the fall. Still, John never gave up on the idea that humanity, made in God's image, was created to share in and display God's likeness. In later sermons he discussed the threefold image of God not as three human faculties but as three human likenesses of God, reflecting humanity's creation by "the three-one God."[20] John called the first the "natural image," by which he meant that humanity was created for immortality and as a spiritual being. He also included the faculties of intellect, will, and freedom from his earlier sermon in the natural image. He called the second image the "political image." John says relatively little about this image except to note that humanity's task

---

[19]John Wesley, sermon 141, "The Image of God," 1.1-3, *WJW* 4:293-95.
[20]John Wesley, sermon 45, "The New Birth," 1.1, *WJW* 2:188.

## John and Charles Wesley on Deification

of stewarding God's good creation reflects God's governance of all creation. The third image, which John emphasized most, was the "moral image":

> [Since] "God is love:" Accordingly, man at his creation was full of love; which was the sole principle of all his tempers, thoughts, words, and actions. God is full of justice, mercy, and truth; so was man as he came from the hands of his Creator. God is spotless purity; and so man was in the beginning pure from every sinful blot; otherwise God could not have pronounced him, as well as all the other work of his hands, "very good" (Genesis 1:31). This he could not have been, had he not been pure from sin, and filled with righteousness and true holiness.[21]

Interestingly, John does not suggest that one of these images reflects the Father, another the Son, and the third the Holy Spirit; rather, the unity of the triune God is of such richness and complexity that it must be reflected, for John, in this threefold image.

Charles was equally emphatic that human beings received, from creation, the gift of likeness to God. A few times in his poetry, Charles writes that human beings are "transcripts" of the Trinity. For example, in the 1740 publication *Hymns and Sacred Poems*, Charles begins a section titled "The Communion of Saints" with an invocation: "Father, Son, and Spirit, hear / Faith's effectual, fervent prayer, / Hear, and our petitions seal; / Let us now the answer feel, / Mystically one with thee, / Transcript of the Trinity, / Thee let all our nature own / One in Three, and Three in One."[22] In "Hymn XCVIII" from the later *Trinity Hymns* collection, he expounds further:

> 1 Remember thy Creators, God
>    In Persons Three confest,
> Who rais'd thee up a breathing clod,
>    And with his name imprest:
> The Persons Three in council join'd
>    To make his earth-born son;
> And, stampt with his immortal mind,
>    He claims thee for his own.
> 2 He challenges thy youthful days
>    Who did thy being give:

---

[21] Wesley, "New Birth," 1.1.
[22] Charles Wesley, "The Communion of Saints, Part I," in *Hymns and Sacred Poems*, by John Wesley and Charles Wesley (London: Strahan, 1740), stanza 1, p. 188.

Created for his only praise,
    For him rejoice to live;
Transcript of holiness divine,
    The Tri-une God proclaim,
And spirit, and soul, and flesh resign
    To glorify his name.[23]

Here the transcript is specifically of the triune holiness of God, and more than that, human beings are also "stampt with [God's] immortal mind." Though Charles does not operate with John's three anthropological categories in these hymns, his high view of humanity's *imago Dei* dovetails with his brother's perspective.

For both Charles and John, sin mars, damages, impedes, and infects the image of God, but it does not destroy the divine image. The gift of the *capax dei*, combined with the work of prevenient grace, means that all people have the possibility of living according to the divine image. Thus, for the Wesleys, the universal availability of saving grace is rooted in how God creates as well as in how God saves humanity.[24] Furthermore, the recovery of this image, with effects in both the present life and in the life of the world to come, is essential to salvation. In another of the *Trinity Hymns*, Charles concluded a selection about a person who received the gift of faith in the triune God: "Father, Son, and Holy Ghost, / Heal thy creature's misery; / Thee, the pearl which Adam lost, / Give us to recover thee, / Give us in pure love renew'd / Higher by our fall to rise, / Image of the Tri-une God, / House of one who fills the skies."[25] The faith that makes possible intimate knowledge of the Trinity through "pure love" culminates in a renewal of the image of God that is so thorough that the renewed image exceeds the original. Elsewhere, in a funeral hymn for a Mrs. Lefevre, Charles testifies that in the deceased woman God had answered such a prayer: "She *was* (what words can never paint) / A spotless soul, a sinless saint, / In perfect love renew'd, / A mirror of the deity, / A transcript of the One in Three, /

---

[23]Charles Wesley, "Hymn XCVII," in *Hymns on the Trinity* (Bristol: Pine, 1767), 63.
[24]The Wesleys' belief in the universal availability of grace and the possibility that every person could respond positively to God's offer of salvation was entirely theocentric and never anthropocentric.
[25]Charles Wesley, "Hymns and Prayers to the Trinity" X, in *Hymns on the Trinity*, stanza 4.

A temple fill'd with God."[26] The emphasis is original; Charles does not intend to say that, now that she has died, Mrs. Lefevre is a "spotless soul, a sinless saint"; rather, he means that while she lived she had been a "temple fill'd with God" because she had borne the image of God, a "transcript of the One in Three."

Because of their convictions about the image of God, for John and Charles the renewal of humanity effected by Jesus Christ is simultaneously a renewal of divinity-in-humanity. Jesus also perfectly displays this image; in a prayer seeking this renewal, Charles pleads, "Now the form divine impress, / True, substantial holiness; / Jesus, thou that image art, / Seal thy name upon my heart."[27] Jesus not only bears the image; he is the image of God. As such, his life is also the life of those who are being saved, both now and also in the world to come, for though the image may be renewed in them now, there still remains a greater gift: "Gain we our high calling's prize, / Feel our sins thro' Christ forgiven, / Rise, to all his image rise, / And meet our head in heaven."[28]

## THE DIVINE EXCHANGE AND CHRIST'S THREEFOLD OFFICE

In turning to sin, human beings abandoned God and neglected the gift of the divine image, which, for John and Charles, should have been visible in every dimension of human life. In one of the great lines of Christian hymnody, Charles comments that, in response to human sin, Jesus "left his Father's throne . . . [and] emptied himself of all but love,"[29] exchanging divine glory for human lowliness, yet nevertheless retaining the image of God perfectly. Accordingly, in Wesleyan theology all of Christ's life is salvific, since Christ accomplishes in his daily life the exact holiness for which human beings were created.[30] This does not mean the Wesleys downplayed the significance of the crucifixion or the atonement; as John Tyson says, "The Wesleys affirmed

---

[26] Charles Wesley, Hymn XXVIII, "On the Death of Mrs. L[efevre], July 6, 1756," in *Funeral Hymns* (London: Strahan, 1759), stanza 5, emphasis original.
[27] Charles Wesley, *Scripture Hymns*, vol. 1 (Bristol: Farley, 1762), #756.
[28] Charles Wesley, Hymn CCXXVII, "Two Are Better Far than One," in *Hymns and Sacred Poems*, vol. 2 (Bristol: Farley, 1749), stanza 5.
[29] Charles Wesley, "Free Grace," in *Hymns and Sacred Poems* (London: Strahan, 1739), stanza 3, p. 118.
[30] See Edgardo Colón-Emeric and Mark Gorman, *The Saving Mysteries of Jesus Christ* (Eugene, OR: Cascade Books, 2019), for a contemporary development of this Wesleyan theme.

the importance of the pardon or *acquittal* that comes to us through God's act in Christ."[31] Regarding Charles's hymns, Joanna Cruickshank notes the frequency of the word *blood*, which "became a common shorthand term signifying Christ's sacrificial work . . . [and] appears nearly 800 times in the later hymns . . . [by which] he repeatedly drew attention to the physical realities of Christ's death."[32] Nevertheless, the Wesleys also understood "Jesus Christ as a 'Second Adam' who came to earth to rectify the plight of humanity who had been despoiled in Adam's fall."[33] Christ's recapitulation or, rather, exceeding of Adam's life means, for the Wesleys, that those who put their faith in Christ can expect him to redeem and transform aspects of human life now.[34]

While an Adamic Christology is commonplace in theologies of deification, that is less true with respect to a key Wesleyan christological emphasis: the threefold office of Christ. The threefold office identifies a connection between three roles in the life of Israel for which persons were anointed and Jesus' title, Messiah. These three roles are prophet, priest, and king, and as the true Messiah, Jesus holds all three offices. He is the prophet who speaks truthfully and faithfully on behalf of the Lord, the priest who offers the perfect atoning sacrifice, and the king who sits both on David's throne and eternally at the right hand of the Father.

The Wesley brothers were hardly the first to emphasize Christ's threefold office; traces of the concept can be found in the patristic era, and John Calvin gave it a central place in his own writings. Still, while the Wesleys did not create the threefold office, they endorsed and promoted it. John famously encouraged his company of preachers to "proclaim [Christ] in all his offices."[35] As John Tyson shows, Charles used the term "threefold office" in some of his poetry, and both brothers structured some of their writings about Jesus according to the offices of prophet, priest, and king.[36]

---

[31] John R. Tyson, *Portraits of Jesus: Charles Wesley's Christology* (Nashville: Wesley's Foundery Books, 2022), 20, emphasis original.

[32] Joanna Cruickshank, *Pain, Passion and Faith: Revisiting the Place of Charles Wesley in Early Methodism* (London: Scarecrow, 2009), 46.

[33] Tyson, *Portraits of Jesus*, 20.

[34] Tyson, *Portraits of Jesus*, 21-22, cites several hymns of Charles Wesley in reference to this second Adam Christology. Rackley, "Recovery of the Divine Nature," devotes most of his chapter 4 to exploring John's use of the same typology.

[35] John Wesley, sermon 36, "The Law Established Through Faith, Discourse II," 1.6, *WJW* 2:37.

[36] See Tyson, *Portraits of Jesus*, 185.

For the Wesleys, the threefold office was another way to explore the breadth of the saving work of Jesus Christ. What Tyson says of a hymn by Charles could be applied more broadly to both John and Charles: "The threefold offices describe the broad and expansive nature of [Christ's] ministry for and in us."[37] This expansive view of salvation, or what acclaimed Wesley scholar Randy Maddox calls the Wesleys' "holistic" understanding of salvation, is of a piece with both the Wesleys' perspective on the image of God and their embrace of Adamic Christology, though neither Wesley ever explores the correspondence explicitly. With respect to Adamic Christology, preaching the threefold office is another form of christological recapitulation; only with the threefold office, instead of Adam, Christ takes on himself the part of God's chosen people: before God he is both Adam and Israel. That, at least, is implicit in the logic of the threefold office. There is, furthermore, a tantalizing possible connection between the threefold image of God (natural, political, and moral) and the threefold offices of Christ. Could it be that in bearing the office of prophet and speaking truthfully and faithfully as the Word of God, he redeems the natural image of God; that in giving himself as the pure, unblemished sacrifice of love, he heals the moral image; and that in instituting the kingdom of God and ascending to God's eternal throne, Christ fulfills the political image of God? While neither John nor Charles ever says so directly, the connections are surely implicit in their writings.

In the divine exchange, the second person of the Trinity condescends to our condition in the incarnation, taking on himself the holy life to which God called first Adam and later Israel but doing so in triumph and victory over sin and death. This divine exchange, however, also means that human beings, in Christ, may exchange their own death-bound, sinful existence for holy life (and holy living) in Jesus Christ. One of Charles's great hymns, "And Can It Be" (originally "Free Grace"), celebrates this very fact in its closing stanza. In that hymn we might expect by way of conclusion something like "Bold I approach . . . / And bow the knee before Christ my own," which would recall Philippians 2 rather nicely, but that is not how Charles finishes. Instead, he concludes audaciously, "No condemnation now I dread; / Jesus, and all in Him is mine! /

---

[37]Tyson, *Portraits of Jesus*, 187.

Alive in Him, my living Head, / And clothed in righteousness divine, / Bold I approach th'eternal throne, / And claim the crown, through Christ my own."[38] For Charles, "Jesus and *all* in him is mine" (emphasis added) means that human nature has not only been forgiven and released but also elevated. *All* means the triumph of the second Adam and the victory over sin and death of the one true prophet, priest, and king, so that reigning with Christ, crowned at his throne, becomes part of human destiny. John echoes this hymn in the invitation at the conclusion of his sermon "The End of Christ's Coming" when he writes, "Only 'come boldly to the throne of grace,' trusting in his mercy; and you shall find, 'He saveth to the uttermost all those that come to God through him!'"[39] In that same sermon, John affirms that "a restoration [of human beings] not only to the favour but likewise to the image of God, implying not barely deliverance from sin, but the being filled with the fullness of God . . . nothing short of this is Christian religion."[40] It is not a partial healing but a full, complete salvation that both John and Charles endorse.

All of this is true for the Wesleys because of the great mystery of the incarnation and the hypostatic union; as S. T. Kimbrough says, "it is the incarnation that makes possible the reality and experience of partaking of the divine nature."[41] If John sometimes emphasizes Christ's divine nature and downplays his human nature, Charles is fascinated by the surplus grace and meaning found in the hypostatic union.[42] "Being's source begins to be, And God himself is BORN!" Charles proclaims in the fourth of his *Nativity Hymns*; elsewhere in the same collection, he writes that in Christ we find "God contracted to a span."[43] The Adam-Christ typology and the threefold office both rest on a deeper, catholic doctrine. Because the incarnation is so great a wonder, human salvation can lead even to deification, as divine love undoes and heals the damage wrought by sin.

---

[38]Wesley, "Free Grace," stanza 6, p. 119.
[39]John Wesley, sermon 62, "The End of Christ's Coming," 3.6, *WJW* 2:484.
[40]Wesley, "End of Christ's Coming," III.5, 2:482.
[41]Kimbrough, *Partakers of the Life Divine*, 44.
[42]See Edgardo Colón-Emeric, *The People Called Metodista: Renewing Doctrine, Worship, and Mission from the Margins* (Nashville: Abingdon, 2022), 52-56, for a summary and some suggestions regarding recent debates about John Wesley's Christology in particular.
[43]Charles Wesley, Hymn IV, "Glory Be to God on High," in *Hymns for the Nativity of Our Lord* (London: Strahan, 1745), stanza 2; Wesley, Hymn V, "Let Earth and Heaven Combine," in *Hymns for the Nativity*, stanza 1.

## THE HOLY SPIRIT AND/AS THE LOVE OF GOD

Throughout their lives John and Charles were relentlessly trinitarian in their theology and preaching. In an age when deism and unitarianism were increasingly popular alternatives to an orthodox doctrine of God, the Wesleys remained steadfast and handed on what they themselves had received. They were practical trinitarians, not trinitarian theorists, but nevertheless they marveled at the splendor of the three-one God and taught their fellow Methodists to do the same.

Consequently, though Jesus Christ was always at the center of their theology, Charles and John taught that the Holy Spirit was equally important in the divine economy. So essential is the Holy Spirit to the Wesleys' theology, and in particular to their soteriology, that it is not an overstatement to say that the grace of God at work in human beings that leads to entire sanctification (i.e., Christian perfection) is in fact the Holy Spirit. Nor does this relegate the Spirit to a passive role. The Spirit is given to humanity similarly to how God gives the eternally begotten Son: that is, to accomplish what God alone can do. The Spirit, for the Wesleys, is at work in and among us. As Kenneth Loyer explains, by the Holy Spirit "Christians experience God through their spiritual senses . . . [and] come to a deeper knowledge of God and a greater love for God and neighbor. . . . In other words, through the work of the Holy Spirit they are renewed in the divine image and drawn increasingly into the life of God."[44] Loyer identifies this as a renewal in and of love.

One of John's favorite Scripture verses is the second half of Romans 5:5, "the love of God is shed abroad in our hearts by the Holy Ghost which is given unto us" (KJV), which for him establishes a direct link between love and the presence of the Holy Spirit. As we see in both John's sermons and Charles's hymns, the restoring, healing work of the Holy Spirit involves drawing out the unholy "tempers," as the Wesleys would have called them, so that the holy tempers would have room to flourish.[45] By *tempers* the Wesleys meant something like a combination of what others might call virtues, passions,

---

[44]Kenneth M. Loyer, *God's Love Through the Spirit: The Holy Spirit in Thomas Aquinas and John Wesley* (Washington, DC: Catholic University of America Press, 2014), 61.

[45]Paul W. Chilcote, *A Faith That Sings: Biblical Themes in the Lyrical Theology of Charles Wesley* (Eugene, OR: Cascade Books, 2016), 64, suggests that "[Charles] Wesley tends to identify the work of restoration . . . with the Holy Spirit."

and emotions. Unholy tempers are motivating forces within human beings that drive them to commit sin; holy tempers are those things at work within that lead to righteousness. The principal difference between the two has everything to do with divine love. A real-world example of this difference from the early days of Methodism is how raucous celebrations of New Year's Eve gave way to Watchnight Services; both were characterized by late-night gatherings and by exuberant singing, but in the Watchnight Services, under the guidance of the Holy Spirit, those activities were directed toward the praise and glory of God rather than indulgent, sinful carousing. Charles pointed to these services as illustrations of the sanctifying effects of the holy love communicated by the Spirit.[46] Another example may be found in one of the most famous passages from John's sermons, in which he describes salvation as a breathing in and out of love, an inhalation of the Holy Spirit and an exhalation of "love, by prayer, and praise, and thanksgiving; love and praise, and prayer being the breath of every soul which is truly born of God."[47] This respiratory analogy underscores the graced and gradual nature of growth in holiness that the Spirit effects in believers.

In *John Wesley's Pneumatology*, Joseph Cunningham explains how love functions for John with respect to other desirable Christian characteristics, writing that "the relationship between love, the core spiritual fruit, and peace, joy, and righteousness in Wesley's theology can be compared to the relationship between prudence and the other cardinal virtues." In other words, "according to Wesley, without love, it is impossible to cultivate the other fruits of the Spirit." Cunningham also makes a direct connection between deification and the work of the Holy Spirit, which, when received by the believer, "is to participate in the divine nature, and to follow the example of Christ by leading the life of Spirit-empowered goodness."[48] Cunningham, however, overplays the significance of human agency in this process, preferring to emphasize human reception, or spiritual perception, rather than divine initiative and action as the chief condition for participation in the godly life. For

---

[46] See Mark Christopher Gorman, "Breathing the Spirit: A Wesleyan Theology of Hymn Singing," *Wesleyan Theological Journal* 48, no. 2 (Fall 2013): 126-45.
[47] John Wesley, sermon 19, "The Great Privilege of Those That Are Born of God," 1.8, *WJW* 1:434.
[48] Joseph W. Cunningham, *John Wesley's Pneumatology: Perceptible Inspiration* (New York: Routledge, 2016), 115, 110.

the Wesleys, human agency matters and is not constrained by Calvinist conceptions of predestination or limited atonement; nevertheless, human agency is always subsequent to and dependent on the prior work of the Holy Spirit. Charles says in one of his hymns, "In my natural estate / Thee, my God, I cannot know: / Let thy grace illuminate, / Thee let thy own Spirit shew ... Thou seest my heart's desire, / Whate'er thy laws require / Freely, faithfully to do; / But I know not how t' obey, / 'Till thy Spirit lend a clue, / Pointing out the living way."[49] For the Wesleys, human agency is not at odds with divine agency but is dependent and enabled by what only God can do.

Charles concludes that same hymn with a petition: "Now, Father, send him [the Holy Spirit] down, / To make thy Godhead known, / Let him thee in Christ reveal, / Now diffuse thy love abroad, / Shew me things unsearchable, / All the heights and depths of God."[50] There is in this petition a parallel drawn between the request for the Father to send the Holy Spirit and the request for the Father to "diffuse thy love abroad." Similarly, in one of his *Whitsunday Hymns* Charles prays, "Spirit of pure and holy LOVE, / We feel thee streaming from above, / In calm unutterable peace, / The LOVE by thee diffus'd abroad / Unites our happy hearts to God, / And seals our everlasting bliss."[51] The identification of the Holy Spirit with divine Love, a name for the Spirit that goes back as far as Hilary of Poitiers and Augustine of Hippo, is a thematic constant for both John and Charles, for whom the Spirit as Love deifies human beings, bringing them into the image and likeness of the God whose "nature and name is love."[52] Charles's poetic commentary on the "new commandment" of John 13:34 makes this connection as boldly as possible: "O put it in our inward parts, / Write thy new precept on our hearts / In characters divine, / Inspire us with thy Spirit's love; / Stronger than death it then shall prove, / A copy, Lord, of thine."[53] In Wesleyan deification, the self is transposed: not eliminated but removed from the key of

---

[49] Charles Wesley, "Hymn XXIV," in *Hymns for Children* (Bristol: Farley, 1763), stanzas 1, 4.
[50] Wesley, "Hymn XXIV," stanza 5.
[51] Charles Wesley, "Hymn XXX," in *Hymns for Ascension Day* (Bristol: Farley, 1746), stanza 8, small caps original.
[52] See Charles Wesley, "Wrestling Jacob," in *Hymns and Sacred Poems*, by John Wesley and Charles Wesley (Bristol: Farley, 1742), 115-18.
[53] Wesley, *Short Hymns on Select Passages*, vol. 2, #455.

death to the key of life but in the process becoming so thoroughly identified with God as to be nearly unrecognizable to the self who once knew only sin and to others who still persist in worldly ways.

### "Lost in Wonder, Love, and Praise"

With the Wesleys' fervent insistence on a transformed, deified life in this world, on the reality of a more complete salvation than forgiveness of sins now, it is fair to wonder what is left to hope for in the life of the world to come. A quick and simple response to such a question is that the life of the world to come is, for John and Charles, a life in which the possibility of backsliding, or losing one's salvation, has been removed. Though they were supremely confident in the present-day work of God, they firmly believed that in this life there was always a possibility of succumbing to temptation, of repeating, once more, the sin of the first Adam, and abandoning a state of grace for the gloom of damnation.

There is, however, a more positive eschatological remainder for Wesleyan deification: the new creation. This term has a double meaning for John and Charles; it is inherently what contemporary theologians might call an inaugurated eschatology. The first meaning has to do with the new creation of the one who is being saved by Christ. In Charles's hymn "Love Divine, All Loves Excelling," this is the definition in play in the great concluding stanza, "Finish then thy new creation, / Pure and sinless let us be."[54] There is an "already" ("Finish," not "Begin" the new creation, is the petition) as well as a "not yet" in this line, but both refer to human beings who are being redeemed, that is, deified. This is also how Charles uses the term in a poem memorializing a Robert Jones, of whom Charles testifies, "Throughout his life the new creation shines, / Throughout his words, and actions, and designs: / Quicken'd with Christ he sought the things above, / And evidenc'd the faith which works by love."[55] Also it is the same sense John uses when he preaches that human beings cannot give their attention to God "till we are new creatures; till we are created anew in Christ Jesus."[56] The second meaning, on the other hand,

---

[54]Charles Wesley, Hymn IX, "Love Divine, All Loves Excelling," in *Hymns for Those That Seek and Those That Have Redemption in the Blood of Jesus Christ* (Bristol: Farley, 1747), stanza 3.
[55]Charles Wesley, *Elegy on the Death of Robert Jones* (Bristol: Farley, 1742), lines 171-74.
[56]John Wesley, Sermon 79, "On Dissipation," §7, *WJW* 3:118-19.

is much wider and more expansive: the renewal not of this or that person, or of humanity in general, but of the whole creation. This second meaning is the central theme of two of John's later sermons, "The General Deliverance," which concerns the future state of the animal creation, and "The New Creation," which describes the hoped-for state of affairs in broad strokes.

While this second sense of new creation does not specifically, or at least exclusively, concern human beings, it still represents a striking dimension of both Wesleyan soteriology and deification. Throughout their lives and ministry, the Wesleys implored the early Methodists to live a social faith. "I lift up my voice, to pardon restor'd, / And bid you rejoice in Jesus my Lord; / I call the oppressed [by sin] my Saviour to own, / I cannot be blessed and happy alone," Charles intones in a hymn called "Thanksgiving."[57] John takes things a step further, declaring, "The gospel of Christ knows of no religion but social; no holiness but social holiness."[58] Social does not mean "concerning societal needs"; it means "done in a society, or community, of other believers." Holiness happens in community, and the structures of early Methodism, the classes, bands, and societies, reinforced this at every step.

The new creation amplifies this sociality of faith to include all that God has made and will redeem. Without the new creation, human deification remains inchoate and incomplete. The crowning of God's saving work rests on the culmination of God's renewal of all things, so much so that John concludes his sermon "The New Creation" with a glorious affirmation: "And, to crown all, there will be a deep, an intimate, an uninterrupted union with God; a constant communion with the Father and his Son Jesus Christ, through the Spirit; a continual enjoyment of the Three-One God, and of all the creatures in him!"[59] Unceasing enjoyment of God and of all creatures in God: for the Wesleys, this is the deified life of the world to come, when at last, in the triune God, eternal holiness of heart and life mean that we are forever "lost in wonder, love, and praise."[60]

---

[57]Charles Wesley, Hymn XXV, "Thanksgiving," in *Hymns and Sacred Poems* vol. 1 (1749), stanza 3.
[58]John Wesley, "Preface," in *Hymns and Sacred Poems* §5 (1739), viii. This document can be found at "John Wesley's Poetry, Hymn, and Verse," Center for Studies in the Wesleyan Tradition, https://divinity.duke.edu/initiatives/wesleyan-methodist/cswt-jw (accessed February 18, 2024).
[59]John Wesley, Sermon 64, "The New Creation," §18, *WJW* 2:510.
[60]Charles Wesley, "Love Divine, All Loves Excelling," stanza 3.

# FROM *BIOS* to *ZOE*

## C. S. LEWIS ON THE DOCTRINE OF DEIFICATION

### JAHDIEL PEREZ

*The experience of deification, it seems, is one of great felicity.*

C. S. LEWIS, *SPENSER'S IMAGES OF LIFE*

ALTHOUGH C. S. LEWIS did not explicitly mention the term *theosis* in his writings, and in fact only used *deification* once in his corpus, he had much to say about how believers can (and should) attain not only to the likeness of God but even union with God's divine nature. Douglas Beyer soundly affirms that Lewis managed to "convey the meaning of theosis better than the word itself."[1] In this chapter, I present four insights about deification drawn from Lewis's theological writings. First, I examine what the deific process means and entails for Lewis. The second part analyzes his metaphorical use of a Great Dance as a model for trinitarian perichoresis. The third part questions whether deification, for Lewis, involves technical knowledge or methodology—that is, the extent to which participating in God's divine life is more like an art or a science. The final section places in the foreground the role that Lewis assigns to divine make-believe in the deific process.

---

[1]Douglas Beyer, "From Kenosis to Theosis: Reflections on the Views of C. S. Lewis," *Inklings Forever: Published Colloquium Proceedings 1997–2016* 5 (2006), article 18, p. 90, https://pillars.taylor.edu/cgi/viewcontent.cgi?article=1118&context=inklings_forever.

## God's Great Experiment

Perhaps the closest approximation of a definition of deification by Lewis is found in *Mere Christianity*: "The business of becoming a son of God, of being turned from a created thing into a begotten thing, of passing over from the temporary biological life into timeless 'spiritual' life."[2] The former kind of life, which Lewis calls *Bios*, is created and corporeal—the kind of life we share with animals—while the latter kind of life, *Zoe*, is eternal, spiritual, and the kind of life human beings can share with God.[3] Bios is created by God, of a different nature from the Creator, while Zoe is begotten of God, of the same nature as God. In these terms, deification is the process whereby Bios *becomes* Zoe—a transformation that has already been achieved in Christ, who, as the Nicene Creed states, is begotten of the Father, not created. Thus, when Lewis observes that the "Son of God became a man to enable men to become sons of God," he affirms the incarnation, which hypostatically unified Bios and Zoe in the person of Jesus, as the sine qua non of deification.[4] It is through Christ that human beings can participate in the divine, uncreated, eternal life of the triune God.

It is vital to note that, for Lewis, the incarnation is a necessary but not a sufficient condition for deification; Christ makes becoming one with God possible but not inevitable. This is in large part because Lewis seems to hold a synergistic view of soteriology. As early as *The Problem of Pain*, he unequivocally states, "The Divine labour to redeem the world cannot be certain of succeeding as regards every individual soul. Some will not be redeemed." Against both universalism and monergism, Lewis believed that the human must cooperate with God to receive the redemption accomplished in Christ and to attain deification through Christ. "We are not merely imperfect creatures who must be improved," writes Lewis; "we are, as Newman said, rebels

---

[2] C. S. Lewis, *Mere Christianity* (New York: Harper, 1952), 181.
[3] The distinction between Bios and Zoe for Lewis is not, as David Meconi suggests, the difference between merely living and flourishing, which is a difference of degree, not kind. For Lewis, Bios is to Zoe what a statute is to a living person—that is, a categorically different kind of being. See Meconi, "Mere Christianity: Theosis in a British Way," *Journal of Inklings Studies*, 4, no. 1 (2014): 16.
[4] This wording is from Athanasius, *On the Incarnation*, trans. John Behr (New York: St. Vladimir's Seminary Press, 2011), 107. Lewis wrote a preface to this text. See C. S. Lewis, "On the Reading of Old Books," in *God in the Dock: Essays on Theology and Ethics*, ed. Walter Hooper (Grand Rapids, MI: Eerdmans, 1970), 217-25.

who must lay down our arms."⁵ Lewis here draws from John Henry Newman's sermon "Christian Repentance," which is based on the parable of the prodigal son. Newman says that "the most decorous conduct in a conscious sinner, is an *unconditional surrender* of himself to God—not a bargaining about terms, not a scheming (so to call it) to be received back again, but an instant *surrender* of himself. . . . He is a runaway offender. . . . He is a rebel, and must lay down his arms."⁶ It is the nature of God and the condition of fallen humanity that renders such scheming impossible. God is, as Lewis experienced in his own conversion, the "reality with which no treaty can be made."⁷

God sets the terms that human beings must submit to if they would be saved, the voluntary submission of which is essential to deification. For Lewis, to say that the total surrender to God that is necessary for redemption and deification can be involuntary, that is, against the will of the individual, is to assert a contradiction in terms. Like Thomas Aquinas and G. K. Chesterton, Lewis did not believe that God's omnipotence applied to logical contradictions. As he puts it in *Miracles*, "Adding 'God can' to a nonsensical proposition doesn't suddenly make it sensible."⁸ Uniting a human being to the divine nature of God against her free will is another such meaningless proposition.

That salvation is not guaranteed to every individual led Lewis to imagine deification in terms of a great experiment, not in the sense that the outcome was unknown to God—Lewis was not an open theist—but in the sense that the ultimate result depended on the variable of human volition. God simply will not deify an individual against his free will. In short, deification is not an experiment in relation to God but in relation to humanity. Lewis affirms as much in a moving passage toward the end of *A Grief Observed*:

> But that, I suppose, is just your grand experiment. Or no; not an experiment, for you have no need to find things out. Rather your grand enterprise. To make an organism which is also a spirit; to make that terrible oxymoron, a "spiritual animal." To take a poor primate, a beast with nerve-endings all over

---

⁵C. S. Lewis, *The Problem of Pain* (London: Collins, 2015), 119, 88.
⁶John Henry Newman, *Parochial and Plan Sermons in Eight Volumes* (London: Longmans, Green, 1907), 3:97.
⁷C. S. Lewis, *Surprised by Joy: The Shape of My Early Life* (New York: Harcourt, 1955), 228.
⁸C. S. Lewis, *Miracles: A Preliminary Study* (London: Collins, 2016), 120.

it, a creature with a stomach that wants to be filled, a breeding animal that wants its mate, and say, "Now get on with it. Become a god."[9]

Here Lewis alludes to the words of Jesus in John 10:34 ("Is it not written in your Law, 'I have said you are "gods"'?" [NIV]) to describe the process of becoming not simply *a* divine being—one among many gods, as some pantheistic readers may want to understand—but one with the divine nature of God himself. In this context, to "become a god" denotes the transformation of Bios into Zoe. Just as in the incarnation Christ did not abdicate his divinity to become human, Lewis believes that we do not completely abandon our humanity to become divine, which is why the result of deification is a "spiritual animal." To summarize Lewis's view, "Deification does not abolish humanity's nature but fulfills and completes it."[10] To use Thomistic language, the nature that grace perfects through deification involves the animality of our humanity, the embodied dimension of our being that is primitive, bestial, sensate, voracious, and libidinous. These "natural loves," once submitted to the supernatural Charity of God, can contribute to deification: "Nothing is either too trivial or too animal to be thus transformed," writes Lewis.[11]

Lewis depicts such a transformation in *The Great Divorce*, where a young ghost allows an angelic spirit, described as "the Burning One," to kill his red lizard (a symbol of lust).[12] After this sacrifice, two transformations occur: the ghost becomes a new man—the only one in the whole narrative who chooses to remain in heaven—while the lizard is resurrected into a glorious stallion, both of whom ride off into the mountains. In this scene, a vital element of the ghost's animality, the sacrifice of his natural but disordered sexual drive, contributes to his deification.

This Lewisian insight can help increase our appreciation for both the object of deification and the paradoxical quality of its outcome. Regarding the former, the raw material on which deification works is less like the transcendentalist divine spark of Ralph Waldo Emerson, according to which human beings possess inherent divinity, and more like the rational animal of Aristotle or the featherless biped of Diogenes, both of which emphasize the

---

[9]C. S. Lewis, *A Grief Observed* (London: Faber & Faber, 2013), 61.
[10]Meconi, "Mere Christianity," 14.
[11]C. S. Lewis, *The Four Loves* (New York: Harcourt, 1988), 134.
[12]See C. S. Lewis, *The Great Divorce: A Dream* (New York: HarperCollins, 1973), 108-12.

animality of our humanity. For Lewis, it is the created Bios of a "poor primate" that deification transforms into the begotten Zoe of God through Christ. Thus, our animal nature can be considered the starting point of the deific process. The outcome of that process, however, Lewis calls a "terrible oxymoron"—an expression that can defamiliarize what a spiritual animal is to help us appreciate its paradoxical nature in a new light. Note that the phrase "terrible oxymoron" is itself oxymoronic. Oxymorons are figures of speech that combine incompatible or contradictory terms, the creation of which usually requires some wordplay. To qualify this kind of witticism with terror sounds odd, if not outright inconsistent, which may be his entire point. Lewis wants us to recapture the wonderful strangeness of what being a spiritual animal means, the two terms of which are as paradoxical as bittersweetness, eloquent silence, open secrets, minor miracles, or joyful sadness. This implies that the natures that deification unifies are not different in degree but in kind, which means that the deific process is not the mere moral improvement of an imperfect person but the total transformation of a natural human being.

## The Great Dance

Because it is the triune life of God that human beings are united to in deification, understanding how Lewis imagines the Trinity would shed more light on his view of the deific process. Lewis uses imagery of a Great Dance—a polysemous metaphor in his writings—to describe the trinitarian perichoresis, or mutual indwelling of the Father, Son, and Holy Spirit. Dance involves the coming together and the moving apart and the intertwining of different dancers. He uses the same image in reference to how the persons of the Holy Trinity interrelate and to how God interacts with humanity.

In *The Problem of Pain*, Lewis writes, "The world is a dance in which good, descending from God, is disturbed by evil arising from the creatures, and the resulting conflict is resolved by God's own assumption of the suffering nature which evil produces."[13] Dance here describes the interplay between God and the world in general and through the incarnation in particular, which is God's great dive into humanity. Lewis suggests that there are three phases or figures to this dance: descent, ascent, and resolution. The goodness

---

[13] Lewis, *Problem of Pain*, 80.

of God descends from heaven, human evil ascends from earth to disrupt that goodness, and the tension between these first two phases is resolved through the incarnation.

For Lewis, this threefold movement—a three-step dance, so to speak—is both a historical event and an ongoing process. It occurred during the incarnation of Jesus two millennia ago, through which Christ overcame the eternal effects of sin and death. This pattern is also how God resolves the temporal effects of evil thereafter. Lewis delineates the structure more clearly by distinguishing the following: "(1) The simple good descending from God, (2) the simple evil produced by rebellious creatures, and (3) the exploitation of that evil by God for His redemptive purpose, which produces (4) the complex good to which accepted suffering and repented sin contribute."[14] Though Lewis enumerates four points here, the last two constitute the same movement in a threefold pattern. Logically, how God redeems human evil is conceptually different from the good that such redemption produces, but both are, causally speaking, part of the same process; God redemptively synthesizes the simple good that he wills for humanity with the evil that humanity does into a greater, richer, more complex good. God and humanity are partners in this dance: the incarnation makes possible a rapprochement between the otherwise eternally separated partners.

Lewis also uses the same image as a metaphor for the inner workings of the Trinity. In *Mere Christianity*, Lewis affirms that what distinguishes Christianity from all other religions is that "in Christianity God is not a static thing—not even a person—but a dynamic, pulsating activity, a life, almost a kind of drama. Almost, if you will not think me irreverent, a kind of dance."[15] Surely it was not lost on Lewis that dance was an essential component of classical drama. The solemn *emmeleia* dances were performed at tragedies, while the obscene *kordax* dance were performed in comedies. Marianne McDonald observes, "When dance was used in ancient Greek ritual, it was the earliest vehicle to try to influence those unknown forces that have power over man: nature and the gods. It was also one of the earliest ways for human beings to express joy and sorrow and all the other

---
[14]Lewis, *Problem of Pain*, 111.
[15]Lewis, *Mere Christianity*, 175.

emotions."[16] The chorus in both classical tragedies and comedies were danced performances, which both appeased the gods and expressed passions in an embodied form. In theory, one could distinguish dance from ancient Greek drama, but both were inseparable in practice. Therefore, in comparing the distinctively Christian conception of God first to a drama and then to a dance, Lewis does not simply offer two different images for the same referent but overlays related images to shift from drama to the dancing element within drama.

Paul Fiddes observes, "It is difficult to find an unambiguous reference to the Trinity as a dance in Christian thinking earlier than Lewis himself."[17] It is one thing to say, as Pseudo-Dionysius and Dante did much before Lewis, that heaven and earth dance *around* God as the fixed point of reality, but it is another thing to suggest, as Lewis himself does, that the triune life of God is itself like a dance. There is movement around the center that is God, but that center has its own inner movement. Thus, God remains the *Primum Mobile*, the Aristotelian "Unmoved Mover," in the sense that he sets the world into motion without being moved by anything outside himself. However, that God is unmoved from without does not mean that he is unmoved or unmoving from within. The distinctively Lewisian image suggests that the Father, Son, and Holy Spirit dynamically move within the Trinity while remaining externally unmoved.

Lewis alludes to both the created order and the uncreated Trinity as a dance across his nonfiction, as we saw in *Mere Christianity*, and in his theological fiction—principally in the scene of the Great Dance in *Perelandra*, which depicts the cosmic dance of the planets and heavens. The Green Lady tells Ransom, "Your world has no roof. You look right out into the high place and see the great dance with your own eyes. You live always in that terror and that delight, and what we must only believe you can behold."[18] In

---

[16]Marianne MacDonald, "Dancing Drama," in *The Oxford Handbook of Dance and Theatre*, ed. Nadine George-Graves (Oxford: Oxford University Press, 2018), 279.

[17]Paul Fiddes, "'For the Dance All Things Were Made': The Great Dance in C. S. Lewis's *Perelandra*," in *C.S. Lewis's Perelandra: Reshaping the Image of the Cosmos*, ed. Judith Wolfe and Brendan Wolfe (Kent, OH: Kent State University Press, 2013), 37. See also Fiddes, "On Theology," in the *Cambridge Companion to C. S. Lewis*, ed. Robert MacSawin and Michael Ward (Cambridge: Cambridge University Press, 2010), 91.

[18]C. S. Lewis, *Perelandra* (London: Lane, 1943), 198. In *The Voyage of the Dawn Treader*, a fallen star, Ramandu, yearns to ascend into the heavens and tread in the great dance. See C. S. Lewis, *The Voyage of the Dawn Treader* (London: Diamond Books, 1998), 158-59.

the Perelandran universe, each planet—with the notable exception of Earth—makes music with other planets, to which the heavenly spheres move in a great cosmic dance. Earth, the "Silent Planet," does not contribute its own sound to the music because it is governed by the Bent One. True to medieval geocentric cosmology, the Earth does not move as the other planets do because it is the fixed point around which the cosmos revolves. Indeed, later in *Perelandra*, Earth is referred to as "the centre of worlds." As such, Earth passively beholds the cosmic dance, in which it does not participate. To live in such a state, the Green Lady suggests, is a paradoxical blend of terror and delight.

Not unlike the beatific vision in the *Divine Comedy*, Ransom's journey culminates in his participation in the Great Dance, where the presiding intelligences of the other planets visit and conference with Tor and Tinidril, the king and queen of Perelandra. One voice affirms,

> All which is not itself the Great Dance was made in order that He might come down into it. In the Fallen World He prepared for Himself a body and was united with the Dust and made it glorious for ever. This is the end and final cause of all creating, and the sin whereby it came is called Fortunate and the world where this was enacted is the centre of worlds. Blessed be He![19]

There is similar language in what Lewis says and a line that he included in his anthology of George MacDonald: "All that is not God is death."[20] Similarly, Lewis suggests here that all that does not participate in the Great Dance (of God) is dead. It is precisely the death that a fallen condition imposes on Thulcandra (Earth) that prohibits its inhabitants and the planet as a whole from joining in the Great Dance. It is through the incarnation of Christ that human beings are drawn into the cosmic harmony and movement of the Great Dance.

It is imperative to note here the sense in which the incarnation is central to the Great Dance. Although the *felix peccatum Adae* (the fortunate or happy sin of Adam) occurred on this planet, its ramifications affect the entire universe. Here the incarnation and death of Maleldil (a Christlike figure) on Earth, which is called both the "Wounded World" and "Darkened

---

[19] Lewis, *Perelandra*, 335.
[20] C. S. Lewis, ed., *George MacDonald: An Anthology of 365 Readings* (London: Collins, 2016), 75.

World," are affirmed as essential to the Great Dance and, what is the same, as the final cause of all creation.

The preceding section enables us to appreciate what deification entails in a new light: to be deified, for Lewis, is to participate in the Great Dance, a dynamic movement that describes not just how the Trinity interacts with the world, making complex good out of human evil, but also the movement of perichoresis. The implication of all this is that being deified is not a static state of having been unified to God but an ongoing, dynamic activity of cooperating with God.

## Deification as God's Art

If deification is like participating in a Great Dance, what is the nature of that participation? Is it more like an art or a science? A central part of what makes a science scientific is the use of a method, a procedural sequence of steps that increases the probability of a desired outcome. To make deification into a science requires articulating a specific technique that would increase the likelihood of our divinization. In such a case, the extent to which individual human beings would participate in the divine life of God would depend more on how each person followed the specific set of rules than on divine grace. For Lewis, that is simply not how it works.

Dance is a performing *art*, not a science.[21] Becoming one with God, writes Lewis, "is more like painting a portrait than like obeying a set of rules."[22] This simile, however, can be misleading if we imagine, with the likes of Friedrich Nietzsche, that we are the artists, the creators in charge of organizing our own chaos into something beautiful.[23] For Lewis, God is the Artist deifying humanity into his masterpiece; he is the Potter, humanity his clay (Jer 18:6). Francis Caponi writes well in describing the deified believer as a "self-portrait of the Triune God."[24] This means that there is no generalizable method, pattern, or sequence of steps that human beings can follow

---

[21] For a seminal articulation of this view, see Graham McFee, *Understanding Dance* (New York: Routledge, 1992), 67-87.
[22] Lewis, *Mere Christianity*, 189.
[23] Friedrich Nietzsche, *The Gay Science*, trans. Adrian Del Caro (Cambridge: Cambridge University Press, 2001), 69-70.
[24] Francis J. Caponi, "Gods and Friends: C. S. Lewis on Divinization," *Expositions: Interdisciplinary Studies in the Humanities* 4, nos. 1-2 (2010): 71.

to achieve divinization. Lewis affirms, "God saves different souls in different ways"—a view he believed was supported by Scripture. As with the performance of miracles, Jesus did not use a uniform method to save his disciples, although he called each to follow him. Elsewhere Lewis observes that some conversions are sharp and dramatic, such as those of the apostle Paul, Augustine, and John Bunyan, whereas others are more gradual, such as his own and, we might add, John Henry Newman's. Lewis stated that it would be dangerous to expect spiritual lives, especially of our loved ones, to "conform to some ready-made pattern of our own."[25] Lewis had an aversion to the theological proclivity of elaborating procedures of salvation or sanctification in which this must precede that because such an approach assumes that how an individual finds God is more important than how God finds that individual. The latter, for Lewis, is infinitely more significant than the former.

"To preach instantaneous conversion," writes Lewis, "and eternal security as if they must be the experiences of all who are saved, seems to me [very] dangerous: the very way to drive some into presumption and others into despair."[26] While those who have not had these experiences can come to lose all hope, others who think they have had them can become arrogant and even complacent about their redemption and deification. A further problem with this internalist approach is that, to no small extent, it depends on introspection to identify the relevant psychological and spiritual indicators of conversion and deification. But what exactly does either *feel* like? What specific sensations are associated with eternal security? What particular cognitions are necessarily linked to deification? For Lewis, these questions are misleading because, as he learned the hard way, introspection is notoriously unreliable when applied to spiritual matters. Part of the reason he abandoned his childhood faith in his early adolescence was his failed attempt to methodize his spiritual life using introspection. He recounts in *Surprised by Joy* the sincere but devastating mistake:

> No clause of my prayer was to be allowed to pass muster unless it was accompanied by what I called a "realisation," by which I meant a certain

---

[25]C. S. Lewis, *Collected Letters*, ed. Walter Hooper (London: HarperCollins, 2000–2006), 3:576. See also *Collected Letters* 2:824.
[26]Lewis, *Collected Letters* 3:1337.

vividness of the imagination and the affections. My nightly task was to produce by sheer will-power a phenomenon which will-power could never produce, which was so ill-defined that I could never say with absolute confidence whether it had occurred, and which, even when it did occur, was of very mediocre spiritual value.[27]

Lewis committed the same error he later warns readers about in the *Screwtape Letters*, where Wormwood is to encourage his "Patient" to evaluate the success of any prayer by the feelings or mental states that accompany it, which is what Lewis did every evening alone in his room at Cherbourg.[28] Unlike Bios, which can be measured, quantified, and controlled, Zoe—the begotten, spiritual life of the Godhead—is not susceptible to techniques of human manipulation. The attempt to evaluate Zoe by methods appropriate to Bios made "religion a quite intolerable burden" for Lewis, which motivated his deconversion.

Lewis later realized that methodological approaches in general, and introspection in particular, are counterproductive, if not outright harmful, to the spiritual life because "we are not always aware of things at the time they happen."[29] Consider the following two descriptions about his conversion:

> It is as if I were carried sleeping across the frontier, or as if I had died in the old country and could never remember how I came alive in the new.[30]

> It was more like when a man, after long sleep, still lying motionless in bed, becomes aware that he is now awake.[31]

In the first, Lewis describes the conversion or baptism of his imagination upon reading George MacDonald's *Phantastes*, while the second describes his conversion from theism in general to Christianity in particular, his newfound conviction that Jesus Christ is God. In both pivotal conversions, Lewis was unaware of the specific time or nature of his transformation, which led him to state in a letter, "No, I don't for a moment think that conversion [that] can be fixed to a definite date is in the least necessary."[32] All Lewis knew was

---

[27]Lewis, *Surprised by Joy*, 61.
[28]See C. S. Lewis, *The Screwtape Letters* (New York: HarperOne, 1996), 17.
[29]Lewis, "Answers to Questions on Christianity," in *God in the Dock*, 53.
[30]Lewis, *Surprised by Joy*, 179.
[31]Lewis, *Surprised by Joy*, 237.
[32]Lewis, *Collected Letters* 3:490. Indeed, Alister McGrath has proven that Lewis did in fact misremember the date of his conversion. See McGrath, *C. S. Lewis—a Life: Eccentric Genius, Reluctant Prophet* (Wheaton, IL: Tyndale House, 2013), 143.

that a border was crossed, a state like sleep left behind, but the exact moment of the change eluded his consciousness. There was no single or set of experiences that specified the definite event. He refused to make such experiences or sensations normative for deification because the way God deals with each and every individual can itself be as unique as that individual. In short, Lewis does not want to circumscribe how God can awaken and draw people to himself. In this sense, God is as good but unpredictable as Aslan in Narnia.[33]

As with the incarnation and other doctrines, Lewis here seeks to shift attention from questions of the methodology of deification to its meaning and mysterious nature. It is less important to understand *how* deification works than it is to *be* deified, that is, to receive the eternal life God offers his children through Christ. For Lewis, imprecision about the former should never function as an excuse for indecision about the latter. Ultimately, becoming one with the divine nature of God should not be reduced to a specific technique.

## Divine Make-Believe

If Lewis affirms that deification cannot be reduced to a specific method, what practical bearing, if any, can the doctrine have for believers? The answer lies in the role that Lewis assigns to make-believe in the spiritual life. He articulates the condition under which pretending can become a spiritually formative practice in the fourth book of *Mere Christianity*, which, according to one author, "is where Lewis's appreciation for human divinization reaches its crescendo."[34] Lewis distinguishes between two kinds of pretending, one negative and one positive. The former kind is intentionally deceptive and hypocritical, "as when a man pretends he is going to help you instead of really helping you." The positive kind facilitates acquiring a good quality; it is one way to accomplish what Augustine preached: "to become what you are not yet."[35] Lewis notes, "Very often the only way to get a quality in reality is to start behaving as if you had it already."[36] Similarly, a decade before this was published, Lewis had Screwtape warn Wormwood, "All

---

[33]For an analysis of this theme in Lewis, see Rowan Williams, *The Lion's World: A Journey into the Heart of Narnia* (London: SPCK, 2012), 63.
[34]Meconi, "Mere Christianity," 14.
[35]Augustine, *The Works of St. Augustine: A Translation for the 21st Century—Sermons III/5*, ed. John Rotelle, trans. Edmund Hill (New York: New City, 1992), 126.
[36]Lewis, *Mere Christianity*, 188.

mortals tend to turn into the thing they are pretending to be."³⁷ A child becomes an adult by pretending to be an adult. By dressing up and playfully mimicking the movements of grownups, children practice and develop the very faculties necessary to grow up.

Josephine Gabelman points out that the childlike, which includes a natural propensity to make-believe, is an irreducible and central element of Christian faith and practice. In every canonical Gospel, Jesus enjoins his followers to enter the kingdom of God like children, giving soteriological value to a childlike posture. Gabelman argues that "the childlike is more than an analogy of peripheral significance to Christianity. . . . [It] is not just a phase in relationship with God, but the essential and abiding formula of that relationship."³⁸ This insight applies first to how Christ relates to the Father and second to how believers ought to relate to Christ. In the immanent Trinity, Jesus eternally relates to the Father through childlike sonship. As Lewis's literary mentor George MacDonald puts it, Christ "could never have been a child if he would ever have ceased to be a child. . . . Childhood belongs to the divine nature."³⁹ For Lewis, it is through childlike make-believe that Christians can participate in that divine nature of God.

Rather than fixating on whether we are in fact becoming more like Christ, Lewis affirms that we should act *as if* we were Christ, that we should pretend to be Christ—in the childlike, transformative sense of the term. He interprets the Lord's Prayer, which is a pattern for all prayer specifically but also the spiritual life generally, as an invitation to what he calls "divine makebelieve." When we say, "Our Father which art in heaven," Lewis suggests that we are putting ourselves in the place of Christ, acting and speaking *as if* we were Christ. This is, of course, nonsensical, if not "outrageous cheek," given how woefully unlike Christ believers should know themselves to be. Yet, through spiritual disciplines such as prayer, God invites us to clothe ourselves with Christ (see Rom 13:14). Speaking of the dance metaphor in *Perelandra*, Erik Eklund rightly notes that in "both dance and music it is grace

---

³⁷Lewis, *Screwtape Letters*, 50.
³⁸Josephine Gabelman, *A Theology of Nonsense* (Eugene, OR: Pickwick, 2016), 137.
³⁹George MacDonald, *Unspoken Sermons: Series I, II, & III—Complete and Unabridged* (Radford, VA: Wilder, 2008), 11-12.

which makes it possible for the various dancers and counterpoints to not only improvise, but also, and perhaps most importantly, to mimic."[40] The only choreography of the Great Dance that believers must follow is to let Christ take the lead, to mirror his movements, as a child at play mimics an adult. In this way, Lewis makes the spiritual discipline of *imitatio Christi* a matter of divine make-believe. In short, to be deified into *a* son of God, a man should pretend to be *the* Son of God.

This Lewisian insight about divine make-believe extends beyond spiritual practices such as prayer and imitation of Christ to the matter of doctrine itself. David Miller states, "Faith is make-believe. It is playing as if it were true."[41] He interprets the biblical definition of faith in Hebrews 11:1—"the substance of things hoped for, the evidence of things not seen" (NKJV)—as thinking and acting *as if* the unseen world were seen. Thus, make-believe can illuminate not only the process of deification, as understood by Lewis, but also what it means to have faith in the doctrine to begin with. The more Christians live as if the doctrine were true, as if the unseen transformation of Bios into Zoe were visible, the more they will come to believe in its truth and act accordingly. This is the practical bearing Lewis gives to the doctrine of deification.

## Conclusion

The preceding discussion has surveyed four Lewisian insights about the doctrine of deification: (1) that deification, God's "grand experiment," is the transformation of Bios to Zoe, which involves the animal nature of human beings as much as it does the soul; (2) that believers are deified to and through something like a Great Dance, a dynamic activity with and within God; (3) that deification is more like an art than a science, which means that it should not be reduced to a specific method, especially one based on introspection; and (4) that a practical implication of the doctrine involves divine make-believe, that through childlike pretending Christians can mimic the movements of Christ, following his lead in the Great Dance of deification.

---

[40]Eric Eklund, "Confessing Our Secrets: Liturgical Theōsis in the Thought of C. S. Lewis," *Journal of Inklings Studies* 10, no. 2 (2020): 122.
[41]David Miller, *Gods and Games: Toward a Theology of Play* (New York: World, 1970), 168.

There is much more that could be said about Lewis's theological approach to deification. For instance, at the end of his best-known sermon, "The Weight of Glory," Lewis touches on the interpersonal nature of the doctrine:

> It is a serious thing to live in a society of possible gods and goddesses, to remember that the dullest and most uninteresting person you talk to may one day be a creature which, if you saw it now, you would be strongly tempted to worship, or else a horror and a corruption such as you now meet, if at all, only in a nightmare. All day long we are, in some degree, helping each other to one or other of these destinations.[42]

Ultimately, Lewis challenges believers to recognize the potential for deification within each person, emphasizing the gravity of our interactions in shaping the destinies of fellow human beings. Elsewhere he illuminates the corporate and ecclesiological dimension of deification through his metaphor of a symphony, wherein the dynamic unity of diverse individuals, orchestrated by divine grace, forms a majestic composition that mirrors the harmony that deification requires.[43] Deification also intersects with Lewis's theological views of transposition, glory, friendship, transformative suffering, and Joy (as *Sehnsucht*). Future research can examine these areas further, offering a more comprehensive understanding of Lewis's perspective on the doctrine of deification.

---

[42]C. S. Lewis, *The Weight of Glory: And Other Addresses* (New York: HarperCollins, 1949), 47.
[43]See Lewis, *Problem of Pain*, 156.

# TOWARD an EVANGELICAL DOCTRINE of DEIFICATION

## Paul Copan

IN HIS *DE INCARNATIONE VERBI DEI*, fourth-century theologian Athanasius affirmed: "For the Son of God became man so that we might become God" (54.3). Such an affirmation may seem audacious to those in the Protestant tradition. It might be less so within the Roman Catholic tradition, as Thomas Aquinas himself used the language of *deification*.[1] But all the more, Eastern Orthodoxy has claimed divinization or deification or theosis as a doctrine that ends up connecting theology proper, Christology, anthropology, soteriology, and eschatology.

Robert Bowman refers to the Eastern Orthodox understanding of theosis as "monotheistic deification." He writes:

> It may surprise some to learn that a monotheistic doctrine of deification was taught by many of the church fathers, and is believed by many Christians today, including the entire Eastern Orthodox church. In keeping with monotheism, the Eastern orthodox do not teach that men will literally become "gods" (which would be polytheism). Rather, as did many of the church fathers, they teach that

---

[1] "Whereas as regards the attainment of the ultimate end, he says, and the thearchy, that is, the principal deity, of those things that are deified [*deificantur*]. For the rational creature is said to be deified [*deificari*] through this: that in his mode, he is united to God; such that deity principally applies to God himself, whereas secondarily and participatively to these who are deified [*deificantur*]." See Thomas Aquinas, *Commentary on the Book on the Divine Names of Blessed Denys* [Pseudo-Dionysius] 4.5, available at Aquinas Text Institute, https://aquinas.cc/la/en/~DeDivNom. See Daria Spezzano, *The Glory of God's Grace: Deification According to St. Thomas Aquinas*, Faith and Reason Studies in Catholic Theology and Philosophy (Ave Maria, FL: Ave Maria, 2015).

men are "deified" in the sense that the Holy Spirit dwells within Christian believers and transforms them into the image of God in Christ, eventually endowing them in the resurrection with immortality and God's perfect moral character.[2]

Theologian and contributor to this volume Carl Mosser observes: "As far as I am aware, no major Western theologian has ever repudiated the patristic concept of deification."[3]

As this book shows, the Protestant tradition has to some degree appropriated this language of divinization as being the goal of the believer—to be transformed from one degree of glory to another into the likeness of Christ (2 Cor 3:18). This volume also emphasizes the corporate dimension of theosis rather than a more individualized understanding. This is significant, as the Protestant Reformation's tradition highlights "the priesthood of all *believers*"—not "the believer" (see 1 Pet 2:9). This tradition of divinization by virtue of our union with the God-man, Jesus Christ, enables us to participate in the transforming divine life of the Trinity. As Jonathan Edwards notes, as we look to Jesus the Sun, we become transformed into little suns that reflect the glory of Christ.

In this more general essay, I note a few connected themes from biblical theology that carve out room for the doctrine of theosis, and then I point out key theotist voices within historical Protestantism who appropriate in some way or other—participation, divinization, deification—the longstanding Athanasian dictum.

## Biblical-Theological Themes

As we undertake the task of biblical theology, we can detect certain a certain connective tissue that draws together key themes.[4] We'll explore a few of the relevant ones.

***The image of God.*** In our discussion of deification, the image of God (e.g., Gen 1:26-28) is a significant hinge-concept that informs both the

---

[2]Robert M. Bowman Jr., "'Ye Are Gods?' Orthodox and Heretical Views on the Deification of Man," *Christian Research Journal* (Winter/Spring 1987): 18.
[3]Carl Mosser, "The Greatest Possible Blessing: Calvin and Deification," *SJT* 55, no. 1 (2002): 38.
[4]James M. Scott, "Jesus' Vision for the Restoration of Israel as the Basis for a Biblical Theology of the New Testament," in *Biblical Theology: Retrospect and Prospect*, ed. Scott J. Hafemann (Downers Grove, IL: InterVarsity Press, 2002), 129.

incarnation (Jn 1:1, 14) and theosis or divinization—that is, our becoming partakers of the divine nature (2 Pet 1:4) and participating in the eternal life of God through his Son (Jn 3:36; 1 Jn 5:12).

Regarding Christ's incarnation, F. F. Bruce observes, "It is because man in the creative order bears the image of his Creator that it was possible for the Son of God to become incarnate as man and in His humanity to display the glory of the invisible God."[5] Indeed, Christ is *the* image of the invisible God (2 Cor 3:18; 4:4; Col 1:15; Heb 1:1-4)—and thus the truest or archetypal human.

In a similar vein to Bruce, Thomas Morris makes the distinction in his *Logic of God Incarnate* between what is *essentially* or *fully* human (e.g., rationality) and what is *merely* or *commonly* human (e.g., sin). Morris argues that being essentially or fully human does not exclude the possibility of being divine. Christ's death, for instance, pertains to his *mere* humanity. But the qualities that are essential to being human are derived from God—a finite subset of certain divine qualities.

Indeed, just as the image of God makes the incarnation possible, so it makes the deification of redeemed humans possible by virtue of their union with Christ. In this divinization, humans do not ascend to the status of the eternally existent, self-sufficient Alpha and Omega. This is no breakdown of the Creator-creature distinction. Rather, humans share in the divine life of the Trinity graciously bestowed on them.

**Priest-kings.** The image of God has implications for us as his creatures: we have been called as priest-kings. For the original humans, being priests involved worshiping—walking or communing with—God in the temple-like sanctuary in Eden (Gen 3:8; see also Gen 5:22, 24; 6:9);[6] as kings, Adam and Eve were to wisely steward and rule over creation as co-regents with God. This included being fruitful, multiplying, and filling the earth (Gen 1:26-28). This point is reinforced in Psalm 8, especially Psalm 8:5: "You have made him a little lower than God [אֱלֹהִים], And You crown him with glory and majesty!" (NASB).

---

[5]F. F. Bruce and E. K. Simpson, *The Epistles of Paul to the Ephesians and to the Colossians* (Grand Rapids, MI: Eerdmans, 1957), 194.

[6]William J. Dumbrell, "Genesis 2:1-17: A Foreshadowing of the New Creation," in Hafemann, *Biblical Theology*, 61.

Humans were assigned the task of putting the finishing touches on God's creation and widening the boundary of God's sacred meeting place with humanity so that God's glory would fill all the earth.

**Table 11.1.** God's image-bearers on earth: Kings and priests

| Priestly Role | Kingly Role |
|---|---|
| Worshiping, communing, walking, and meeting with God as priests in the temple-garden at the center of God's creation | Ruling the earth with God, naming animals, being fruitful and multiplying, and extending God's glory |

Alas, human beings failed to carry out their vocation in leading a good creation to perfection.[7] They allowed the serpent to rule over them rather than their ruling over it.[8] Instead of *expanding* the divine presence in the earth, they were *expelled* from that blessed presence. Even so, Adam and Eve were the original priest-kings.

Ancient Israel was to carry on this vocation as a royal priesthood and holy nation (Ex 19:6). God called his son Israel out of Egypt (Hos 11:1), but the nation of Israel proved to be a disobedient son (Is 1:2-3; Hos 11:2). Thus the kingdom would be granted to a "people, producing the fruit of it" (Mt 21:43).[9] The New Testament picks up this emphasis on the priest-king. Christ in his incarnation, atoning death, and resurrection has come to restore humanity to that task. Christ himself comes to fallen humanity as a faithful high priest (Heb 2:17; 3:1; 4:14-15) and as king (Jn 1:49; 12:15; 18:37). He came to bring into existence a new people of God who would be a royal priesthood and a holy nation (1 Pet 2:9). Through the death of the Lamb, he will raise up a "kingdom and priests" who will "reign upon the earth" (Rev 5:10; see Rev 1:6; 20:4-6)—that is, in the completed new creation (Rev 21:1-2; 22:1-5). God's original intention for humanity to live out the divine image as priest-kings over all creation will finally be realized. So from the very beginning, the democratization of kingship is clear:

---

[7]John Goldingay, *Old Testament Theology: Israel's Story* (Downers Grove, IL: InterVarsity Press, 2003), 1:112.

[8]G. K. Beale, *The Temple and the Church's Mission* (Downers Grove, IL: InterVarsity Press, 2004), 81-87.

[9]Unless otherwise indicated, Scripture quotations in this chapter are from the NASB 1995. Unless otherwise noted, italics in Scripture from the NASB 1995 are original, not the author's emphasis.

we are intended to rule God's creation with him.[10] As N. T. Wright observes, "We are made for God: for God's glory, to worship God and reflect his likeness."[11]

***Two central images: The second Adam and the true Israel.*** The New Testament takes up two central images that inform what Christ came to accomplish as the inaugurator of the new creation and the new exodus. Jesus—the true image of God—is the new (or second) Adam, who came to reverse what the first Adam had done and to bring about a new creation and a new humanity (Rom 5:12-19; 1 Cor 15:20-28; 2 Cor 5:17). Jesus is also the true Israel—the obedient Son that national Israel was not (Mt 2:15; 3:17). Jesus fulfills what both Adam and national Israel should have been, living out Adam's and Israel's story, restoring creation and leading his people out of bondage to sin and Satan as a newly gathered covenant people of God.[12]

As the image of God, Jesus brings creation and redemption together (Jn 1:1-18; Col 1:15-20). He is the archetypal human and the truest Israelite. William Dumbrell writes:

> Genesis 2 sets the basic course of biblical eschatology [the end of times]. The biblical movement is from creation and the Fall to the creation of Israel and its fall, to Christ as representative Israel, to the new Israel in Christ putting into effect Israel's mission to the new creation, to the final, full complement of the redeemed people of God who are kings and priests in the new creation. Thus in Genesis 2 we find a preliminary picture of the end of the age, in which redeemed humanity experiences [everlasting] and indefectible fellowship with the Creator. Temple theology, which attests to the sovereign presence of God with his people, takes its rise in Eden.[13]

**Table 11.2.** New Adam/true Israel: Creation and covenant

| Creation | Covenant |
| --- | --- |
| As the new **Adam**, Christ is the head of a new **humanity**. | As the true **Israel**, Christ (the beloved Son of God) is head of a renewed covenant (chosen) people. |
| Christ **reverses the curse** and brings about a **restored creation**. | Christ (as portrayed at his baptism) leads a new people out of bondage in **a new exodus**. |

---

[10]Goldingay, *Old Testament Theology* 1:100.
[11]N. T. Wright, *The Challenge of Jesus* (Downers Grove, IL: InterVarsity Press, 1999), 16.
[12]See N. T. Wright, *Paul* (Minneapolis: Fortress, 2005).
[13]Dumbrell, "Genesis 2:1-17," 64-65.

***The one and the many: The individual and the corporate.*** We see this new creation (new Adam/new man) and new covenant language (Israel/Son) in both individual and corporate terms. First, consider our *corporate identity with Christ as part of the new creation and the new exodus*. Romans 6:6 brings both of these together: "Our old man [in Adam] was crucified with him that our body of sin might be rendered inoperative that we should no longer be slaves to sin [in the new exodus]." The "old man" should not be translated in individualistic terms—namely, as the "old self" (NIV). This refers to our fallen humanity and past status in Adam, the "first man" (1 Cor 15:45, 47).[14] This status stands in contrast to "the one man Jesus Christ" (Rom 5:15), who is also called "the last man" (1 Cor 15:45). Romans 5:19 states: "Through the one man's [Adam's] disobedience the many were made sinners," and Romans 5:15 speaks of another man, "much more did the grace of God and the gift by the grace of the one Man, Jesus Christ, abound to the many." These two men are representative heads of two races—the unredeemed and the redeemed, respectively. In light of Christ's death, there is *no middle ground* with God: one is either (1) "in Adam" (the old man) or (2) "in Christ" (the new man). Before we were believers in Christ, we were all "in Adam."[15]

To be "in Christ" or in the "new man" means the redeemed is a solidarity of people whose destinies have been wholly affected by Jesus' work on the cross. We are part of a corporate new man, whose head is Christ (1 Cor 15:47; Eph 2:14-15; 4:22; Col 3:9-11). We are called to grow up into "a mature man, to the measure of the stature which belongs to the fullness of Christ" and "grow up in all *aspects* into Him who is the head, *even* Christ, from whom the whole body, being fitted and held together by what every joint supplies, according to the proper working of each individual part, causes the growth of the body for the building up of itself in love" (Eph 4:13, 15-16). Paul affirms

---

[14]As Carl B. Hoch Jr. writes, "It is unfortunate that the NIV has translated 'old man' as 'old self' in [Rom 6:6]. This makes the old man individualistic and ontic. The term, rather, is corporate and relational. The aorist passive [of 'crucified'] does not mean that the 'old self' continues to stir men and women to sin as in the 'two natures doctrine' but that the old relationship in Adam was abrogated by Christ's work on the cross." See Hoch, "The New Man of Ephesians 2," in *Dispensationalism, Israel, and the Church*, ed. Craig Blaising and Darrell Bock (Grand Rapids, MI: Zondervan, 1992), 117.

[15]See Douglas J. Moo, *The Epistle to the Romans* (Grand Rapids, MI: Eerdmans 1996), 372-76.

both the one and the many—individuals belong to one or another grouping under one of two heads, either "in Adam" or "in Christ."

Carrying over from the first point, we can add, second, that Scripture reveals *a strongly corporate language of reigning over creation with Christ*. In addition, by virtue of our union with Christ, who is seated at God's right hand in the heavenly places above all angelic powers (Eph 1:20-21), we too share in the reign of Christ in those heavenly places (Eph 2:6). Earlier, Jesus told his disciples, "Do not be afraid, little flock, for your Father has chosen gladly to give you the kingdom" (Lk 12:32). And to John the Seer Jesus himself proclaimed coregency with his people: "He who overcomes, I will grant to him to sit down with Me on My throne, as I also overcame and sat down with My Father on His throne" (Rev 3:21).

This corporate understanding of reigning with Christ is rooted in Old Testament texts like Daniel 7, where we see the Son of Man is "given . . . a kingdom" just as the saints of the Most High "receive the kingdom and possess the kingdom forever" with the Son of Man:

> I saw in the night visions,
> and behold, with the clouds of heaven
>     there came one like a son of man,
> and he came to the Ancient of Days
>     and was presented before him.
> And to him was given dominion
>     and glory and a kingdom,
> that all peoples, nations, and languages
>     should serve him;
> his dominion is an everlasting dominion,
>     which shall not pass away,
> and his kingdom one
>     that shall not be destroyed. (Dan 7:13-14 ESV)

> But the saints of the Most High shall receive the kingdom and possess the kingdom forever, forever and ever. (Dan 7:18 ESV)

Third, we could add an *individual-corporate dimension* in Isaiah's Servant Songs (Is 40–55), which highlight the theme of an *anticipated new exodus*. In some places, the Servant appears to be the nation of Israel—the "servant"

Jacob is also the "worm" Jacob (Is 41:8, 14). But we also see an individual Servant, who bears with the sins and rebellion of Israel. He would be "a tender shoot . . . like a root out of parched ground"; he would be "despised and forsaken . . . a man of sorrows" who will "sprinkle many nations" (Is 53:2-3; 52:15). Isaiah already anticipates an individual messianic rescuer who is coming (in Is 9; 11). Furthermore, consider the "plant" language of Isaiah 53. This language ("tender shoot"/"root") sounds looks very much like what other prophets say about the Messiah:

- Jeremiah 23:5: "I will raise up for David a righteous Branch [צֶמַח]; And He will reign as king" with "justice and righteousness," which sounds like Isaiah 9:7; 11:4-5.
- Jeremiah 33:15: "I will cause a righteous Branch [צֶמַח] of David to spring forth."
- Ezekiel 17:22-23: "I will also take a *sprig* from the lofty top of the cedar. . . . I will plant *it* on a high and lofty mountain . . . that it may . . . bear fruit. . . . Birds of every kind will nest under it."
- Zechariah 6:12: "a man whose name is Branch [צֶמַח] . . . will build the temple of the LORD."

This fits in with Jesus as the true Israel, as God's Son who is the corporate head of the new people of God, the true or genuine and fruitful vine that Israel was not (Jn 15:1; see Ps 80:8; Is 5:1-7). By believers' abiding in Christ, the true vine, they will bear fruit (Jn 15:1-8).

Thus, in Isaiah, the Servant *is* Israel (Is 49:3), but his mission is *to* Israel (Is 49:5-6). David's son is the *representative Israelite*, yet *he is true Israel while serving Israel* ("I will be a father to him and he will be a son to Me" [2 Sam 7:14]).[16]

In this section, we have taken a looked at certain related themes in biblical theology—the image of God, the priest-king motif, the Adam-Israel language appropriated by New Testament authorities—and the individual-corporate language found in union-with-Christ texts that highlight how believers share in the status and privileges of Christ the God-man.

---

[16]Taken from Michael L. Brown, "Jewish Interpretations of Isaiah 53," in *The Gospel According to Isaiah 53*, ed. Darrell L. Bock and Mitch Glaser (Grand Rapids, MI: Kregel, 2012), 62-63; Graeme Goldsworthy, *According to Plan* (Downers Grove, IL: InterVarsity Press, 2001), 191.

## A Protestant Theosis Tradition

For over a decade, I have been in conversation with a group of orthodox Christians that both reflects the stamp of Protestantism but also has incorporated the language of theosis into its tradition—namely, "the local churches" founded by Watchman Nee and furthered by his successor, Witness Lee. Their publishing arm is Living Stream Ministry. A number of its representatives have been trained at evangelical institutions and are members of the Evangelical Theological Society, whose doctrinal statement affirms the doctrine of the Trinity. As mentioned in the introduction, I have copresented papers with one of its members, Chris Wilde, in two annual Evangelical Theological Society meetings (2015 and 2016). More recently (November 2022), I chaired a string of presentations on deification, and these presentations are included in the book. Some of these presenters belong to the local churches tradition.

Living Stream Ministry and the apologetics group Defense and Confirmation Project have jointly published statements affirming the common faith aligned with evangelical/biblical orthodoxy. A growing number of evangelicals have extended the right hand of fellowship to them.[17] Indeed, true evangelicals could readily sign their seven-point doctrinal statement, which looks like a standard document at any respected evangelical institution.[18] While evangelicals may disagree here and there with certain views held by the local churches, the local churches are certainly within the mainstream of Protestant evangelicalism. Indeed, they more readily embrace the language of Athanasius than most of us evangelicals typically do: "For He was made man that we might be made God" (Αὐτὸς γὰρ ἐνηνθρώπησεν, ἵνα ἡμεῖς θεοποιηθῶμεν, *Inc.* 54.3).

The sometimes-misunderstood language of theosis in Witness Lee's theology—and his soteriology in particular—can be clarified and also defended. The kinds of charges that critics have leveled against Lee could potentially be made against Isaiah and Paul, if we are to be consistent: the anticipated

---

[17] See "Dialogues with Other Christians," Contending for the Faith, https://contendingforthefaith.org/en/dialogues-with-other-christians/ (accessed February 18, 2024), and "An Open Letter From the Local Churches and Living Stream Ministry Concerning the Teachings of Witness Lee," https://an-open-letter.org/en/ets-eps-papers/ (accessed February 18, 2024).

[18] See Defense and Confirmation Project's Contending for the Faith website: https://contendingforthefaith.org/en/.

Messiah is called "everlasting Father" (Is 9:6), and "the Lord" is called "the Spirit" (2 Cor 3:17). Moreover, the doctrine of deification espoused by the local churches maintains a clear ontological distinction between the divine Trinity and human beings, between Creator and creature. As we have seen, this stands in contrast to, say, Mormon theology, in which Creator and human beings are on a continuum rather than being ontologically distinct.

Now, Eastern Orthodoxy acknowledges that we do not share in the "essence" of God—namely, "the substance, nature and being of God." Rather, we share in the "energies" of God—"that which radiates from the hidden essence or nature of God."[19] Commenting on 2 Peter 1:4, Richard Bauckham points out that for us to be "sharers [κοινωνοί] of divine nature" is to be divine only in the loose sense; by God's grace we become God*like*: "To share in the divine nature is to become immortal and incorruptible."[20] Indeed, we are called to "imitators of God" himself (Eph 5:1). By participating in the life of God, we come to share in his glory through his grace. Perhaps we could compare this to the moon's receiving or reflecting the sun's glory—that when we walk in a manner worthy of our calling, "the name of our Lord Jesus will be glorified in you, and you in Him, according to the grace of our God and the Lord Jesus Christ" (2 Thess 1:12).

The majority of Protestant evangelicals would shrink from using Athanasius's theotic language of "becoming God," declaring that such language is not sufficiently explicit in biblical texts. They would more readily appropriate the explicit language of being "in Christ," "united with Christ," "hidden with Christ in God," and being "transformed into the image of Christ."

Just as Protestant theologians have not condemned Eastern Orthodoxy as heretical on this score, neither should they speak against Lee and the local churches.[21] Now, some evangelical Protestants who readily affirm Eastern Orthodoxy's theosis as theologically acceptable have criticized Witness Lee for teaching theosis in language that turns out to be quite balanced. For

---

[19]Kallistos Ware, in *The Orthodox Study Bible: New Testament and Psalms*, ed. Peter E. Gillquist, Alan Wallerstedt, and Joseph Allen (Nashville: Thomas Nelson, 1993), 797.
[20]Richard Bauckham, *Jude, 2 Peter*, Word Biblical Commentary 50 (Waco, TX: Word, 1983), 181. I would disagree, however, with Bauckham's claim that this language is "inherited from Hellenistic religion."
[21]For a lengthy discussion, see Mosser, "Greatest Possible Blessing."

example, Norman Geisler and Ron Rhodes rightly affirm as orthodox the doctrine of theosis in Eastern Orthodoxy: "Eastern Orthodox call this process [of sanctification] 'Christification' or 'deification,' not to be confused with the New Age pantheistic belief that we can actually come to realize that we are God. Nor is sanctification to be confused with the Mormon idea that believers may become gods in the world to come."[22]

However, in joining a 2007 call for Living Stream Ministry and the local churches to disavow Lee's deification language, Geisler and Rhodes did not treat that language in the same way they did Eastern Orthodoxy's.[23] Living Stream Ministry and the local churches have taken great care in responding to these criticisms, showing that the document Geisler and Rhodes signed is selective in its citations and simply ignores many of Lee's defenses and clarifications.[24]

I could add that Geisler and Rhodes make the additional claim that Lee is heretical for calling God "a person"; after all, God is tripersonal. But is this a fair charge? Not at all. Noted orthodox Christians such as Alvin Plantinga, J. P. Moreland, Martyn Lloyd-Jones, and Billy Graham have referred to God as "a person." Ironically, even Geisler and Rhodes *themselves* occasionally refer to God as "a person" in their writings![25]

But enough of these preliminaries. Let me bring in some noted Protestant thinkers who use this language of theosis. This is just a sampling of what some other chapters in this book draw out at great length.

---

[22]Norman Geisler and Ron Rhodes, *Conviction Without Compromise* (Eugene, OR: Harvest House, 2008), 279.

[23]"An Open Letter to the Leadership of Living Stream Ministry and the 'Local Churches,'" 2007, www.open-letter.org; also see Defense and Confirmation Project, *A Confirmation of the Gospel: Concerning the Teachings of the Local Churches and Living Stream Ministry* (Fullerton, CA: DCP, 2009); Defense and Confirmation Project, *A Defense of the Gospel: Responses to an Open Letter from "Christian Scholars and Ministry Leaders"* (1) (Fullerton, CA: DCP, 2009). The contents of these two books are also available at lctestimony.org/OpenLetterDialogue.html.

[24]Defense and Confirmation Project, *A Defense of the Gospel: Responses to an Open Letter from "Christian Scholars and Ministry Leaders"* (2) (Fullerton, CA: DCP, 2010). The Christian Research Institute also wrote on this subject in its reassessment of the teachings of Witness Lee and the local churches. See Christian Research Institute, "Part 2: Addressing the Open Letter's Concerns: On the Nature of Humanity," *Christian Research Journal* 32, no. 6 (2009): 24-31.

[25]See various citations of Geisler and Rhodes in Defense and Confirmation Project, *Brothers, Hear Our Defense: Concerning the Trinity* (Fullerton, CA: DCP, 2011), 24-25. The entire volume addresses the criticisms of Geisler and Rhodes.

### Evangelical/Protestant Theotists

Earlier we cited Robert Bowman in his affirmation of theosis as consistent with Christian orthodoxy. However, he himself finds the language of humans as "gods" to be problematic; some theotists will appeal to the affirmation in Psalm 82:6 that "you are gods," but Bowman considers this to be unbiblical, inconsistent, and confusing, as it smacks of polytheism. He acknowledges, though, that "the substance of what the Eastern Orthodox are seeking to express when they speak of deification is actually faithful to the monotheistic world view." As such, the view is not heretical, as it would condemn theologians such as Athanasius and Augustine and the Christian branch of Eastern Orthodoxy.[26]

But more than this, it would condemn stalwart pillars of Protestantism as well. Who are these? Let me give just a sampling below.

**Martin Luther.** Luther, who was as good a Protestant as any, followed the logic and language of Athanasius in a 1526 sermon: "God pours out Christ His dear Son over us and pours Himself into us and draws us into Himself, so that He becomes completely humanified [*ganz und gar vermenschet wird*] and we become completely deified [*ganz und gar vergottet werden*] and everything is altogether one thing, God, Christ, and you."[27] Earlier, in a Christmas sermon in 1515, Luther declared:

> As the Word became flesh, so it is certainly necessary that the flesh should also become Word. For just for this reason does the Word become flesh, in order that the flesh might become Word. In other words: God becomes man, in order that man should become God [*Deus fit homo, ut homo fiat Deus*]. Thus strength becomes weak in order that weakness might become strong. The Logos puts on our form and figure and image and likeness, in order that He might clothe us with His image, form, likeness. Thus wisdom becomes foolish, in order that foolishness might become wisdom, and so in all other things which are in God and us, in all of which He assumes ours in order to confer upon us His [things] We who are flesh are made Word not by being substantially changed into the Word, but by taking it on [*assumimus*] and uniting it to ourselves by faith, on account of which union we are said not only to have but even to be the Word.[28]

---

[26] Bowman, "'Ye Are Gods?,'" 18.
[27] WA 20:229, 30; translation cited in Kurt E. Marquardt, "Luther and Theosis," *Concordia Theological Quarterly* 64, no. 3 (July 2000): 185.
[28] WA 1:28; translation cited in Marquart, "Luther and Theosis," 186-87.

And again, Luther writes: "Faith makes a man God"; and Luther reasons as follows: "The one who has faith is a completely divine man, a son of God, the inheritor of the universe.... Therefore the Abraham who has faith fills heaven and earth; thus every Christian fills heaven and earth by his faith."[29]

Here is another mention in a 1525 sermon:

> And that we are so filled with "all the fulness of God," that is said in the Hebrew manner, meaning that we are filled in every way in which He fills, and become full of God, showered with all gifts and grace and filled with His Spirit, Who is to make us bold, and enlighten us with His light, and live His life in us, that His bliss make us blest, His love awaken love in us. In short, that everything that He is and can do, be fully in us and mightily work, that we be completely deified [*vergottet*], not that we have a particle or only some pieces of God, but all fulness. Much has been written about how man should be deified; there they made ladders, on which one should climb into heaven, and much of that sort of thing. Yet it is sheer piecemeal effort; but here [in faith] the right and closest way to get there is indicated, that you become full of God, that you lack in no thing, but have everything in one heap, that everything that you speak, think, walk, in sum, your whole life be completely divine [*gottisch*].[30]

**John Calvin.** Calvin was well aware of the doctrine of deification and appropriated it in his own writings.[31] Calvin in his commentary on 2 Peter uses lofty language about believers being "partakers of the divine nature." He says, "Let us then mark, that the end of the gospel is, to render us eventually conformable [*conformes*] to God, and, if we may so speak, to deify [*quasi deificare*] us." Calvin qualifies what he means: "The word nature is not here essence but quality," which Calvin takes to mean not that God's nature "swallows up our nature" but rather that "we shall be partakers of divine and blessed immortality and glory, so as to be as it were one with God as far as our capacities will allow."[32]

In the 1545 version of the *Institutes of the Christian Religion*, Calvin affirms that we are "made one substance with him" and that "daily he more and more unites himself to us in one, same substance." This conjoining of

---

[29] *WA* 40 I:182, 390; translation cited in Marquart, "Luther and Theosis," 191.
[30] *WA* 17 1:438; translation cited in Marquart, "Luther and Theosis," 196-97.
[31] For a lengthy discussion, see Mosser, "Greatest Possible Blessing."
[32] John Calvin, *Commentaries on the Catholic Epistles*, trans. and ed. John Owen (repr., Grand Rapids, MI: Baker, 1996), 371.

divine and human substances was later removed in the 1559 edition of the *Institutes*.[33] This kind of language is used for sharing in the "substance of Christ," but again Calvin is not speaking of the mixing of divine and human substances, but speaks more of "participation," "communion," and "putting on Christ"—of being engrafted into Christ's body.[34]

**Jonathan Edwards.** While it does not appear that Edwards ever read Gregory Palamas's *On the Divine and Deifying Participation* or other such works of Eastern Orthodoxy, he does use theotic language. Though he does not refer to *deification* or *divinization*, he uses the language of participation in the glory of God, being increasingly transformed to higher degrees of glory toward God's perfect likeness, eternally progressive union, and so on. In his work *The End for Which God Created the World*, Edwards writes:

> There are many reasons to think that what God has in view, in an increasing communication of himself through eternity, is an increasing knowledge of God, love to him, and joy in him. And it is to be considered, that *the more those divine communications increase in the creature, the more it becomes one with God*: for so much the more is it united to God in love, the heart is drawn nearer and nearer to God, and the union with him becomes more firm and close: and, at the same time, the creature becomes more and more conformed to God. *The image is more and more perfect, and so the good that is in the creature comes for ever nearer and nearer to an identity with that which is in God.*[35]

Edwards adds:

> In this view, those elect creatures which must be looked upon as the end of all the rest of the creation, considered with respect to the whole of their eternal duration, and as such made God's end, must be viewed as being, as it were, one with God. They were respected as brought home to him, united with him, centering most perfectly in him, and as it were *swallowed up in him*: so that his respect to them *finally coincides and becomes one and the same with respect*

---

[33]See David Willis-Watkins, "The Unio Mystica and the Assurance of Faith According to Calvin," in *Calvin: Erbe und Auftrag*, ed. Willem van't Spijker (Kampen: Kok Pharos, 1991), 80. But see also James Weiss, "Calvin Versus Osiander on Justification," *The Springfielder* 30 (1965): 31-47; Clive S. Chin, "Calvin, Mystical Union, and Spirituality," *Torch Trinity Journal* 6 (2006): 183-209.
[34]John Calvin, *Commentary on Galatians, Ephesians, Philippians, Colossians*, trans. John Owen (Edinburgh: Calvin Translation Society, 1843), 209.
[35]WJE 8:443, emphasis added.

*to himself*. The interest of the creature is, as it were, God's own interest, in proportion to the degree of their relation and union to God.[36]

A further quotation by Edwards reflects this deification theme:

> As the creature's good was viewed in this manner when God made the world for it, viz. with respect to the whole of the eternal duration of it, and the eternally progressive union and communion with him; so the creature must be viewed as in infinite strict union with himself. In this view it appears that God's respect to the creature, in the whole, unites with his respect to himself. Both regards are like two lines which seem at the beginning to be separate, but aim finally to meet in one, both being directed to the same center. And as to the good of the creature itself, if viewed in its whole duration, and infinite progression, it must be viewed as infinite; and so not only being some communication of God's glory, but as coming nearer and nearer to the same thing in its infinite fullness. The nearer anything comes to infinite, the nearer it comes to an identity with God. And *if any good, as viewed by God, is beheld as infinite, it can't be viewed as a distinct thing from God's own infinite glory.*[37]

So strong is this theme in Edwards that he says some things that, according to Princetonian Charles Hodge and others, border on the pantheistic (i.e., everything is God; God is identical to all that exists; God is altogether immanent).[38] However, scholars such as Oliver Crisp consider Edwards to be more panentheistic (i.e., all is in God; God is in all). In this particular version of panentheism, God and the world are distinct; the universe is entirely dependent on, and even emanating from, God.[39] This view was influenced by the idealist and emanationist Plotinus, filtered through Cambridge Platonist Henry More and Reformed theology.[40] However Edwards's view is to be teased out, the following expressions suggest the theme of theosis:

---

[36] WJE 8:443, emphasis added.
[37] Edwards, *Ethical Writings*, 459, emphasis added. See also Kyle Strobel, "Jonathan Edwards and the Polemics of Theosis," *Harvard Theological Review* (July 2012): 259-79.
[38] For a nuanced discussion of concurrence, idealism, pantheism, and the other themes associated with Edwards, see Nathan J. Archer, "Inscrutable Providence: The Doctrine of Divine Concurrence and the Theology of Charles Hodge" (PhD diss., Calvin Theological Seminary, 2015), https://digitalcommons.calvin.edu/cts_dissertations/4.
[39] On the varieties of panentheism, see John W. Cooper, *Panentheism: The Other God of the Philosophers: From Plato to the Present* (Grand Rapids, MI: Baker Academic, 2006).
[40] Oliver Crisp, "On the Orthodoxy of Jonathan Edwards," *SJT* 67, no. 3 (2014): 304-22.

"more and more conformed to God . . . more and more perfect . . . nearer and nearer to an identity with that which is in God," "swallowed up in him," and "infinite strict union."

**John and Charles Wesley.** John Wesley is known for his theology of Christian perfection, drawn from passages such as Matthew 5:48 and 2 Peter 1:4. His hymn-writing brother Charles held to a variation on this theme. Both of them draw on the long-standing tradition of deification. Charles's hymn "Since the Son Hath Made Me Free" reflects this doctrine of theosis:

> Heavenly Adam, life divine,
> Change my nature into thine;
> Move and spread throughout my soul,
> Actuate and fill the whole;
> Be it I no longer now
> Living in the flesh, but thou.

And in "Let Heaven and Earth Combine":

> He deigns in flesh to appear,
> Widest extremes to join;
> To bring our vileness near,
> And make us all divine:
> And we the life of God shall know,
> For God is manifest below.

And again in "All-Wise, All-Good, Almighty Lord":

> Didst thou not in thy person join
> The natures human and divine,
> That God and man might be
> Henceforth inseparably one?
> Haste then, and make thy nature known
> Incarnated in me.

**C. S. Lewis.** Citing Psalm 82:6 and John 10:30, Lewis uses the language of deification in his *Mere Christianity*:

> God said that we were "gods" and he is going to make good His words. If we let Him . . . He will make the feeblest and filthiest of us into a god or goddess, dazzling, radiant, immortal creatures, pulsating all through with such energy

and joy and wisdom and love as we cannot now imagine, a bright stainless mirror which reflects back to Him perfectly.[41]

In addition to all of these, we could add other contemporary scholars who are evangelical Protestants (aside from contributors to this book) who view deification as an appropriate biblical inference. Consider Old Testament scholar Iain Provan, who comments on Psalm 8's affirmation of the human as being "a little lower than God": "He is a divine king, this human being, and he plays a crucial role in the cosmos. . . . Each and every individual has been raised to the status of *divinity and royalty* from the status only of a *slave*." Following Hamlet, Provan says, "'How like a God' . . . is the human person." And again, "If there are gods in the cosmos apart from God, they are women as well as men. The divine image that is to rule in the temple-cosmos is male *and* female."[42] Earlier, evangelical theologian Robert Rakestraw reminds and admonishes us in the *Journal of the Evangelical Theological Society*:

> While the concept of theosis has roots in the ante-Nicene period, it is not an antiquated historical curiosity. The idea of divinization, of redeemed human nature somehow participating in the very life of God, is found to a surprising extent throughout Christian history, although it is practically unknown to the majority of Christians (and even many theologians) in the west. . . . With the growing interest in Eastern Orthodox/evangelical rapprochement it is essential that theosis studies be pursued. Evangelicals may receive considerable benefit from a clear understanding and judicious appropriation of the doctrine.[43]

I could add more such quotations—and the essays in this book certainly do the job. However, I hope this sufficiently shows that this deification language ranging from Athanasius through Luther, Calvin, Edwards, the Wesleys, Lewis, and Witness Lee not only is embraced by the Eastern Orthodox but is also used by certain theological heroes of Protestantism. As we look in our Protestant theological side mirrors, this doctrine of deification is closer than it appears.

---

[41] C. S. Lewis, *Mere Christianity* (New York: Macmillan, 1952), 174-75.
[42] Iain Provan, *Seriously Dangerous Religion* (Waco, TX: Baylor University Press, 2014), 84, 93.
[43] Robert V. Rakestraw, "Becoming Like God: An Evangelical Doctrine of Theosis," *JETS* 40, no. 2 (June 1997): 257.

PART 3

# CONSTRUCTIVE INVESTIGATIONS *into the* DOCTRINE *of* DEIFICATION

# DEIFICATION *as a* THEOLOGICAL FOUNDATION *and* GOAL *for* FORMATIONAL THEOLOGICAL EDUCATION

BRIAN SIU KIT CHIU

CONTEMPORARY YALE UNIVERSITY THEOLOGIAN Willie James Jennings (1961– ) holds that, just like any other form of education, the nature of theological education lies in a process of formation.[1] The Christian use of the word *formation* has its origin in the New Testament, which refers to the process of Christ growing to maturity in his believers.[2] In Galatians 4:19, Paul compares his suffering for the Galatians' spiritual growth to giving birth: "Until Christ is formed [μορφωθῇ] in you," the word μορφόω meaning "give shape to, mold, fashion."[3] Theological education aims at facilitating the process of the formation of God's people through educating them in biblical truth and the knowledge and wisdom of God, with the goal of presenting every believer as "full-grown in Christ" (Col 1:28).[4] As believers are maturing, they are able to participate in the building of Christ's body by

---

[1] Willie James Jennings, *After Whiteness: An Education in Belonging* (Grand Rapids, MI: Eerdmans, 2020), 4-5.
[2] Evan B. Howard, *A Guide to Christian Spiritual Formation: How Scripture, Spirit, Community, and Mission Shape Our Souls* (Grand Rapids, MI: Baker Academic, 2018), 4.
[3] William D. Mounce, *Mounce's Complete Expository Dictionary of Old and New Testament Words* (Grand Rapids, MI: Zondervan, 2006), 1214.
[4] See Fritz Deininger, "Foundations for Curriculum Design in Theological Education," in *Leadership in Theological Education*, vol. 2, *Foundations for Curriculum Design*, ed. Fritz Deininger and Orbelina Eguizabal (Carlisle, UK: Langham, 2017), 27.

becoming the very gifts (the gifted ones) whom the resurrected and ascended Christ bestows on the church, "toward the perfecting of the saints unto the work of the ministry, unto the building up of the body of Christ, until we all may attain to the oneness of the faith and of the full knowledge of the Son of God, to a full-grown man, to the measure of the stature of the fullness of Christ" (Eph 4:12-13, literal translation). Hence, theological education should not be viewed merely as professional training that offers practical courses or as an academic program that focuses solely on intellectual development. Theological education should be viewed more as a process of spiritual formation. The nature of theological education is to nurture the lives of believers, helping them mature in their understanding of the Son of God so that they can be fully equipped to fulfill their purpose and contribute to the building and unity of the body of Christ.

## The Modern History of Protestant Theological Education in the West

The development of theological education in the West spans nearly two millennia. However, during the initial fifteen centuries of church history, the church did not rely on organized institutions like today's theological seminaries to provide specialized theological education. The concept of theological seminaries gradually emerged much later, after the Reformation, and they were established to meet the need for training clergy.[5] In reviewing the history of Protestant theological education, Justo González points out that the Western theological disciplines in the modern age were modeled after the German theological education model in Berlin.[6] Ironically, German Pietists such as Philipp Spener (1635–1705) and August Francke (1663–1727), who are more central to the personal/spiritual formation of the clergy, were instrumental in the rise of theology in its modern sense of a specialized discipline in the eighteenth century.[7] To correct the overly scholastic and rational approach to theology, Pietists introduced, in addition to personal/

---

[5] Justo L. González, *The History of Theological Education* (Nashville: Abingdon, 2015), 117.
[6] González, *History of Theological Education*, 105-8, 110-11, 115.
[7] Philipp Spener, *Pia Desideria: Or, Heartfelt Desires for a God-Pleasing Improvement of the True Protestant Church*, trans. Theodore G. Tappert (Philadelphia: Fortress, 1964), 107; Roger E. Olson and Christian T. Collins Winn, *Reclaiming Pietism: Retrieving an Evangelical Tradition* (Grand Rapids, MI: Eerdmans, 2015), 39, 46-47.

spiritual formation, training for professional ministerial activities as a second telos of theological education.[8]

After the later influence of Friedrich Schleiermacher (1768–1844), theology came to be considered a science—a discipline—and the goal of theological education has since shifted to becoming more intellectual, professional, and ministerial. In his *Theologia*, Edward Farley demonstrates how the concept of theology turned from knowing God to a very fragmented field of professional qualification since the church's efforts to provide education followed the secular educational institutions that resulted from the Enlightenment.[9] The early model for evangelical theological education in North America was adopted from this mainline Protestant model in Western Europe.[10]

## A FORMATIONAL APPROACH TO EVANGELICAL THEOLOGICAL EDUCATION

In the past two decades, the subject of theological education has gradually become a focal point of concern within Western evangelical churches and the academic community. This is due to the close connection between theological education and the future development of the church. Issues surrounding theological education, including its purpose, nature, models, teaching methods, and goals, have sparked unprecedented discussions and debates within the Western Christian sphere since the 1980s. These debates originated in evangelical Protestant circles in North America and subsequently spread to Europe and other regions.[11] Many evangelical theological educators have recently proposed models of formation in theological education and ideas to further develop them. For example, Bruce Powers suggests a formation model for theological education curriculum that connects the experience of the students in the learning environment with the reality of the ministry context.[12]

---

[8] Edward Farley, *Theologia: The Fragmentation and Unity of Theological Education* (Minneapolis: Fortress, 1983), 41.

[9] Farley, *Theologia*, 74–95.

[10] D. G. Hart and R. Albert Mohler Jr., "Introduction," in *Theological Education in the Evangelical Tradition* (Grand Rapids, MI: Baker, 1996), 15.

[11] Key figures participating in the debates include scholars such as H. Richard Niebuhr (1894–1962), Edward Farley (1929–2014), Max L. Stackhouse (1935–2016), David Kelsey (1932– ), Robert Banks (1939– ), Daniel Aleshire (1947– ), Bernhard Ott (1952– ), and others.

[12] Bruce P. Powers, "Developing a Curriculum for Academic, Spiritual, and Vocational Formation," in *C(H)AOS Theory: Reflections of Chief Academic Officers in Theological Education*, ed. Kathleen D. Billman and Bruce C. Birch (Grand Rapids, MI: Eerdmans, 2011), 302–18.

"We are in a time of transition from one prevailing paradigm in theological education to another," write Ted Smith, Marti Jewell, and S. Steve Kang in their introduction to the 2018 special issue of *Theological Education* titled "Theological Education Between the Times."[13] In that issue, Daniel Aleshire, the leading scholar in North American theological education and the former executive director of the Association of Theological Schools, traces the rise of the professional model of theological education from the early nineteenth century until the present. At the turn of the century, Aleshire suggested a new model that is more formational and puts more emphasis on the human and spiritual aspects of ministry than the current model.[14] He explained that this does not imply that theological education is no longer focused on pastoral development, nor does it signify a reduction in rigorous academic standards. Instead, it emphasizes a broader cultivation that encompasses the spiritual, human, and interpersonal aspects of the students.[15] In this light, Aleshire defines formational theological education as follows: "the development of a wisdom of God and the ways of God, fashioned from intellectual, affective, and behavioral understanding and evidenced by spiritual and moral maturity, relational integrity, knowledge of the Scripture and tradition, and the capacity to exercise religious leadership."[16] As the model of evangelical theological education is being shifted to be more formational, however, what is frequently overlooked or lacking in developing curriculum and programs within evangelical traditions is a discussion of the theological basis and goals of theological education, which investigates what theological education is truly about and what distinguishes it from secular education.

In his book *One with God: Salvation as Deification and Justification*, Veli-Matti Kärkkäinen argues that salvation is seen as deification in Eastern Orthodox tradition and as justification in Protestant tradition, and that they do not exclude each other. He suggests that the idea of union with God is a

---

[13] Ted A. Smith, Marti R. Jewell, and S. Steve Kang, "A Special Issue with Essays from Theological Education Between the Times," *Theological Education* 51, no. 2 (2018): 1.

[14] Daniel Aleshire, "The Emerging Model of Formational Theological Education," *Theological Education* 51, no. 2 (2018): 25-37; Aleshire, *Beyond Profession: The Next Future of Theological Education* (Grand Rapids, MI: Eerdmans, 2021), 79.

[15] Aleshire, "Emerging Model," 35-36.

[16] Aleshire, *Beyond Profession*, 82.

common motif between the Eastern and Western traditions.[17] From the evangelical perspective, Goran Medved argues that the doctrine is not only biblical and historical, but also Protestant and evangelical.[18] Michael Austin discusses several points related to the practice of deification in the context of a local church, showing the doctrine can act as a corrective to help evangelical Christians to have a deeper union with Christ, coupled with the cultivation of intellectual and moral virtue in Christ.[19] In this light, I suggest that the biblically sound, theologically meaningful, and historically faithful retrieval of the doctrine of deification can profoundly reshape the very framework of evangelical theological education for the future.

## DEIFICATION AS A BIBLICAL-THEOLOGICAL FOUNDATION AND GOAL FOR THEOLOGICAL EDUCATION

In Christian theology, the doctrine of deification (also known as theosis, divinization, or participation in God), literally meaning "the process of becoming God," was coined by the great fourth-century theologian Gregory of Nazianzus to refer to the mystical union of believers in Christ with God and their progressive transformation into the likeness of God.[20] The early church, particularly the Eastern churches, understood the process of human deification as the goal of salvation as well as the purpose and destiny of humanity. In the patristic view, theosis is perceived not only as the ultimate goal of human beings but also as a lifelong guiding principle for a Christian's life, and hence carries crucial implications for human development and theological education.

Theological education is in many ways a lifelong process of human development and formation that undergoes a metabolic process of transformation in which students are being conformed into the image of God's Son, Jesus

---

[17]Veli-Matti Kärkkäinen, *One with God: Salvation as Deification and Justification* (Collegeville, MN: Liturgical Press, 2004), 4.
[18]Goran Medved, "Theosis (Deification) as a New Testament and Evangelical Doctrine," *KAIROS: Evangelical Journal of Theology* 13, no. 2 (2019): 176.
[19]Michael W. Austin, "The Doctrine of Theosis: A Transformational Union with Christ," *Journal of Spiritual Formation & Soul Care* 8, no. 2 (2015): 184-85.
[20]Stephen Finlan and Vladimir Kharlamov, "Introduction," in *Theosis: Deification in Christian Theology*, ed. Stephen Finlan and Vladimir Kharlamov (Cambridge: Lutterworth, 2006), 1:1. Throughout this chapter, the terms *theosis*, *deification*, and *divinization* will be used interchangeably.

Christ (Col 1:15; 2 Cor 3:18). This chapter argues that introducing the doctrine of deification into the educational curriculum can provide a theological foundation and goal for students in their personal transformation and relationship with God. The inclusion of the view of deification can more effectively enhance students' development and formation as disciples of Christ, thus reaching the telos of true theological education.

The following will draw on insights from patristic theology to advocate for incorporating the doctrine of deification into theological education in the postmodern milieu.[21] The rest of the chapter will first identify several distinctives of deification that should propel the renewal of evangelical theological education in both its theory and praxis. Second, I present a Bible training program adopting Watchman Nee and Witness Lee's view of deification. The intention is to use this training program as a forum to discuss possible future developments in theological education.

## DEIFICATION: WHAT IT IS AND WHAT IT IS NOT

In an attempt to define the variety of concepts found in the Greek fathers, Norman Russell analyzes four different senses of deification used in the early church.[22] For the patristic fathers, as Daniel Keating indicates, human deification indicates becoming gods and sons of God by grace without any sense of pantheism, any confusion of Creator and creature, or any absorption or annihilation. Believers' participation in God's divine nature does not bring about a change in their human nature from created to uncreated but rather exalts, glorifies, and brings it to the goal for which humans were made.[23] Believers can never become part of the Godhead, whom John of Damascus in his classic *An Exact Exposition of the Orthodox Faith* defines as the one God who is "known in three perfect Persons [the Father, the Son, and the Holy Spirit] and adored with one adoration, believed in and

---

[21]I was inspired by Anthony Oladotun Akinsuire's proposal in "The Shema as a Theological Foundation for Christian Education in a Postmodern Context," *Sapientia Global Journal of Arts, Humanities and Development Studies* 4, no. 4 (2020): 287-96.

[22]Norman Russell, *The Doctrine of Deification in the Greek Patristic Tradition* (Oxford: Oxford University Press, 2004), 1-2.

[23]Daniel A. Keating, "Deification in Greek Fathers," in *Called to Be the Children of God: The Catholic Theology of Human Deification*, ed. David V. Meconi and Carl E. Olson (San Francisco: Ignatius, 2016), 55.

worshiped by every rational creature."²⁴ Thus, one in the process of deification will always remain a created being in relation to the Creator and never become part of the Godhead to be an object of worship.

From the Orthodox perspective, theosis is not just a mystical concept; it is also a living reality in the life of a believer. The Eastern Church calls the way Christians are called to live and be transformed into God's image and likeness φρόνημα, a New Testament Greek term meaning "mind, mindset."²⁵ The word is used four times in Romans (Rom 8:6-7, 27). According to the Orthodox tradition, attaining the state of φρόνημα is regarded as the first step toward theosis.²⁶ Another Greek term in this tradition used to summarize a spiritual practice toward theosis is νῆψις—wakefulness or watchfulness. In its cognate verb form, this term can be translated as "be sober-minded" (see 1 Pet 5:8: Νήψατε). A νῆψις mindset recognizes the reality of the spiritual battle in Christian life and can be cultivated through different spiritual practices, such as prayer, contemplation, solitude, Scripture meditation, and fasting.²⁷

## DISTINCTIVE CHARACTERISTICS OF DEIFICATION IN THEOLOGICAL EDUCATION

There are several theological distinctives that are embedded in the doctrine of deification, and thus it deserves to be a foundation for formational theological education in an environment in which popular trends and culture continue to foster postmodern thought in all of its instability, plurality, tentativity, and suspicion.²⁸

***Centered on Scripture and God's purpose.*** First, the concept and language of deification are uniquely Christian and deeply rooted in the Scriptures. This

---

²⁴John of Damascus, *Saint John of Damascus Writings*, trans. Frederic Hathaway Chase, FC 37 (New York: Fathers of the Church, 1958), 165, 177.
²⁵William Joseph Mascitello, "*Theosis*: Union with God as a Foundation for Religious Education in Roman Catholicism" (PhD diss., Felician College, 2015), 4, 6, https://research.library.fordham.edu/dissertations/AAI10014276/.
²⁶Patrick Whitworth, *Three Wise Men from the East: The Cappadocian Fathers and the Struggle for Orthodoxy* (Durham, UK: Sacristy, 2015), 197.
²⁷Daniel Clendenin, "Partakers of Divinity: The Orthodox Doctrine of *Theosis*," *JETS* 37 (1994): 378; cited in Austin, "Doctrine of *Theosis*," 184.
²⁸See Michael Paul Gama, *Theosis: Patristic Remedy for Evangelical Yearning at the Close of the Modern Age* (Eugene: OR: Wipf & Stock, 2017).

fact goes against what late nineteenth-century Protestant historian of dogma Adolf von Harnack (1851–1930) proposed in his Hellenization thesis: that deification is a pagan corruption of the Bible's primitive message.[29] Although the word *deification* is not used expressly, the idea of deification has a strong foundation in both the Old and New Testaments (see Ps 82:6; 2 Cor 3:18; Gal 2:20; Phil 1:21; 2 Pet 1:4; 1 Jn 3:2). The anthropological ground of deification is found at the forefront of Scripture: we were created in the *image* and *likeness* of God to share in his life and his dominion to become one with him, with the result that we express him as his reflection and represent him as his co-regents over the earth while maintaining a perfect relationship with him (Gen 1:26-28).

Pauline theology in particular reflects the New Testament idea of deification. David Litwa points out that Paul's statement "we ... are being transformed into *the same image* [τὴν αὐτὴν εἰκόνα]" (2 Cor 3:18 NASB) has surprised many interpreters because Paul seems to advance the idea that believers are spiritually (or even ontologically) unified with Christ.[30] Believers are being transformed into the "same" image of Christ, who is later designated as the image *of God* (2 Cor 4:4). The adjective *same* serves to underscore that the image of 2 Corinthians 3:18 is identical to the image of Christ himself. Thus, Litwa proceeds to argue that Paul's teaching here on transformation presents a Christian version of deification, a divine life ordained by God as the telos for believers. In Paul's view of human destiny, Christians are not being transformed into a lesser image than the true image, which is Christ. The image of God can thus be predicated, eschatologically, on both redeemed humanity and Christ. Robert Rakestraw similarly claims that deification can be thought of as "the restoration and reintegration of the 'image' or ... 'likeness' of God, seriously distorted by the fall, in the children of God" (Jn 1:12; Rom 8:16; 1 Jn 3:1). Rakestraw appeals to 2 Corinthians 3:17-18 in support of Paul's affirmation of deification.[31]

---

[29]John Lenz, "Deification of the Philosopher in Classical Greece," in *Partakers of the Divine Nature: The History and Development of Deification in the Christian Traditions*, ed. Michael J. Christensen and Jeffrey A. Wittung (Teaneck, NJ: Fairleigh Dickinson University Press, 2007), 56.

[30]M. David Litwa, "2 Corinthians 3:18 and Its Implications for *Theosis*," *Journal of Theological Interpretation* 2, no. 1 (2008): 118.

[31]Robert V. Rakestraw, "Becoming Like God: An Evangelical Doctrine of *Theosis*," *JETS* 40, no. 2 (1997): 261.

Thus, Scripture presents itself as a foundation for the doctrine of deification and a contribution to the development of the theme. What is hinted at in Scripture later became explicit in the early church. Following this pattern, theological educators should integrate deification into their curriculum to help students understand, interpret, and teach the Bible in a manner that is better grounded in Scripture's metanarrative of salvation; thus, they could more effectively relate biblical teachings to various aspects of spiritual formation.

**Historical and apologetic.** In the context of apologetics, the early church believed that salvation was a process of human deification. As Keating notes, "The doctrine of deification took shape through engagement and conflict primarily within the Church, as the early Christians wrestled with and opposed the various Gnostic systems of the second and third centuries and the varieties of Arian teaching of the fourth century."[32] As various heresies influenced by pagan philosophies emerged, the church fathers responded with the concept and language of deification.

In the early centuries, patristic writers justified the divinity of the Son and the Spirit with reference to the doctrine of deification, with deification being the purpose of the Son's work and the function of the Spirit. For instance, Irenaeus of Lyons, in his response to various Gnostic teachings, used Scripture to provide a theological framework for the doctrine of deification. He connects Psalm 82:6 with Romans 8:15, showing the link between Christians' being made many sons of God by grace and "becoming gods" (*Haer.* 3.6.1).[33] In his argument against the varieties of Arianism, Athanasius employs the doctrine of deification to defend the person of Christ, affirming that if "being made god" (theosis) is to be possible, Christ the Savior must be both fully God and fully human (*Contra Arianos* 1.38-39).[34] Following Athanasius, Gregory of Nazianzus, in refuting the Pneumatomachians (semi-Arians), argues that for the Holy Spirit to activate the process of human deification, the Spirit must be fully God rather than simply a creature.[35]

---

[32]Keating, "Deification in Greek Fathers," 42.
[33]*ANF* 1:419.
[34]*NPNF* 2/4:329; see also *Contra Arianos* 1.9, 3.53.
[35]Gregory of Nazianzus, *Oration* 34.12: "I cannot believe that I am saved by one who is my equal. If the Holy Ghost is not God, let Him first be made God, and then let Him deify me His equal";

The doctrine of deification has been scripturally and theologically integrated into the formulation of Christian orthodoxy, while the doctrine was shaped, formulated, and deepened by the church.[36] In fighting against heretical teachings, a soteriology of deification motivated many patristic arguments for the Trinity and two-nature Christology, thus contributing to the birth of ecumenical orthodoxy.[37] The doctrine of deification can help students rediscover the heritage of ancient Christianity and the authentic faith, seeing it not as a dead tradition but as relating themselves to the universal church throughout history. This can be done, for instance, by renewing the theological education curriculum by introducing the doctrine into a church history course.

***Christological, anthropological, and eschatological.*** The doctrine of deification is centered on Christ and his incarnation. For patristic writers, the divine incarnation includes the entire divine economy (οἰκονομία) in Christ, that is, his entire human living, teaching, ministry, suffering, resurrection, ascension, and glorification. In his incarnation, Christ, the second man, in contrast with the first man, Adam, opens the way for a new humanity; and now, in human deification, believers in Christ are being conformed to his image (Rom 8:29; Gal 4:19) and led into glory as he has entered (Rom 8:30; Heb 2:10; 1 Tim 3:16). The Greek fathers steadfastly adhered to deification as the anthropological purpose and destiny of humanity in God's creation.[38]

In brief, the doctrine of deification helps to call students back to a living faith and to cultivate in them an ecumenical spirit so that they can share the same rich heritage with fellow believers who come from different traditions. As Carl Mosser suggests, deification is a truly ecumenical concept.[39] Moreover, incorporating a proper understanding of deification into theological education can give students, especially evangelical students, a shift of attention from self-centered Christian life toward Christ's call to discipleship, as well as

---

Oration 31.28: "For if He is not to be worshipped, how can He deify me by Baptism?" English translation from *NPNF* 2/7:655, 674.

[36]Meconi and Olson, *Called to Be the Children*, 48-50.

[37]Carl Mosser, "Deification: A Truly Ecumenical Concept," *Perspectives: A Journal of Reformed Thought*, 30, no. 4 (2015): 8.

[38]Markos Orphanos, "The Destiny of the Human Person," *Phronema* 11 (1996): 21.

[39]Mosser, "Deification," 8.

from individualism toward living as a member of Christ's body in a community of faith. Orthodox theological educator Cristian Sonea concludes, "If the theological education does not aim towards this theological goal—how to reach *theōsis*—but only towards the notions related to it, recoverable as theological information, and therefore formalizable through academic knowledge, the work of grace is abandoned for the empty gesture of passing knowledge."[40] The retrieval of language and concepts of deification in theological education preserves educators from the danger of only building effective channels for transmitting information of a theological nature without experiencing the central work of the grace of God (1 Cor 15:10; Phil 2:12-13).

## A Case Study of a Formational Approach to Theological Education

I use "the local churches," a worldwide Christian group that originated in China at the beginning of the twentieth century, as a case study to show an alternative approach to theological education in the aspect of the spiritual formation of believers and to make the doctrine of deification foundational and central to its theological education.[41] The group appears to employ a formational approach to theological education, with apparent success in comprehensive discipleship and vibrant mission. As Kärkkäinen writes,

> Nowadays one cannot do justice to the rich diversity of Christian communities on Asian soil without mentioning other nontraditional church forms. One of them is called "Local Churches," a movement currently present in the Global North as well, particularly in the United States. This vibrant movement is stronger in mainland China and Taiwan, and it is also spreading elsewhere

---

[40]Cristian Sonea, "The Missionary Formation in the Eastern Orthodox Theological Education in Present Day Romania," *Transformation* 35, no. 3 (2018): 153.

[41]Note that Watchman Nee, Witness Lee, the coworkers associated with their ministry, and the churches with which they are affiliated reject the exclusive use of the term with capital letters—"Local Churches" or "Local Church"—as a name or a movement designated for them. They maintain that the only name they hold and honor is the name of the Lord Jesus Christ. They consider the term "local church" to be simply a general description of the local nature and expression of the church, that is, the expression of the universal church in a locality. According to Nee and Lee's ecclesiology, the church in a locality stands on the ground of genuine oneness that includes all genuine believers from any background, race, or nationality in that locality. See "Frequently Asked Questions," the local churches, 2023, www.localchurches.org/faq/ (accessed December 29, 2023). Therefore, I use the lowercase terms "local church" and "the local churches" here to reflect Nee and Lee's understanding.

thanks to its missionary outreach. Founded by Watchman Nee and Witness Lee, this movement focuses on lay ministry and mission and a comprehensive Christian discipleship.[42]

In the first half of the twentieth century, the local churches began an attempt to make theological education more formation oriented. This was first proposed and practiced by Watchman Nee (1903–1972) and later expanded in other parts of the world by Nee's closest coworker, Witness Lee (1905–1997). Both Nee and Lee were prominent church leaders in China in the twentieth century.[43]

**Deification in Nee's and Lee's teaching.** Nee and Lee taught the doctrine of deification, which was at the core of not only their soteriology but also their whole theology. Even though the word *deification* is not explicitly found in the works of Nee, this salvific view of deification and its related subjects is used by Nee, as particularly seen in his early classic work *The Spiritual Man*, in which the term "union [with God]" appears at least 229 times.[44] Nee says, "God's original goal was for [humans] to receive and digest God's spiritual life with the truth and reality in this spiritual life. . . . [Humans] could receive God's life and become a spiritual person, sharing God's nature."[45]

Based on Nee's thought, Lee taught deification more explicitly and, particularly in his later ministry, affirmed Athanasius's significant statement, "For He was made man that we might be made God" (*Inc.* 54.3).[46] Lee was

---

[42]Veli-Matti Kärkkäinen, *An Introduction to Ecclesiology: Historical, Global, and Interreligious Perspectives*, 2nd ed. (Downers Grove, IL: IVP Academic, 2021), 129.

[43]J. Gordon Melton, *Melton's Encyclopedia of American Religions*, 8th ed. (Farmington Hill, MI: Gale, 2009), s.v. "The (Local) Church." Watchman Nee was born into a Christian family, with his grandfather serving as a Congregationalist minister and his parents being faithful Methodists. Nee's coworker Witness Lee was also born into a Christian family and was a former Brethren member. He joined Nee in ministry in 1932 and soon became Nee's closest coworker. With the labor of these two workers, over seven hundred local churches were started by 1949. On the eve of the 1949 Communist Revolution, Nee sent Lee to Taiwan, where the church flourished and spread to neighboring countries, eventually reaching the United States. Lee moved to California in 1962 and led the church to spread over the country and other continents. See Melton, *Melton's Encyclopedia of American Religions*, 552-54; George N. Patterson, *Christianity in Communist China* (Waco, TX: World Books, 1969), 72-73, 79-80.

[44]*CWWN* 14:581.

[45]*CWWN* 12:30-31. Note on the English edition translation in *CWWN* of "man" for "human," "men" for "human beings."

[46]*NPNF* 2/4:65. See Christopher Wilde, "'In Life and Nature but Not in the Godhead': Witness Lee's Contribution to a Biblical Understanding of *Theosis*" (presentation, Evangelical Theological Society, Atlanta, November 17-19, 2015), https://an-open-letter.org/en/ets-2015-in-life-and-nature-but-not-in-the-godhead. See Witness Lee, *Life-Study of 1 & 2 Samuel* (Anaheim, CA:

aware of the concern that the deification language may be misunderstood and possibly mislead readers to the idea of pantheism.[47] To resolve this concern, Lee added a phrase to exclude any possibility of pantheism and refined Athanasius's iconic statement, "God became a man so that man may become God in life and in nature (but not in the Godhead)."[48] In saying this, Lee expressed his caution that the word *deification* be applied only with proper qualification and used only "in a limited sense to convey the fact that we have been born of God to become sons of God."[49] In other words, in speaking of "human beings becoming God," Lee rejects the concept that human beings become the divine one, God himself, because God is the only Creator and the only one who deserves the worship of creatures. There is no question that Lee recognizes and affirms that God always exists apart and remains distinct from his creatures from eternity past to eternity future.[50] Furthermore, both Nee and Lee use the term *nature* not in the metaphysical or philosophical sense but in the biblical sense of the same term that Peter uses in 2 Peter 1:4, to indicate God's communicable attributes such as holiness (1 Pet 1:15-16; 2:5, 9; 3:5; Heb 12:10) and love (Rom 5:5), of which believers are able to partake.[51]

Concerning Lee's use of the language of "life/nature-Godhead" distinction, Wilde observes, "The classic distinction between God's communicable energies and his incommunicable essence is useful as a bridge to understand Witness Lee's teaching that regenerated man is made God in his communicable 'life and nature' but not in his 'Godhead,' which is

---

Living Stream Ministry, 1994), 166. The term *deification* appears at least thirty-two times and the phrase "become/becoming God" over two hundred times throughout Lee's publications. In the early 1950s, Lee already began to teach deification. For example, "Incarnation is for God to become man to live out a human life, and death and resurrection are for man to become God to live out God's life" (*CWWL 1954* 2:428). The *CWWL* contains the entirety of Lee's ministry from 1932–1997, comprising 138 volumes containing over 78,000 pages; it was published in 2020. Lee's work is published by Living Stream Ministry, Anaheim, CA, and is available at www.ministrybooks.org and www.livingstream.com.

[47]Witness Lee, *Life-Study of Philippians* (Anaheim, CA: Living Stream Ministry, 1995), 407.
[48]Witness Lee, *Life-Study of 1 & 2 Chronicles, Ezra, Nehemiah, Esther* (Anaheim, CA: Living Stream Ministry, 1995), 5.
[49]Witness Lee, *Life-Study of Galatians* (Anaheim, CA: Living Stream Ministry, 1984), 175.
[50]Witness Lee, *One Body, One Spirit, and One New Man* (Anaheim, CA: Living Stream Ministry, 2000), 47.
[51]See *CWWN* 36:189; Witness Lee, *Life-Study of Hebrews* (Anaheim, CA: Living Stream Ministry, 1992), 158.

incommunicable."[52] Just as a number of traditions hold the Creator-creature distinction or communicable-incommunicable distinction, so also does Nee's and Lee's basic understanding of deification exclude philosophically and theologically objectionable ideas such as "equality with God," "elevation to divine status," or "absorption into God's essence."[53]

For Nee and Lee, this understanding of deification is scripturally sound and theologically rooted, which led them throughout their ministry to pay much attention to believers' personal and corporate experiences of the triune God for spiritual formation, that is, to help believers grow spiritually in life unto maturity.[54] In this regard, both Nee and Lee considered deification not to be a teaching held exclusively by patristics or the Orthodox Church. Instead, it is a teaching based on the central theme of the Bible—God's economy—and is thus of great value in bringing believers into a deeper experience of the transformative union with Christ.

***The calling and ethos of the training program.*** The contextual challenge that Nee and Lee encountered during their ministry served as inspiration to create a training program in order to more successfully carry out God's mission in the country. In the mid-1930s, numerous local churches were established in China by Nee and Lee's ministry, but the majority of these churches lacked spiritually proper and mature local church leaders. Nee recognized the importance of training for the Lord's testimony in the country, and he conducted various kinds of trainings throughout the course of his ministry in the face of different challenges.[55] The churches in China's need for leadership and workers was the primary reason for Nee's proposal. Although Bible knowledge was needed for Christian workers, the kind of workers that the country most needed were those who truly knew God in the original sense of the word *theology* (*theologia*)—the personal knowledge of God, instead of merely objective knowledge about

---

[52] Wilde, "'In Life and Nature,'" 7.
[53] Wilde, "'In Life and Nature,'" 19; James Starr, "Does 2 Peter 1:4 Speak of Deification?," in Christiansen and Wittung, *Partakers of the Divine Nature*, 90.
[54] Wilde, "'In Life and Nature,'" 2.
[55] *CWWN* 26:479. See "Watchman Nee's Use of Trainings," *"Having This Ministry . . ."* (newsletter), no. 11 (March 2022), https://newsletters.lsm.org/having-this-ministry/issues/Mar2022-011/need-for-training-02.html.

God.[56] Nee never rejected the need for theological education per se but saw that most seminaries at his time failed to guide students to know God experientially and that the traditional model did not fit the setting in China and the biblical standard.[57] Therefore, as early as the early 1930s, Nee had a profound burden to provide training to the emerging young workers and church leaders, and he considered this an important way to fulfill his ministry.

Another factor that drove Nee's philosophy and practice in theological education was his eschatological ecclesiology, regarding the vision of the building up of the church as the one body of Christ expressed in local churches before Christ's second coming (Rom 12:4-5; Eph 4:12-16; 1 Cor 12:12-27; 14:4, 26). Nee's vision was a church in which all believers function as priests instead of just a few ordained ministers or priests.[58] This echoes the idea of the "priesthood of all believers," the Reformation's rallying cry, which finds its key biblical expression in Exodus 19:4-6; Ephesians 4:12-16; 1 Peter 2:9; and Revelation 5:10. Nee referred to Ephesians 4, where the building up of Christ's body depends on the growth in life of each member of Christ and the functioning of all members as priests, which must be fulfilled as Christ prophesied (Mt 16:18) before he comes again.[59] From Nee's perspective, the professionalism promoted by the traditional theological education model in his time solidified the clergy-laity system and deepened the grassroots-ministerial divide. Rather, Nee affirmed that all regenerated members of Christ's body were truly priests of God's kingdom, and thus each member had to grow spiritually and become a priest to build up the church and equally participate in God's mission on earth.[60]

---

[56] CWWN, 10:532-33: "Let me also say a few words to those brothers and sisters who are co-workers. No one can work for God without knowing God.... We have to learn to know God before we can work for God.... Indeed, a man can only preach what he is touched by in the Word; he can only help others in the areas that God has touched him. What can we preach if we do not know God?"

[57] CWWN 11:867: "Concerning the perfecting of the young ones, the Bible does not speak of any seminary. Although some tried to start a school for the prophets in the Old Testament, it did not produce any prophets. Studying in a seminary will not make a person a worker. The training of a worker comes from following a pattern and from submission. Timothy and Silas both followed Paul. In the Bible, we only see the way of apprenticeship; we do not see the way of scholarship."

[58] CWWN 57:221.

[59] CWWN 57:13, 220-21.

[60] CWWN 57:199-203. See Volker Glissmann, "Grassroots Theological Education," *InSights Journal* 5, no. 1 (2019): 53-67.

Nee aimed for training that went beyond professionalism, with various types of training for believers of different ages and focuses, from perfecting young people to training workers, from edifying newly saved ones to preparing a family for migration. In 1933 Nee initiated a small, informal training in Shanghai that lasted for two years on and off.[61] The trainees were required to live together, study the Bible, and spend time with Nee personally for spiritual help. In 1936 he began preparing a facility for young people's training and expressed his burden concerning this training. He testified that he was called by God to focus his ministry on four aspects, one of which was to establish a program to train believers to grow in life and serve in local churches across the country, ultimately for the building up of the universal body of Christ.[62] This particular calling of Nee had a significant impact on the design of his training program and later the ethos of the training centers.

From 1948 to 1949 in the Kuling Mountains, Fujian, Nee launched two terms of a training program for his coworkers and the church leaders throughout the country, with a total of more than two hundred trainees. This program later made a substantial contribution to the great spiritual revival in the country after the civil war.[63] Taking the same educational vision, philosophy, and methods as Nee, Lee, after being sent by Nee to Taiwan, further developed such training programs for over a thousand Chinese believers in the diaspora in the 1950s. The training programs offered by Nee and Lee focused on developing trainees' personal dedication, spiritual growth, and pastoral skills related to church service, producing numerous dedicated believers and effective workers.[64] In 1986, Lee made the program more official in Taiwan—a two-year, postgraduate, nondegree Bible-training program with the goal of aiding college graduates in their

---

[61] Witness Lee, *Watchman Nee—a Seer of the Divine Revelation in the Present Age* (Anaheim, CA: Living Stream Ministry, 1991), 214.

[62] *CWWN* 26:479: "When the Lord called me to serve Him, . . . the Lord revealed to me that He wanted to build up local churches in other localities to manifest Himself, to bear testimony of unity on the ground of locality so that each saint might perform his duty in the church and live the church life. My thought is not to establish a seminary or a Bible institute, but to have young people staying together to live the Body life and practice the spiritual life."

[63] Lee, *Watchman Nee*, 215-16.

[64] Che Bin Tan, "Chinese Protestant Theological Education in the Diaspora Since 1949," *Missiology: An International Review* 13, no. 3 (1985): 299.

Christian development in life, truth, service, and character.⁶⁵ In establishing this formal training program, Lee resonated with and shared the same burden as that of Nee in his founding vision, as reflected in the purpose statement of the program.⁶⁶ Thus far, there are eighteen affiliated training centers with similar goals and programs of study that have been established around the globe, such as in Mexico City, London, Tokyo, Moscow, and Pretoria, South Africa.⁶⁷

*The educational philosophy of the program.* Lee named the doctrine of deification as one of the goals of the training program in his explanation of the program's mission statement.⁶⁸ From Lee's perspective, deification was realized by the growth of each member in the experience of the Head, Christ, in life and the functioning of all members, which issues in the building up of the body of Christ (see Eph 4:12-16).⁶⁹ In designing the program's curriculum, Lee adopted a comprehensive view to reflect his and Nee's understanding of theological education with the view of deification in at least five areas: spiritual, character, moral, communal, and missional formation.

## Integrating Deification into Training Programs

*1. Spiritual formation.* For Nee and Lee, the spiritual growth of individual believers began with regeneration, that is, having God's divine life added into their human lives and participating in God's nature, which is the beginning of the deification process. As believers continually partake of God's nature, this divine life will keep growing in them unto maturity until Christ is formed in them (Gal 4:19). According to Nee and Lee, God's desire is to bring believers to be deified, as the apostle Paul states, "For to me, to live is Christ" (Phil 1:21).⁷⁰

---

⁶⁵"History of the Training," Full-Time Training in Taipei, 2022, www.fttt.org.tw/?page_id=87.
⁶⁶*CWWL 1994–1997* 1:39. See also "Purpose & Goal of the Training," Living Stream Ministry, 2024, https://ftta.org/about/purpose.php.
⁶⁷"Full-Time Training Around the Globe," Full-Time Training in Malaysia, 2024, www.fttmy.org/related-link/; "Full-Time Training in Pretoria," Ministry of Life, 2024, https://ministryoflife.co.za/fttp.
⁶⁸*CWWL 1994–1997* 1:39. See also "Purpose & Goal of the Training": one of the three goals of the training is "to reach the highest peak of the divine revelation—God becoming a man that man may become God in life and in nature, but not in the Godhead."
⁶⁹"Truth, Life, Gospel & Service," Living Stream Ministry, 2024, https://ftta.org/.
⁷⁰*CWWL 1952* 1:369-70.

Both Nee and Lee held the spiritual principle that genuine service to God is not just a matter of method or activity but of *person* and *character*. In light of this principle, there are two classes that specifically focus on spiritual growth in the program curriculum, namely, Experience of Christ as Life and Life of Service, in which trainees explore basic spiritual and life principles necessary for service. These classes orient trainees toward a proper view of service by experiencing Christ as life and growing in this life. Apart from the classes on the development of spiritual life, trainees are required to follow a regular weekly schedule. Through a variety of spiritual practices, such as calling on the Lord, spiritual solitude, pray-reading of Scripture, singing hymns, writing prayer, and spiritual journals, students are empowered to deepen their loving relationship and union with Christ (Eph 3:16-17; Rom 12:2).

**2. Character formation.** Nee and Lee realized the importance of character development and formation in theological education. It is essential for Christians, especially Christian workers, to have traits such as godliness, endurance, meekness, righteousness, faith, and particularly love (ἀγάπη; 1 Tim 6:11) formed in them. For Lee, becoming God implies that we become beings of love.[71] Human beings are made in God's image, that is, according to his divine attributes, and God is love (1 Jn 4:16). Hence, love is one of the foremost virtues that needs to be cultivated in believers' deification.

In the program curriculum, there is one class specifically focusing on character formation, with two books as assigned readings, namely, Nee's *The Character of the Lord's Worker* and Lee's *Character*. The content focuses on a series of character traits that are crucial for Christian workers, including being a good listener, loving humanity, and being prepared to suffer for Christ. Character formation aligned with spiritual formation is another intentional nurturing of Christlike traits that aims at the goal of deification, transforming the whole person into the likeness of Christ.

**3. Moral formation.** Lee speaks of morality in terms of deification. For Lee, the highest morality of human beings, who are made in God's image, is to live to the standard of life that God requires.[72] The first man, Adam,

---

[71]Witness Lee, *Vital Groups*, 2nd ed. (Anaheim, CA: Living Stream Ministry, 2021), 71; Lee, *Life-Study of 1 John* (Anaheim, CA: Living Stream Ministry, 1984), 61, 234.

[72]Witness Lee, *Life-Study of Luke* (Anaheim, CA: Living Stream Ministry, 1986), 18.

failed to receive God's life in him and hence failed to live out the highest morality. Jesus Christ, in becoming the second man as well as the first God-man, became our prototype for life in God's kingdom; he is the true human who lives by God's life and manifests divine attributes through his human virtues.[73] Through deification—union with Christ and partaking of the divine nature—believers, who are many "god-men" are enabled to live here with the highest standard of morality, as Jesus lived.[74] The life of the first God-man, Jesus, was characterized by humility and cruciformity (Mk 10:45; Phil 2:8), which Lee describes as a life "from the manger to the cross."[75] Hence, according to Lee, to be deified (i.e., to become Christ in expression and function) is to follow the Lord Jesus Christ, who took this narrow way of a manger and a cross. We likewise must humble ourselves, pouring ourselves out to serve others, even suffering for others. Lee always reminded his trainees, "The children of God are the God-men. . . . We should not forget our status as God-men. . . . A God-man needs to have a God-man living."[76]

This is the primary reason that trainees in the program are required to serve one another with practical tasks. Some practical services in the training include meal preparation, meal cleanup, mopping, restroom cleaning, and setting up chairs in dining areas and classrooms, in which practices trainees can take experience the humble and serving life of Christ within them. Many graduates now serving around the world in their respective churches have testified to the value of what they learned through various services during their training.[77]

**4. Communal formation.** Austin writes that deification has implications for formation not only individually but also communally, which he calls "corporate *theōsis*."[78] In the training programs, students learn to live as members of Christ's body and are built up with fellow members to their full

---

[73] Witness Lee, *The Conclusion of the New Testament: Experiencing, Enjoying, and Expressing Christ* (Anaheim, CA: Living Stream Ministry, 2010), 2:3662.
[74] Lee, *Life-Study of Luke*, 18-19. The language of "god-men" is to parallel the God-man, Jesus, and not meant to exclude women—indeed, they shall be "god-women."
[75] *CWWL 1994–1997* 3:462-63.
[76] *CWWL 1994–1997* 3:462.
[77] "Training Services," Full-Time Training in Anaheim, https://ftta.org/prospective-trainees/life-ftta/service.php (accessed February 19, 2024).
[78] Austin, "Doctrine of Theosis," 185.

extent within a community. The ecclesiology of Nee and Lee plays an important role in the communal formation of believers. Nee was not content with training believers to be merely zealous, victorious, and holy Christians while remaining individualistic, like fragmentary stones. Rather, he envisioned establishing and building up many local churches in different cities as a miniature manifestation of the new Jerusalem collectively, and hence communal formation was an indispensable element in training.[79]

Lee built on Nee's ecclesiology with the doctrine of deification.[80] Living together was required for all trainees in Nee's early model of Kuling training and also in Lee's later training program, with trainees staying together to learn how to live the body life. Besides attending lectures given by Nee, trainees meet according to the principle of mutuality described in 1 Corinthians 14.[81] Classes include both lectures and opportunities for trainees to share their experience and questions from class material. Learning how to meet in mutuality in local church meetings is also part of communal formation.

**5. Missional formation.** Last, in accordance with Nee and Lee's perspective, one of the main goals of the training program is to fulfill Christ's Great Commission (Mt 28:19-20).[82] The burden for Nee and Lee to establish training centers went along with their burden for missionary work. While proposing to set up a training center in the mid-1930s, Nee published his book *Concerning Our Mission* in 1937 to express his evangelistic plan for the country. Moreover, when Nee was conducting the Kuling training, he was doing it in the context of evangelizing China.[83]

Lee conducted several training sessions to carry out evangelistic work after he was sent to Taiwan. The training was fruitful; graduates were sent throughout the island, and many new local churches were raised up. Later, he used the terminology "the God-ordained way" to describe the way God ordained believers to serve together as a priesthood to build up the church as Christ's body in the New Testament, including reaching out to nonbelievers and shepherding the new believers, and made it a strong emphasis in

---

[79]*CWWN* 22:10.
[80]Lee, *Conclusion of the New Testament* 3:4362.
[81]*CWWN* 59:2.
[82]*CWWL 1994–1997* 5:244-45.
[83]*CWWN* 53:3.

the program curriculum. In class, students studied the biblical foundation of the God-ordained way, discussed case studies in study groups, and practice these steps in various local churches. Under the supervision of trainers, trainees were assigned to gospel teams to labor among specific age groups (teenagers, college students, or other communities) on a weekly basis, and coordinated closely with one or two other people in their team to meet people and shepherd those they met.[84] Lee believed that the Great Commission of Christ was properly fulfilled by including deification in the training program. In order to carry out the Great Commission of Christ in resurrection, what we are is more important than what we say or do. Sent disciples must be those who experience the reality of deification, that is, are united with the resurrected Christ and live out the resurrection life of Christ so that they might become the witnesses of the resurrected one to the uttermost parts of the earth (Acts 1:8; 2:32; 3:15; 26:16).[85]

In 1991, after receiving a special training, a large number of program graduates immigrated to the former Soviet Union and Eastern Europe. By the time of his passing in 1997, there were seventy-four local churches in Russia and 169 cities in the former Soviet Union countries. Later, several hundred graduates also migrated to Western Europe, Africa, India, and many other places.[86]

## EDUCATIONAL IMPLICATIONS IN A CONTEMPORARY GLOBALIZED WORLD

As mentioned earlier, theological educator Aleshire, in his *Beyond Profession*, proposes that theological education in the future be formational.[87] Nee and Lee's approach to theological education has three important implications for today's evangelicals in constructing a model of theological education that is both integrative and formative.

---

[84]"The Full-Time Training Curriculum," Full-Time Training in London, 2022, https://fttl.org/curriculum.
[85]*CWWL 1994–1997* 5:97-98. *CWWL 1994–1997* 5:114: "When we are one with God, *we become God*. Then we have God and *are God* in our shepherding of others. To shepherd according to God is to shepherd according to what God is in His attributes" (emphasis added).
[86]"Local Church Members Take the Gospel to the Former Soviet Union" (unpublished manuscript, March 18, 2024), 192.
[87]Daniel O. Aleshire, *Beyond Profession: The Next Future of Theological Education* (Grand Rapids, MI: Eerdmans, 2021), 80-81.

**1. Revising the current curriculum to be transformative.** As Robert Banks notes, "The curriculum is formational, and formation is curriculum."[88] Practitioners of theological education should consider placing greater emphasis in the current curriculum on spiritual growth, which occurs not solely in an individual context but also in a communal context. Spiritual formation should not be marginalized in curriculum design; instead, it should permeate the entire curriculum, connect the entire campus community, and evolve into a daily way of life for students. Curriculum developers could incorporate the doctrine of deification, in terms of its scriptural basis, theological grounds, history, and implications, in the current curricular offerings by creating modules and content and by including spiritual practices within courses.

**2. Viewing teaching and learning as a transformation process.** The teaching and learning process can be viewed as a transformation process of both knowledge and qualities from teachers to students. Educators should endeavor to foster spiritual transformation within the communal settings, both inside and outside the classroom. This requires instructional reforms that are not confined to the lecture format but go beyond focusing solely on one-way knowledge transmission within the classroom.

**3. Changing the role of teachers.** To take on a transformative role, teachers must first be deified—be united with God in their personal lives—to rededicate themselves to being spiritual examples. During the teaching-student interaction, students should explore the challenges that hinder their spiritual growth and draw on the lived experiences of their teachers. Institutional leaders can promote faculty development by promoting spiritual practices, building relationships with students, mentoring younger faculty or organizing peer mentoring, and developing a mutual shepherding community to strengthen spiritual growth.

## Conclusion

Living in the new face of Christianity in the twenty-first century, we must recognize the urgency of reenvisioning the paradigm for theological

---

[88]Robert Banks, *Reenvisioning Theological Education: Exploring a Missional Alternative to Current Models* (Grand Rapids, MI: Eerdmans, 1999), 223.

education to be formational. Evangelical educators are to reengage with the patristic understanding of deification, retrieve the doctrine and its practice, and realign their curriculum with contemporary realities in relation to the foundational issues of theological education to better ensure the transformation of a rising generation in the postmodern era.

Nee's and Lee's training program can be viewed as an example of an attempt at a formational approach to theological education. The program highlights the inadequacy of the traditional fragmented approach to theological education and demonstrates the possible implications of the doctrine of deification for training Christ's seekers in every context across the globe. Lee was not the first Bible teacher to teach the doctrine of deification, nor was he the first to make deification the goal of theological education, which we see in Eastern Orthodoxy. However, after receiving many insights from Nee, Lee was probably the first Bible teacher and Christian educator from the Global South to recover the doctrine in the twentieth century, incorporate it into the curriculum as the goal of theological education, adopt an alternative approach to theological education, and bring this across the globe. Thus Nee and Lee contributed to the global church in theological education for the twenty-first century.

By adopting a new approach that revives deification language and incorporates this idea into educational philosophy and practice, we could see great benefit brought to evangelical theological education with this turn toward Christ's call to discipleship as a part of what it truly means to be Christian and human.

# SHARING *in the* LIFE *of* GOD

## Considering the Relationship Between Justification and Deification

### Ben C. Blackwell

ONE SIGNIFICANT THEOLOGICAL DEVELOPMENT of the past century is a greater attention to ecumenical dialogue. Discussions between Protestants and Roman Catholics have often returned to topics that have been perennial issues of debate since the Reformation, but the dialogue between Protestant and Orthodox Christians has raised new questions that have not yet been fully explored. A number of doctrines have generated a great deal of interest, but a central question regards the relationship of deification and justification as soteriological models. Further to this conversation, I will explore how sharing in the life of God and being acquitted by God relate to each other.

Though the Reformers periodically used the language of deification, they did not employ it consistently or in the context of justification. Traditional Protestant views on the relationship between justification and deification argue that they stand distinct from each other, reflecting similar inconsistencies between wider Protestant and Roman Catholic approaches to soteriology. Using John Calvin's *Institutes of the Christian Religion* as a representative of the Protestant synthesis on justification, in *Institutes* 3.11.1 we find an essential distinction between justification and regeneration (or what was later styled sanctification). Both arise from union with Christ as a *duplex gratia* (a double grace), so they are not separated but are essentially distinct. The key difference is that justification is a legal status declaration wherein believers are acquitted before God and therefore forgiven, whereas in regeneration believers are made alive spiritually to walk the spiritual life. Showing the importance of the spiritual life, Calvin explores this later aspect extensively in the previous chapters with his discussion of vivification and mortification in *Institutes* 3.3-10. Life (vivification) is set as distinct from justification, which is his focus in 3.11-19.

Though in many ways Calvin reclaims an Augustinian root for his theology, Calvin's critique of Augustine in this context is telling. He charges Augustine with confusing spiritual renewal with justification (3.11.15), a problem also evident in Catholic contemporaries (3.14.11). Justification is not antithetical to regeneration (μὴ γένοιτο!), but confusing one for the other leads to great error. Though Calvin does not address deification in this context, we can be sure that its inherent focus on life means that it cannot be a part of justification.[1] If a part of soteriology at all, deification would have to be a part of regeneration, since that is where life resides theologically. Accordingly, within broader Reformational settings, justification and deification cannot refer to the same reality. Other Protestant traditions, particularly the Lutheran tradition via the Finnish school, have been more sanguine about the relationship of justification and deification, but questions remain since the forensic nature of justification seems to be sacrificed to achieve this rapprochement.[2]

If difficulties on the Protestant side of the discussion have been raised, Orthodox theologians also note the distinct problem with recognizing an interconnection between the two soteriological systems. When describing the role of deification within the Orthodox context, Andrew Louth specifically points out the different structures that lie behind Protestant and Orthodox models.[3] To make this comparison, he identifies two arcs that

---

[1] Calvin's critiques of Osiander do not directly address deification, but they are telling (*Inst.* 3.11.5-12).
[2] Bruce D. Marshall, "Justification as Declaration and Deification," in *The Holy Trinity in the Life of the Church*, ed. Khaled Anatolios (Grand Rapids, MI: Baker Academic, 2014), 113-43, here 141-43. For an example of an approach that is more sanguine about the relationship of justification and deification, see Veli-Matti Kärkkäinen, *One with God: Salvation as Deification and Justification* (Collegeville, MN: Liturgical Press, 2004).
[3] Andrew Louth, "The Place of Theosis in Orthodox Theology," in *Partakers of the Divine Nature: The History and Development of Deification in the Christian Traditions*, ed. Michael J. Christensen and Jeffery A. Wittung (Grand Rapids, MI: Baker, 2008), 32-44.

inform the nature of soteriology. The inner arc is that of the fall of humanity in Genesis 3 to the cross, with the cross as the basis of restoration and forgiveness. The outer arc is that of original creation to Jesus' resurrection, which is the basis of new creation. He notes that Protestant models of soteriology (focused on justification) prioritize the inner arc, with the outer arc lacking requisite structural attention. In sharp distinction, Orthodox theology is framed around the outer arc, such that the cross is necessary to address the fall, but the telos of soteriology is not forgiveness but deification. The inner is necessary for the outer, but the outer sets the frame. The whole divine economy is oriented toward cosmic restoration by means of the incarnation, death, and resurrection of the Son, and these spiritual realities are expressed through the divine mysteries within the church.

Louth is not overtly critical of Protestant theologies of justification, but the direct implication is that the Protestant system is inadequate because it makes a (potentially) reductive account of soteriology a theological pillar. Thus, justification is too narrow and struggles to connect to the scope of restoration evident in deification. With few attempts by Orthodox theologians to bridge the gap between deification and justification, Louth's articulation of the disconnect is representative of the wider tenor.

Is there, then, any substantive relationship between justification and deification? Does the forensic nature of the justification metaphor make it incompatible with deification? Does the cosmic framework of deification set it at odds with a doctrine of justification focused primarily on the cross? These and other questions regarding the relationship of justification and deification will be my focus in this essay.

My approach to this conversation will be from a Protestant perspective, in that I am conscious of historical debates but also attempt to return to Scripture as the basis of my theological affirmations.[4] Accordingly, as I address justification and deification, I will attempt to norm these to scriptural patterns over against where some traditional positions have been

---

[4] By speaking of a Protestant (or Catholic) perspective, I do not see these as impositions on Scripture but an affirmation of common ways of reading and understanding the details we encounter. The nature of the comparison would look differently from a Catholic perspective. For example, see Daniel A. Keating, *Deification and Grace* (Naples, FL: Sapientia, 2007), 63-71.

advanced, particularly with regard to justification. I provide a reassessment according to direct concerns that Paul specifically raises regarding death and life. In particular, my participationist reading of Paul's justification theology recognizes his focus on being made alive (ζωοποίησις) as a forensic reality. This attention to the intersection of justification and life in Paul's letters creates the space for reengaging the question of the relationship of justification and deification, of being made alive and of sharing in God's life. Not only are both concerned with life, but the basis of participation in God serves as the ground for both. Thus, the two are not simply synonymous but attend to aspects of the same soteriological arc. To establish this comparison between the two, I will explore deification and justification in turn and then explore the intersection of the two. I first discuss deification.

## Exploring Deification: Sharing in God's Life

As a soteriological doctrine, deification speaks to the restoration of believers from the problem of sin, but as I noted above in discussing Louth, the framework of restoration is cosmic in nature. That is, deification speaks to the whole divine economy of the church being eschatologically united with God by means of the work of Christ and the Spirit. While attention here will be on the individual experience of this union with God, recognizing the wider divine economy expressed by the incarnation, death, and resurrection of the Son and the ministry of the Spirit is essential. Likewise, the communal experience expressed through the divine mysteries within the church is inseparable from a holistic theology of deification. Space does not afford the opportunity to attend to such a broad scope; so I will focus more specifically here on the individual experience, while always recognizing this wider context. As I proceed, I will explore the nature of deification according to the common description of sharing in God's life. Given the influential role of patristic theologians in these discussions, I will attend most closely to patristic formulations of this doctrine. Norman Russell's monograph *The Doctrine of Deification in the Greek Patristic Tradition* continues to stand as the premier work discussing the wider traditions arising during this time frame.[5] I extended and refined

---

[5]Norman Russell, *The Doctrine of Deification in the Greek Patristic Tradition* (Oxford: Oxford University Press, 2004). See also Jules Gross, *The Divinization of the Christian According to the Greek Fathers*, trans. Paul A. Onica (Anaheim: A&C, 2002). As the rest of the essays in this

Russell's treatment in my monograph *Christosis*, and this refined analysis will be the basis for the discussion here.[6]

The basic meaning of deification is "becoming (a) god," with θεοποίησις being one of the first terms used by patristic theologians. Though addressing a holistic transformation, deification is always a metaphor within this tradition. That is, patristic theologians hold to an eternally existing ontological distinction between the Creator and creation that is never crossed in this experience. An affirmation of this ontological distinction stands at the basis of most of the primary theological debates among patristic theologians, such as in the disputes about Gnosticism, Arianism, monophysitism, and monothelitism. In each of these conflicts, attending to the distinction between the Creator and creation (or more specifically between the divine and human natures) is essential for the orthodox position. Accordingly, an orthodox perspective on deification is best described as "attributive deification" rather than "essential deification": humans take on attributes of the divine rather than having the divine nature themselves.[7] The term *ontological* is used in various ways in reference to these approaches. While deification is metaphorical, a true change occurs. Human nature (οὐσία, or the human λόγος) itself is not changed, as believers always remain human; rather, their mode of being (τρόπος τῆς ὑπάρξεως) changes as they take on divine attributes.[8] Both types

---

volume attest, deification is not a static doctrine with a fixed definition. Depending on the context of discussion—biblical, historical, or ecumenical—one's lens on deification will help shape the aspects that are highlighted. Without acceding to the modernist aversion toward later tradition as a corruption of the original source, I will, however, focus on the patristic sources of deification as most significant. This is not to say that there is "the patristic" view of deification, as I will discuss below, but there are central themes that emerge and converge over the earliest centuries of the church. Given the influence of these patristic sources on the later traditions that emerge from them, not only the later Orthodox confession, which gives the most overt attention, but also the Western confessions—Roman Catholic and Protestant. I am addressing the issue of deification (and that of justification) from a confessional perspective. This is important because there are a number of other deification traditions that stand adjacent to the orthodox stream of Christian approaches to deification, among them Mormon approaches, which are outside the scope of my discussion here.

[6]Ben C. Blackwell, *Christosis: Engaging Paul's Soteriology with His Patristic Interpreters*, rev ed. (Grand Rapids, MI: Eerdmans, 2016), and more recently Blackwell, "Deification in the Pauline and Petrine Letters," in *The Oxford Handbook on Deification*, ed. Paul Gavrilyuk, Andrew Hofer, and Matthew Levering (Oxford: Oxford University Press, forthcoming).

[7]Blackwell, *Christosis*, 99-110; see also xx-xxv.

[8]Maximus the Confessor's discussion of these topics is especially helpful. For further discussion, see Ben C. Blackwell and Kris Miller, "Theosis and Theological Anthropology," in *Ashgate*

of change could be described as ontological, but the latter form of change is the focus of (attributive) deification. Extending beyond the direct affirmation of becoming gods, a common way to describe deification is "sharing in the life of God." In this phrase, we encounter two foci expressed through it—likeness (ὁμοίωσις) and participation (μέθεξις). We will consider each in turn.

As we consider becoming *like* God, a number of aspects arise for consideration. If we attend to the aspect of sharing God's *life*, this helps give initial focus to a discussion of likeness. The contrast of death and life is a leitmotif within the Bible explaining the nature of sin and salvation or the fall and new creation. Drawing from this leitmotif, deification is often, even primarily, articulated in terms of participating in eternal life as believers experience incorruption and immortality. Key biblical texts contrast death with being gods (esp. Gen 2–3; Ps 82), and experiencing life is a restoration of Adamic creation in the image and likeness of God (1 Cor 15). *Life* speaks to a specific reality while also serving as a synecdoche regarding a wider participation in covenant blessing. For example, in Deuteronomy 30:15-16 (LXX) ζωή ("life") represents holistic covenant flourishing in its various forms—individual, communal, and terrestrial. It is this wider form of life, characterized in creational and covenantal blessing, that shapes an ancient understanding of deification as sharing in God's life.

Extending this more general conception of becoming like God, the tradition draws out certain divine attributes that receive more attention such as impassibility, holiness, and incorruption. Perhaps incorruption is the most general of these, addressing separation from both moral and somatic corruption. While deification is sometimes identified as moral transformation (historically labeled sanctification in Protestant discussions), deification forms a wider arc that links the process of salvation from regeneration to resurrection. In the present life, believers pursue holiness and flee from moral corruption (see 2 Pet 1:2-8; 2 Cor 3:3-18). The Spirit's initial work of transformation in the present life is oriented to its culmination in resurrection (2 Cor 5:1-5; Rom 8:1-11). Thus, deification captures this wider arc oriented to this telos of the restoration of all creation. As texts such as

---

*Research Companion to Theological Anthropology*, ed. Joshua R. Farris and Charles Taliaferro (Burlington, VT: Ashgate, 2015), 303-17.

Romans 8:28-30 show, being "conformed to the image of the Son" characterizes this holistic process of transformation, such that likeness to God is expressed in terms of the Son and the Spirit.

We could explore much more with regard to likeness of God, but I will turn now to the concept of participation. At a basic level, participation describes how one (greater) entity shares something with a (lower) entity.[9] A vision of participation not only describes the divine-human relationship but is essential to the whole created order, hence the importance of the incarnation of the Son as modeling healthy participation and restoring this to creation. Accordingly, deification goes well beyond the individual, including ecclesial and cosmic aspects. We see the intersection of these various aspects, for instance, in the sacraments because God uses part of the created order to communicate divine mysteries.[10]

Regarding participation in God, God's trinitarian identity, unsurprisingly, shapes the doctrine of becoming gods.[11] Perhaps the primary metaphor for deification is that of adoption, as believers become children of the Father. As with Romans 8 and Galatians 4, adoption speaks not merely to a new relationship but to an ontological change (in the mode of being) particularly identified with resurrection, where believers become coheirs with Christ by means of the Spirit. The Son is a child by nature, whereas believers become adopted children by grace. The Spirit's agency is central to this deifying reality. Due to similar instances of the language of participation, "participating in the divine nature" (2 Pet 1:4) is often equally and ubiquitously expressed by "participation in [or 'fellowship of'] the Holy Spirit" (2 Cor 13:13; Phil 2:1; Heb 6:4) in deification discussions.[12] The incarnation of the divine Son draws all these elements together to express the fullness of the divine-human engagement. The hypostatic union thus serves as the best model for the experience of deification. Throughout the tradition, the illustration of the iron in fire is used to

---

[9]This key point is drawn out by Torstein Theodor Tollefsen, *Activity and Participation in Late Antique and Early Christian Thought*, OECS (Oxford: Oxford University Press, 2012), 6-7. I also address the topic of participation more widely in Ben C. Blackwell, "You Become What You Worship: Theosis and the Story of Bible," *Ex Auditu* 33 (2017): 1-20.

[10]Mediation, then, is part of the ontology of participation.

[11]I explore the trinitarian and christological aspects of deification in Blackwell and Miller, "Theosis and Theological Anthropology."

[12]Scripture translations in this chapter are my own.

describe both the hypostatic union and deification, with the goal of expressing the shared attributes and the preserved distinction of natures within a context of participation. Ultimately, God's identity as Father, Son, and Spirit distinctly shapes both the nature of imaging God and participating in him.

This necessarily cursory discussion of deification provides only a window onto the wider discussions of this doctrine.[13] We see the story progressing from creation to new creation by means of the divine economy through Christ and the Spirit. As believers more fully experience that reality, they share in God's life through union with God in the present age as they await the fullness of consummation eschatologically. With this picture of deification in mind, we can now turn our attention to the topic of justification.

## Exploring Justification: Being Made Alive

Central to theological debates for the last five centuries in the West, the doctrine of justification continues to receive close attention in biblical and theological scholarship. Although Reformational emphases helped to shape the majority of these conversations, a diversity of approaches has arisen since the mid-twentieth century. Since a comparison of deification to each of the various approaches would be unwieldy, I will clarify how contemporary perspectives to justification relate to one another and then articulate a fresh reading of the Pauline letters that attends to the primary forensic issue he addresses with justification, namely, the reversal of condemnation and death by being made alive in Christ through the Spirit.[14]

***Contemporary approaches.*** In the Reformation, distinct attention was given to the metaphor of justification and its role in theology. Heretofore, it was not that justification was ignored, but it did not hold the central prominence that it came to hold for Protestant theology. Attending to the key moment in the timing of justification is central to understanding the nature of the doctrine within Protestant theology. By timing, I speak primarily of initial and final justification. By "initial justification" I am referring to the

---

[13]For wider approaches to deification from a biblical perspective, see especially Michael M. C. Reardon, "Becoming God: Interpreting Pauline Soteriology as Deification," *Currents in Biblical Research* 22, no. 1 (2023): 83-107.

[14]I explore all these issues in greater detail in a forthcoming book, *Participating in the Righteousness of God* (Grand Rapids, MI: Eerdmans, forthcoming), chaps. 5-9.

entrance of the believer to the Christian experience, namely, through faith and baptism. By "final justification" I am referring to the final judgment. While these are not the only moments in relation to justification, they are points of orientation (or centers of gravity) that shape the nature of the metaphor.

Augustine was not the first to discuss justification, but his work has been distinctively influential for subsequent Western formulations. Augustine's approach attends to both initial and final justification, and this is captured by the descriptions of his justification theology as both event and process.[15] The event nature of justification speaks to the initial entry into Christian faith, or (initial) justification. The process aspect addresses the ongoing transformation but also its orientation toward final judgment, or (final) justification. At the initial experience of justification, Augustine discusses being forgiven and having the soul made alive (e.g., *De spiritu et littera* 29.51; *De Trinitate* 4.2.4–3.5). This helps set the orientation to the final judgment, as captured in his discussion of meriting eternal life and thus having the body made alive in resurrection.[16] In this way justification is a reorientation of the believer to God and to the created order.

Over time medieval debates about penance, purgatory, and falling from grace shifted theological attention away from initial justification toward final justification, and we see this expressed (though with modification) in the Counter-Reformation, as articulated in the Council of Trent. Initial justification occurs at baptism, but a continued focus on final justification remains the center of gravity for justification within Catholic theology. We see this through the close attention to meriting eternal life and the process of reconciliation (i.e., penance) after committing mortal sin.[17] In this wider context, Reformation theologians rejected this orientation to final justification and called attention to the initial moment of justification as of primary importance for Paul's theology.

---

[15]See Alister E. McGrath, *Iustitia Dei: A History of the Christian Doctrine of Justification*, 4th ed. (New York: Cambridge University Press, 2020), 46-49.

[16]See Augustine, *De gratia et libero arbitrio* 7.18 and *In Evangelium Johannis tractatus* 3.9, where eternal life is described as "grace" in accord with righteous living, which is also by grace. See David F. Wright in his "Justification in Augustine," in *Justification in Perspective: Historical Developments and Contemporary Challenges*, ed. Bruce L. McCormack (Grand Rapids, MI: Baker Academic, 2006), 69-71.

[17]Council of Trent, session 6: Decree on Justification, chaps. 7, 9, 14–16.

Martin Luther was instrumental for critiquing the penitential system and centering the soteriological moment on initial justification. While he is not at odds with later Reformers, his approach to justification was less systematic. The synthesis achieved in the works of John Calvin and Philipp Melanchthon, what I style the Reformational approach, forms the foundation for most contemporary discussions.[18] A key point of unity is a common recognition of Paul's focus on initial justification as the basis for an assurance of salvation at the final judgment. If initial justification is the theological center of gravity for Paul, the Reformers thus gave requisite attention to divine agency over against human agency. If humans cannot merit initial justification, their acts after initial faith cannot merit final justification. An important aspect is their distinct recognition of the legal (or forensic) aspect of the metaphor of justification, and they focused on forgiveness as the primary experience related to this legal acquittal in (initial) justification.

This Protestant synthesis set the basis for discussion, but other Protestant proposals have arisen within the past century. Though they define the nature of justification differently, these proposals attend to the historical Protestant emphasis of locating justification at initial justification, along with a prioritization of divine agency. I note here the four chief approaches to justification in contemporary scholarship and include the primary experience arising from justification in parentheses: the Reformational perspective (forgiveness), the New Perspective (covenant membership), the apocalyptic perspective (liberation), and the participationist perspective (being made alive). I will briefly explain the key tenets of the first three in turn before more fully explaining the participationist approach separately.[19]

The Reformational perspective identifies justification as God's positive judgment, namely, the acquittal of a criminal defendant (a two-party legal model), as a declaration of a positive status before the court as "not

---

[18] A sensitive account of the similarities and differences between these key reformers is found in Stephen J. Chester, *Reading Paul with the Reformers: Reconciling Old and New Perspectives* (Grand Rapids, MI: Eerdmans, 2017), 173-318.

[19] Besides the extended discussion in my *Participating in the Righteousness of God*, I also explore these four approaches in Ben C. Blackwell, "Paul and Salvation," in *The State of Pauline Studies: A Survey of Recent Research*, ed. Nijay K. Gupta, Erin M. Heim, and Scot McKnight (Grand Rapids, MI: Baker, forthcoming). See also Scot McKnight and Joseph B. Modica, eds., *Preaching Romans: Four Perspectives* (Grand Rapids, MI: Eerdmans, 2019).

guilty."²⁰ Humans outside Christ are sinners before God who experience his wrath as condemnation, and justification by faith is a means to relational reconciliation, with forgiveness being the primary aspect of this restoration. With the New Perspective, the focus is on God's adjudication as in a civil trial that arises between his people and the opposing nations (a three-party legal model). Rather than justification as a distinctly soteriological metaphor, New Perspective interpreters focus on the judge's identification of believers as covenant members over against the condemnation of exile with the nations. Like the Reformational model, justification is the declaration of the judge. This declaration plays a role within a wider soteriological movement of God but primarily as affirming a right standing within the covenant. Thus, *adoption* is a key synonym for *justification* since it similarly addresses family membership. The apocalyptic perspective also situates justification in a three-party model, but instead of the nations as the opponents, humans are oppressed and enslaved by cosmic powers. In this model, God's act of justification brings restoration as liberation, as God makes right (rectifies) the world. The focus is not God's declaration as central to the metaphor but his act of release.

These differing interpretations attend to the varieties of contexts and issues that Paul raises in his letters. Several interpretive questions arise that are necessary to answer to make proper sense of justification as a legal (or forensic) metaphor: How is Paul's theology focused between initial and final justification? When Paul contrasts condemnation and justification, what is the primary focus of this antithesis? What legal model serves as the basis of the forensic metaphor—two-party or three-party? What is the nature of God's act as judge—a declaration or some other kind of enactment? How does justification relate to God's covenant promises to Israel?

While each of the prior three approaches provides partially helpful answers to these questions, they struggle to articulate an approach that attends to the full scope of data in his letters. Not only that, they generally ignore some of most important data Paul provides. This seems to happen because justification is framed as a Protestant theology in response to medieval

---

[20] The two-party and three-party setting greatly illuminates a key distinction between justification approaches. This is very helpfully explained by James B. Prothro, *A Pauline Theology of Justification* (Eugene, OR: Cascade, 2023), 18-75.

Catholic emphases. They rightly capture Paul's focus on initial justification, but the topic of life plays little structural role in most articulations of justification due to concerns about meriting eternal life. The problem is that life is the central focus of Paul's forensic metaphor of justification, as drawn from his primary Old Testament verse (Hab 2:4) as its basis: "the one righteous by faith will live" (Rom 1:17; Gal 3:11). In the following section, I will demonstrate how a participationist perspective best accounts for Paul's justification theology in terms of the questions above and how this relates to the topic of life. This setting does not provide space to build this model from the separate data; so I will articulate a holistic picture of Paul's portrayal.[21]

**Justification within a participationist perspective.** By attending to a participationist perspective of Paul, we are drawn into a stream of interpretation that arises well before the Reformation. I and others have argued that wider patristic readings of Paul also stand within this stream of interpreting his letters, and so today Orthodox, Catholic, and some Protestant readings fall within this wider umbrella. The nomenclature of *participation* highlights the fundamental structure of theology as grounded in a personal encounter with the triune God in which humans share in God's divine attributes. Of course, many Protestant traditions attend to some aspect of this, as evident in the theology of union with Christ. The difference here is the structural nature of this participationist ontology as grounding the breadth of theological discussion.[22] As such, participation is as fundamental to justification as the rest of Paul's theology. What distinguishes a Protestant reading is not then the mode (through participation) but more so the timing (initial justification).

What is distinctive of the participationist reading I advance here is attention to Paul's language of life as the primary concept concurrent with his justification theology.[23] That is, for Paul justification primarily entails being

---

[21]For exegetical support for this wider vision, see my *Participating in the Righteousness of God*.

[22]For a wider biblical theology from the perspective of participation, see Klyne R. Snodgrass, *You Need a Better Gospel: Reclaiming the Good News of Participation with Christ* (Grand Rapids, MI: Baker, 2022).

[23]For an articulation of this reading that attends more closely to Paul's letters, see Ben C. Blackwell, "Justification as Participation in Divine Glory in Romans 1–4," in *The Beginning of Paul's Gospel: Theological Explorations in Romans 1–4*, ed. Nijay K. Gupta and John K. Goodrich (Eugene, OR: Cascade, 2023), 197–219. For a similar perspective, see Michael J. Gorman, "Reading Galatians 2:15-21 Theologically: Beyond Old and New, West and East," in *Participating in Christ: Explorations in Paul's Theology and Spirituality* (Grand Rapids, MI: Baker, 2019), 115–49.

made alive (ζωοποίησις). Though life is not normally considered a legal category, as we encounter Paul's justification theology within its Old Testament covenant lawsuit context, we will see that God's forensic act of restoration from sin, as a move from condemnation to justification, is exactly a move from death to life.

Justification fits within Paul's wider focus on restoration eschatology: God has made promises to restore Israel from the problems arising from sin, and Paul stands in the tradition of Second Temple Jews who were expecting God to bring restoration to the people of Israel. One development from the Old Testament into the Second Temple period is an increasing focus on God's final judgment on individuals at the great assize, in which humans would encounter either condemnation or justification, and respectively experience eternal death or eternal life. One could be considered righteous in the present age, but the center of gravity was on final justification with the enactment of God's judgment in death or life in the afterlife. It is important to note that the legal focus is the judge's enacted verdict at this final judgment, not simply the verdict alone. While this forensic metaphor takes on a more individual tone, we should not forget the wider restoration eschatology from the Old Testament that grounds the basis of this theology. That is, death and life serve as the primary focus of covenant curses and blessings for the people as a whole (see Deut 30:15-20). Building on this foundation, the experience of death and life in God's judgment is an extension of the covenant lawsuit as we see expressed in the prophets.

Paul's encounter with the promised Messiah Jesus and the promised Spirit distinctly shape his justification theology. In the death and resurrection of Jesus the Messiah, God's restoring grace is poured out by the Holy Spirit as an expression of new covenant renewal. The definitive turning point in history is no longer God's future judgment by means of the Messiah's future advent but rather the Messiah's first advent. The eschatological turn has already happened, and believers participate in Christ as an eschatological reality. One central way that Paul articulates this eschatological reality is through justification—the final judgment has been brought forward to the present for those who believe in Jesus. God's eschatological judgment of acquittal is enacted in the present at conversion, and so Paul's focus is on initial justification.

Paul's emphasis on initial justification is not strongly disputed, but what happens at this initial justification is. In coherence with the forensic character of the metaphor, we should expect that the nature of God's act in initial justification should be commensurate with that of final justification—participation in eternal life (rather than eternal death). This is in fact what we encounter in Paul's theology, particularly through the discussion of the antithesis of condemnation and justification (esp. Rom 5:12-21; 2 Cor 3:6-9; Gal 2:15–3:21). *Death* is the primary and repeated emphasis of Paul's discussion of the covenant curse by means of condemnation.[24] Likewise, *life* is the primary and repeated emphasis of the covenant blessing of justification. In this way, death and life serve as a synecdoche, as central parts of the covenant curse and blessing, which represent the whole. Forgiveness is also a part of this wider covenant restoration, but not the primary focus of justification.

Condemnation does not simply *mean* death, nor justification, life. Condemnation and justification arise from a legal metaphor as the *enacted verdict* of a judge. Death is the negative enactment of the judge as condemnation, and life the enactment of justification, just as in Jewish final judgment traditions. In this way, then, condemnation entails the enactment of death (i.e., killing), and justification entails the enactment of life (i.e., making alive). Accordingly, the clearest term in Greek to describe the experience of justification is ζωοποίησις ("being made alive"), and we find Paul specifically using this language in terms of justification in Galatians 3:21; 2 Corinthians 3:6-9; and Romans 4:17-25. A number of other passages articulate this idea by means of the language of life (ζωή): Galatians 2:16-21; 3:10-14; Romans 1:17; 5:12-21; 8:1-10. Paul's well-known affirmation "I no longer live, but Christ lives in me" (Gal 2:20) is the climax of his most celebrated argument regarding justification—Galatians 2:15-21. Likewise, the thesis of Romans highlights this hope of justification as life by means of the prophetic text that proclaimed the gospel beforehand (see Rom 1:2): "The one righteous by faith will live" (Hab 2:4 in Rom 1:17). Or later we read, "There is therefore now no condemnation [i.e., there is now justification] for those who are in Christ because the law of the Spirit of life has set you free from the law of sin and death" (Rom 8:1-2). The

---

[24]This data notably stands in opposition to positions that see guilt (Reformational), exile (new perspective), or enslavement (apocalyptic) as central to condemnation.

focus throughout Paul's letters is on the enactment of the judge, not merely a verdict (or status declaration) alone.[25]

The language of *life* in terms of the promised Messiah and Spirit thus expresses the restoration of covenant blessing. The hope of restoration at the final judgment helps set the focus of the act of justification, but the legal structure of the covenant lawsuit helps establish the nature of the legal model that undergirds Paul's theology. In the Reformational approach, the appeal is to a two-party structure (God versus sinful humans), and in the other two approaches, the appeal is to a three-party structure with God as judge (new perspective: covenant community versus the nations; apocalyptic: humanity versus cosmic powers). Which structure best accords with the Old Testament background and with Paul's letters? Actually, both structures are evident in the Old Testament and both in Paul. James Prothro expertly details the interconnecting reality of these two-party and three-party legal structures within Old Testament covenant lawsuits and in Paul.[26]

Paul's use of both forms of this covenant lawsuit as a legal metaphor is important in two respects. First, Paul's justification theology is fundamentally covenantal in nature. Though he disputes the "works of the law" as the basis of justification, the foundational use of the covenant lawsuit structure and the covenant outcomes (blessing/life and cursing/death) establishes the directly covenantal nature of his justification theology. Second, a holistic perspective on Paul's justification theology must attend to both legal structures—both the two- and three-party models. The Reformational, New, and apocalyptic perspectives each make use of only one structure but cannot include the other. However, the participationist reading incorporates both without placing them in opposition. Whether the condemnation arises from God as judge (two-party) or the opposing powers (three-party), death is the result. Likewise, whether restoration is before God or before these opposing powers, justification as life for the dead is the result of God's acquittal. The focus is not the declaration of the judge but the enacted verdict.

---

[25]Similarly, the problem with the law and justification is not that the law declares sinners guilty but rather that the law kills, and it cannot make alive (Rom 7:7-21; Gal 3:10-11, 21; 2 Cor 3:6-9).
[26]See Prothro, *Pauline Theology of Justification*, 18-75.

Ultimately, justification is an expression of Paul's most basic soteriology: "The wages of sin is death, but the gift of God is eternal life in the Messiah Jesus our Lord" (Rom 6:23). In this already-not yet eschatological experience of life, ascertaining the extent to which believers are made alive in the present in (initial) justification is important. In Romans 8:10-11, we have clear evidence of a human duality (though not a dualism)—the inner-outer distinction. Paul stipulates that although the body is mortal presently, "the Spirit is life on account of righteousness" (Rom 8:10). The presence of the life-giving Spirit presently in justification (Rom 8:10) is thus the basis for the hope that God will also make alive our bodies in the future (Rom 8:11). Initial justification (being made alive internally) is the basis for the hope of final justification (being made alive physically—resurrection) at the final judgment, thus linking the beginning with its telos.

This participationist reading of justification not only attends to Paul's direct statements; it also better explains his ethics arising from it. Many have struggled in the past to see the connection between justification as solely God's act and sanctification as a divine-human partnership: the former is done without works, but works are necessary for the latter. A distinction between divine and human agency is important to Paul's argument, as the Reformers carefully noted. They tried to protect this distinction by arguing that justification entails only a verdict (a status declaration), over against nonforensic approaches. However, the enactment of the verdict is as much forensic as its declaration, and both aspects are ascribed to only the judge's activity. No one makes oneself alive; this is the act of an external agent.[27] However, once one is made alive, one can live. In this connection, then, we see the intimate relationship between justification and sanctification: God makes us alive so that we can live in obedience. Justification is thus inherently connected to sanctification, while still being distinct.

To summarize the key elements, justification is a legal metaphor arising from covenant lawsuits in the Old Testament. Moving into the Second Temple period, the nature of God's eschatological adjudication at the final judgment became more of the focus, particularly with regard to God enacting

---

[27] A dependence on God's sole sufficiency is the distinct focus of 2 Cor 3:3-9, where Paul interweaves being made alive and justification.

his verdict of eternal death or eternal life. Because of Paul's prior experience of the Christ-event through the promised Spirit, Paul eschatologically reinterprets the nature of this trial. God's positive enacted verdict of making people alive is no longer a future judgment; it becomes a present reality through faith by participation in the Messiah and the Spirit. Though the experience of life does not immediately seem forensic, God's making believers alive as initial justification is absolutely forensic. It is a legal reality shaped by the Messiah's own vindicating (that is, justifying) resurrection (Rom 4:25; 1 Tim 3:16), rescuing him from death and condemnation. As God makes believers alive, this grounds his ethical challenge to live in obedience.

By attending to Paul's focus on initial justification and divine agency in the process, my reading accords with key Protestant distinctives. Though Calvin and (later) Melanchthon made a firm distinction between justification and regeneration (vivification), Martin Luther did not.[28] This is not to say that Luther held to the covenantal structure I have noted here; however, Luther was much more comfortable presenting life as a necessary companion to justification. Indeed, he is just as happy to talk about an "alien life" as he is an "alien justification," both of which arise from union with Christ.[29] While my reading might not appear to attend to Protestant concerns, it both has Protestant roots historically and follows in the distinct Protestant focus of always returning to Scripture to test our previous readings. Once we capture the centrality of becoming alive to the doctrine of justification, we now see a distinct avenue for engaging the discussion between justification and deification—being made alive and sharing in God's life.

## JUSTIFICATION AND DEIFICATION: LIFE AND PARTICIPATION

Having now articulated an approach to deification and justification, I can address our primary question regarding the relationship between these two theological loci. Both speak to the issue of life and arise by means of participation, so there is an immediate connection, yet they are not simply synonymous. Deification speaks to the wider arc of salvation, and justification sits within this arc, primarily addressing one's entrance. With this connection

---

[28] On this, see Chester, *Reading Paul with the Reformers*, 213-17.
[29] Luther, "Lectures on Galatians" (1535), *LW* 26:170.

in mind, let us consider the relationship at a more granular level. I will specifically address the nature of the respective experiences and the process for experiencing each.

***Comparing experiences.*** Both justification and deification are soteriological doctrines; so they speak to the restoration of humanity from the problem of sin and separation from God. In popular Protestant theology, the relationship of justification and deification is mapped onto the justification-sanctification distinction, as two distinct realities arising from union with Christ.[30] Justification addresses the restored relationship before God as an objective reality—a status declaration made by the Father. In contrast, sanctification addresses the personal transformation that arises from this divine-human encounter—a subjective reality through participation. While this appears heuristically helpful, this articulation arises from reductive perspectives of both justification and deification. Justification is not merely the verdict (as a status declaration) but rather an enacted verdict—being made alive. Deification is not merely the process of sanctification but rather the whole arc of salvation as God's new creation restoration. When attending the full picture of each, we can best attend to the specific relationship of how each addresses the experience of life.

Deification speaks to the wider arc of salvation, though with more focus on the present (moral) life and the life of the world to come. Sitting within this wider arc, justification likewise addresses the experience of life but primarily addresses the initiation of life at conversion, while also pointing to resurrection at the final judgment. While both speak of the experience of life, deification mostly addresses the process of transformation in the present and future, whereas justification primarily addresses the initiation. The relationship of justification to other biblical images—namely, sanctification and adoption—helps to clarify the nature of these relationships. We do not want to collapse these metaphors, but we recognize that they correlate with each other.

Paul does not seem as uniquely concerned to separate justification and sanctification as some readers do, but we can discern a distinction between

---

[30]Of course, this traditional use of *sanctification* can be problematic. It does not only speak to progressive holiness because Paul just as often speaks of sanctification as punctiliar, definitively established at conversion, hence his regular address of believers as "saints."

the beginning of the Christian life and what results from it.[31] Paul particularly argues that believers have been made alive, so they should live. We see this in Romans 6, where Paul uses the transition from death to life in baptism as the foundation for his ethical encouragement not to continue to live in sin. Importantly, in Romans 6:7 Paul identifies the freedom from sin in baptism as a "justification from sin," thus clarifying that the initial transition of death to life in baptism is none other than justification. In other words, the Reformation model is right that justification is a point that leads to a process of sanctification, but the segregation of inward renewal from justification is not. Though traditional in order, Paul's goal is not to emphasize forgiveness leading to obedience but a freshly planted tree bearing fruit as the natural result.

We also see a direct correlation between justification and adoption rather than a sharp differentiation. Calvin rightly notes that justification and adoption are distinct soteriological metaphors, in which God is judge and Father (*Inst.* 3.11.1). This raises the question of how justification and adoption are related. While we might see these images as distinct, Kevin Vanhoozer articulates how justification and adoption are both legal transactions that create a new reality, and he helpfully argues that we should not overextend the differences.[32] Paul importantly addresses adoption in two key passages that also explore his justification theology (Gal 3–4; Rom 8). Whereas the justification-sanctification relationship speaks to beginning and continuing, justification and adoption appear to overlap more in the beginning and completion aspects, at least in the Pauline usage. By means of these metaphors, Paul primarily emphasizes the initial relational transition, but they also both speak to the culmination of believers' salvation, the assured hope of resurrection. Being made alive inwardly in the present as justification assures believers that they will be made alive bodily in the future (Rom 8:10-11). Likewise, adoption in the present (Rom 8:14-17) also assures believers of their future "adoption, the redemption of our bodies" in resurrection (Rom 8:23).

---

[31]One cannot simply make an identification of following the works of the law and sanctification.

[32]Kevin J. Vanhoozer, "Wrighting the Wrongs of the Reformation? The State of the Union with Christ in St. Paul and Protestant Soteriology," in *Jesus, Paul, and the People of God: A Theological Dialogue with N. T. Wright*, ed. Nicholas Perrin and Richard B. Hays (Downers Grove, IL: IVP Academic, 2011), 235-61, here 254-57. That said, he identifies justification with only a status declaration.

Though Paul uses adoption to focus on these two points in time, the wider canonical discussion of believers as children of God serves to address the moral life in the present. Similarly, God's act of justification focuses on the initiation of the Christian life in Paul, whereas the language of righteous living (e.g., Mt 6) places the focus on the present life as a basis for future realities. Thus, we experience some tension from comparison of these metaphors because Paul uses them in specific ways that are either not present in other works or are expanded in ways he does not. We do not need to collapse the metaphors, making God the Father-judge as a single reality, but we can also appreciate the ways the metaphors overlap while remaining distinct. These insights regarding the comparison of justification with the metaphors of sanctification and adoption similarly apply to the comparison of justification and deification. That is, justification is primarily used in Paul's letters, and so while there are debates about what justification entails, we encounter a fairly consistent portrayal across his letters. Deification, however, does not arise from singular linguistic center but rather a conglomeration of topics related to life, such as image of God, incorruption, adoption, and glory. As such, deification is much more wide-ranging and flexible as a doctrine, which makes a neat comparison impossible.

Ultimately, these metaphors of justification and deification address overlapping areas in complementary ways. Rather than a *duplex gratia* model where justification and sanctification are simultaneous but distinct, the deification model identifies an organic coherence between being made alive (justification) and living (sanctification), which is part of the whole arc of sharing in God's life, from conversion to resurrection. Though justification primarily speaks to conversion (initial justification), its purpose is to assure resurrection (final justification), and this shows how justification and deification both speak to the wider arc of salvation. Going beyond mere comparison, the distinct focus on life central to both—being made alive (justification) and sharing in God's life (deification)—shows that they speak to the same reality, just highlighting specific aspects. In this way, we could better speak of a *simplex gratia* model, not only because of the single focus on life but because of the single source of that life in participation, which I will now explain.

***Comparing processes.*** If the common soteriological experience of life grounds the intersection of justification and deification, the common foundation of participation between each is even stronger. In this way, both arise from the same basis—a personal encounter with the triune God, such that humans participate in divine realities. Two key aspects of this common foundation of participation are important to address: divine and human agency and the trinitarian foundation.

The role for human agency seems to place a theology of deification at direct odds with the doctrine of justification, where there is a distinct focus on divine agency over against human agency. In particular, one reason justification rose to the forefront of theological debate was due to its determinative function in rebutting the role of human agency to achieve salvation. Deriving from the likes of Augustine, medieval Roman Catholic theologians affirmed that humans, by means of divine grace, could merit eternal life.[33] The Reformers rejected the notion that human agency could influence (or merit) salvation, as evidenced by Paul's distinction of faith over against works (of the law) as the basis for justification. The segregation of divine and human agency was protected even further by the later but distinct emphasis on the objective status declaration by God as judge (justification) over against the subjective internal renewal by the Spirit (sanctification). While the latter is still a divine work, identifying justification with only a status declaration of the judge meant there could be no hint of human involvement. This differentiation thus allows divine agency alone with justification and a partnership between divine and human with sanctification.

Since partnering with God in the walk of faith is a central focus the present spiritual life, deification seems to stand at odds with justification, or it is at least structurally different.[34] Though some might express concern about being absorbed into God with deification, it is actually the elevation

---

[33] Augustine, *De gratia et libero arbitrio* 7.18 and *In Evangelium Johannis tractatus* 3.9; Council of Trent, session 6: Decree on Justification, chap. 16. Of course, the human agency described by Trent is based on the enlivening work of the Spirit and founded on the ultimate merits of Christ (chap. 7).

[34] Norman Russell's excellent introduction to the topic of deification even captures this in his title: *Fellow Workers with God: Orthodox Thinking on Theosis* (Crestwood, NY: St. Vladimir's Seminary Press, 2009), as drawn from 1 Cor 3:9.

of human agency that seems to create one of the biggest problems. We see this explicitly in the christological controversies that simultaneously shaped the doctrine of deification. In particular, deification arose concurrently with the effort to defend the full humanity of Christ against Apollinarian and monothelite positions. Thus, the climax of christological debates affirmed the distinct human nature of Christ, and this is most evident in a separate but fully acquiescent human will, as defended by Maximus the Confessor and affirmed in Constantinople III (680–681). If Christ's humanity has a fully functioning will, then vivified believers likewise can and should expect to exercise their human will in partnership with that of the divine.[35]

Does this mean that the two theological systems are incommensurate? As we consider the issue of divine and human agency, we should first note that the doctrines of justification and deification are both grounded in the absolute dependence of humanity on God for life and flourishing. The importance of divine agency is evident in justification, whether the context of the discussion is faith and works or God's life-giving activity. As God makes believers alive in justification, this is for the purpose that they would live. That is, restored agency for humanity is inherent to justification and thus the telos of a human partnership with God in the life of faith. With regard to patristic theology, human nature is not sufficient for existence on its own; rather, life and flourishing is found through participation in God, who self-exists. Thus, with the doctrine of deification, the emphasis throughout is on God's initial gift of life in creation and the culmination of the gift in new creation. This is not merely a restoration of what was lost in the fall, but rather humans grow throughout eternity as finite people who continually engage an infinite God.

Thus, while I would disagree with the segregation of inward renewal from justification, the fundamental thesis of the progression from justification to sanctification is correct.[36] John Barclay's work on the nature of grace is quite important for helping distinguish elements of Paul's argument regarding grace. In particular, Barclay highlights that perhaps the most consistent theme in Paul's theology of grace is that of incongruity, which in more

---

[35]This is grounded on a model of noncompetitive agency.
[36]Regarding the segregation of inward renewal from justification, Paul never seems to go out of his way to distinguish justification and sanctification in the way that dogmatic theology has.

traditional terms means "unmerited grace." Human agency, corrupted and mortally wounded by sin, would always be insufficient to influence our salvation.[37] Thus, the inward renewal and forgiveness inherent in justification must be a distinct work of divine agency.[38] In fact, it is the efficacy of this divine agency that makes the possibility of human agency in the journey of life a reality, and this is the very basis for the circularity of grace.[39]

If, then, we attend to the different moments of salvation, the question of divine and human agency need not be at odds in deification and justification. Deification traditions that focus on the present walk of faith do not tend to emphasize initial conversion, where divine agency is the singular act, but neither do they negate the focus on divine agency. Rather, their focus is on the partnership of humans with God in obedience to the divine will, similar to wider Reformation traditions. Deification traditions typically are much freer with the language of cooperation (not unlike Roman Catholic theology) in a way that makes many Protestants uncomfortable, but this appears to be a matter of emphasis than a contradiction, with Orthodox and Catholic theologians most similar to Wesleyans when referring to postconversion cooperation in sanctification. Ultimately, we should not lose sight of the absolute dependence that deification traditions place on the divine source of human flourishing through participation. It is God's life that humans share in, and this similarly is the foundation for justification.

To fully capture the nature of participation, we must attend to the trinitarian nature of God, which highly shapes the nature of soteriology. The doctrine of deification is inextricable from the doctrine of the Trinity, whereas historically Protestant discussions of justification have focused on union with

---

[37] Roman Catholic doctrine also affirms this focus on incongruity before conversion. The primary distinction between Protestant and Catholic doctrine on agency relates to the human agency in restoration from mortal sin by means of the process of penance, which includes works of satisfaction (Council of Trent, session 6: Decree on Justification, chap. 14). Cf. John M. G. Barclay, *Paul and the Gift* (Grand Rapids, MI: Eerdmans, 2015), 97-99.

[38] No one raises themselves. In the same way that even Jesus' own resurrection was a distinct work of the Father and Spirit, not Christ raising himself, the act of making alive is also a singularly divine work.

[39] Barclay highlights "incongruity" and "circularity" in Paul's theology but fails to appreciate efficacy holistically. For an assessment, see Ben C. Blackwell, "Justification in Cyril of Alexandria," in *The New Perspective on Grace: Paul and the Gospel After Paul and the Gift*, ed. Stephen Chester et al. (Grand Rapids, MI: Eerdmans, 2023), 197-214.

Christ as the foundation, and even more so on the importance of Jesus' human obedience. In contrast to Catholic affirmations of the Spirit's righteousness or affirmations such as that of Andreas Osiander, who points to Christ's divine righteousness in justification, Reformation traditions focus on the obedience of the man Jesus that is imputed to believers (see Calvin, *Inst.* 3.11.5-12).[40] The Father serves as the impartial judge, and the Spirit draws believers to faith, but the primary mechanism of Reformational approaches to justification is christological, in that it is by means of union with Christ and the imputation of Christ's righteousness. In distinction, the trinitarian shape of deification is more evident—believers are adopted as children of the Father, as they are conformed to the image of Christ, by participating in the Holy Spirit. Thus, one might raise the question whether justification and deification so easily arise from a common root of trinitarian participation.

While traditional readings of justification are more christological, participationist readings more easily cohere with deification theologies in which believers share in the life of God through Christ and the Spirit. Believers are made alive (ζωοποιέω), just as their crucified Messiah was made alive as his own vindication (Rom 4:25; 1 Tim 3:16). Accordingly, as a climax of one of his earliest justification arguments in Galatians 2:16-21, Paul writes: "I have been crucified with Christ and I no longer live, but Christ lives in me" (Gal 2:19-20). This echoes participation in Jesus' death and life through baptism in Romans 6:1-11. Not only is this the life of the Messiah, but it is also the life of the Holy Spirit. In 2 Corinthians 3:6-9 and Romans 8:1-2, 10, Paul identifies the life-giving work of the Spirit with justification.[41]

Accordingly, the one who is in Christ and in the Spirit participates in the life of God as justification. This participationist understanding of justification is no less christological than the Reformational reading, but I would argue it is more holistically christological. It does not so quickly separate the divine from the human in Jesus' obedience, and it more holistically accounts

---

[40] With regard to Jesus' passive and active obedience within the Reformed tradition, see Brandon Crowe, "The Passive and Active Obedience of Christ: Retrieving a Biblical Distinction," in *The Doctrine on Which the Church Stands or Falls: Justification in Biblical, Theological, Historical, and Pastoral Perspective*, ed. Matthew Barrett (Wheaton, IL: Crossway, 2019), 441-68.

[41] The Nicene Creed recognizes this life-giving and therefore justifying role of the Spirit when it affirms the Spirit as "the Lord and Giver of life" (τὸ κύριον τὸ ζωοποιόν).

for the Spirit's work in raising Jesus and those who follow the Messiah as believers.⁴² In addition, Paul highlights the personal encounter with the Messiah and the Spirit, not just imputation as the means of justification. The grace necessary for justification is experienced in Christ and through the Spirit personally. For this reason, participation arises from a hypostastization of grace, not that grace has (or is) a hypostasis, but grace is communicated through the hypostases of the Son and Spirit for those who are "in" them.

Believers thus experience a *simplex gratia* as we encounter the triune God personally. The *duplex gratia* model separates the elements of grace—justification comes from the obedience of the human Jesus, but sanctification from the divine indwelling of the Spirit. This articulation arises from divisions externally imposed, not ones arising from Paul's letters. On the contrary, the participationist model attends to the triune economy evident in Paul's theology. It thus accounts for the interdependent missions of the Son and the Spirit toward humanity in returning humanity to the Father. Associating justification solely with Jesus' human obedience echoes problems that the third through sixth ecumenical counsels sought to overcome.⁴³ Rather, believers encounter a *simplex gratia* through the God-man Jesus as mediated through the Spirit. This best accords with dogmatic trinitarianism and the biblical data regarding sharing in the divine life.

Ultimately, the nature of participation that grounds deification is the same participation that grounds justification. Of course, a wider series of issues remain to be considered, such as the role of sacraments, the distinction between extrinsic and intrinsic grace, and the relationship of faith

---

⁴²There is no indication, e.g., in Rom 5 that Paul is trying to make that distinction between the divine from the human in Jesus' obedience.

⁴³As we attend to the hypostatic union in Christ as the best model for deification, this means that, yes, we should recognize the distinction between the fullness of divinity and the fullness of humanity in the incarnation of the Son and the distinct properties of the natures. However, we also should attend to the hypostatic union where these two natures are experienced in the single person of the incarnate Son. Indeed, Maximus the Confessor (*Ambiguum* 5, 41) uses the language of *perichoresis* to describe this interpenetration of natures in the hypostatic union. Korb summarizes this well: "In the incarnation the Word enhypostasises his own human nature in himself; in deification he enhypostasises human beings within himself by identifying them (by grace) with the same humanity with which he is hypostatically one, as members of his own body. Seen in these terms, deification can be nothing but incarnation—the Word's gracious incorporation of humanity into his own hypostasis." Samuel Korb, "Whole God and Whole Man: Deification as Incarnation in Maximus the Confessor," *SJT* 75 (2022): 308-18, here 309.

to love. However, this common foundation of participation in God through Christ and the Spirit distinctly shapes the experience of God's life in justification and deification, thus uniting them together.

## Conclusion

In our study to explore the possible intersection of deification and justification, I articulated the key aspects of each and determined that they do indeed have a distinct overlap by means of the experience of life in the context of participation. The key questions about the cosmic nature of deification and the forensic nature of justification proved not to be the anticipated dividing walls. The Reformers were right that justification is absolutely a forensic metaphor. This forensic foundation has been seen as wall of division, but it actually becomes the bridge: the judge's enacted verdict to make alive consummates the covenant lawsuit of the Old Testament and articulates the restoration of covenant blessing through the Messiah and the Spirit. With the direct connections between covenant restoration and new creation, particularly expressed by *life* as a synecdoche for holistic restoration, we see that the hope of being made alive is both a personal reality and part of a cosmic framework. We thus encounter grace as participation in the divine life, articulated in particular modes within the wider divine economy.

As we continue the conversation about justification and deification, let me commend two patristic theologians, Cyril of Alexandria and Augustine, as insightful partners to model a fruitful dialogue. They both provide extensive treatments of justification and relate this to a theology of deification.[44] Like them, we see that justification and deification both speak to the reality of being made alive through participation in the life of God through Christ and the Spirit. Though we find a basic harmony, much more work is yet to be done to continue these conversations.

---

[44]Within their wider treatments of justification, they each draw in deification explicitly: e.g., Cyril, *Commentarii in Iohannem* 17.18-19; Augustine: *De Trinitate* 4.2.4–3.5 and *Enarrationes in Psalmos* 49.2. For Cyril's theology of justification, see Blackwell, "Justification in Cyril of Alexandria." For Augustine's theology of justification, see Blackwell, *Participating in the Righteousness of God*, chapter 2.

# JUSTIFICATION as UNION and CHRIST'S PRESENCE

## A Lutheran Perspective

### Veli-Matti Kärkkäinen

## A New Emerging Paradigm of Considering Luther's Theology of Justification

Reformation theology in general and Lutheran tradition in particular have had a hard time in trying to reconcile the idea of theosis with the doctrine of justification. Historically, these two traditions have been considered diametrically opposed to each other. A corollary problem is that, for Lutherans, Eastern Orthodox soteriology entertains problematic notions of the freedom of the will, too positive an anthropology, and, worst of all, the idea of human-divine *synergia* in salvation. It is not uncommon among Lutheran theologians to consider any reference to theosis a form of Osiandrism, that is, a Lutheran heresy according to which "the presence of God in Christians amounts to a participation in the majestic divine essence."[1] Too bad that too many Protestants know too little about the Orthodox doctrine.[2] It is safe to say that until

---

This essay is a republication of my "Justification as Union and Christ's Presence: Deification in Lutheran Tradition," in *With All the Fullness of God: Deification in Christian Tradition*, ed. Jared Ortiz (Minneapolis: Lexington Books/Fortress Academic, 2020), 59-81; permission granted by the publisher. That essay borrows liberally from a wider discussion in chapter 11 of my *Spirit and Salvation*, vol. 4 of A Constructive Christian Theology for the Pluralistic World (Grand Rapids, MI: Eerdmans, 2016).

[1]Risto Saarinen, "Justification by Faith: The View of the Mannermaa School," in *The Oxford Handbook of Martin Luther's Theology*, ed. Robert Kolb, Irene Dingel, and L'ubomír Batka (Oxford: Oxford University Press, 2014), 259-60. This essay (pp. 254-64) helps put the new Mannermaa school interpretation (to be discussed in this article) in a wider historical context in Lutheranism and its traditional resistance to the doctrine of theosis and related emphases.

[2]Georg Kretschmar, "Die Rezeption der orthodoxen Vergöttlichungslehre in der protestantischen Theologie," in *Luther und Theosis: Vergöttlichung als Thema der abendländischen Theologie*, ed.

recent decades, the standard Lutheran assessment of theosis as a controlling metaphor has been ignored or, if need be, resisted and rejected. I am not aware of any major historical Lutheran theologian or Lutheran theological community that has lifted up theosis as a favorable soteriological concept, notwithstanding the fact that related concepts such as union and participation, of course, belong to the Lutheran theological thesaurus.

Against this historical background, one of the most unexpected and theologically-ecumenically most promising developments in international Lutheran studies is the rise of a new perspective on Martin Luther's soteriology that can be named as "salvation as union" or "salvation as Christ's 'real' presence in faith through the Holy Spirit." Under the leadership of the late Finnish professor Tuomo Mannermaa, a number of Luther scholars at the University of Helsinki have not only helped to radically revise the canons of the interpretation of the Reformer's own theology but also accomplished unprecedented ecumenical achievements.[3]

It was a great surprise that important commonalities were discerned between Luther's theology of justification and the ancient concept of theosis, *widely embraced by Eastern Christianity*—notwithstanding the largely negative (or dismissive) reception of deification among Protestants. The breakthrough came at the end of the 1970s, thanks to ecumenical contacts with the Orthodox tradition (of Russia). The Lutheran-Orthodox dialogue produced a highly influential soteriological document in Kiev (Ukraine) 1977 titled "Salvation as Justification and Deification." The preamble to the theses claims, "Until recently, there has been a predominant opinion that the Lutheran and Orthodox doctrines of salvation greatly differ from each other. In the conversations, however, it has become evident that both these important aspects of salvation discussed in the

---

Simo Peura and Antti Raunio, Schriften der Luther-Agricola-Gesellschaft 25 (Helsinki: Martin-Luther Verlag, 1990), 61-80.

[3] In English, see Tuomo Mannermaa, *Christ Present in Faith: Luther's View of Justification*, ed. Kirsi Stjerna (Minneapolis: Augsburg Fortress, 2005); consult also Carl E. Braaten and Robert W. Jenson, eds., *Union with Christ: The New Finnish Interpretation of Luther* (Grand Rapids, MI: Eerdmans, 1998); for a succinct introduction, see Mannermaa, "Why Is Luther So Fascinating? Modern Finnish Luther Research," in Braaten and Jenson, *Union with Christ*, 1-20. A full-scale presentation of Helsinki scholars' interpretation of Luther's theology at large is Olli-Pekka Vainio, ed., *Engaging Luther: A (New) Theological Assessment* (Eugene, OR: Wipf & Stock, 2010).

conversations have a strong New Testament basis and there is great unanimity with regard to them both."[4]

It was found that the doctrine of deification covers the idea of a Christian's life as righteous and sinful at the same time, as Lutheran theology has always emphasized. The idea of deification makes more explicit what is sometimes in danger of being underemphasized in Lutheranism, namely, the sanative role of grace: "When the Christian has been justified, he takes a new road leading to deification."[5] Soon it was also discovered that important convergences could be discerned between the soteriologies of Luther and of Catholics—and even beyond.

The basic theses and claims of this new Lutheran interpretation can be summarized as follows:

1. Luther's understanding of salvation can be expressed not only in terms of the doctrine of justification but also as *deification*. Thus, while there are differences between the Eastern and Lutheran understandings of soteriology, over questions such as free will and understandings of the effects of the fall, Luther's own theology should not be set in opposition to the ancient idea of deification. Concepts such as union and participation speak the same language as deification.

2. For Luther, the main idea of justification is Christ present in faith (*in ipsa fide Christus adest*, "in the faith itself Christ is present/indwells"). Justification for Luther means a participation in God through the indwelling of Christ in the heart of the believer through the Spirit. Obviously, this is more than merely an external forensic declaration of justification, although it does not have to dismiss it.

3. In contrast to the theology of the Lutheran confessions, the Reformer Luther himself does not typically make a categorical and programmatic separation between forensic (that is, the believer is pronounced righteous, similarly to an accused person in the court) and effective justification (that is, the change of the believer) but rather argues that justification includes

---

[4] Hannu Kamppuri, ed., *Dialogue Between Neighbours: The Theological Conversations Between the Evangelical-Lutheran Church of Finland and the Russian Orthodox Church, 1970–1986* (Helsinki: Luther-Agricola Society, 1986), 73.

[5] Kamppuri, *Dialogue Between Neighbors*, 75.

both. In other words, in line with Roman Catholic theology, justification means both declaring righteous and making righteous.

4. Therefore, justification means not only sanctification but also good works, since Christ present in faith makes the Christian a "christ" to the neighbor.[6]

The purpose of this essay is to consider carefully the possibility and conditions of the new perspective on Luther's understanding of salvation. Furthermore, it also seeks to assess what the liabilities of this new interpretation under the leadership of Helsinki Mannermaa school might be and what the areas of further investigation are. While a *new* interpretation and in many ways strongly contested, some leading ideas of Mannermaa's interpretation have been echoed by some other contemporary scholars as well. The late Wolfhart Pannenberg, with the concept of adoption as the key metaphor of explaining the meaning of the Lutheran doctrine of justification with a focus on the transformative union, comes to mind here. That said, he did not specifically address the Helsinki school paradigm, although he was aware of it, and in his theology deification plays no role in his soteriology. Furthermore, the essay also seeks to advance ecumenical discussion of Luther's theology of salvation by looking at resources in a trinitarian-pneumatological orientation, oftentimes left to a junior role in this theological tradition.

This essay will not attempt an ecumenical dialogue between either Lutherans and Orthodox or Lutherans and Roman Catholics; that task has been attempted elsewhere. The focus will be on Lutheran contributions to and perspectives on salvation as union and participation.

## Justification as Renewing Union with and Participation in Christ

The standard account of Lutheran doctrine of justification by faith is something like this: whereas the forensic declaration of the sinner as just is

---

[6]For various aspects of the discussion, see Veli-Matti Kärkkäinen, *One with God: Salvation as Deification and Justification* (Collegeville, MN: Liturgical Press, 2004); Kärkkäinen, "Justification as Forgiveness of Sins and Making Righteous: The Ecumenical Promise of a New Interpretation of Luther," *One in Christ* 37, no. 2 (April 2002): 32-45; Kärkkäinen, "The Ecumenical Potential of Theosis: Emerging Convergences Between Eastern Orthodox, Protestant, and Pentecostal Soteriologies," *Sobornost/Eastern Churches Review* 23, no. 2 (2002): 45-77.

something that happens outside the believer in the sense that it is not conditioned on the inner change of the justified, sanctification as the second step is meant to refer to the improvement of life. But as important as the latter is (sanctification), the success (or lack) thereof has little or no effect on the foundational status of the sinner as the justified. As a result, in some popular preaching—or at least anecdotally—Lutherans may even speak of "bold sinning."[7] No wonder that Roman Catholic theology at the mid-sixteenth-century Council of Trent, in response to Protestant Reformation, vehemently and fiercely attacked the alleged lack of pursuit of holiness. Similarly, the Orthodox tradition casts serious doubts on an account of salvation that is divorced from the renewal and holiness of life. Be this caricature true or not, it helps us set the stage for an interpretation of Luther's own view in which even when forensic declarative terminology is being deployed, the big picture is that of linking tightly together justification as the change of status and change of the believer's life as the follower of the triune God.

Justification in Luther can be described with the help of several closely related concepts such as participation in God, the presence of Christ in the believer through the Holy Spirit, union with God, perichoresis (mutual indwelling between God and the human person), and occasionally also deification. Regardless of the term used, Luther sees justification as the union between Christ and the believer, as Christ through faith abides in the Christian through the Spirit. In fact, Luther says, Christ is "one with us" and "Christ lives in us through faith."[8] For the Reformer, Christ is the divine and inestimable gift that the Father has given to us to be our Justifier, Life Giver, and Redeemer. To put on Christ according to the gospel, therefore, is to put on not the law or works but an inestimable gift, namely, the forgiveness of sins, righteousness, peace, comfort, joy in the Holy Spirit, salvation, life, and Christ himself.[9]

---

[7]An excellent up-to-date account with rich and comprehensive bibliography is Mark Mattes, "Luther on Justification as Forensic and Effective," in Kolb, Dingel, and Batka, *Oxford Handbook of Martin Luther's Theology*, 264-73. Highly useful and accessible is also Robert Kolb, "Contemporary Lutheran Understandings of the Doctrine of Justification: A Selective Glimpse," in *Justification: What's at Stake in the Current Debate?*, ed. Mark Husbands and Daniel Treier (Downers Grove, IL: InterVarsity Press, 2004), 153-76.
[8]Martin Luther, "Heidelberg Disputation" (1518), *LW* 31:56.
[9]Martin Luther, "Lectures on Galatians" (1535), *LW* 26:353.

For the reception of this wonderful gift, the Wittenberg theologian uses the important term *apprehension* (*apprehendere*), rendered in English as "taking hold": "Faith itself is a gift of God, a work of God in our hearts, which justifies us because it takes hold of [*apprehendit*] Christ the Savior."[10] The Latin term *apprehendere* (which occurs in various forms in his mature commentary on Galatians [1535] about 300 times!) is a key scholastic philosophical concept denoting not only "intellectual apprehension when seen in terms of understanding and comprehension" but also the idea that "the object of knowledge becomes the property of a knowing subject." For Luther this means "knowing Him as God who gives Himself to and on behalf of all sinners," in other words, participation and union; Christ indeed is the righteousness of the Christian.[11] The frequent use of this key term alone tells us how very deeply union-driven Luther's conception of justification is.

While insisting on this idea of union and participation, Luther also has in the background of his thinking an important medieval Catholic teaching that he saw as detrimental to a proper understanding of grace and salvation. It is often referred to in its Latin form simply as the principle of *ordo caritatis*. It was a central theological motif for St. Thomas Aquinas. It means that love as a natural capacity may reach out to the highest end, which is God. In other words, the human being is able (and, under certain conditions, willing) to love God, the highest good. Technically put, love is the "form of faith" (*fides caritate formata*). In other words, faith coupled with love is the key to loving God, to be saved. While Luther himself highly appreciated love correctly understood, he adamantly denied any such capacity to fallen human person when it came to access to salvation. To express his opposition to the Thomistic teaching, he rather insisted on making "Christ the form of faith" (*fides Christo formata*).[12] In place of love, he put faith in Christ, indeed Christ himself, as the key to justification. Hence, as cited above, "Therefore faith justifies because it takes hold of [*apprehendit*] and possesses this

---

[10] *LW* 26:88.
[11] Olli-Pekka Vainio, *Justification and Participation in Christ: The Development of the Lutheran Doctrine of Justification from Luther to the Formula of Concord (1580)* (Leiden: Brill, 2008), 20-22, 26. Luther often uses the expression of Christ as the "form of faith" (*forma fidei*), for which see 27.
[12] Among many other passages, representative is *LW* 26:128-30.

treasure, the present Christ."[13] It is helpful to keep in mind that the thick meaning of "taking hold" of Christ helps us appreciate his union-driven view of justification totally focused on Christ, not on the human person and her natural capacities.

For Luther himself, justification is not only—and perhaps not even primarily—a matter of forensic declaration of the sinner (although it is of course also that). Rather, as a union and participation—"taking hold of" Christ—justification is an inner change, renewal, sanctification. Theologians often name the latter aspect of justification as effective justification, as it speaks of the effects to the believer of God's renewing work. Having been trained and immersed in late medieval debates and thought forms, Luther was fond of expressing this coupling of forensic and effective justification with the help of two widely used scholastic concepts, namely, gift (*donum*) and favor (*favor*), the latter of which was usually understood as the forgiveness of sin.[14] Whereas Lutheran confessions typically (but not exclusively) focus justification on the latter aspect, namely, the forgiveness of sins, Luther himself typically (but not exclusively!) wished to keep the gift and favor tightly linked with each other. Luther states it unambiguously: "But 'the grace of God' [*favor*] and the 'gift' are the same thing, namely, the very righteousness which is freely given to us through Christ."[15] This is also at the heart of Roman Catholic teaching before and after the Reformation. In this regard, with all his critique of the *ordo caritatis* principle, Luther remained a faithful son of the Catholic Church.

The focus of Luther's conception of justification just explicated here is important in the sense that it can be found both in Luther's earlier and one of the latest main writings, which is the final form of the *Commentary on Galatians* (1535), from which the above references to "taking hold" mainly come. Recall that it is this major writing of the mature Luther that is endorsed officially by the drafters of the Formula of Concord (the official summation of Lutheran confessional teaching on disputed issues among various fractions in

---

[13]*LW* 26:130; see Vainio, *Justification and Participation*, 27-36.
[14]For discussion on the Galatians commentary (1535), see Vainio, *Justification and Participation*, 36-42.
[15]Martin Luther, "Lectures on Romans. Glosses and Scholia" (1515–1516), *LW* 25:306.

the emerging new church) as a reliable guide to the Lutheran doctrine of salvation.[16] Importantly, this commentary presents justification as participation in Christ and thus goes beyond and amplifies the forensic paradigm.[17]

## JUSTIFICATION AS CHRIST PRESENT IN FAITH

In an important passage, already alluded to above, Luther makes this programmatic statement of the nature of true faith: "It takes hold of Christ in such a way that Christ is the object of faith, or rather not the object but, so to speak, the One who is present in the faith itself [*in ipsa fide Christus adest*]."[18] In this light it is understandable that, as discussed above, the distinction between effective and forensic righteousness does not play an important role in Luther. That said, another kind of distinction is crucial, that between two kinds of righteousness: the righteousness of Christ and the righteousness of the human being. The first kind of righteousness Luther defines as alien righteousness. It is being infused to us from outside in a sense that it does not come from within human resources. It comes from Christ, and it is that kind of righteousness that Christ is in himself, Christ who is the righteousness of faith. This kind of righteousness of Christ makes the human being just. This type of righteousness is given without our own works, solely on the basis of grace.[19] This is the famous *sola gratia*, "grace alone." Any allegedly meritorious human activity is totally excluded in this process. As explained, the infusion of this righteousness is more than mere forensic imputation, though; it also means the realization of the righteousness of Christ in the believer.

On that basis, Luther calls the other kind of righteousness "our righteousness." It is a result of the first kind of righteousness and makes it effective, perfects it. Even though it is called our righteousness, its origin and source are outside the human being, in the righteousness of Christ. In other words, it is not something the human person brings about; it is ours in a sense that it indwells us. Indeed, Luther says, Christ present in faith "absorbs

---

[16]*Formula of Concord*, part 2, chap. 3, #67, in *The Book of Concord: The Confessions of the Evangelical Lutheran Church*, trans. Theodore G. Tappert (Philadelphia: Fortress, 1959), 571.
[17]For a detailed analysis, see Vainio, *Justification and Participation*, chap. 2.
[18]*LW* 26:129.
[19]Martin Luther, "Two Kinds of Righteousness" (1519), *LW* 31:297, 299.

all sin in a moment," since the righteousness of Christ infused into the human heart is infinite; at the same time, the power of sin and death is deteriorating day by day but is not fully destroyed until death.[20] This means that the central Lutheran principle of *simul iustus et peccator*, "simultaneously just and sinner," is not dismissed. It is in the daily repentance and return to the regenerating grace given in the sacrament of water baptism that the old Adam is being drowned and put to death. The believer is not partially just and partially sinner but simultaneously both, waiting for the final eschatological consummation of God's renewing, justifying work.

Finnish theologian Arto Seppänen summarizes the core idea of Luther's doctrine of justification in a succinct manner:

> Through faith the Christian and Christ are one, the union of which is pictured in the union between a bride and bridegroom. On the basis of this union [literally: being one] the Christian possesses all that Christ has in the same way the bride has everything that belongs to her bridegroom. Similarly, the sins of the human being become Christ's possession. It is the *unio* which makes possible this participation. The whole of Christ is donated to the believer. The donation takes place through faith in Christ. "Happy exchange" is related to the essence of faith and is a natural consequence of the union with Christ.[21]

The indwelling of Christ through faith in the Holy Spirit, the union, results in continuous renewal to the measure that, rightly understood, the Christian can be called "christ" (lowercase) to the neighbor.

## The Christian as "christ" to the Neighbor

What is truly important to Luther's union-driven account of justification is that as a result, good deeds follow "our" righteousness.[22] Good deeds are the fruit of justification, not a human merit—a suspicion among the drafters of Lutheran confessions in their mixed relationship to good works. Similarly to the fact that the human person depends solely on grace, *sola gratia*, with regard to initial justification, the resulting good deeds are also attributed to

---

[20] *LW* 31:298-300.
[21] Arto Seppänen, *Unio Christi: Union ja vanhurskauttamisen suhde Anders Nohrborgin postillassa*, Suomalaisen Teologisen Kirjallisuusseuran julkaisuja 211 (Helsinki: STKJ, 1997), 37 (my translation).
[22] *LW* 31:299-300.

the indwelling Christ rather than human achievements. To repeat: good works spring from the union, Christ's presence through Spirit in the believer.

> All works except for faith have to be directed to the neighbor. For God does not require of us any works with regard to himself, only faith through Christ. That is more than enough for him; that is the right way to give honor to God as God, who is gracious, merciful, wise and truthful. Thereafter, think nothing else than that you do to your neighbor as Christ has done to you. Let all your work and all your life be turned to your neighbor. Seek the poor, sick, and all kinds of wretched people; render your help to those; surrender your life in various kinds of exercises. Let those who really need you enjoy you, insofar as that is possible with regard to your body, possessions, and honor.[23]

Indeed, opines the Reformer, if we do not use everything that we have to serve the neighbor, we rob him or her of what we owe her according to God's will.[24]

In keeping with his idea of justification as participation in the triune God through the indwelling of Christ in the heart through the Spirit, Luther simply believes that the human being also participates in the characteristics or attributes of God, or as he often puts it, of the Word of God. On the one hand, this participation means putting down those human traits that are contrary to the righteousness of God, and on the other hand, this means participating in the goodness, wisdom, truthfulness, and other characteristics of God. Luther also expresses this truth by saying that God in fact becomes truthful, good, and just in the human person when God himself makes the person truthful, good, and just. Never is there reason to boast, though, since even the presence of Christ and its consequences are always hidden in the Christian.[25]

Astonishingly, Luther is so bold as to claim that the Christian not only becomes a "work of Christ" but even more, a "christ" to the neighbor; the Christian begins to do what Christ does. "Since Christ lives in us through

---

[23] Martin Luther, "Advent Postil" (1522), WA 10/1:2 (my translation).

[24] Luther also describes the essence of sin as "robbery of God," e.g., in "Against Latomus" (1521), LW 32:224.

[25] Antti Raunio, *Die Summe des christlichen Lebens: Die "Goldene Regel" als Gesetz der Liebe in der Theologie Martin Luthers von 1510 bis 1527*, Publications of the Systematic Theology Department 13 (Helsinki: Yliopistopaino, 1993), 172-77 especially. This monograph is a major study on the concept of love, both divine and human, in Luther's theology and its relation to Christ's presence through faith in the believer. Unfortunately, it is not available in English.

faith . . . he arouses us to do good works through that living faith in his work, for the works which he does are the fulfillment of the commands of God given us through faith."[26] Says Luther, "I will therefore give myself as a Christ to my neighbor, just as Christ offered himself to me; I will do nothing in this life except what I see is necessary, profitable, and salutary to my neighbor, since through faith I have an abundance of all good things in Christ."[27] Mannermaa succinctly summarizes:

> Therefore "sanctification"—that is, the sanctity or holiness of the Christian—is, in fact, only another name for what Luther speaks when discussing the communication of attributes, the happy exchange, and the union between the person of Christ and that of the believer. Christ is the true agent of good works in the Christian. . . . Because of the Christian's union with Christ, his or her works are works of Christ himself. . . . In this argumentation Luther's view of Christians as "Christs to their neighbors" finds its ontological realization. Luther argues that Christ who is present in faith becomes, as it were, incarnate in Christian's works.[28]

Of course, the human being left to his own devices would be incapable of fulfilling this divinely mandated law of love—and Luther would be the first to remind us of it. It is possible only through Christ, who fulfilled the law. Those who participate in Christ, in other words those Christians in whose hearts through faith Christ indwells, are capable of fulfilling the law. They do the works of Christ through Christ's presence in them and so meet the requirement of the second table of the law:

> Love is the common virtue of all virtues, their fulfillment and source. Love feeds, gives drink, clothes, consoles, prays, makes free, helps, and saves. What do we say then? It gives itself, body and life, possessions and honor and all its power internally and externally to meet the desperate need of the neighbor for his benefit. It does not hold back anything either from a friend or fiend with which it can serve other people. Therefore, no virtue can be compared to it, neither is

---

[26]*LW* 31:56-57. See further Veli-Matti Kärkkäinen, "Christian as Christ to the Neighbor," *International Journal of Systematic Theology* 6, no. 2 (April 2004): 101-17.

[27]Martin Luther, "Treatise on Christian Liberty" (1520), *LW* 31:367. Speaking of Paul, Luther explains the agency of Christ in the believer: "Paul, living in himself, is utterly dead through the Law but living in Christ, or rather with Christ living in him, he lives an alien life. Christ is speaking, acting, and performing all actions in him" (*LW* 26:170).

[28]Mannermaa, *Christ Present in Faith*, 50.

it possible to describe or name any specific work for it as with regard to other virtues, which are actually partial virtues, such as purity, charity, patience, and goodwill, etc. Love does everything . . . so much so that Saint Paul says that all the commandments are included in this summa: love your neighbor.[29]

It is to be noted that Luther differs from those well-meaning contemporary (to us) teachers who emphasize that in order to be able to love the neighbor, one has to love oneself first. Realistically, Luther believes that every person already knows how to love oneself; what is lacking, rather, is the capacity and desire to love another person, especially when nothing good is to be expected in return.[30]

Before turning to an assessment of this new interpretation of Luther's soteriology and connecting it to a wider Lutheran thought, for the sake of the focus of this current set of essays in the book, it is worth asking whether the term *deification* has any currency in Lutheran theology.

## WHAT ABOUT DEIFICATION? IS IT A PART OF LUTHER'S VOCABULARY?

Following Western Christian tradition, differently from the East, Lutheran theology rarely deploys the ancient term *deification*. That said, for Luther himself it is not a totally foreign concept. Indeed, Helsinki scholars have credibly shown evidence that at times Luther's view of justification can also be called deification.[31] The term *deification* and its cognates appear about thirty times in Luther's corpus.[32] It is not much in ratio to his extensive writings, but neither is it meaningless.

---

[29] Martin Luther, "Lent Postil" (1525), WA 17/2:100.26–101.4 (my translation).
[30] "Therefore I believe that with this commandment 'as yourself' man is not commanded to love himself but rather is shown the sinful love with which he does in fact love himself, as if to say: 'You are completely curved in upon yourself and pointed toward love of yourself, a condition from which you will not be delivered unless you altogether cease loving yourself and, forgetting yourself, love your neighbor. For it is a perversity that we want to be loved by all and want to seek our interest in all people; but it is uprightness that if you do to everyone else what in your perverseness you want done to yourself, you will do good with the same zeal as you used to do evil'" (*LW* 25:513).
[31] A whole monograph on the topic has been written by one of the students of Mannermaa, Bishop Simo Peura, *Mehr als ein Mensch? Die Vergöttlichung als Thema der Theologie Luthers von 1513 bis 1519*, Veröffentlichungen des Instituts für Europäische Geschichte (Mainz: Philipp von Zabern, 1994). Unfortunately, this work is not available in English.
[32] Simo Peura, "Vergöttlichungsgedanke in Luthers Theologie 1518–1519," in *Thesaurus Lutheri*, ed. T. Mannermaa et al. (Helsinki: Luther-Agricola-Society, 1987), 171–72.

The core of the doctrine of deification from Luther's viewpoint is the idea of real participation in the divine life in Christ. We receive the salvific gifts through participation in Christ. This is in keeping with the wider Lutheran tradition that holds to the idea of God living in the believer (*inhabitatio Dei*). This for Mannermaa is analogous with the doctrine of deification even when the term itself is not employed. He reminds us that, according to Luther, Christ, and thus his person and work, is present in the faith itself.[33] Justification and deification, then, as the participation of the believer in Christ, are also a participation in the triune God himself because Christ is God. Of this participation, Luther says boldly, "It is true that a man helped by grace is more than a man; indeed, the grace of God gives him the form of God and deifies him, so that even the Scriptures call him 'God' and 'God's son.'"[34] And: "Just as the Word of God became flesh, so it is certainly also necessary that the flesh become Word. For the Word becomes flesh precisely so that the flesh may become Word. In other words: God becomes man so that man may become God."[35]

It is easy to see that Luther presents here the idea of deification with the help of formulations from the church fathers such as Athanasius and Irenaeus, as a union of logos (Word) and "flesh" (human nature). This is what the patristic doctrine of theosis foundationally means: "Divine life has manifested itself in Christ. In the church as the body of Christ, man has a share in this life. Man partakes thereby of 'the divine nature' (2 Pet 1:4). This nature, or divine life, permeates the being of man like a leaven in order to restore it to its original condition as *imago Dei*."[36] In other words, Luther himself joins the ancient patristic line of teaching as a key formulation of his soteriological doctrine.

Pneumatological implications of this new approach of Luther scholarship are obvious. The leading idea, Christ present through faith, can also be expressed pneumatically: it is through the Spirit of Christ that the mediation

---

[33]Tuomo Mannermaa, "Theosis as a Subject of Finnish Luther Research," *Pro Ecclesia* 4, no. 1 (1995): 42-44.
[34]Martin Luther, "Defense and Explanation of All the Articles" (1521), *LW* 51:58.
[35]WA 1:28.25-32, quoted in Mannermaa, "Theosis as a Subject," 43.
[36]Mannermaa, "Theosis as a Subject," 42.

of salvific gifts is accomplished. Participation in God is possible only through the Spirit of Christ, the Spirit of adoption.[37]

Yet another way of considering the idea of justification and deification in Luther is in reference to the concept of giving and gift. For Luther, the divinity of the triune God consists in that God gives himself. The essence of God, then, is identical with the essential divine properties in which he gives of himself, called the names of God: Word, justice, truth, wisdom, love, goodness, eternal life, and so forth. Says Mannermaa, "The *theosis* of the believer is initiated when God bestows on the believer God's essential properties; that is, what God gives of himself to humans is nothing separate from God himself."[38] God is, as Luther says, the whole "beatitude" (*beatitudo*) of his saints:

> And so He gives Himself, and He does not give, but is Himself the good and complete blessing of the saints. For as it is said that "God gives Himself to the saints," which means that "God is the good [*beatitudo*] of his saints," so also His name gives Him to them, that is, it is their good. But the name of God is Christ Himself, the Son of God, the Word by which He verbalizes Himself and the name by which He calls Himself in eternity.[39]

We can summarize hence like this: while the idea of union and participation points to the same direction as does *deification* and its cognate terms, understandably it is not typical for Lutheran tradition to deploy that language.

## Reaffirming and Restating the Mannermaa School's Ecumenical Proposal for Orientation

To no one's surprise, responses to the Mannermaa school's reinterpretation of Luther have been varied.[40] Roughly put, the responses can be classified like this: Whereas the Continental, particularly German, Luther scholarship

---

[37]For a brief summary of the idea of adoption in Luther, see Risto Saarinen, "The Presence of God in Luther's Theology," *Lutheran Quarterly* 3, no. 1 (1994): 9-10. For pneumatological implications, see Kenneth L. Bakken, "Holy Spirit and Theosis: Toward a Lutheran Theology of Healing," *St. Vladimir's Theological Quarterly* 38, no. 4 (1994): 409-23.

[38]Mannermaa, "Why Is Luther So Fascinating?," 10.

[39]Martin Luther, "First Lectures on the Psalms" (1513-1514), *LW* 10:253; see Simo Peura, "Christ as Favor and Gift," in Braaten and Jenson, *Union with Christ*, 50.

[40]An important dialogue with critics is Olli-Pekka Vainio, "Luther and Theosis: A Response to the Critics of the Finnish Luther Research," *Pro Ecclesia* 24, no. 4 (2015): 459-74.

has been deeply critical, a number of leading American Lutherans have enthusiastically endorsed it.[41] Understandably, conservative Lutherans (Missouri Synod), along with many evangelicals, to whom the forensic-imputational template is the only correct interpretation, have expressed deep reservations.[42] The reasons for the German and conservative American criticism of Mannermaa's paradigm are the ones listed in the beginning of the essay, that is, a general hostility toward any notion of deification and corollary misunderstandings of its nature, for example, a danger of pantheism. Furthermore, these critics are not convinced at all that a critical distinction between Lutheran confessional and Luther's own theology can or should be drawn; or, if it be made, then the confessional side should be followed.

While I myself materially adopt the basic insights of the Mannermaa school, there is also a felt need for the sake of ecumenical rapprochement to critically assess its liabilities and propose some new revisions.

Let me list here what I see as some of the liabilities not only of this particular Lutheran school but also more widely and then suggest briefly some constructive ideas for a remedy:

- the need to envision salvation as justification as union and participation in pneumatological-trinitarian terms, not only in christological terms;
- to imagine justification, while being one with and participating in Christ, also through the lens of the eccentric nature of faith, that is, faith resides in Christ;
- while critiquing the one-sided Lutheran confessional focus on justification by faith as forensic declaration, there is also a need to rehabilitate, so to speak, the proper role of forensic justification as an integral part of justification as union and participation;
- coupling justification as union and participation with an "active reception of gift" in order not to make the justified merely passive recipients of justification without any effects on life and ethics.

---

[41]See Braaten and Jensen, *Union with Christ*, among others. Leading German scholar Bernhard Lohse virtually dismisses the Mannermaa school's insight altogether. See Lohse, *Martin Luther's Theology: Its Historical and Systematic Development* (Minneapolis: Fortress, 1999), 221.
[42]See Kolb, "Contemporary Lutheran Understandings," 153-76.

## The Pneumatological-Trinitarian Form of Salvation as Participation in Divine Life

There is a curious trinitarian deficit in most Protestant soteriological accounts in general and Lutherans in particular when it comes to the doctrine of justification. Quite striking is the passive (or almost nonexistent) role of the Spirit in most accounts of justification as opposed to the Eastern theology of deification.[43] In a typical Protestant conception of justification, the Spirit's role is somewhat external; as Pentecostal Frank Macchia puts it, "The Spirit function[s] from the outside, inspiring faith in the gospel" without having to do with the "substance of justification," and the Father "seems to be a relatively passive spectator who happily accepts Christ's advocacy" without having an active role to play.[44]

Referring to passages such as Titus 3:5-7, which speaks about the "washing of regeneration and renewal in the Holy Spirit, which he poured out upon us richly" (RSV), the Reformed Jürgen Moltmann laments the pneumatological deficit. He rightly emphasizes that "'regeneration' as 'renewal' comes about through the Holy Spirit" when the "Spirit is 'poured out.'"[45] By making further reference to John 4:14, the metaphor of the divine wellspring of life that begins to flow in a human being, he contends that "through this experience of the Spirit, who comes upon us from the Father through the Son, we become 'justified through grace.'"[46]

Indeed, the Christ-event itself, reconciliation, has an integral trinitarian form.[47] The identification with humanity in incarnation and the voluntary suffering at the cross through which the Father shows himself to be just

---

[43] Frank Macchia, *Justified in the Spirit: Creation, Redemption, and the Triune God* (Grand Rapids, MI: Eerdmans, 2010), 5; see also Macchia, "Justification Through New Creation: The Holy Spirit and the Doctrine by Which the Church Stands or Falls," *Theology Today* 58, no. 2 (July 2001): 202-17.
[44] Macchia, *Justified in the Spirit*, 5; see also 39.
[45] Jürgen Moltmann, *The Spirit of Life: A Universal Affirmation*, trans. Margaret Kohl (Minneapolis: Fortress, 2001), 146. See further Veli-Matti Kärkkäinen, "'By the Washing of Regeneration and Renewing by the Holy Spirit': Toward a Pneumatological Account of Justification in Christ," in *Spirit and Christ: Essays in Honour of Max Turner*, ed. Howard Marshall, Cornelis Bennema, and Volker Rabens (Grand Rapids, MI: Eerdmans, 2012), 303-22.
[46] Moltmann, *Spirit of Life*, 146; see also Bakken, "Holy Spirit and Theosis," 410-11.
[47] For a trinitarian theology of reconciliation (and atonement), see chap. 13 in Veli-Matti Kärkkäinen, *Christ and Reconciliation: Constructive Christian Theology for the Pluralistic World*, vol. 1 (Grand Rapids, MI: Eerdmans, 2013).

(Rom 3:25) are followed by the raising to new life "for our justification" (Rom 4:25) of the Son by the Father, and then the ascension, which propel the Pentecostal pouring out of the Spirit.[48] Even when the forensic/legal aspects of justification are in the forefront, the Spirit's role is not excluded: the Spirit as the Paraclete is both Advocate and Judge according to the Johannine testimony (Jn 14; 16).[49] The *Joint Declaration on the Doctrine of Justification* between Roman Catholics and Lutherans got it right: "Christ himself is our righteousness, in which we share through the Holy Spirit in accord with the will of the Father."[50]

Perhaps unbeknownst to many, Luther's theology of salvation is not void of this proper pneumatological-trinitarian element, although most Lutheran accounts do not usually highlight it. His focus on justification as the presence of Christ through the Spirit exhibits an integral trinitarian-pneumatological focus, as evident in his remarkable comment on Galatians 3:7. Therein, Luther equates righteousness imputed to the believer with the gift of the Spirit:

> Now is not the fact that faith is reckoned as righteousness a receiving of the Spirit? So either he proves nothing or the reception of the Spirit and the fact that faith is reckoned as righteousness will be the same thing. And this is true; it is introduced in order that the divine imputation may not be regarded as amounting to nothing outside God, as some think that the apostle's word "grace" means a favorable disposition rather than a gift. For when God is favorable, and when He imputes, the Spirit is really received, both the gift and the grace. Otherwise grace was there from eternity and remains within God, if it signifies only a favorable disposition in the way that favor is understood among men.[51]

The Spirit's role comes into play also in the central concept of Luther concerning the ecstatic nature of faith as something rooted in and finding its source outside the believer, that is, in Christ.

---

[48]See also Macchia, *Justified in the Spirit*, 7-8.
[49]Macchia, *Justified in the Spirit*, 6, emphasis original.
[50]Lutheran World Federation and the Roman Catholic Church, *Joint Declaration on the Doctrine of Justification* (Grand Rapids, MI: Eerdmans, 2000), #15. www.vatican.va/roman_curia/pontifical_councils/chrstuni/documents/rc_pc_chrstuni_doc_31101999_cath-luth-joint-declaration_en.html.
[51]*LW* 27:252 (on Gal 3:17); for comments, see Macchia, *Justified in the Spirit*, 63-64.

## Union and the Ecstatic Nature of Faith

Every Lutheran trained in catechism knows this statement of Luther's:

> I believe that by my own reason or strength I cannot believe in Jesus Christ, my Lord, or come to him. But the Holy Spirit has called me through the Gospel, enlightened me with his gifts, and sanctified and preserved me in true faith, just as he calls, gathers, enlightens, and sanctifies the whole Christian church on earth and preserves it in union with Jesus Christ in the one true faith.[52]

Luther rightly saw not only the necessary role of the Spirit in making possible faith in Christ but also the eccentric (or "ecstatic," as in *ek-stasis*, "to stand outside oneself") nature of faith. Faith places trust outside itself, in Christ. Luther's profound statement in the early pamphlet *The Freedom of a Christian* (1520) puts it succinctly:

> We conclude, therefore, that a Christian lives not in himself, but in Christ and in his neighbor. Otherwise he is not a Christian. He lives in Christ through faith, in his neighbor through love. By faith he is caught up beyond himself into God [*rapitur supra se in deum*]. By love he descends beneath himself into his neighbor. Yet he always remains in God and in his love.[53]

It is the Spirit who makes this eccentric nature of faith possible. Building on this key insight, Pannenberg states that through faith in God, the Spirit lifts us "up to participation in the sonship of Jesus Christ" and "binds believers together in the fellowship of the body of Christ."[54] Faith has this "outside ourselves" (*extra nos*) character and at the same time "links believers to Jesus Christ as they rely on him and on the promise of salvation that is given in his message and history"; indeed, this means nothing less than the believer's participation in the filial relation of the Son to the Father.[55]

As a result, Pannenberg selects—surprisingly to his Lutheran readers—adoption as the overarching and determining concept of his *ordo salutis*. Whereas the importance of the concept of adoption is of course nothing new in the Lutheran (or Reformed) tradition, making it an overarching concept

---

[52]From the third article of the *Small Catechism* (1531) in Tappert, *Book of Concord*, 345.
[53]*LW* 31:371.
[54]Wolfhart Pannenberg, *Systematic Theology*, trans. Geoffrey W. Bromiley (Grand Rapids, MI: Eerdmans, 1998), 3:134-34.
[55]Pannenberg, *Systematic Theology* 3:136-37, 211.

that also regulates justification is new.[56] The surplus of opting for adoption as the main framework, namely, that "being God's children is thus of the essence of the Christian life," helps use not only Pauline theology (Rom 8:16, among others) but also Jesus' teaching (Lk 18:17; Mk 10:15; Mt 5:9).[57] Adoption in this theological template means that the believer is lifted up by the Spirit through faith into the filial relationship with Christ and is united with other believers in the same body.

## What About the Theological Significance of the Forensic Aspect of Justification?

Although the rediscovery of the centrality of union, participation, and adoption as controlling metaphors has helped contemporary Finnish Lutheran theology to establish a more satisfactory and integral account of justification, an account that materially approximates deification, the downplaying of the forensic element (particularly by the Mannermaa school) also calls for reconsideration.[58] It does not do—nor is it necessary—to pit union against forensic justification; that was the valid critique of the Council of Trent against the Protestant Reformers. In this respect, Lutherans have had a chance to correct themselves as in that joint declaration with the Roman Catholics they affirm justification as both forgiveness of sins (forensic) and making righteous (effective).[59]

Those interpreters who advocate the effective understanding of justification (that is, justification includes also the inner change) understandably have undermined the idea of imputation (of Christ's righteousness), a key mainstream Protestant idea. The reason is self-evident: in Protestantism at large, imputation has been seen merely as a forensic act. But does it have to be so? I do not think so. Only if justification as imputation is understood *exclusively* as a forensic act that blocks the way for making righteous is the opposition justified. But what if, as the most recent research has allowed us

---

[56]See the long and detailed section 4, titled "Adoption as God's Children and Justification," in Pannenberg, *Systematic Theology* 3:211-36.
[57]Pannenberg, *Systematic Theology* 3:211-12.
[58]See Risto Saarinen on the downplaying of the forensic element, "De iustificatione," *Teologinen aikakauskirja* 118, no. 4 (2013): 291-304 (this section is indebted to it).
[59]See "4.2 Justification as Forgiveness of Sins and Making Righteous," in *Joint Declaration on the Doctrine of Justification.*

to understand, the concept of imputation of Christ's righteousness does not have to be solely (or even primarily) forensic but could also include the process of change and renewal?[60]

Indeed, as argued above, Luther's own concept of "Christ present in faith" (*in ipsa fide Christus adest*) is just that: the imputed Christ's real presence in the believer also instantly brings about the lifelong process of change.[61] Even semantically, *imputation* has a number of meanings, from commercial exchange and accounting (the primary meaning in Protestant orthodoxy), to personal (not to count the friend's mistake as a reason for breaking relationship), to hermeneutical (to consider one's own experience as the key to understanding), and so forth.[62] What clearly comes to the fore in Luther's theology is the personal orientation. As Mannermaa's successor in Helsinki, Risto Saarinen, importantly argues: whereas in Augustine righteousness could be imputed to the believer in a nonpersonal manner (as a liquid is poured into a container), in Luther it is always a matter of personal trust, personal relationship.[63] That justification is more than forgiveness (forensic declaration, "favor"), however, should not hinder us from lifting up its significance in a proper manner.

### Active Reception of the Gift of Justification

Back to the concept of gift and giving: I noted above several times that another way of speaking of union and participation is to speak of gift. In Luther's theology, the meaning of divine gift serves as a defining feature: God's love seeks that which is worthless in itself and donates not only gifts but oneself. The basic Greek verb δίδωμι ("to give or donate") appears over four hundred times in the New Testament alone.[64] Macchia rightly reminds us

---

[60]The key investigation is the massive study by Sibylle Rolf, *Zum Herzen sprechen: Eine Studie zum imputativen Aspekt in Martin Luthers Rechtfertigungslehre und zu seinen Konsequenzen für die Predigt des Evangeliums* (Leipzig: Evangelische Verlagsanstalt, 2008). Unfortunately, it is not available in English. See also Alister McGrath, *Iustitia Dei*, 4th ed. (Cambridge: Cambridge University Press, 2020).

[61]This is the brilliant conclusion of Saarinen ("De Iustificatione," 295-97), combining Rolf's and the Mannermaa school's insights.

[62]Saarinen, "De Iustificatione," 296, with reference to Rolf, *Zum Hertzen sprechen*, 27.

[63]Saarinen, "De Iustificatione," 296; for details, see Rolf, *Zum Hertzen sprechen*, 33-40.

[64]For a detailed discussion, see Risto Saarinen, *God and Gift: An Ecumenical Theology of Giving* (Collegeville, MN: Liturgical Press, 2005), 36-45.

that "'justification' refers fundamentally to the gift of *righteousness* (or 'just relation') that is granted to the sinner."[65]

With this in mind, worth hearing among the Lutherans (and others) is the justified critique of the British Radical Orthodox John Milbank of the overly passive reception of justification in mainstream Protestant tradition. Rightly, he demands that "an account of the arrival of grace must . . . also mean an account of sanctification, and of ethics." This is what Milbank names "active reception" of gift.[66] Although common sense is not always the best guide in matters theological, I believe it is here: it just does not make any sense to think of the recipient of a gift—say, a child at a birthday party or a spouse on an anniversary—as totally passive; a gift can also be unreceived, as when a spouse who is transgressed against by the partner in adultery wishes to forgive. "After all, the creature is not destined to act without any element of choice involved, and God does not commit violence on creation."[67] Christian tradition at large agrees that all human response is *graced* and that—again, following common sense—no parent (the heavenly Father in this case) would enjoy giving a gift to a robot rather than to a child who passionately and actively looks forward to a gift (say, for Christmas).

I argue that the paranoid fear of works-righteousness of much of Protestantism, certainly including Lutheranism, has to be challenged and corrected by the synergistic (Eastern Orthodox) and cooperational (Roman Catholic) understanding of (prevenient) grace—while at the same time (in agreement with the whole of Christian tradition) all forms of Pelagianism must be resisted.[68] Here John Wesley's robust theology of grace as therapeutic is a needed reminder for other Protestants; sanctifying grace begins to heal and change a person the moment the person is justified, the founder of Methodism taught.[69]

---

[65] Macchia, *Justified in the Spirit*, 3, emphasis original.
[66] John Milbank, *Being Reconciled: Ontology and Pardon* (New York: Routledge, 2003), 138. Milbank coins the term "active reception" in his essay "Gregory of Nyssa: The Force of Identity," in *Christian Origins: Theology, Rhetoric, and Community*, ed. Lewis Ayres and Gareth Jones (London: Routledge, 1998), 95.
[67] Macchia, *Justified in the Spirit*, 25.
[68] On the necessity of good works in the Christian life, see Thomas H. McCall, Caleb T. Friedeman, and Matt T. Friedeman, *Doctrine of Good Works* (Grand Rapids, MI: Baker Academic, 2023).
[69] See further Theodore Runyon, *The New Creation: John Wesley's Theology Today* (Nashville: Abingdon, 1998), 27-30.

Luther's profound theology of the Christian as "christ" to the neighbor is the needed pointer in this direction.

## Concluding Remarks

The purpose of this essay is to shed light on Lutheran, particularly Luther's, resources for conceiving of salvation as union and participation, features that approximate materially what the ancient doctrine of theosis means to say. Rather than a comparative exercise between Lutheran and Eastern Orthodox soteriologies, the current one chose to delve into defining texts in Reformer's own theology of justification. (Another comparative task, namely that between Luther's own theology and the theology of Lutheran confessions, was also forfeited.)

As can be guessed from the get-go, Luther did not speak of salvation in terms of deification. When he very rarely and occasionally chose to deploy that terminology, he was linking his soteriology with that of church fathers, particularly Irenaeus and the Eastern fathers.

Luther's own way of speaking of justification is focused on the idea of union and participation. The key motif has to do with the presence of Christ in faith through the Spirit in the believer that integrally also leads to the daily renewal of life as the Christian begins to seek to do the kinds of deeds the indwelling Christ did while on earth. Although in Lutheran diagnosis the Christian is simultaneously just and a sinner, the indwelling Christ effects continuous renewal.

The wellspring of justification is Christ's righteousness. Therefore, it can be called alien righteousness, as its origin is Christ rather than the human person. This same alien righteousness, however, becomes ours as it is graciously donated to the Christian through the indwelling of Christ in faith through the Spirit. Therefore, to the nature of faith belongs its eccentric, "outside us," characteristic. Faith springs from and resides in Christ but not so externally as not to be also ours as Christ indwells us.

This is a short, nontechnical explanation of what I call in this essay a new interpretation of Luther's theology of justification. It is not necessarily a total alternative to what is more commonly known as a two-stage account of salvation found typically in Lutheran confessions, in which initial justification as a forensic declaration is separated, or at least definitively distinguished, from the need for renewal (sanctification). But, as I argued, Luther's own account links these two aspects integrally together and focuses on indwelling Christ's sanative, efficient work in the believer.

In the constructive part I suggested that a more robust role be given to the whole Trinity in the account of justification as union and participation. Christ's justifying and renewing work comes to us through the Spirit and is founded on the Father's participation in the economy of salvation. Similarly, I recommended that Lutherans imagine the divine gift in more active terms so that they not be content with merely passive reception.

Insightful and constructive ecumenical exchanges between Lutherans (and other Protestants) and Eastern Orthodox await the ecumenical guild. The work so far has yielded remarkable results, but much more is needed, for example, to tackle the dramatically differing accounts of theological anthropology, particularly the nature of human will and the effects of fall. The Roman Catholic–Lutheran joint declaration on justification further enriches and inspires this kind of continuing ecumenical exploration.

# DEIFICATION *and* WORLD CHRISTIANITY

## Hesychasm and "Calling upon the Name of the Lord"

### Shu-chen Hsu Hsiung

THE THEOLOGICAL EFFORT TO RETRIEVE theosis or deification as a doctrine has been ongoing for decades. However, this endeavor has largely focused on Christianity in the West. This chapter explores the potential relationship between deification and world Christianity by drawing a comparison between the theology of Gregory Palamas (1296–1359) and Witness Lee (1905–1997). In the fourteenth century, Gregory Palamas gained renown for defending the orthodoxy of hesychasm and its significance for mystical participation in divine energy. Fast-forward six centuries, and Witness Lee, a Chinese immigrant Bible teacher to the United States, encouraged his followers to engage in a practice known as "calling upon the name of the Lord." Both practices are a form of concentrated prayer with a focus on the holy name. Lee, whose teachings are closer to evangelicalism than Eastern Orthodoxy, intriguingly drew parallels between this practice and the goal of theosis, and faced theological challenges reminiscent of those encountered by Palamas.

This chapter begins with an exploration of Lee's theological foundations and the potential connection to the motif of deification. It is followed by a comparative analysis of the teachings of Lee and Palamas. In advocating for their followers to engage in prayers by invoking the holy name, they both found it necessary to delineate a boundary for deification. Nonetheless, they provided different praxes to reach spiritual union.

## DEIFICATION AND CHINESE THEOLOGY

In 2013, Alexander Chow published his *Theosis, Sino-Christian Theology and the Second Chinese Enlightenment: Heaven and Humanity in Unity*.[1] In this book, Chow proposes an alternative to the fundamentalist-modernist dichotomy in categorizing Chinese theologians. He borrowed Justo González's model, which differentiates theologies and their efforts of contextualization into three types, A, B, and C.[2] Chow found in China the representatives of type-A (law-oriented and confrontational toward culture) and type-B (affirming the inherent truth in human nature and culture) theologians. Still, he believes that type-C theology (theosis and divine-human synergism) has not yet emerged in this country. In his conclusion, he advocates for type-C theology, as it is compatible with the project of contextualizing Christian theology in China, especially in the moment of what Chow refers to as the "second Chinese enlightenment" since the 1980s.

Chow's book was one of a few attempts to creatively summarize Chinese theology in the twentieth century and may be the only one to interact with the theme of deification. While he could not find a suitable representative of type-C theology in China, some reviewers pointed out that Chow's choice of type-A representative, Watchman Nee (1905–1972), incorporated some deification themes in his teaching and inspired his followers to elaborate on this.[3] Nee was one of the most well-known Chinese Christians in the West due to the success of his English publications on spirituality in the 1960s. Chow categorized Nee as a type-A theologian based on his soteriology, which aligned with twentieth-century English evangelicalism to emphasize Christ's atoning death as the unique foundation for salvation. However, Chow also noticed that Nee taught a kind of synergism concerning sanctification according to the Keswick theology, while other type-A theologians

---

[1] Alexander Chow, *Theosis, Sino-Christian Theology and the Second Chinese Enlightenment: Heaven and Humanity in Unity* (New York: Palgrave Macmillan, 2013).

[2] Justo L. González, *Christian Thought Revisited: Three Types of Theology* (Maryknoll, NY: Orbis Books, 1999).

[3] For example, see Michael M. C. Reardon's review on *Orthodoxy in Dialogue*, September 13, 2017, https://orthodoxyindialogue.com/2017/09/13/theosis-sino-christian-theology-and-the-second-chinese-enlightenment-heaven-and-humanity-in-unity-reviewed-by-michael-reardon/.

often emphasized monergism.⁴ Unable to pinpoint the presumed origin of Nee's synergism, Chow suggested that it might come from the idea of *Tianrenheyi* or harmony between the heavenly and human realms, a common theme found in Chinese religions and philosophies.⁵

The notion that Nee's theological influence came from his Chinese background has obvious flaws—not least that Nee himself repudiates the use of Chinese philosophy in Christian formation and theology—but some recent studies continue to advance this claim by implying a link between his theology and Taoism or neo-Confucianism.⁶ These studies presume the continual relevance of Chinese culture but seem to fail to consider the country's context at the beginning of the twentieth century, a time when tradition was heavily criticized. At that time, most people turned outward for solutions to the problems they saw in China. Nee was strongly influenced in his early ministry by Christian authors from the West, and he maintained an extensive library of classical Christian writings. The ideas he culled from these sources seem to have contributed to receptiveness among both native Chinese and Western missionaries. Instead of trying to synthesize Christianity and Chinese culture, Nee was mainly translating and incorporating new Western spiritual writings in his earliest publications, and his public messages often summon examples and anecdotes from Western church history. Chinese cultural idioms rarely featured in his illustration of the Christian faith.

This does not mean that China never held a place in Nee's theology. Similar to how Jonathan Edwards described America, Nee appreciated China as a "virgin soil" for God's new move on earth, which was for the birth of a pure and unified church free from any denominational institutions.⁷ Nee proposed the vision of the "local church" in the mid-1920s. In reaction to the Plymouth Brethren and what he believed to be an impractical ecclesiology held by T. Austin Sparks, Nee suggested that all Christians in each

---

⁴On this point, Chloë Starr questioned the applicability of Chow's type. See Starr's review article in *Studies in World Christianity* 19, no. 3 (December 2013): 271-83.
⁵Chow, *Theosis, Sino-Christian Theology*, 53. Also see 41-44, 52-54, 61-63 for Chow's discussion of Nee's contextual theology.
⁶E.g., Chin Ken Pa, "The Theological Anthropology of Watchman Nee: In the Context of Taoist Tradition," *Sino-Christian Studies* 12 (December 2011): 159-87.
⁷Diarmaid MacCulloch, *Christianity: The First Three Thousand Years* (New York: Penguin, 2011), 759. Watchman Nee's quotation was reiterated by Witness Lee. See *CWWL 1973-1974* 1:27.

locality be joined together as one church under the name of Jesus only.[8] At that time, missionary societies in China operated independently and sometimes competed with each other, largely reflecting how imperial powers were dividing spheres of influence in China. The situation appeared inconceivable and abhorrent to many Chinese converts. This model, which Nee considered to be scripturally informed, was also intended for Christians beyond China and later inspired a global audience.

Even though Chow could not locate the source of Nee's synergism and other ideas aligning with deification, recent scholarship suggests that the Wesleyan-holiness tradition, the upstream source of the Keswick Convention, retains some continuity with the teaching of deification.[9] The following section argues that the mystical teachings of Madame Jeanne Guyon (1648–1717) also influenced Nee's and Lee's turn toward the doctrine of deification.[10] By 1949, under Nee's leadership, the local churches grew to be one of the largest independent Christian groups among the Chinese people. After Nee was detained in 1952, Witness Lee continued to spread the local churches to Taiwan and the United States. Much ignored in English scholarship, Lee's theology inherited a great deal from Nee, though he further developed several prominent themes in Nee's theology.

## Witness Lee's Theology: *The Experience of Life and Calling upon the Name of the Lord*

From 1949 to 1962, Lee was primarily based in Taiwan, though he traveled throughout southeast Asia on a regular basis. Besides helping the local churches' attendance to significantly increase on the island, he published

---

[8] Watchman Nee, *The Assembly Life* (Shanghai: Gospel Book Room, 1934). A more complete version is seen in the more famous *Concerning Our Mission* or *The Normal Christian Church Life*, which was first published in 1939. For Nee's interaction with the Plymouth Brethren, the best source is William E. Buntain, "The Exclusive Brethren, Watchman Nee, and the Local Churches in China," *Brethren History Review* 15 (2019): 40-72.

[9] S. T. Kimbrough, *Partakers of the Life Divine: Participation in the Divine Nature in the Writings of Charles Wesley* (Eugene OR: Cascade Books, 2016). Similarly, recent scholarship has found the theme of theosis in Latin church fathers and prominent Protestant figures, suggesting that the teaching of deification might not have disappeared in Western Christianity until recently. See Jared Ortiz, ed., *Deification in the Latin Patristic Tradition* (Washington, DC: Catholic University of America Press, 2019).

[10] For the deification themes in Guyon's mysticism, also reference George Balsama, "Madame Guyon, Heterodox . . ." *Church History* 42, no. 3 (1973): 350-65.

two sets of books summarizing Lee's teaching. *Crucial Truths in the Holy Scripture* (1949) includes Lee's teachings on sixty biblical topics, and *The Experience of Life* (1953) lists nineteen spiritual experiences in four spiritual stages. The idea of these four stages may be sourced from Madam Jeanne Guyon's *Spiritual Torrents* (1682). In this book, Guyon talks about different ways and degrees in which "the souls are led to seek after God." Guyon clearly states that the highest form of spirituality is where the soul experiences deification:

> There the soul is filled with a love of suffering and of the good pleasure of God: here it is a loss of the will in God by a state of deification, where all is God without its being recognized as such. . . . God does not make the life divine all at once, but by degrees. Then, as I have said, He enlarges the capacity of the soul, and can continually deify it more and more, God being an unfathomable depth.[11]

In 1896, Mrs. Jessie Penn-Lewis (1861–1927), a speaker in the Keswick Convention and witness of the Welsh Revival in 1904–1905, wrote a summary of *Spiritual Torrents* called *Life Out of Death* (1896). In this pamphlet, Penn-Lewis condenses Guyon's guides of mysticism into four spiritual planes. According to Penn-Lewis, the four spiritual planes are as follows:

> *The first plane we may call the evangelistic plane*: that is, the plane where the soul knows the new birth, knows that he has eternal life in Christ. . . . Then there is *the second plane, which may be called the revival plane*—the stage in personal experience where the believer receives the fullness of the Holy Spirit; where he learns to know Him and to obey Him, to rely upon Him and to look to Him to work as he co-operates with Him. . . . Then there is *the third plane, which we may call the plane of the path of the cross*, where the believer experientially apprehends his position in Romans 6 in fellowship with Christ's death; where he is brought into "conformity" to His death (Philippians 3:10), learns the fellowship of His sufferings, and is led to walk in the path of the cross in every detail of practical life. . . . *The fourth plane is the plane of spiritual warfare*. It is really the *"ascension" plane*, where the believer knows his union with Christ, seated with Him "far above all principality and power" (Ephesians 1:21, KJV); and where, in service, he is in aggressive warfare against the powers of darkness; learns to have spiritual discernment to detect the working

---

[11] Jeanne Guyon, *A Short Method of Prayer and Spiritual Torrents*, trans. A. W. Marston (London: Sampson Low, Marston, Low, & Searle, 1875), 242–43.

of the devil; and learns the authority of Christ over all the power of the enemy (Luke 10:19).[12]

In a sense, this summary arranges the core spiritual experiences of evangelicalism on a vertical ladder. At that time, Guyon's quietist spirituality was enjoying a renewed interest in the Keswick movement; therefore, Penn-Lewis put it on the third plane, above the born-again (first plane) experience and the following change of lifestyle as the sign of one entering genuine revival (second plane). On the very top of that, "spiritual warfare" is how Penn-Lewis categorized her (and her close companion Evan Roberts's [1878–1951]) experience in participating and discerning the early expressions of Pentecostalism in the Welsh revival.[13]

In his early career, Nee came to appreciate much of Penn-Lewis's writings and became friends with her disciple T. Austin-Sparks (1888–1971). In 1927, Nee translated the "four planes" chapter and published it in Chinese.[14] In *The Experience of Life*, Lee maintains this structure and fills in more content from Nee's teachings (see table 15.1). Although Lee was still far from using the term *deification* at the time he wrote this volume, a seed from Jeanne Guyon may have been preserved. In the concluding chapter of *Experience of Life*, Lee considered the highest experience in this progression to be "full of the stature of Christ," which is when a believer is full of the life and nature of Christ, shares the heavenly position of Christ, and reigns with Christ.[15]

**Table 15.1.** Four stages of spiritual experiences according to *The Experience of Life*

| The First Stage (Salvation): In Christ | 1. Regeneration<br>2. Clearance of the past |
|---|---|
| The Second Stage (Revival): Abiding in Christ | 3. Consecration<br>4. Dealing with sins<br>5. Dealing with the world<br>6. Dealing with the conscience<br>7. Obeying the teaching of the anointing<br>8. Knowing the will of God |

---

[12]Jessie Penn-Lewis, *Life Out of Death: A Brief Summary of Madame Guyon's Spiritual Torrents and Other Papers on the Spiritual Life* (Poole, UK: Overcomer Literature Trust, 1896), 27.

[13]In the fuller version of Penn-Lewis's chapter, it is clear that she thinks the higher form of spirituality is an active cooperation with God in spiritual warfare and helping others to experience the same, instead of what Guyon suggested as the passive way of light and faith. Nee did not include this difference in his translation.

[14]Nee published it as a chapter of his *The Christian Life and Spiritual Warfare* (Shanghai: Bible Truth Dept, 1927). The chapter can be found today in *CWWN* 1:179-84.

[15]Witness Lee, "Full of the Stature of Christ," *CWWL 1953* 3:531-38.

| | |
|---|---|
| **The Third Stage (the Cross): Christ Living in Me** | 9. Dealing with the flesh<br>10. Dealing with the self<br>11. Dealing with the natural constitution<br>12. Accepting the discipline of the Holy Spirit<br>13. Dealing with the Spirit<br>14. Being filled with the Holy Spirit |
| **The Fourth Stage (Spiritual Warfare): Christ's Full Growth in Us** | 15. Knowing the body<br>16. Knowing the ascension<br>17. Reigning<br>18. Spiritual warfare<br>19. Full of the stature of Christ |

Another route through which Madame Guyon inspired the Nee's and Lee's teaching of deification is concerning the monastic spiritual practice of *lectio divina*, or divine reading. Guyon spent considerable time in a convent during her childhood, which might be where she learned the practice. In 1938, one local church member in Shanghai translated Guyon's *A Short and Easy Method of Prayer* into Chinese.[16] In this book, she recommends that "meditative reading" or "prayerful reading" of the Bible is the best way to introduce one's soul into prayer. It incorporates *lectio divina*'s core approach—that is, that one needs to taste and digest the Scripture until the significance in the text is exhausted.[17]

Around 1966, some Taiwanese local church members began praying with the Bible directly (*Zhiduzhidao*) in meetings, a practice that would later be called "pray-reading." Already shifting his emphasis to the United States, Lee immediately endorsed this exercise and encouraged American believers to practice it. In a conference in San Francisco in 1967, Lee and his followers promoted this practice more broadly.[18]

Lee's teaching often resulted in a fervent and lively atmosphere in the church life and was especially conducive to lay participation. The practice of pray-reading is different from most contemporary versions of *lectio divina*. Even though they both emphasize the incremental approach and prayerful atmosphere, pray-reading is more often a group exercise. It requires practitioners to use an audible voice and interact with others. The

---

[16] The translation was by C. H. Yu (Chenghua Yu, 1901–1956). He also translated Guyon's autobiography and other notable works.
[17] Guyon, *Short Method of Prayer*, 8-10.
[18] Witness Lee, "Enjoying Christ Through the Word by Pray-Reading the Word," *CWWL 1969* 2:193-94.

process is dynamic and mutual, and can have unexpected effects of community building. Generally speaking, it is not difficult to join this group improvisation of interpreting the Word of God in real time because it is possible to enter into the corporate pray-reading of Scripture with short phrases such as "Amen" or "Hallelujah!"

Members of the local churches in the United States and Taiwan quickly adopted pray-reading. It became a component of almost every church meeting. On a Lord's Day in 1966, Lee introduced a four-word prayer—"O Lord, Amen, Hallelujah"— to encourage more people to corporately engage in the practice.[19] This phrase, along with other related phrases, became quite popular and Lee began to refer to it as "calling upon the name of the Lord." This grew to become another distinctive practice of Lee's teachings. The phrase differs from other ways of audibly praying. While corporate prayers often rely upon unified chanting (e.g., liturgy), the communal practice of "calling on the Lord" is spontaneous and organic. It varies between gatherings and can include the interspersion of individual prayers followed by corporate "Amens" from the congregation.

Lee rarely addressed theological sources or predecessors of this practice, but instead, drew from many examples from Scripture. In the 1930s, both he and Nee are recorded as employing forms of audible solitary prayer, even in a loud manner, to inflame their spirituality.[20] When talking about the practice, Lee most often referred to Acts 2:21, Romans 10:9, and 2 Timothy 2:22. Some Old Testament examples, such as Psalm 18:6, Isaiah 12:4, and Lamentations 3:55 were also referenced as support for the practice of audibly invoking the Lord's names in times of exultation or depression. For Lee, the commands to "pray without ceasing" (1 Thess 5:17) and "always persevere in supplication" (Eph 6:18) also necessitate this practice in a consistent way since calling upon the name of the Lord is the shortest and most convenient form of prayer.

How were these two practices, pray-reading and calling upon the name of the Lord, connected to the themes of deification? A distinctive

---

[19] Witness Lee, "The Up-to-Date Presentation of the God-Ordained Way and the Signs Concerning the Coming of Christ," *CWWL 1990* 3:535.

[20] Angus Kinnear, *Against the Tide: The Unforgettable Story of Watchman Nee* (Fort Washington, PA: CLC, 2017), 188-89; Witness Lee, *Watchman Nee, a Seer of the Divine Revelation in the Present Age* (Anaheim, CA: Living Stream Ministry, 1991), 286.

characteristic of Lee's theology is his profound engagement with the biblical passages about eating, drinking, and breathing.[21] Lee believed that Christians, through daily practices such as pray-reading and calling upon the Lord, truly obtained spiritual nourishment from God, and that this "regular diet" was necessary for spiritual health, strength, and maturity. For Lee, there was no specific style of worship that guarantees increasing spiritual intimacy. Notwithstanding this issue, he highly recommended pray-reading and calling upon the name of the Lord. The key was not to fall into a passive, idle state of mind or formulaic religiosity but to have a living contact with Christ.

The imagery of ruminating the Word of God in Psalm 1:1-3 supports the connection between pray-reading and eating. As an example, Lee greatly appreciated a hymn written by A. B. Simpson, and promoted it in support of calling upon the name of the Lord as a kind of spiritual "air-change" in which the negative elements of fallen humanity are exhaled, and the positive elements of the divine life, nature, and spiritual vitality are inhaled:

> O Lord, breathe Thy Spirit on me, teach me how to breathe Thee in,
> Help me pour into Thy bosom all my life of self and sin.
> I am breathing out my sorrow, breathing out my sin,
> I am breathing, breathing, breathing—all thy fullness in.[22]

To further employ this image of spiritual breathing, Lee uses Acts 2:17-21 to associate calling upon the name of the Lord with the receiving of the Holy Spirit, the πνεῦμα as air or wind. Along with the allegories of eating and drinking, Lee builds the case to argue that during this kind of spiritual cultivation, a spiritual metabolism happens where God dispenses himself into humans to transform and renew them.[23]

Along with this idea of spiritual union, Lee eventually adopted the language of deification in his mature age. In 1994, Lee concluded that the "highest peak" of the divine revelation was that "God does intend to make the believers God in life and in nature but not in the Godhead."[24] As he had

---

[21] These themes were ubiquitous in Lee's writings. But the best example was a book called *The All-Inclusive Christ*, CWWL 1962 4:194-353.
[22] *Hymns*, 2nd ed. (Anaheim, CA: Living Stream Ministry, 1985), #255.
[23] Witness Lee, *Lessons on Prayer* (Anaheim, CA: Living Stream Ministry, 1981), 7-20.
[24] Witness Lee, "The Seed of David and the Son of God," in *Life-Study of 1 & 2 Samuel* (Living Stream Ministry: Anaheim, 1994).

no previous exposure to Eastern Orthodoxy, it is readily apparent that he developed the doctrine by reflecting upon the teachings he inherited from Nee. However, he later cited Athanasius of Alexandria, the *Catechism of the Catholic Church*, and various patristic fathers to vindicate this doctrine, and contended that the practices of pray-reading and calling upon the name of the Lord were helpful for one to experience deification.[25]

In his statement, Lee makes it clear that he considers there is a limit to deification: humans can only become God in life and nature, not in the Godhead. This limitation, for Lee, is plain in scriptural references such as 1 John 5:12; 2 Peter 1:4; and Acts 14:15. Lee clarifies that human beings will never become omnipotent, omniscient, omnipresent, or objects of worship.[26] In his interpretation, the benefit we receive in participating in the life of God is basically in spirituality and morality. He boldly asserts that in deification, humans may become many "God-men" to "express the divine attributes in human virtues" and live a life that is "mysterious yet human," just like the one lived by Jesus Christ.[27]

## INTRODUCING GREGORY PALAMAS: HESYCHASM AND THE DISTINCTION BETWEEN THE ESSENCE AND ENERGIES OF GOD

Interestingly, Lee's teaching about deification has many parallels with that of Gregory Palamas (1296–1359). Palamas was born into a noble family and was highly educated before becoming a monk at age twenty. He entered into monastic life in Lavra on Mount Athos but was forced to leave because of an invasion by Turkish forces. When he was thirty, he was ordained to the priesthood while living in the hermitage. Also at this time he began to follow the pattern of hesychastic life. Later, he returned to the Athonite community and started publishing his writings on spirituality. He persisted in this profession, even though the rest of his life was marked by theological debates and political turmoil.[28]

The most important debate in Palamas's life, which occurred in Constantinople, was against Barlaam the Calabrian. The issue at hand was part of the

---

[25]Witness Lee, *Living a Life According to the High Peak of God's Revelation* (Anaheim, CA: Living Stream Ministry, 1994).
[26]Lee, *Life-Study of 2 Peter* (Anaheim: Living Stream Ministry, 1985), 28.
[27]Witness Lee, *The God-Man Living* (Anaheim, CA: Living Stream Ministry, 1997).
[28]Gregory Palamas, *The Triads*, ed. John Meyendorff, trans. Nicholas Gendle, Classics of Western Spirituality (New York: Paulist, 1983), 5-6.

larger debate about the *filioque*. Barlaam thought that the debate itself proved the dialectical nature of scriptural and patristic statements, and the inaccessibility of the direct knowledge of the person of God.[29] On the contrary, Palamas believed that direct knowledge of the truth primarily applied in personal experience but not in conceptual exercise. When Barlaam was trying to conceptualize what this experience was, he was aghast by the practice of hesychasm and the claim that this practice allowed for the physical human body to participate in seeing and knowing divinity. To champion the life of hesychast and the deifying benefits of hesychasm, Palamas wrote *The Triads* as three discourses against Barlaam.

Theologically speaking, it is not hard to see why the association of deification with any bodily or spiritual praxis might be controversial. How could any exercise or practice initiated by human beings and through human efforts have a deifying effect? And how could the fallen human body be a part of it and not an obstacle? Barlaam's contempt for the hesychasts concerning their view and use of the body is obvious in his mockery of them as *omphalopsychoi*—"people-whose-soul-is-in-their-navel." To justify their practice, Palamas began by defending the role of the body.

The flesh, contends Palamas, is not condemned by the apostle Paul because it is evil but because it is inhabited by evil. Whenever the matter begins to live and acquires the form of life conformable to the union with Christ, it becomes compatible with the essence of mind. Palamas strongly suggests that our body is suitable for any divine activity because it is the "temple of the Holy Spirit within you" and that "we have this treasure in clay jars" (1 Cor 6:19; 2 Cor 4:7). In the physical body, Palamas indicates that the human heart is where the rational faculty is located. To grow in spirituality, it is essential to force the mind to return within our body. The only direction our soul should be led to is inward; he condemns the suggestion of keeping the mind *outside* one's body during prayer and calls those who make such suggestions the accomplices of the father of lies.[30]

---

[29] Palamas, *Triads*, 6.
[30] Palamas, *Triads*, 41, 43-45. According to *The Triads*, Palamas clearly embraced the idea of ecstasy as a pursuable experience in mysticism. However, we do not know how he explains the literal meaning of the term "standing outside oneself."

To circumscribe one's mind within the body, Palamas recommended hesychasm. He learned hesychasm through the inherited tradition, best seen in the writings of Pseudo-Macarius and Nicephorus the Hesychast. It is a combination of repetitive prayer and mindful regulation of one's breathing. He follows Macarius of Egypt's (300–391) teachings that the body, soul, and spirit were originally one organism, dissolved and disordered later only by sin. It was Jesus who reestablished this order; therefore, constantly calling his name will best help the grace of redemption remain in one's heart.[31] It was later developed as the Jesus Prayer, or "the prayer of the heart." The prayer gradually assumes the form of repeating a brief sentence: "Lord Jesus Christ, Son of God, have mercy on me, a sinner." The exercise is mental and physical, requiring one to place the holy name in one's heart while attaching it to one's breath. Nicephorus the Monk introduces the following breathing technique to help one concentrate one's mind during this kind of prayer:

> You know that we breathe our breath in and out, only because only our heart.... So, as I have said, sit down, recollect your mind, draw it—I am speaking of your mind—in your nostrils; that is the path the breath takes to reach the heart. Drive it, force it to go down to your heart with the air you are breathing in. When it is there, you will see the joy that follows: you will have nothing to regret. As a man who has been away from home for a long time cannot restrain his joy at seeing his wife and children again, so the spirit overflows with joy and unspeakable delights when it united again to the soul.[32]

Hesychasm not only involves the body; the practice also enables its physical deification. To refute the accusation of Barlaam, Palamas says that the involvement of the body corrupts the soul only when the body serves as the source of pleasure itself. What happens in the hesychasm is spiritual, not pleasurable, activity. This activity descends from the soul down to the body and brings joy to the whole being. As promised in the Scripture, the transformation and glorification of the body can only consist in the corrected order. To prove this point, he posits the model of Christ: "He has deified the flesh through the mediation of the soul to make it also accomplish the works

---

[31] John Meyendorff, *Gregory Palamas and Orthodox Spirituality* (Crestwood, NY: St. Vladimir's Seminary Press, 1974), 58.
[32] Palamas, *Triads*, 16.

of God; so similarly, in spiritual man, the grace of the Spirit, transmitted to the body through the soul, grants to the body also the experience of the things divine, and allows it the same blessed experiences as the soul undergoes." Palamas raises Stephen and the saints who beheld the transfiguration on Mount Tabor as the examples of "spiritual man."[33] They experienced the transformation of the body through their corporeal vision of the theophany. These visions became a further point of contention in their debate.

Another point of disagreement related to the createdness of the light seen on Mount Tabor. Barlaam viewed this light as "natural" and purely created: "This light was a sensible light, visible through the medium of the air, appearing to the amazement of all and then at once disappearing. One calls it 'divinity' because it is a symbol of divinity." Palamas was irritated by this statement. He claims that this light was a "hypostatic light," which means that the light was of concrete and divine reality, and that the saints, being purified in mind and illuminated through contacting this light, saw it with the "second eye" of their soul, which was for the glory of his nature.[34]

By asserting that the divine light seen by the saints was hypostatic, Palamas was formulating the boundaries and/or limitations of deification. As history demonstrates, any theologian who engages the concept of deification is immediately confronted with its inherent danger and challenges in relation to the Creator/creature distinction. How far can humans legitimately claim to attain divinity? To what extent can humans, through divine grace, become what God is by nature? What is the boundary that human beings cannot cross? What defines the forbidden territory where humans pursuit leads not to glory but blasphemy? Establishing this demarcation is an arduous task. The challenge, some argue, is insurmountable due to the inherent paradox of two possible heresies: either humans can participate entirely in God, a God fully participatory, or there exists a differentiation within God's own essence, a God divisible. Palamas took on

---

[33] Palamas, *Triads*, 51-52.
[34] Palamas, *Triads*, 72-73, 131n2, 60. "The symbol of divinity" as an expression is not totally unacceptable to Palamas, but it must be put in the right way. It must be in the sense that the nature of the symbol was generated from the object but not gained elsewhere independently. The relationship between the natural symbol and its object that Palamas had in mind is in fact the same with the energy and essence of God.

this task, and his proposal stands as perhaps the most significant exploration of this question by a renowned theologian, albeit one accompanied by significant controversy.[35]

What Palamas proposes is that a distinction exists between the essence of God and the essential energy of God. Deification, thus, is confined to participation only in the latter. Many questions and discussions have been raised about this distinction and what the energies of God actually are. What Palamas aimed to articulate in *The Triads* is that there is only one reality that transcends all things: the superessential. The essence or superessence of God as such is unique and beyond all affirmation and negation in speculation. However, the essence of God holds its own energy, just like every other essence. For example, the essence as the person of God holds the energy as the will of God. Energy is inseparable from the essence. This is not to say, however, that there are infinite couples of essence and energy; on the contrary, while the energies are many, the essence is only one. Although the energies of God are participable, experienceable, and even visible to the eyes of those deemed worthy, it is definitely unoriginated, uncreated, and not intelligible. The existence of divine energies are not eternal; they consist in the essence itself but do not proceed from it. The most succinct example of this distinction is the one that Palamas borrowed from Pseudo-Dionysius: "There is a glory of God beyond participation, an eternal reality, and thus identical to the divine essence; and there is a participable glory, different from this essence and not eternal, for the universal Cause has given it existence."[36]

Nonetheless, no matter how it is articulated, it is still unclear how this distinction may avoid the problem of splitting God into half. Palamas simply attaches the existence of energy to essence. He fails to explain how human participation in the divine energies does not open the door to participation in the divine essence. John Meyendorff says, "The distinction in God between 'essence' and 'energy' is nothing but a way of saying that the transcendent God remains transcendent, as He also communicates Himself to

---

[35]Louis Dupré and James A. Wiseman, eds., *Light from Light: An Anthology of Christian Mysticism*, 2nd ed. (New York: Paulist, 2001), 208.
[36]Dupré and Wiseman, *Light from Light*, 81-82, 99.

humanity."[37] In their introduction to *The Triads*, Louis Dupré and James A. Wiseman also write, "It is hard to see how God's energies can be distinguished from God's nature."[38] What Palamas accomplished is perhaps not a perfect doctrine, yet during his lifetime, he was the only person who aimed to articulate an answer to this difficult question.

One thing that must be added is that although he lacked clarity in the mechanics of how humans might participate in God's energies versus his essence, he excels in explaining how human beings can participate in God practically. The distinction here he makes is clearer—between the purification by human beings themselves and deification through illumination by God. The purification, which is suggested through the practice of hesychasm, does not entail deification. Deification is purely a gracious act from God.[39] From this side, his answer is coherent and worth reference in our discussion of Witness Lee's teaching on similar questions.

## Comparing Witness Lee and Gregory Palamas

In comparing Lee and Palamas in terms of their contributions to the praxis and/or means of deification, one immediately notices that both attempted to define the limit of deification. Lee closely followed the biblical expression to assert that human beings can only become God in life and nature, while Palamas taught that participation in God was only in the divine energy, not essence. Both definitions were not without challenges from their contemporaries, yet their contribution to this meaningful question is still worth reference today.

Lee and Palamas also similarly recommended matching spiritual practices to people who desire to experience the mystical union with God. Calling upon the name of the Lord and hesychasm are both repetitive prayers centered on the holy name. This repetitive aspect invited opposition and concerns about pagan origins for both thinkers. For hesychasm, the suspected influence was the Hindu *Yoga* and Islam *Dhikr*; for calling upon the name of the Lord, there were comparisons with other "Eastern" chanting

---

[37]Dupré and Wiseman, *Light from Light*, 20.
[38]Dupré and Wiseman, *Light from light*, 209.
[39]Palamas, *Triads*, 59, 83.

and mantras.[40] However, no serious connection exists here except geographical and cultural proximity.

Although certain aspects of their practices are similar, there are significant theological differences between calling upon the name of the Lord and hesychasm. The first one is about breathing. Physical exercise in hesychasm is essential; it involves detailed breathing techniques and requires movement of specific body parts. However, Lee's understanding of breathing as it happens in calling upon the name of the Lord is solely spiritual, though due to his tripartite anthropology, this spiritual benefit yields soulish and even physical interactions; the participation in God happens in the spiritual realm simultaneously, not consequentially. This follows Nee's understanding of the human spirit as the organ needed to directly contact and participate in God. In line with this outlook, Lee never mandated any physical form of the practice.

Even though Lee did not teach a standard form of calling upon the name of the Lord, he did teach certain virtues of this practice. He often encouraged practitioners to become more "open"—that is, spiritually receptive to God—during the process, to release one's spirit by opening one's mouth and heart.[41] Calling upon the name of the Lord is not to circumscribe the soul inside the body, but, on the contrary, it is to liberate the human spirit from deep within. One may argue that both practices are trying to bring the human body and mind under control; yet hesychasm teaches people to close down, but calling upon the name of the Lord asks for opening up. One thing separating them is that Lee does not promote silence to the extent that the mystics do, though still finding a place for it within the individual Christian walk. He promotes a lively, active spirituality; silence may indicate lukewarmness, death, or empty piety.

## Conclusion

This chapter began with the question of why and how Watchman Nee and the local churches, as an important component of world Christianity, picked up the theme of deification. It argued that, instead of any inherent Chinese

---

[40]Meyendorff, *Study of Gregory Palamas*, 62.
[41]Witness Lee, "The Organic Building Up Requiring Organic Prophesying," *CWWL 1989* 1:166.

religiosity, the mystical teaching of Madam Guyon was a more obvious source of influence. Inheriting this influence, Lee developed a spiritual practice and theological statement about the limit of deification. These developments are analogous to Gregory Palamas's teachings in *The Triads*. This chapter suggests that calling upon the name of the Lord and hesychasm are a meaningful pair for comparison. Even though Lee and Palamas pictured different ways to reach mystical union, the prayer methods they proposed have many resemblances in form, metaphor, and theological significance.

The findings of this chapter ask for future seeking of more possible parallels in the history of world Christianity. Even though the retrieval of deification has expanded to most of the Western churches, there still may be developments that are much under the radar. Recently, there has been a resurgence of the interest in hesychasm in contemporary global spirituality.[42] Through the immigration of different branches of Orthodox Christians, hesychasm spread to more countries and invited keen practitioners from outside the church. Researchers indicate that there are some worries about not having enough masters to guide the practice. Additionally, our analysis of Lee demonstrates that his understanding of deification, which does not require the same level of "guidance" as hesychasm, may allow the practical implications of the doctrine to be accessible to believers outside of the Eastern Orthodox tradition, as it allows for the actuation of deification through spiritual practices in their daily lives. Regardless, the inheritance and appropriation of any cultural and spiritual tradition are often beyond anyone's control. An interplay between the stimulating doctrine of deification and the many diverse actors in world Christianity can call for more unexpected yet surprising developments.

---

[42]Christopher D. L. Johnson, *The Globalization of Hesychasm and the Jesus Prayer: Contesting Contemplation* (New York: Continuum, 2010).

# TRANSHUMANISM *as* ACTIVE EFFORT *of* TECHNOLOGY VERSUS DEIFICATION *as* ACTIVE RECEPTION *of* GRACE

### Kimbell Kornu

To understand how deification should position itself in relation to transhumanism, we must first see how the transhumanist movement understands itself. At its core, transhumanism explicitly seeks to go beyond the human. Humanity+, the transhumanist organization that publishes the Transhumanist Declaration, the Transhumanist Manifesto, and the Transhumanist FAQ, formally defines *transhumanism* in two parts:

> (1) The intellectual and cultural movement that affirms the possibility and desirability of fundamentally improving the human condition through applied reason, especially by developing and making widely available technologies to eliminate aging and to greatly enhance human intellectual, physical, and psychological capacities.

> (2) The study of the ramifications, promises, and potential dangers of technologies that will enable us to overcome fundamental human limitations, and the related study of the ethical matters involved in developing and using such technologies.[1]

Looking more closely at the definition, we can highlight the major themes of transhumanism: power, radical life extension, maximizing intellectual

---

[1] H+Pedia, "Transhumanist FAQ Live," https://hpluspedia.org/wiki/Transhumanist_FAQ_Live (accessed November 1, 2023).

capacity, and freedom to overcome finitude, all through radical biotechnological enhancement. A key assumption in the transhumanist project of improving the human condition is conquering suffering and death through a "techno-can-do-ism."[2]

The themes and goals of transhumanism constitute a kind of religion with its own doctrine of God and theology of nature, as humans become god and exert power over nature. Ray Kurzweil encapsulates the transhumanist religious vision, comparing the never-ending progress of evolution with the attributes of God. It is worth quoting him in full:

> Evolution moves toward greater complexity, greater elegance, greater knowledge, greater intelligence, greater beauty, greater creativity, and greater levels of subtle attributes such as love. In every monotheistic tradition God is likewise described as all of these qualities, only without any limitation: infinite knowledge, infinite intelligence, infinite beauty, infinite creativity, infinite love, and so on. Of course, even the accelerating growth of evolution never achieves an infinite level, but as it explodes exponentially it certainly moves rapidly in that direction. So evolution moves inexorably toward this conception of God, although never quite reaching this ideal. We can regard, therefore, the freeing of our thinking from the severe limitations of its biological form to be an essentially spiritual undertaking.[3]

Here we see that Kurzweil places a trust in evolution to move us toward more truth, goodness, and beauty, which are divine transcendentals. He has enough awareness to know that these are found in God but is careful to say that evolution will never reach them in their fullness. It is important to note here that the evolution of which Kurzweil speaks is not biological evolution, since biology has "severe limitations," but rather a spiritualized technological evolution. Through a never-ending advancement of biotechnology, biological restrictions are overcome in a spiritual striving toward the God

---

[2]Max More, "The Philosophy of Transhumanism," in *The Transhumanist Reader*, ed. Max More and Natasha Vita-More (Malden, MA; Wiley-Blackwell, 2013), 4; Ted Peters, "Theologians Testing Transhumanism," *Theology and Science* 13, no. 2 (2015): 130-49. For an account of how suffering is a means to deification over against transhumanism, see Kimbell Kornu, "Transfiguration, Not Transhumanism: Suffering as Human Enhancement," *The Heythrop Journal* 63, no. 5 (2022): 926-39.

[3]Ray Kurzweil, *The Singularity Is Near: When Humans Transcend Biology* (New York: Penguin, 2006), 389.

of truth, goodness, and beauty. Key to this spiritual undertaking is that the transhumanist's never-ending striving is an infinite restlessness, a rest that is endlessly deferred and never attained. So for Kurzweil and other transhumanists, one of the essentials of the transhumanist religious vision is techno-evolutionary restless striving to become divine, which is essentially pure active effort.[4] It is all effort and no grace.

Recent theologians have actively engaged transhumanism, showing their differences and affinities with Christianity through the doctrine of deification. Ron Cole-Turner has been a cautious yet optimistic interpreter of how transhumanism and deification relate to each other. On the one hand, Cole-Turner wants to make it clear that secular transhumanism and biblical deification are fundamentally incompatible. The goal of secular transhumanism is a never-ending self-expansion and self-protection; it is not other-oriented. Biblical deification or theosis, however, is essentially about self-emptying. Theosis is kenosis: there is a need to embrace and live a collective, cruciform life to challenge the culture of human enhancement.[5]

On the other hand, Cole-Turner argues provocatively that transhumanism is a fundamentally Christian concept, tracing the idea back to Dante in the term *transmanar*, precisely because of deification. The word *transmanar* is invented to describe how a great transformation lies ahead for humans on their way from grace to glory. This way of glorification is rooted in the incarnation, in God becoming human so that humans can become God. In this way transhumanism is essentially deification. Cole-Turner compares transhumanism and Christianity as two different means of deification: the former by technology and the latter by grace. He sees technology as a proper way for humans to contribute to the transformation of humans and creation, as long as one grants that it is ultimately God's work. Christ is the purpose of Christian transhumanism because humanity and all of creation are brought up into transfiguration.[6]

---

[4]For another example of transhumanist religion, see Giulio Prisco, "Transcendent Engineering," in More and Vita-More, *Transhumanist Reader*, 234-40.
[5]Ron Cole-Turner, "Theosis and Human Enhancement," *Theology and Science* 16, no. 3 (2018): 330-42.
[6]Ronald Cole-Turner, "Going Beyond the Human: Christians and Other Transhumanists," *Theology and Science* 13, no. 2 (2015): 150-61.

Cole-Turner's proposal is provocative and alluring. On the one hand, he does not want to conflate transhumanism and deification when it comes to its moral core: self-centeredness flies in the face of the gospel of the kenotic Christ of Philippians 2. On the other hand, he seeks to carve out a space for a robust theology of creation and transfiguration such that creative human efforts through technology will be an active agent in transforming the world in glory.

However, I challenge his proposal, showing how transhumanism in any stripe, whether secular, Christian, or other, is fundamentally incompatible with Christian deification because of their incompatible views on human agency in deification. But how are we to investigate human agency in this context? As Cole-Turner suggests, the proper diagnostic questions for theology's engagement with transhumanism must interrogate the foundational assumptions regarding evolution and technology, both of which come under a theology of nature and grace.[7] (In this chapter, I will focus mainly on evolution as part of a philosophy of nature and will set aside an in-depth engagement with technology for another time.)

I suggest that the proper way to understand human agency, transhumanism, and deification must contrast the active effort of transhumanism with the active receptivity of deification. Simone Kotva has recently shown that within the recent discussion of philosophy as spiritual exercise, a division has been made between active effort and passive receptivity.[8] Kotva draws on the insights of Simone Weil, who sets up a distinction between "muscular effort" and "negative effort."[9] Muscular effort is the elevation of effort in praise of the virtue of activity and human accomplishment. In contrast, negative effort is inspired by the tradition of Augustinian mystical prayer, which recognizes that not all things are under our control. Mystical prayer entails the passive receptivity of relaxation, effortlessness, and desire. Following the model of mystical prayer, philosophy as spiritual exercise entails both activity and passivity, willing and waiting, effort and grace, such

---

[7]Cole-Turner, "Going Beyond the Human," 153-54.
[8]Simone Kotva, *Effort and Grace: On the Spiritual Exercise of Philosophy* (London: Bloomsbury Academic, 2020).
[9]Simone Weil, *Waiting for God* (New York: Harper Perennial Modern Classics, 2009), 57-66.

that it does not depend solely on active effort—that is, not on will-to-power—but rather is paradoxically enmeshed with passive receptivity. Taken together, active effort and passive receptivity combine in a singular action in what I call active receptivity.

Active receptivity entails effort, but it is a negative effort, which Weil calls the effort of attention. Attention is not pure activity in contrast to inactivity. Rather, attention is an active receptivity. Weil applies the notion of attention to school studies and connects it to prayer. For example, in the effort of trying to solve a problem in geometry, even if there is no sense of progress after an hour, there is still progress being made each minute because there is "another more mysterious dimension. Without our knowing or feeling it, this apparently barren effort has brought more light into the soul. The result will one day be discovered in prayer." In other words, endless striving in solving the problem will not bring about the solution. Instead, in following the model of prayer, one must expend intellectual effort but then must effortlessly receive the light that illumines the mind. This light is the light of desire, for "the intelligence can only be led by desire." The substance of this desire is pleasure and joy in the work at hand. The joy of work is what makes work a spiritual exercise, "for desire directed toward God is the only power capable of raising the soul." Practicing the effort of attention "will help form in them the habit of that attention which is the substance of prayer." One must expend active effort to accomplish something but passively receive grace. Indeed, accomplishment is ultimately a gift to be received: "We do not obtain the most precious gifts by going in search of them but by waiting for them."[10] As Kotva puts it succinctly, "In the organic as well as the moral life, active effort and passive receptivity depend upon one another."[11]

I extrapolate Kotva's account of the spiritual exercise of philosophy as active receptivity more generally to human agency in relationship to nature, such that effort and grace are both necessary to properly understand deification. In this chapter I will argue that transhumanism maps onto active muscular effort of accomplishing auto-deification by technology through will-to-power over nature and over self, whereas Christian deification follows

---

[10]Weil, *Waiting for God*, 58, 61, 59, 62.
[11]Kotva, *Effort and Grace*, xii.

the active receptivity of effort and grace: in seeking to become like God, one must desire God, exert effort, but ultimately must receive the grace to become like God in Christ.

The argument proceeds as follows. First, I will provide a historical account of how science changed during the early modern period after the transformation of natural philosophy, which provides the conditions for active effort to predominate. Active effort informs both evolution and technology and grounds transhumanist philosophy. Second, I will explore Félix Ravaisson's philosophy of graced nature as the basis for understanding active receptivity within nature and agency. Third, I will highlight Maximus the Confessor's cosmic motion of active receptivity in his metaphysics of created desire, which culminates in deification as an ever-moving rest. I conclude that a proper understanding of Christian deification makes it impossible to be a transhumanist, whether secular or Christian.

## Transformation of Science from Active Receptivity to Active Effort

The transformation of science and its philosophy of nature provides the philosophical and historical background for how transhumanism became paradigmatic of an agency of pure active effort. The change in how we understand the practice of science was accompanied with a change in how we understand the essence of nature and humanity's relationship to nature, epitomized in Francis Bacon's transformation of natural philosophy and Nietzsche's modification of Darwinian evolution, which gives priority to power and control.

Drawing on Peter Harrison's intellectual history of the relationship between science and religion to help tell this story, I contend that the transformation of science from a virtue to a body of knowledge created the conditions for active effort to take precedence. Science as it is currently understood is a recent invention since the early modern period. *Scientia* was initially understood to be an intellectual virtue, but through a process of objectification, science became a body of practice and knowledge.[12]

---

[12] Peter Harrison, *The Territories of Science and Religion* (Chicago: University of Chicago Press, 2015), ix-x.

Before the seventeenth century, *scientia* was primarily a personal quality. Virtue was not merely moral but also a habit that perfected the powers the individual possessed. Following Aquinas, *scientia* was an intellectual virtue, a habit of mind gradually acquired through rehearsal of logical demonstrations, such as studying geometry (as we saw from Weil's example). The purpose of science was to grow in clear and ordered thinking as an interior quality of the mind. However, after the seventeenth century, science became a system of belief and practice, and the purpose and method of gaining knowledge changed. *Scientia* was transformed from an interior quality as intellectual virtue to science as an objectification of method and doctrine. From the premodern understanding to the early modern understanding of *scientia* to science, there was an inversion of internal and external aims. In the premodern understanding, scientific knowledge was instrumental for the purpose of growing the intellectual virtue of *scientia*, whereas the intellectual virtue of *scientia*—that is, the habit of clear and ordered thinking—was cultivated as an instrument for the production of scientific knowledge.[13]

How does this apply to human agency and active effort? Harrison tells a long history that starts with ancient Greek philosophy and the early church. There were two common ancient assumptions. First, moral order was built into the structure of the cosmos. For example, for Plato mathematical study of the cosmos contributed to the moral and intellectual formation of the philosopher. Second, natural philosophy was essential for moral and spiritual formation. Knowledge of nature allowed the philosopher to align her life with the rational principle that animated the cosmos. Natural philosophy was a spiritual exercise that helped transform the philosopher's mode of seeing and being, leading to a spiritual ascent to the mind of God. Early Christianity was not a religion but understood as a new kind of philosophy, a way of life. The only way to understand Christianity as a philosophy is if philosophy is primarily concerned with moral and spiritual formation. Christian spiritual formation occurred in part through natural philosophy because it was a form of spiritual practice. The Christian contemplated visible things through natural philosophy and then progressed to the

---

[13]Harrison, *Territories of Science and Religion*, 1-19.

invisible things of truths about God.¹⁴ The active effort of studying nature was meant to transform the one doing the studying through a passive receptivity to have new spiritual eyes to see the divine through nature, akin to Weil's "negative effort" of attention.

However, with the early modern period, this framework was turned on its head. Central to the premodern understanding of nature was the Aristotelian framework of fourfold causation. Natural entities have formal, final, material, and efficient causes. Formal cause identifies what the entity is, and the final cause is the intrinsic purpose of the entity. In the early modern period, the conception of nature with an intrinsic teleology was challenged.¹⁵ Modern science set aside formal and final causes and focused exclusively on material and efficient causes.¹⁶ Virtue understood as both moral qualities of persons and inherent dispositions of natural bodies was overturned. This meant that nature no longer had an inherent purpose. The understanding of nature in terms of intrinsic teleology changed to laws of nature. The goodness and order of nature was no longer intrinsic to nature but rather became dictated by the will of God, manifested in God's law and, consequently, the laws of nature. The laws of nature governed a kind of extrinsic teleology—that is, will is imposed on nature. With the imposition of God's will on nature, it shaped the scientific imagination to impose human will on nature.¹⁷ Nature became a standing reserve for humans to manipulate, control, and bend to their wills.¹⁸

What resulted was a transference from inward dominion to outward dominion. Harrison explains, "The motifs of self-cultivation and self-mastery that had been central to classical accounts of philosophy, and which to some degree found their way into medieval understandings of human ends would now be directed outward onto the world."¹⁹ The shift from inward to outward

---

[14] Harrison, *Territories of Science and Religion*, 21-54.
[15] Simon Oliver, "Teleology Revived? Cooperation and the Ends of Nature," *Studies in Christian Ethics* 26, no. 2 (2013): 158-65.
[16] Edwin A. Burtt, *The Metaphysical Foundations of Modern Science* (Mineola, NY: Dover, 2003).
[17] Amos Funkenstein, *Theology and the Scientific Imagination from the Middle Ages to the Seventeenth Century* (Princeton, NJ: Princeton University Press, 1986).
[18] Martin Heidegger, "The Question Concerning Technology," in *The Question Concerning Technology, and Other Essays*, trans. William Lovitt (New York: Harper & Row, 1977), 3-35.
[19] Harrison, *Territories of Science and Religion*, 90.

dominion was inaugurated by Bacon's transformation of natural philosophy. Bacon reoriented the purpose of natural philosophy away from growth of moral and intellectual virtue toward a new goal of relieving the human condition, which has been called the Baconian project.[20] Not surprisingly, transhumanists claim Bacon as an inspiration for transhumanism's philosophy as a kind of theological project, as scientific experimental knowledge enabled a return to Eden and sovereign dominion over nature.[21]

Bacon's natural philosophy has the two key elements of utility and progress, characterized by dominion over nature. The utility of knowledge reflects the changing view of knowledge from self-improvement to usefulness. Knowledge is only good if it wields power to help relieve the human condition. For Bacon, knowledge is power: "Those two goals of man, knowledge and power, a pair of twins, are really come to the same thing."[22] Progress also took on new meaning. Premodern progress was teleological and personal: human progress is the natural motion of the individual toward the goals of wisdom and virtue, fulfilled in life with God. In contrast, modern progress is objective and cognitive in an ever-increasing external body of knowledge, like an encyclopedia. Instead of nature being a source of self-improvement through contemplation, nature becomes the object of improvement. The goal of progress is not personal improvement but rather contributing to an external body of knowledge. The utility of progress is growing a mass of information for the purpose of materially improving human welfare. The means of progress is technological, since it exerts ever-greater power over nature.

The difference between premodern self-dominion versus modern dominion over nature is clear. Premodern dominion over nature is self-dominion over the passions. Controlling the passions enables growth in virtue. Modern dominion over nature is exercise of control over the natural

---

[20]Gerald P. McKenny, *To Relieve the Human Condition: Bioethics, Technology, and the Body* (Albany: State University of New York Press, 1997).

[21]Joseph Wolyniak, "'The Relief of Man's Estate': Transhumanism, the Baconian Project, and the Theological Impetus for Material Salvation," in *Religion and Transhumanism: The Unknown Future of Human Enhancement*, ed. Calvin Mercer and Tracy J. Trothen (Santa Barbara, CA: Praeger, 2015), 53-70.

[22]Francis Bacon, *The New Organon*, ed. Lisa Jardine, trans. Michael Silverthorne (Cambridge: Cambridge University Press, 2000), 24.

world. Bacon separated self-dominion from physical dominion over nature. Self-dominion was relegated to faith and religion and had nothing to do with nature outside humans. Physical dominion over nature was exercised through the experimental sciences. Baconian natural philosophy seeks transformation of the world rather than the soul of the philosopher. Bacon proclaims, "Our design is to discover whether in truth we can lay firmer foundations for human power and human greatness, and extend their limits more widely."[23] The purpose of natural philosophy is active effort over nature for the sake of relieving the human condition. Natural philosophy has lost the core element of passive reception of inward transformation of the mind.[24]

Now that the historical conditions for the active effort of natural philosophy have been identified, we can see how this speaks directly to discourse on transhumanism and deification. I want to take seriously Cole-Turner's suggestion that the two most important diagnostic questions in theology's engagement with transhumanism are how we think about evolution and how we think about technology. Rooted in a materialist philosophy, transhumanism affirms Darwinian evolution but thinks that evolution should be enhanced for the purpose of human enhancement, since waiting and relying on Darwinian evolution for human fitness is too slow of a process. Rather, precisely because of the Baconian moral imperative to relieve the human condition, radical enhancement technologies should accelerate and direct evolution. They could redefine what it is to be human or even go beyond the human by linking Darwinian evolution with "enhancement evolution."[25] The notion of "directed evolution" has been challenged as incoherent since, by definition, Darwinian evolution is blind, random, and not willfully purposeful, while transhumanism is inherently purposed toward breaking bonds of biological evolution.[26] So is directed evolution incoherent?

A Nietzschean Darwinist evolution provides the way forward for transhumanist-directed evolution. It is rooted in a Nietzschean *power ontology*.

---

[23] Bacon, *New Organon*, 90.
[24] Harrison, *Territories of Science and Religion*, 117-44.
[25] John Harris, *Enhancing Evolution: The Ethical Case for Making Better People* (Princeton, NJ: Princeton University Press, 2010), 24.
[26] Andrew Askland, "The Misnomer of Transhumanism as Directed Evolution," *International Journal of Emerging Technologies & Society* 9, no. 1 (2011): 71-78.

Power ontology means that there is an ontic priority given to will-to-power, such that will-to-power is a kind of cosmic force that drives all things. Nietzsche is unsatisfied with mere mechanistic explanations because they still do not explain the "why" of things. However, will-to-power does explain the nature of things.[27] What is interesting is when this power ontology is applied to evolution and humans.

The power ontology in evolution selects for power as a strategy that outcompetes all other strategies for fitness maximization. Power as a competitive strategy entails control over nature and the environment. Nietzschean Darwinian evolution presumes the necessity of direct struggle between organisms. Selection for will-to-power is a result of the Darwinist direct struggle among organisms, as it is a naturalistic explanation for organismic drives for control. Humans are the pinnacle in Nietzsche's conception of evolution. The good of human beings is the preservation of the human species through a drive for power, which "constitutes *the essence* of our species and herd."[28] John Richardson explains: "Nietzsche's will-to-power idea is . . . a naturalistic thesis about a class of drives—tendencies toward power as control. These drives have control as their explaining goal, insofar as they've been selected for producing it; such drives are widespread, because control is *strongly* selected for."[29]

The essence of Nietzschean Darwinist evolution is power and control over nature. We can see how this applies directly to transhumanism and its notion of directed evolution. Through the power of radical bioenhancement technologies, humans can fulfill their "natural" goal of power and control over nature, including the nature of their own physical bodies through enhancement or even leaving their bodies behind in the maximization of power and control. Even leaving the body behind follows Nietzsche's logic of nature and will-to-power. When Nietzsche declares, "*Long live physics!*" he is proclaiming that human beings must become physicists to be creators,

---

[27]John Richardson, *Nietzsche's New Darwinism* (New York: Oxford University Press, 2004), 49–50.
[28]Friedrich Nietzsche, *The Gay Science*, §1. For an English translation, see Friedrich Nietzsche, *Nietzsche: The Gay Science; With a Prelude in German Rhymes and an Appendix of Songs*, ed. Bernard Williams, trans. Josefine Nauckhoff and Adrian Del Caro (New York: Cambridge University Press, 2001), 27, emphasis original.
[29]Richardson, *Nietzsche's New Darwinism*, 59.

that is, must understand the natural laws of necessity in order to overcome necessity and thereby self-create: "We, however, want to *become who we are*—human beings who are new, unique, incomparable, who give themselves laws, who create themselves! To that end we must become the best students and discoverers of everything lawful and necessary in the world: we must become *physicists* in order to be creators in this sense."[30]

Here is the rub: the Nietzschean power ontology of evolution perfectly aligns with the Baconian project of relieving the human estate by exercising dominion over nature. The Nietzschean power ontology of will-to-power to maximize power answers the urgent call of the Baconian project to relieve the human estate. This Nietzschean and Baconian coupling provides the philosophical underpinning for transhumanism that is wholly grounded on active effort through technology.[31] Transhumanism is muscular effort on steroids.

Transhumanism as an auto-deification is not only a problem of lust for power and control over nature through technology. Nor is it merely a problem of how one directs the will for self-exaltation or self-denial. Based on Nietzsche's power ontology, transhumanism as active effort presupposes a metaphysics of nature that begins and ends with power. Evolution should be enhanced because humans have the moral imperative to go beyond being human and become god(s). But this is not the only way to understand the essence of nature. For Félix Ravaisson and Maximus the Confessor, the metaphysics of nature begins and ends with love, which underscores an agency of active receptivity and directly shapes how to understand deification. So the opposition between transhumanism and deification and between active effort and active receptivity can be grounded on an opposition between philosophies of nature rooted either in power or in love. Transhumanism has a Nietzschean Darwinian power ontology that exalts will-to-power with endless effort, whereas deification assumes a created nature that is directed toward God in ever-moving rest. Let us now turn to Ravaisson and Maximus to a metaphysics of nature and deification of active receptivity.

---

[30] Nietzsche, *Gay Science*, §335, trans. Nauckhoff, 189, emphasis original.
[31] Not all transhumanists affirm inspiration from Nietzsche, but affirmation is not important for my argument. For differing views on the role Nietzsche plays in transhumanism, see Yunus Tuncel, ed., *Nietzsche and Transhumanism: Precursor or Enemy?* (Newcastle upon Tyne: Cambridge Scholars, 2017).

## Félix Ravaisson and the Active Receptivity of a Graced Nature

Félix Ravaisson comes from the French spiritualist tradition in the nineteenth century, as a third way between German idealism and British empiricism, such that it does not fall either into pure mind or into pure nature but rather a kind of spiritual nature. Ravaisson is not well-known in the Anglophone world, but he is prominent within the French philosophical tradition, given both his philosophy and his position within the French academy in the mid-nineteenth century.[32] His commissioned work *French Philosophy in the Nineteenth Century* was required reading for every French philosophy student in the latter part of the nineteenth century, which set the agenda for the French spiritualist tradition that shaped his student Henri Bergson and later Simone Weil.[33]

The French spiritualism of Ravaisson is a throwback to understanding nature in the premodern, Aristotelian way we saw in Harrison's story of the transformation of science and the philosophy of nature. For Ravaisson, nature is inherent with purpose, which he calls "prevenient grace," drawing on the Augustinian mystical tradition of François Fénelon.[34] Nature is already graced with love. This language of grace from theology has its equivalent in philosophy as formal cause. Ravaisson compares materialism with his philosophy of graced nature.[35] He calls materialism and its positivist variants a "philosophy of the brain." In materialism, there is by definition no preexistent reason for order or beauty—that is, there is no formal cause—as everything proceeds chaotically, as in Nietzschean power ontology. There is no organizing beauty or fittingness, as it is war of all against all. The history of the world is a "perpetual progress" that starts from nothingness (again, there is no preexistent order) and raises itself up to thought and consciousness. In this historical evolution, out of nothingness comes a self-generated

---

[32]For more on Ravaisson's philosophy and influence, see Mark Sinclair, *Being Inclined: Felix Ravaisson's Philosophy of Habit* (New York: Oxford University Press, 2019).

[33]Félix Ravaisson, *French Philosophy in the Nineteenth Century*, ed. Mark Sinclair (New York: Oxford University Press, 2023); Kotva, *Effort and Grace*, 59-172.

[34]Félix Ravaisson, *Of Habit*, trans. Clare Carlisle and Mark Sinclair (London: Continuum, 2008), 123n61.

[35]The rest of this paragraph and the next paragraph draw heavily from Félix Ravaisson, *Selected Essays*, ed. Mark Sinclair (London: Bloomsbury Academic, 2016), 325n16.

rationality, of which transhumanism is the culmination. Transhumanism exalts the intellect and its exercise of power through technology, and humans prevail in the conflict over nature by mastering and controlling it, including one's own body. Transhumanists then seek to exceed and go beyond the human to become god(s). It is auto-deification through pure active effort.

In contrast, for Ravaisson a philosophy of graced nature is a "philosophy of the heart," in which beauty reigns. Where there is beauty, desire plays a key role as a passive receptivity. This spiritualist reality is understood as "the movement of nature by a pre-existent love, by a prevenient grace," which is a "principle of life" that proceeds "from humiliation to inspiration to, to deification."[36] Nature is moved by the preexistent love, the prevenient grace. Nature's motion is not self-generated, as in transhumanism, but is received. But received from where? Or from whom? Ravaisson is explicit about the divine source of this love: "The truth is the divinity lowering itself by love to the forms that both hide it and make it visible, it is the soul inspired by divinity, filled by it with the desire to pour out its goods into the world, to clothe it in splendor and glory, to intoxicate it with goodness. . . . This movement is first abasement and then recovery, or resurrection."[37] The divine condescends in love, fills the soul with the desire for the good, and glorifies it. While Ravaisson is not writing as a theologian, this has a clear resonance with the incarnation and resurrection of Christ in an *exitus-reditus* framework. The descent of love must be received in one's nature in order to ascend up to the good. There is an active receptivity in the metaphysics of love.

But this given desire does not make one an automaton. On the contrary, desire is a tendency toward something; so there is a passive receptivity, as one cannot merely conjure desire through effort. In Ravaisson's framework, the will is already impelled by primal desire, so the will is not an uninformed, naked actor. The relationship between desire and will is part of a larger framework of a philosophy of habit. Habit is a disposition, a virtue. Ravaisson develops Aristotle's notion that "habit is a second nature."[38] Habit as

---

[36]Ravaisson, *Selected Essays*, 325n16.
[37]Ravaisson, *Selected Essays*, 325n16.
[38]Aristotle, *On Memory and Recollection* 452a30. This quotation serves as the epigraph to Ravaisson's *Of Habit*.

disposition becomes a part of the agent's nature, and habit entails an inverse relationship between receptivity and what Ravaisson calls the spontaneity of nature. The double law of habit is that "the continuity or the repetition of passion weakens [habit]; the continuity or repetition of action exalts and strengthens it." As receptivity decreases, spontaneity increases.[39] In other words, the more one repeats an action, the more one spontaneously does that action without thinking; and conversely, the more one is passive about an action, the less one will do that action.

Habit is acquired precisely through the inverse relationship between effort and resistance, such that there is a change in disposition. Effort requires a preexisting resistance. The conscious will resides in the space of effort and resistance. What has been received in desire is the setting of resistance for the will to exert effort. Habit is a necessity of desire, which becomes naturalized, so willing against a given desire requires effort. In the exertion of effort, the will becomes conscious: "Therefore effort necessarily requires an effortless antecedent tendency, which in its development encounters resistance; and it is at this point that the will finds itself in the self-reflection of activity, and is awakened through effort." So voluntary movement finds its source and origin in desire. The will sets the goal of an action, but desire works out the production of movement, for the depth of desire is "where the idea of nature becomes being and substance."[40] This is an insight from Augustinian anthropology, that our desires shape who we are. As one continues to will an action, it becomes a habit, which is driven by desire. In habit acquisition, it becomes natural to do that very thing that is desired such that it becomes a second nature.

So the philosophy of graced nature that works out in human agency looks like this: prevenient grace → desire → will → habit → fulfilled nature. This schema represents the interplay of active receptivity: in order to will through active effort, one must first have desire, which is passively received. Then, in the acquisition of habit, those received desires become realized in action, and as those habits are strengthened, one's nature is further conformed with the desire of the action. In the philosophy of graced nature, one's nature

---

[39]Ravaisson, *Of Habit*, 49, 31.
[40]Ravaisson, *Of Habit*, 61, 71.

moves to be in conformity with the heart of nature, which is love. As one repeatedly acts in love, one is habituated in the virtue of love, and one's nature becomes loving. Ravaisson equates the motion of love with nature, which unifies desire, intellect, and conscious will:

> The mediated intelligence and will relating to the extremities envelop, then, an immediate understanding and will relating to the milieu. Immediate intelligence and will are like the middle term within movement across the entire milieu. The poles touch each other everywhere, the principle and the end merging. This immediate understanding is concrete thought, within which the idea is fused with being. This immediate will is desire, or rather love, which possesses and desires at the same time. This thought and this desire, this idea substantiated in the movement of love, is Nature.[41]

The fulfillment of desire and goal of the will fuses with nature. If we read this in light of Ravaisson's previous statement about the principle of life moving from humiliation to inspiration to deification, it can be understood that the telos of the philosophy of graced nature is deification in love. What results is that the fulfillment of nature is not out of natural necessity but rather is the realization of freedom—the freedom to love in accordance with the love that is the purpose of nature. In other words, true freedom is nature being fully itself.[42]

Ravaisson's philosophy of graced nature provides a philosophical account of an agency of active receptivity for deification over against a transhumanist agency of pure active effort. However, Ravaisson's account is incomplete for a full account of deification, as it does not have a place for suffering and does not feature Christ at its heart.[43] In a surprising connection, Maximus the Confessor's account of deification has striking similarities to Ravaisson's philosophy of graced nature, explained in part because they share a framework of Aristotelian teleological motion for nature. Yet, Maximus goes beyond Ravaisson on deification by giving a central place to suffering with Christ at the very heart of his metaphysics of cosmic motion.

---

[41] Ravaisson, *Of Habit*, 75.
[42] Ravaisson, *Of Habit*, 77.
[43] Kotva argues that the successors of Ravaisson came to emphasize active effort in the spiritual exercise of philosophy at the expense of passive receptivity, naming Henri Bergson specifically (*Effort and Grace*, 95).

## Maximus the Confessor and the Active Receptivity of Deification in Love

Maximus's doctrine of the two wills of Christ brings together suffering and Christ to show how suffering plays into deification and acts as a powerful critique of the transhumanist will-to-power, summarized in the Transhumanist Declaration, propositions 8 and 1, respectively: "We favour allowing individuals wide personal choice over how they enable their lives"; and "We envision the possibility of broadening human potential by overcoming aging, cognitive shortcomings, [and] involuntary suffering."[44] Taken together, will-to-power works to overcome limitations in life, intellect, and suffering, all through active effort.

In direct contrast to the intuition that suffering must be overcome, Maximus's doctrine of the two wills of Christ gives primacy to the importance of suffering of Jesus in Gethsemane, which enables deification and provides the paradigmatic model of active receptivity. It is significant that the account of Jesus in Gethsemane focuses on Christ in prayer. Prayer is the paradigm for active receptivity: one actively prays, but must wait to receive grace from God. A related point is that the manner in which one responds to suffering is also an important instance of active receptivity. In suffering, one submits to the affliction but responds in faith, hope, and love to what God will give. The key point is that Christ's human will aligns with the divine will out of love of the Son for the Father for the sake of deification. Over against the monothelite position, which held that in Christ there were two natures but one activity and one will, Maximus affirmed that Christ had two wills and two activities in accord with two natures. Maximus held that will was a capacity and process that could not be removed from activity, and that activity was nature in action.[45] In other words, human beings share a common human nature that exhibits an activity, one of which is will.

Because death entered by the exercise of free will in the Garden of Eden, death needed to be reversed by Christ's human free will, which occurred in

---

[44] H+Pedia, "Transhumanist Declaration," 2009, https://hpluspedia.org/wiki/Transhumanist_Declaration.

[45] Maximus, *Opusculum* 7. For an English translation, see Maximus the Confessor, *Maximus the Confessor*, trans. Andrew Louth (New York: Routledge, 1996).

the Garden of Gethsemane.[46] Christ submitted his human will to the divine will, foregoing active effort of human will, and instead accepted the divine will, which then deified his human will. In submission, Christ suffered, which manifested as sweating blood, which is an identified medical condition called hematidrosis, typically found in persons who experience extreme mental anguish, such as acute fear of death.[47] Gethsemane demonstrated the weakness of Christ's flesh (in accordance with human flesh) and the perfect concordance between the will of the Father and the human will.[48] Jesus' suffering in Gethsemane liberates the human will to align with the will of the Father, for "although he was a son, he learned obedience through what he suffered" (Heb 5:8 ESV).[49] Christ came to deify human nature in the hypostatic union and to show that deification entails obedient sonship to the Father.[50] For human nature to be truly free, it must submit to the divine will. As part of the divine economy, obedience to the will of the Father deifies the human nature.

Expanding beyond the will, Maximus gives an account of cosmic motion, which is a "metaphysics of created desire."[51] This metaphysics culminates in an ever-moving repose of an eschatology of active receptivity, which counters the transhumanist endless striving of active effort. Maximus's metaphysics is fundamentally a creaturely metaphysics, which is a study of motion.[52] Its basic structure is the triad of coming-to-be, movement, and rest. Maximus's clearest expression of motion as the mark of creation is found in *Ambiguum* 7, which is a response to Origenism, which holds to the cosmological triad of rest, motion, and becoming with the view that motion

---

[46]Maximus, *Ambiguum* 7, PG 91:1076A-B. For an English translation, see Maximos the Confessor, *On Difficulties in the Church Fathers: The Ambigua*, trans. Nicholas Constas, 2 vols. (Cambridge, MA: Harvard University Press, 2014).
[47]Joe E. Holoubek and Alice B. Holoubek, "Blood, Sweat and Fear: 'A Classification of Hematidrosis,'" *Journal of Medicine* 27, nos. 3-4 (1996): 115-33.
[48]Maximus, *Opusculum* 7, PG 91:80C-D, 81C-84A.
[49]Paul M. Blowers, *Maximus the Confessor: Jesus Christ and the Transfiguration of the World* (Oxford: Oxford University Press, 2016), 234.
[50]Maximus, *Opusculum* 7, PG 91:77B-80B, trans. Louth, 184-85.
[51]I borrow this phrase from Adam G. Cooper, "Spiritual Anthropology in *Ambiguum* 7," in *The Oxford Handbook of Maximus the Confessor*, ed. Pauline Allen and Bronwen Neil (New York: Oxford University Press, 2015), 363.
[52]Hans Urs von Balthasar, *Cosmic Liturgy: The Universe According to Maximus the Confessor*, trans. Brian E. Daley (San Francisco: Ignatius, 2003), 154.

is a result of the fall. In contrast, Maximus demonstrates that motion is not a result of the fall but rather constitutive of created existence. He argues that created existence is in motion toward its ultimate object of desire:

> If, in the first place, we accept that the Divine is immovable (since it fills all things), whereas everything that has received its being *ex nihilo* is in motion (since all things are necessarily carried along toward some cause), then nothing that moves has yet come to rest, because its capacity for appetitive movement has not yet come to repose in what it ultimately desires, for nothing but the appearance of the ultimate object of desire can bring to rest that which is carried along by the power of its own nature. It follows, then, that nothing that is in motion has come to rest, since it has not yet attained its ultimate desired end, because that which can arrest the motion of whatever is moved in relation to it has not yet appeared.[53]

We can see that this metaphysics of created desire can cut both ways. The transhumanist desire is for absolute power over nature through willed active effort, but because the ultimate object of desire has not yet arrived and will never arrive, there can be no rest. In contrast, in deification the ultimate object of desire is God, the only one who can bring the creature to rest. In other words, rest must be actively received, not strived for.

Maximus goes on to show that rest is not intrinsic to the thing itself because it is not uncaused. If rest were intrinsic, then the thing "would be uncreated, without beginning, and without motion, having no way of being moved toward something else." Only that which is uncaused, namely, God, transcends motion because he exists for the sake of nothing outside himself. Thus, all created things are in motion until they have rest in the ultimately desirable, who is God the Beautiful. "For from God come both our general power of motion (for He is our beginning), and the particular way that we move toward Him (for He is our end)."[54] With God as the beginning, the manner, and the end of one's motion, Maximus describes the order of motion as a motion of ecstatic love culminating in deification:

> If an intellective being *is moved* intellectively, that is, in a manner appropriate to itself, then it will necessarily become a knowing intellect. But if it knows, it

---

[53]Maximus, *Ambiguum* 7, PG 91:1069B, trans. Constas, 1:77-79.
[54]Maximus, *Ambiguum* 7, PG 91:1069D-1072C, 1073C, trans. Constas, 1:83, 87.

> surely loves that which it knows; and if it loves, it certainly *suffers* an ecstasy toward it as an object of love. If it *suffers* this ecstasy, it obviously *urges itself onward*, and if it urges itself onward, it surely *intensifies and greatly accelerates its motion*. And if its motion is intensified in this way, it will not cease *until it is wholly present in the whole beloved, and wholly encompassed by it, willingly receiving* the whole saving circumscription by its own *choice*, so that it might be wholly qualified by the whole circumscriber, and, being wholly circumscribed, will no longer be able to wish to be known from its own qualities, but rather from those of the circumscriber, in the same way that air is thoroughly permeated by light, or iron in a forge is completely penetrated by the fire, or anything else of this sort.[55]

There are several important dimensions to highlight. Following the cosmic motion of active receptivity, humans are moved by God through knowing him as the object of love. God moves us by desire for him. We know this through Maximus's use of the word *suffers*. We must receive the beginning of our motion toward him. But God does not merely implant desire that then follows mechanical necessity. A human person "suffers this ecstasy" of love and "urges [herself] onward" and then accelerates her motion in the manner of active effort. The goal of this accelerated motion is being completely enveloped by the love of God, but it must be willingly received. The consequence of attaining this goal is deification, signaled by the language of an iron in a forge that is completely penetrated by fire. The one deified retains human nature but is suffused by divine love. In short, Maximus's cosmic motion is a metaphysics of created desire that ends in deification based on an agency of active receptivity. At every step of the way, the motion of love must be received and willed. Maximus's metaphysics of created desire transfigures the schema of Ravaisson's philosophy of graced nature: desire for the beautiful, will-to-love, habit of love, and true human nature deified and suffused by love.

The active receptivity of deification culminates in ever-moving rest, a paradoxical concept of motion and rest. Ever-moving rest is a complete envelopment of divine love when one is in union with God.

The aim of faith is the true revelation of the object of one's faith. The true revelation of the object of one's faith is the ineffable relation of mutual love

---

[55]Maximus, *Ambiguum* 7, PG 91:1073C-1076A, trans. Constas, 1:87-89, emphasis added.

with that object according to the measure of each one's faith. The relation of mutual love with the object of faith is the final return of the faithful to their own beginning. The final return of the faithful to their own beginning is the fulfillment of every desire. The fulfillment of desire is the *ever-moving rest* around the object of desire by those desire it. The *ever-moving rest* around the object of desire by those who desire it is the perpetual enjoyment of the object of desire unbroken by any interval. Perpetual enjoyment of the object of desire unbroken by any interval is participation in divine realities that transcend nature. Participation in divine realities that transcend nature is the likeness of the participants to the participable. The likeness of participants to the participable is the actualized identity of the participants with the participable, which they receive through the likeness. The actualized identity of participants with the participable received through the likeness is the *divinization* of those made worthy of it.... When I say "realities that transcend nature," I mean the divine and incomprehensible pleasure of God, which God inherently brings about by nature when He unites Himself according to grace to those who are worthy.[56]

In the context of faith and its aim, Maximus uses the language of motion toward fulfillment of desire in the object of desire. What is significant is the explicit language of participation in the divine realities that transcend nature. In participation, the participant becomes identified with the one who is participated, who is God, and yet the creature maintains ontological difference. In union with God, one is deified. But the nature of this deification is an ever-moving rest. How do we reconcile this paradox? Because God is infinite and is love, the motion of love for the creature is everlasting. Yet, because the motion of love is completed in union with God by grace, not effort, then there is rest. Ever-moving rest is the eschatology of active receptivity. In contrast, the eschatology of the transhumanist is never-ending active effort.

## Conclusion

In this chapter, I have attempted to show the stark contrast between transhumanism as an auto-deification by active effort through technology and Christian deification through grace as the paradigm of becoming like God by

---

[56]Maximus the Confessor, *Ad Thalassium* 59.8. For an English translation, see Maximos the Confessor, *On Difficulties in Sacred Scripture: The Responses to Thalassios*, trans. Maximos Constas (Washington, DC: Catholic University of America Press, 2018), 416-18, emphasis added.

active receptivity. I argued that there was a historical shift in how we understand science, away from Aristotelian causation that gave primacy to intrinisic teleology of nature and toward a mechanistic view of nature that is governed by an extrinsic teleology of will—first God, then human. Baconian natural philosophy transformed science to be a pursuit of knowledge as merely useful to relieve the human condition. The means of usefulness became dominion over nature through power. Nietzschean power ontology then gave primacy to the will-to-power as the central drive in Darwinian evolution. Transhumanists are inspired by Nietzsche to break the bonds of natural necessity and exert technological power to direct evolution for the maximization of (trans)human power and control over nature, including one's own body. The agency of active effort completely suffuses the transhumanist logic.

In contrast, I explored Félix Ravaisson's philosophy of graced nature to show how nature is already given by love, which is received by humans as desire, which in turn drives the will. Through repetitions of willed actions, habits are acquired, which become second nature. As one develops the habit of love, one becomes loving by fulfilled nature. This provides an agential model of active receptivity and a philosophical account for the process of deification. However, because Ravaisson does not account for suffering, and neither does he invoke Christ, I turned to Maximus's account of cosmic motion that is fulfilled in union with God and deification by grace, culminating in an ever-moving rest.

Because of their mutually opposing views of agency in deification, I conclude that transhumanism and Christian deification are fundamentally incompatible. Transhumanism and Christian deification function as limit cases for human agency and Christian spirituality in general. Given Maximus's cosmic vision of deification as encompassing all creaturely reality, what we think about deification touches every part of human life. If deification necessarily follows a model of active receptivity, then how much more should active receptivity inform our day-to-day human agency? We should follow Simone Weil and shy away from muscular effort in favor of negative effort. We actively receive the grace of God in prayer and in suffering, not by technological striving. We should suffer the love of God so that we might become like God.

# LIST OF CONTRIBUTORS

**Nathan Betz** (PhD, Katholieke Universiteit Leuven) is a research fellow at the Beyond Canon Centre for Advanced Studies at the University of Regensburg in Germany. His primary research pertains to the diverse historical reception of the idea of the new Jerusalem from John's Revelation. He is the author of *City of Gods: The New Jerusalem of John's Revelation in Early Christianity (Through ca. 313)* (Brill, 2024) and coeditor of *Revelation's New Jerusalem in Late Antiquity* (Mohr Siebeck, 2024). A founder of the Revelation Reception Network and Seminar, he holds master's degrees from Oxford and St. John's College (Annapolis).

**Ben C. Blackwell** (PhD, Durham University) is professor of early Christianity at Houston Christian University and director of Houston Theological Seminary. He earned his PhD in early Christianity at Durham University, where he worked under John Barclay and N. T. Wright. Blackwell's primary research is in Pauline theology and the reception history of Paul in early Christian texts. He is currently coeditor for two monograph series: New Testament Theology (Cambridge University Press) and Lectio Sacra (Cascade).

**Brian Siu Kit Chiu** (PhD, Talbot School of Theology) is interested in several research areas, including theological education, spiritual formation, Chinese Christianity, and Christianity in China. He received his master's degree in theology from Wheaton College (Illinois) in 2017. A sampling of Brian's recent publications include "The Sinicization of Christian Pietism: Jia Yuming's and Watchman Nee's Approaches to the Problem of Rationality Versus Spirituality" and "Beyond Localization: Theological Education in China and Watchman Nee's Concepts and Practices in Spiritual Education." Brian also cotranslated *Entrance to the Kingdom* by Robert Govett into Chinese in 2021. He is currently an institutional researcher at Logos Evangelical Seminary in Southern California.

**Paul Copan** (PhD, Marquette University) is professor and Pledger Family Chair of Philosophy and Ethics at Palm Beach Atlantic University (West

Palm Beach, Florida), and teaches in the master of arts philosophy of religion program there. He is the author and editor of nearly fifty books, including *Creation Out of Nothing: A Biblical, Philosophical, and Scientific Exploration* (Baker Academic), *Is God a Moral Monster? Understanding the Old Testament God* (Baker), *Is God a Vindictive Bully? Reconciling Portrayals of God in the Old and New Testaments* (Baker Academic), and *Loving Wisdom: A Guide to Philosophy and Christian Faith* (Eerdmans). He has contributed chapters to over sixty books, and he has written many articles and book reviews for various professional and popular journals. For six years he served as the president of the Evangelical Philosophical Society. He has been a visiting scholar at Oxford University in 2017 and 2024. He is cochair of the Tyndale Fellowship Philosophy of Religion Study Group (UK). He is a member of the Institute for Biblical Research and the Society of Biblical Literature. Paul and his wife, Jacqueline, have six children and reside in West Palm Beach, Florida. His website is www.paulcopan.com.

**Jacob Chengwei Feng** (PhD, Fuller Theological Seminary) was born and raised in China as an atheist. He became a Christian while pursuing his PhD in physics. After graduating with a master's degree in electrical and computer engineering, he worked in the financial institutions on Wall Street in New York City for ten years. His church affiliation is the local church, or the "Little Flock," founded by Watchman Nee in 1922 in China. His research interests include systematic theology, Chinese theology, theology-religion-science trialogue, and ecumenical and interfaith dialogue with world religions. Feng has published several journal articles, the most recent of which include "Seven Spirits from Patmos: Towards a Decolonial Chinese Theology for the Third Millennium," "Alister McGrath and China: Toward a Chinese Theology and Science on Transhumanism for the Third Millennium," and "*Pneumasis/Pneumafication* Based on Romans 8:1-17: Highlighting the Spirit's Role in Deification."

**Mark Gorman** (ThD, Duke University Divinity School) is a pastor in the United Methodist Church and teaches systematic theology and worship studies at St. Mary's Ecumenical Institute in Baltimore, where he is a core faculty member. With Edgardo Colón-Emeric, he coauthored *The Saving Mysteries of Jesus Christ* (Cascade Books, 2019). His research interests include Wesleyan/Methodist theology, ecumenism, and the intersection of systematic theology and Christian worship.

**Michael J. Gorman** (PhD, Princeton Theological Seminary) holds the Raymond E. Brown Chair in Biblical Studies and Theology at St. Mary's Seminary and University in Baltimore. He has taught at St. Mary's since 1991, serving from 1995 to 2012 as the dean of St. Mary's Ecumenical Institute. A specialist in the Pauline and Johannine writings, he has published twenty books, including *Cruciformity: Paul's Narrative Spirituality of the Cross*; *Inhabiting the Cruciform God: Kenosis, Justification, and Theosis in Paul's Narrative Soteriology*; *Romans: A Theological and Pastoral Commentary*; and *Abide and Go: Missional Theosis in the Gospel of John*.

**Shu-chen Hsu Hsiung** (PhD, University of Alberta) engages in multiple areas of research, including historical theology, globalization of religion, and Chinese Christianity in the world. His publications appear in *Religious Studies Review* and *Reading Religion*. Shu-chen holds a master of arts from National Taiwan University and a master of arts in theological studies from Princeton Theological Seminary.

**L. Ann Jervis** (ThD, University of Toronto) is emerita professor of New Testament at Wycliffe College, University of Toronto. She is cross-appointed to the Department for the Study of Religion at University of Toronto and an Anglican priest in the Diocese of Toronto. Ann is the author of numerous articles and several books, including *Paul and Time: Life in the Temporality of Christ* (2023) and *At the Heart of the Gospel: Suffering in the Earliest Christian Message* (2007). She is a member of the Center for Theological Inquiry, Princeton; Studiorum Novi Testamenti Societas; and Massey College, University of Toronto.

**Rev. Dr. Veli-Matti Kärkkäinen** (DTheolHabil, University of Helsinki) is professor of systematic theology at Fuller Theological Seminary, Pasadena, California, and docent of ecumenics at the University of Helsinki. A native of Finland, he has also lived and taught theology in Thailand and continues participating widely in ecumenical, theological, and interreligious work. He is an author and (co)editor of more than thirty books and hundreds of essays. His major project is the five-volume series titled *Constructive*

*Christian Theology for the Pluralistic World* (Eerdmans, 2013–2017), which develops a full-scale systematic theology in a critical dialogue with Christian tradition and four living faiths. Kärkkäinen is an ordained Lutheran minister (ELCA) and serves also as a part-time associate pastor for the Finnish Lutheran Church in California and Texas.

**Kimbell Kornu** (PhD, MD) is the inaugural Provost's Professor of Bioethics, Theology, and Christian Formation at Belmont University and is a palliative care physician. He holds an MD from the University of Texas Southwestern and a PhD in Theology from the University of Nottingham (UK). He is currently working to help start a new medical school at Belmont University. He has taught palliative medicine, bioethics, and theology across the university to undergraduates, medical students, PhD students, and medical residents and fellows. His research focuses on the historical, social, philosophical, and theological determinants that shape the metaphysics and practices of modern medicine. He has published widely in the philosophy and theology of medicine.

**Chao-Chun Liu** (PhD, Durham University) completed his bachelor's in music from Johns Hopkins University and master's degree with an artist diploma also in music at Yale University. Thereafter he felt called to attend a two-year Bible school. Afterward, he went to the United Kingdom for mission work, during which he completed a master's degree in translation at the University of Bath (UK) and a master's degree in the reception of the Bible at the University of Bristol (UK). Since then, he has served as a translator and editor of Christian literature for several publishers, has translated and published multiple works both in Chinese and in English, and has worked on several translation projects with the Israel Museum. Chao has published three peer-reviewed journal articles and several book reviews on the subject of Bible translation and Chinese Christianity.

**Alister E. McGrath** is a senior research fellow at the Ian Ramsey Centre for Science and Religion in the Faculty of Theology at Oxford University, having previously been professor of historical theology and subsequently Andreas Idreos Professor of Science and Religion at Oxford. His research interests focus on the interaction of theology, philosophy, and the natural sciences, and he is presently working on a major monograph on the parallels between the development of scientific theories and Christian doctrines. His most recent monograph is *Natural Philosophy: On Retrieving a Lost Disciplinary Imaginary* (Oxford University Press, 2022).

**Carl Mosser** (PhD, University of St. Andrews) has served as professor of Christian theology at Gateway Seminary in Ontario, California; visiting research professor and analytic theology fellow at the University of Notre Dame; and associate professor of biblical studies at Eastern University. Currently he is an independent scholar living in Southern California, where he serves as the pastor of House of God Lutheran Church. His publications include several articles on the origin of the doctrine of deification in patristic theology, how deification came to be mislabeled an Eastern doctrine, and the place of deification in early Reformed theology.

**Jahdiel Perez** (DPhil, Oxford) is assistant professor of humanities and the sciences at Villanova University. In 2023, Perez earned his DPhil in theology and literature at the University of Oxford, where he wrote the first dissertation on C. S. Lewis with the Faculty of Theology and Religion. While at Oxford, Perez was president of the Oxford C. S. Lewis Society and a doctoral fellow with the OCCA Oxford Centre for Christian Apologetics. He researches and teaches at the intersection of philosophy, theology, literature, and psychology of religion. Before attending Oxford, Perez earned his BA in philosophy from the University of Massachusetts in Boston and his MDiv in Christian theology from Harvard University.

**Michael M. C. Reardon** (PhD, University of Toronto) is the academic dean and professor of New Testament and historical theology at Canada Christian College and School of Graduate Theological Studies. He has written and spoken extensively about deification in invited lectures, podcast interviews, conference papers, and recent articles in *Currents in Biblical Research* and *Horizons: The Journal of the College Theology Society*. Michael has contributed to multiple anthologies and reviewed monographs for *Review of Biblical Literature, Reading Religion, Toronto Journal of Theology*, and *Journal of Evangelical Theological Society*. He is also the director of the Eckstein Institute for Jewish-Christian Relations, where he creates and teaches courses on Jewish and Christian theology, engages in dialogue with Jewish theologians, and is coediting a volume titled *The Seed of Abraham: Intersections of Jewish and Christian Thought*. Michael and his wife, Joyce, have three children.

**James Salladin** (PhD, University of St. Andrews) serves as rector at Emmanuel Anglican Church in New York City, where he lives with his wife, Amber, and two sons, Caleb and Peter. Jim earned a PhD from the University of St. Andrews and has served as a pastor in Canada, the United Kingdom, and the United States. He is the author of the recently published *Jonathan Edwards and Deification: Reconciling Theosis and the Reformed Tradition* (IVP Academic).

# GENERAL INDEX

Adam, 20, 22, 49-50, 74-75, 85, 174, 176-77, 191, 201-4, 228, 236
   second, 176, 178, 203
adoption, 30, 32, 75, 123, 128, 131, 141, 248, 252, 259-61, 281, 285-86
Aquinas, Thomas, 28, 110, 112, 128, 169, 179, 186, 199, 314
assimilation, 31, 49, 110
Athanasius of Alexandria, 16, 18, 24-26, 28, 54, 58, 105, 155, 207, 210, 215
Augustine of Hippo, 18, 26-30, 32, 106, 116-17, 193, 195, 243, 250, 262, 267
authority, 33, 53, 61, 78, 91, 296
Barth, Karl, 17
Bauckham, Richard, 208
Bavinck, Herman, 17
birth, 13, 30, 52-54, 219, 228, 293
Blackwell, Ben, 18, 20, 105, 110, 121, 242, 246, 248, 251, 253, 264, 267, 331
blessing, 71, 78, 132, 254-55
blood, 26, 46, 142-43, 176, 182, 325
body of Christ, 18, 20-21, 23-26, 28-29, 34-37, 51-54, 90, 93, 99, 101, 220, 233, 235
Buntain, William, 294
Bunyan, John, 193
Calvin, John, 17, 84, 120-21, 124, 130-44, 176, 200, 211-12, 215, 242-43, 251, 258, 260, 265
Cappadocian Fathers, 28, 125, 225
character, 12, 58, 98, 101, 235-36, 285
Chinese Christianity, 87, 102, 331, 333-34
Chinese Recovery Version, 82, 86-87, 89-102
Chinese Union Version, 82-102
Christ, 10-39, 43-54, 58-61, 71-72, 85-99, 114, 116-22, 127-29, 133-44, 158-62, 175-78, 195-97, 200-206, 223-24, 226-28, 232-37, 252-55, 265-90, 295-99, 323-25
   and humanity, 44, 46, 53
   metaphor, 46-47, 49-50, 61
   pneumatic, 59, 88-89
   present, 119, 274
   present in faith, 111, 269-71, 275, 278, 287
   resurrected, 51, 88, 239
Christ's body, 14, 143, 212, 219, 229, 233, 237-38
   death, 176, 201, 204, 295
   flesh, 125, 133, 142, 325
   humanity, 24, 46, 48, 136-38, 140-41, 144, 263
   life, 12, 23, 49, 95, 175
Christification, 38, 98, 105-22, 209
Christosis, 20, 38, 105, 121, 246
church, 10, 16-37, 70, 99, 101, 138-39, 147, 160, 162, 166, 220-21, 225, 227-30, 232-34, 243-46
   early, 16, 18, 22, 36, 138, 140, 223-24, 227, 314
church fathers, 28, 43, 49, 125, 130, 169, 199, 227, 280, 289, 325
communion, 26, 32-33, 142-43, 146-47, 156, 160, 169, 171, 212-13
communities, 183, 219, 229, 238-39, 288
corporate Christ, 34-35
corporate identity, 24, 28, 37, 204
covenant, 10-12, 203, 252
creation, 39, 41, 75, 77, 145-65, 167, 172-73, 188, 192, 201-3, 205, 246-49, 310-11
Creator-creature distinction, 123-24, 151, 201, 232
Crisp, Oliver, 213
cross, 36, 44-47, 51, 116, 122, 204, 237, 244, 295, 297, 303
Cruickshank, Joanna, 176
declaration, 120, 123, 127, 243, 251-52, 256-57, 324
deification and justification, 135, 222-23, 243-45, 258, 264, 267, 271
deification of Christ's humanity, 137-38, 140-41, 144
Deininger, Fritz, 219
deity, 16, 23, 27, 72, 123, 141, 154, 174, 199
divine agency, 181, 251, 258, 262-64
divine attributes, 136-37, 142, 144, 149, 236, 246-47, 253, 300
divine energies, 291, 304-5
divine essence, 158, 304
divine filiation, 64, 75-76
divine glory, 78, 150, 164, 253
divine grace, 156, 192, 198, 262, 303
divine image, 151, 174-75, 179, 202, 215
divine immortality, 123, 132, 134, 137
divine life, 93, 95, 97-101, 124, 126, 129, 131, 133, 135, 149, 152, 235, 266-67, 280, 283

divine love, 156, 178, 180-81, 327
divine nature, 22, 48-49, 59, 61, 87-88, 105-6, 111-12, 136, 138-42, 156-57, 168-69, 171, 178, 180, 186-87, 195-96, 208
  partakers of the, 57, 159, 211
divinity, 11-12, 48, 50, 52-54, 59-60, 136-37, 140, 146, 153, 225, 227, 303, 321
divinization, 30-31, 132, 134, 136, 145, 165, 167, 169, 192-93, 200-201, 212, 215, 223
dominion, 205, 226, 316, 319, 329
earth, 46, 48, 81, 85, 131, 143, 145, 163, 165, 189-91, 201-2, 211, 285
Eastern Orthodox, 57-58, 89, 106, 124, 167-69, 199, 208-10, 212, 215, 241, 271, 288-91, 300
ecumenical, 110, 246, 332-33
Eden, 201, 203, 316, 324
Edwards, Jonathan, 17, 145-65, 200, 212-13, 215, 293, 336
effort, 154, 263, 292, 310-13, 319-23, 328
eternal life, 15, 43, 85-86, 91-94, 97, 99-100, 247, 250, 253-55, 257-58, 262
eternity, 35, 151-52, 212, 231, 263, 281, 284
evil, 57, 74-76, 118, 156-57, 188-89, 279, 301
exchange, 40, 118, 131, 145, 159, 177, 278
existence, 32-33, 35, 66, 92, 108, 110, 152, 202, 263, 304, 326
faith, 15-16, 87-88, 93-94, 105-6, 117-20, 129, 171, 173-74, 176, 197, 210-11, 252-53, 262-66, 268-73, 275-78, 280, 282, 284-86, 289, 327-28
  and baptism, 87-88, 250
Father, 15-16, 24-26, 39, 51-54, 57, 72, 146-47, 156, 159-60, 162, 173-74, 181, 196, 205-6, 224-25, 248-49, 259-60, 264-66, 283-85, 324-25
favor, 274, 284, 287, 329
Finlan, Stephen, 17, 112, 223, 244-45
forensic, 16-17, 57, 108-9, 120, 243, 249, 251-55, 258, 267, 270-75, 278, 282-84, 286, 290
forgiveness, 56-57, 61, 135, 244, 251-52, 255, 260, 264, 274, 287
Gavrilyuk, Paul, 17, 65, 109, 111, 153, 246
Geisler, Norman, 209
glorification, 51, 75, 95, 138, 171, 228, 302, 310
glory, 59-61, 64, 123, 132-33, 135, 137, 148-52, 157, 159, 162-64, 198-203, 205, 211-13, 303, 310-11
  of God, 45, 58, 66, 129, 152, 180, 212, 304
God, 10-17, 23-27, 29-33, 37-46, 48-55, 57-61, 63-81, 91-95, 97-101, 126-37, 145-56, 158-65, 170-97, 199-215, 222-37, 247-67, 280-81, 298-306, 309-16, 326-29
God-man, 30, 48, 59, 98, 200, 206, 237

good works, 16, 100, 129, 171, 271, 276, 278, 288
Gorman, Michael, 38, 121, 169, 253, 333
gospel, 27, 29, 72, 75, 81, 84, 109, 129, 132, 134, 209, 211, 283, 285, 333
grace, 30-31, 137, 153-60, 162-65, 167, 169-70, 181-82, 208, 250, 263-64, 266, 273-76, 284, 288, 302-3, 310-13, 320, 323-24, 328-29
  of God, 179, 204, 229, 280, 329
  prevenient, 174, 320-22
  special, 153-56
Gregory the Great, 28
Gregory of Nazianzus, 28, 81, 223, 227
Gregory of Nyssa, 28, 119, 227, 288
Gregory of Pontus, 79
growth, 45, 60, 76, 95-101, 131, 180, 204, 233, 235, 316
Guyon, Jeanne, 295-96
Harnack, Adolf, 109-11, 226
Hays, Richard, 18
heresies, 63-64, 68, 139, 227
Hilary of Poitiers, 18, 25-26, 28, 181
holiness, 58-59, 118, 120, 160, 163, 170-71, 175, 180, 183, 247, 272, 278
holy, 87, 89, 117, 119, 136, 139, 142, 177
Holy Spirit, 30, 39, 48, 59-60, 74, 85, 87-88, 136, 150, 156, 159-60, 172-74, 179-81, 227, 265, 272, 283, 297
human, 52, 54, 64-65, 68-69, 75-76, 173-75, 177-83, 185-89, 191-92, 197-98, 208, 230-31, 236, 251-52, 254, 262-64, 299-301, 303, 305, 309-10, 315, 317-19, 321
  nature, 46, 48-49, 54, 136-37, 140-42, 144, 156-57, 178, 246, 263, 266, 325, 327
  soul, 118, 162
  spirit, 90, 306
humanity, 44-50, 52-55, 59-60, 113, 145-46, 151, 153, 156-58, 162, 165, 168, 171-72, 174-76, 186-89, 192, 201-3, 263, 266, 292
  fallen, 186, 202, 204, 299
  new, 51-54, 203, 228
hymns, 35, 48, 59, 169, 171, 174-78, 181-83, 299
identification, 32, 37, 181, 260, 283
identity, 10, 27-28, 32, 117-18, 127, 212-14, 249, 288
image, 64, 73, 75-76, 78, 172-75, 188-90, 201, 210, 212, 223, 225-26, 228, 236, 247-48
  of Christ, 60, 98, 208, 226, 265
  of God, 128, 149, 171-72, 174-75, 177-78, 200-201, 203, 206, 261
  and likeness of God, 69, 76, 172, 247
  natural, 172, 177
*imitatio Christi*, 28, 197
  imitation of Christ, 119, 197

immortality, 21, 75-76, 123-24, 131, 133, 142-43, 172, 200, 247
in Christ, 89, 204-5, 208
incarnation, 13, 48, 105-6, 129, 137-40, 162, 177-78, 185, 188-89, 191, 201-2, 228, 244-45, 248, 266
incorporation, 31-32, 44, 49, 51-54, 60-61, 64, 122, 266
incorruption, 123, 132-33, 137, 247, 261
indwelling of Christ, 116, 270, 276-77
Irenaeus of Lyons, 18, 20-21, 24, 28, 57-58, 73, 75-76, 79, 81, 105, 109, 168, 227, 280
Israel, 10, 14, 24, 176-77, 200, 202-6, 252, 254
Jesus, 10-11, 13-15, 24-25, 41, 162, 164, 175-77, 183, 196, 203, 205-6, 237, 254, 264-66, 324-25
Jewish interpretations, 123, 206
judgment, final, 250-51, 254, 256-57, 259
justice, 81, 169, 173, 206, 229, 281
justification, 38-39, 57-58, 61-62, 106-11, 113, 115-16, 119-21, 124, 134-36, 169, 171, 222-23, 242-46, 249-77, 279-90
    and adoption, 260
    and deification, 61, 135, 242-45, 258-59, 261, 263, 265, 267, 269, 280
    and participation in Christ, 109, 119, 273
    and regeneration, 242, 258
    and sanctification, 120, 257, 259, 261, 263
Justin Martyr, 66, 68-69, 73-75, 79, 81
Kärkkäinen, Veli-Matti, 38-39, 110-11, 222-23, 230, 243, 268, 271, 278, 283, 333
Kimbrough, S. T., 168-69, 178, 294
kingdom, 15, 69, 85, 130, 135, 177, 196, 202, 205, 233, 237
knowledge, 76, 100-101, 151, 219-20, 222, 240, 273, 309, 313-14, 316, 329
    of God, 100, 130, 179
language, 82, 85, 124, 127-28, 130, 205-10, 212, 229, 231, 255-56, 261, 264, 266, 327-28
law, 51, 58, 72, 76, 181, 187, 255-56, 260, 262, 272, 278, 315, 319
Lee, Witness, 34-36, 38, 40, 43, 45, 48-49, 51, 59, 86, 90, 93, 207-9, 229-32, 234-39, 241, 291, 293-94, 296-300, 305-7
Lewis, C. S., 17, 184-98, 214-15, 335
life, 25, 33-35, 44-46, 48-49, 90-101, 133, 136-37, 139-40, 142-43, 163, 169-71, 174-76, 179-80, 182-85, 230-37, 242-67, 277-78, 282-83, 294-96, 299-301
    alien, 258, 278
    of Christ, 12, 45, 50, 122, 237
    deified, 182-83
    moral, 261, 312

new, 25, 85, 93, 284
triune, 188, 190
light, 11-12, 98, 102, 124, 128, 161-63, 165, 168, 222-23, 303-5, 312, 323, 327
likeness, 69, 76, 96, 130, 134, 172-73, 181, 210, 226, 247-48, 328
    to God, 119, 130, 134, 153, 173, 248
Litwa, David, 15, 18, 38, 64, 67-69, 226
Living Stream Ministry, 34-35, 45, 48, 51, 90, 207, 209, 231, 234-37, 298-300
local churches, 85, 207-9, 223, 229-30, 232-34, 238-39, 293-94, 298, 306, 332
Lord, 14, 22, 24-25, 32, 36, 48-49, 128, 171-72, 176, 178, 181, 234, 291, 298-300, 305-7
Lord's Supper, 131, 167
Louth, Andrew, 152, 243, 324
love, 129, 160, 171-73, 175, 177, 179-83, 211-12, 236, 273, 277-79, 281, 285, 319-21, 323-24, 327-29
    of God, 179, 327, 329
de Lubac, Henri, 148
Luther, Martin, 17, 38, 61, 105-22, 126, 210-11, 215, 251, 258, 268-82, 284-85, 287, 289-90
Lutheran doctrine of justification, 109, 271, 273
Lutheranism, 106, 109, 167, 268, 270, 288
Luther's theology, 111, 114-16, 121-22, 269, 271, 277, 281, 287, 289
Mannermaa, Tuomo, 17, 111, 113, 269, 278-81
Mannermaa school, 268, 281-82, 286-87
Maximus the Confessor, 246, 263, 266, 319, 323-28
McCormack, Bruce, 134, 136-37, 250
McGrath, Alister, 105-6, 108, 113, 116, 122, 194, 250, 334
Meister Eckhart, 126-27
Mersch, Émile, 18, 20, 25, 27, 29-31, 35
metaphors, 34-35, 38-46, 49, 51, 53-57, 60-61, 77-79, 250, 252, 255, 259-61, 283, 286
Meyendorff, John, 58, 300, 302, 304
mingling, 48-49, 53-54
ministry, 29, 34, 81, 87, 93, 177, 183, 220, 222, 228-30, 232-35
morality, 39, 57, 236-37, 300
nature, 16-17, 32-33, 75-76, 131-32, 137-44, 147-48, 153-58, 161-65, 185-89, 214, 230-32, 235, 244-45, 248-50, 255-59, 266, 299-300, 303, 311-24, 328-29
Nee, Watchman, 34-35, 38, 40, 43-46, 49, 53-55, 58-59, 61, 224, 229-36, 238, 241, 292-94, 296-98, 300, 306
New Jerusalem, 35, 39, 43-44, 49, 51-54, 59-61, 64-67, 69-79, 81, 238, 331.

Newman, John Henry, 186, 193
Nietzsche, 146, 164-65, 318-19, 329
obedience, 15, 23, 26, 72, 136, 257-58, 260, 264-66, 325
Oecolampadius, Johannes, 124, 128, 144
Oecumenius, 49, 64, 77-79
Old Testament, 56, 66, 215, 233, 254, 256-57, 267
Origen of Alexandria, 18, 22-24, 28, 66, 69-71, 73, 79-81, 155
Orthodox, 57, 59, 115-16, 152, 207, 242-44, 307
   Christians, 207, 242, 307
   doctrines, 179, 225, 268-69
   theologians, 57, 59, 116, 243-44
   theology, 115, 152, 243-44
Owen, John, 17, 132, 136, 156, 159, 211-12
Palamas, Gregory, 169, 212, 291, 300-305, 307
Pannenberg, Wolfhart, 285-86
partakers, 105, 111-12, 131-32, 136, 141-42, 146, 152, 169, 171, 178, 226, 232
partaking, 43, 49, 131, 133-34, 155, 160-61, 169, 178, 237
participation, 17, 31-32, 38, 128, 151-53, 155, 161, 191-92, 212, 223, 245, 247-49, 251, 253, 258-59, 261-71, 273-77, 280-83, 285-87, 289-90, 304-6, 328
participationist perspective, 251, 253
participatory metaphysics, 153, 156
passions, 170, 176, 179, 316, 322
Paul, 10-15, 18, 26, 28, 36-38, 40, 45, 81, 123, 132-34, 136, 193, 203-4, 226, 251-61, 263-66, 278, 301, 331-33
Pauline soteriology, 15-16, 18, 20, 36, 105, 121
Pauline theology, 10, 38, 226, 250, 252-53, 255-56, 263-64, 266, 286, 331
Paul's letters, 116, 245, 253, 256, 261, 266
Penn-Lewis, Jessie, 295-96
Peura, Simo, 111, 113, 116, 269, 279, 281
philosophy, 26, 39, 170, 199, 234, 311-12, 314-15, 319-21, 323, 331-32, 334-35
Plato, 119, 130, 132, 213
pluralism, 42, 268, 283, 333
power, 30, 61, 75-76, 131-32, 140-41, 143, 145-46, 170-71, 256, 276, 295-96, 308-9, 312-14, 316, 318-19
praise, 174, 180, 182-83, 311
prayer, 167, 174-75, 180, 193-94, 196-97, 291, 295, 297-99, 301-2, 311-12, 324, 329
process, 19, 42, 75, 117, 119, 180, 182, 185, 187-89, 219-20, 223, 227, 250, 258-59, 262
prophets, 176, 206, 233, 254

Protestant, 56, 58, 60, 220, 223, 243-44, 246-47, 251, 253, 264, 268-69, 271, 288, 290
   theology, 107, 126-27, 249, 252
   traditions, 199-200, 222, 243, 253
Pseudo-Dionysius, 190, 199, 304
Pseudo-Macarius, 302
Recovery Version, 23, 90
redemption, 36, 39, 128, 130, 132, 135, 139, 152, 159, 163-64, 182, 185-86, 189
Reformation, 28, 105, 108, 110, 124, 135, 220, 242, 249, 253, 260
Reformed Tradition, 84, 87, 89, 93, 98, 100-101, 123-44, 155-56, 265, 336
Reformers, 116, 124-26, 130, 242, 251, 257-58, 262, 267, 269, 272, 277
regeneration, 59, 90, 117, 235, 242-43, 247, 258, 283, 296
renewal, 168, 174-75, 179, 183, 224, 272, 274, 283, 287, 290
restoration, 106, 172, 178-79, 200, 244-45, 247, 252, 254, 256, 259, 263-64
resurrection, 3, 5, 10, 20, 37, 45, 48, 51, 95-96, 124, 132, 135, 200, 202, 228, 239, 244-45, 247-48, 254, 257-59, 261, 321
righteousness 109, 113, 116-17, 120, 249, 251, 253, 267, 275-77, 289
   alien, 120, 275, 289
   of Christ, 109, 117, 275-76
   of God, 113, 116-17, 249, 251, 253, 267, 277
Roman Catholic, 29, 169, 170, 225, 242, 271, 286, 288, 290
Russell, Norman, 17, 38, 42-43, 65, 111, 147, 153, 157, 224, 245, 262
sacraments, 26, 31, 36, 48, 131, 143, 170, 248, 266, 276
saints, 73-74, 77-78, 156, 158-65, 173, 205, 220, 234, 259, 281, 303
salvation, 16-17, 42-43, 56-58, 105-6, 110-14, 123-24, 128, 135-36, 158-60, 170-71, 174, 177, 222-23, 227, 247, 258-62, 264, 268-73, 283-85, 289-90
sanctification, 25, 28, 167, 170-71, 209, 257, 259-64, 266, 271-72, 274, 288, 290, 292
Sarisky, Darren, 26
science, 37, 41, 184, 192, 197, 309-10, 313-14, 320, 329, 332, 335
sin, 39-40, 55-61, 118, 136, 170-71, 178, 182-83, 191, 203-4, 254, 259-60, 271-72, 274, 276-77, 286, 299
   and death, 85, 136, 172, 177-78, 189, 255, 276

sinners, 56, 58-59, 117, 135, 204, 252, 256, 271-74, 276, 288-89, 302
Son, 12-14, 16, 21, 23, 26, 30-33, 49, 51-52, 65-67, 69-76, 90, 137, 139-41, 156, 158-62, 173-74, 203-6, 248-49, 266, 283-85
sons of God, 21, 25, 67, 69, 72-76, 78-79, 128, 131, 141, 185, 224, 227, 231
sonship, 123, 285
soteriology, 32, 37, 58, 179, 185, 199, 242-44, 264, 270-71, 289, 292
soul, 22-23, 30, 74, 90, 117-18, 130, 133, 135-36, 142, 156, 161, 295, 301-3, 312, 321
spirit, 30, 37-39, 46-48, 51-54, 68, 87-90, 124, 126-28, 133, 158-61, 173-74, 179-81, 227, 245, 247-49, 256-58, 262, 264-67, 283-86, 288-90
Spirit of Christ, 88, 90, 143, 280-81
Spirit of God, 48, 88, 127
spiritual formation, 220, 227, 229, 232, 235-36, 240, 314, 331
spirituality, 30, 38, 119, 124, 157, 164, 292, 295-96, 298, 300-301, 306
spiritual life, 154, 185, 193-96, 230, 234, 236, 243, 296
systematic theology, 29, 112, 153, 155, 278, 285-86, 332-33
Tertullian of Carthage, 18, 21-22, 24, 28
theological anthropology, 168, 172, 246-48, 290
theological education, 80, 219-25, 228-30, 233, 235-36, 239-41, 331
*theosis*, 17, 38, 57-58, 105-7, 110-16, 118, 120-23, 145-49, 151-54, 157-59, 167-69, 184-85, 199-201, 207, 209-10, 223, 225-27, 268-69, 280-81, 291-94
time, 14-15, 20-21, 65, 67, 71, 85-86, 93, 112-13, 194, 222, 230-31, 233-34, 287-88, 293-94, 296-98

transfiguration, 78, 303, 309-11, 325
transformation, 15, 18, 33, 49-50, 97-98, 118-20, 123, 125, 127, 157, 185, 187, 247-48, 250, 302-3
    progressive, 28, 223
Trinity, 31, 43-44, 114, 140, 160, 173-74, 188-90, 192, 200-201, 207, 209
truth, 19, 29, 33, 39, 230, 235, 277, 281, 295, 309-10, 315, 317, 321
union, 30-32, 38-39, 42-45, 48, 53-54, 86-87, 89, 92, 95-97, 118, 133-36, 142-44, 151-52, 156-57, 212-13, 222-23, 258-60, 264-65, 268-89, 327-29
    believer's, 114, 117, 120-21
    deifying, 20, 124, 135
    hypostatic, 137, 178, 248-49, 266, 325
    mystical, 92, 212, 223, 305, 307
    and participation, 269-70, 273-74, 281-82, 287, 289-90
    transformative, 120, 127, 232, 271
Vainio, Olli-Pekka, 109, 111, 269, 273, 281
Vanhoozer, Kevin, 26, 38, 260
Vermigli, 123-44
vision, 113, 116, 126, 128, 147, 149, 151-52, 155, 157, 164-65, 293
Ward, Michael, 190
Wengert, Timothy, 108, 111
Wesley, Charles, 17, 166-83, 214, 294
Wesley, John, 166-67, 169-73, 176, 178-83, 214, 288
women, 80, 95, 117, 170, 204, 215, 237
worship, 40, 66, 77-78, 80-81, 178, 198, 225, 231, 248, 299-300
Wright, N. T., 10-14, 203, 260, 331
Zizioulas, John, 18, 29, 31
Zwingli, Huldrych, 17, 123-43

# SCRIPTURE INDEX

**OLD TESTAMENT**

**Genesis**
1:26, *69, 85*
1:26-28, *200, 201, 226*
1:31, *173*
2, *203*
2–3, *247*
2:1-17, *201, 203*
3, *244*
3:8, *201*
4:13, *56*
5:22, *201*
5:24, *201*
6:9, *201*

**Exodus**
7:1, *57*
19:4-6, *233*
19:6, *202*
34:30, *57*

**Leviticus**
1–16, *24*
2:1-10, *39, 46, 47, 49*
2:3, *49*
16:21-22, *56*

**Deuteronomy**
30:15-16, *247*
30:15-20, *254*

**2 Samuel**
7:14, *206*

**Psalms**
1:1-3, *299*
8, *201, 215*
8:5, *201*
18:6, *298*
80:8, *206*
81, *26, 80*
82, *64, 65, 67, 68, 70, 71, 72, 73, 74, 75, 77, 79, 80, 123, 247*
82:1, *65, 67, 70, 71, 72, 80*
82:6, *57, 67, 68, 73, 123, 210, 214, 226, 227*
82:6-7, *65, 69, 70, 71, 72, 76*
82:7, *68, 70*

**Proverbs**
16:4, *164*

**Isaiah**
1:2-3, *202*
5:1-7, *206*
9, *206*
9:6, *208*
9:7, *206*
11, *206*
11:4-5, *206*
12:4, *298*
40–55, *205*
41:8, *206*
41:14, *206*
49:3, *206*
49:5-6, *206*
51:17, *69*
52:15, *206*
53, *206*
53:2-3, *206*

**Jeremiah**
18:6, *192*
22:15, *206*
23:5, *206*

**Lamentations**
3:55, *298*

**Ezekiel**
17:22-23, *206*
28, *69, 70*

**Daniel**
7, *205*

7:13-14, *205*
7:18, *205*

**Hosea**
11:1, *202*
11:2, *202*

**Habakkuk**
2:4, *253, 255*

**Zechariah**
6:12, *206*

**NEW TESTAMENT**

**Matthew**
1:18, *48*
2:15, *203*
3:17, *203*
5:3, *87*
5:9, *286*
5:48, *171, 214*
6, *261*
7:14, *93, 94*
16:18, *233*
17:4, *57*
18:6, *91*
21:43, *202*
28:19, *85, 91*
28:19-20, *238*

**Mark**
1:8, *87, 88*
9:42, *91*
10:15, *286*
10:45, *237*

**Luke**
1:17, *89*
9:13, *81*
10:19, *296*
10:21, *88*
12:32, *205*
18:17, *286*
20:36, *74*

**John**
1:1, *201*
1:1-18, *105, 203*
1:4, *94*
1:12, *91, 226*
1:14, *129, 201*
1:16, *159, 165*
1:33, *88*
1:49, *202*
2:11, *91*
2:16-21, *51*
2:23, *91*
3:2, *129*
3:3, *68*
3:5, *68*
3:6, *51, 68, 90*
3:8, *57*
3:15, *51*
3:15-16, *91*
3:16, *85, 91, 92, 100*
3:18, *91*
3:34, *158*
3:36, *91, 201*
4:14, *283*
4:24, *90*
4:39, *91*
6:29, *91*
6:35, *91*
6:40, *91*
6:57, *49*
7:5, *91*
7:31, *91*
7:38-39, *91*
7:48, *91*
8:30, *91*
9:35-36, *91*
10, *71, 72, 73*
10:30, *214*
10:34, *187*
10:34-36, *57*
10:42, *91*
11–21, *134*
11:25, *94*
11:25-26, *91*
11:45, *91*

11:48, *91*
12:11, *91*
12:15, *202*
12:36-37, *91*
12:42, *91*
12:44, *91*
12:46, *91*
13:34, *181*
14, *284*
14:1, *91*
14:2, *51*
14:6, *94*
14:10, *51*
14:12, *91*
14:16, *85*
14:16-17, *51*
14:20, *51*
14:21-23, *57*
15:1, *46, 47, 51, 206*
15:1-8, *206*
15:4-8, *57*
16, *284*
16:9, *91*
16:13-16, *51*
16:19-22, *51*
17:20, *91*
17:21-23, *57*
18:37, *202*

**Acts**
1:5, *88*
1:8, *239*
2:17-21, *299*
2:21, *298*
2:32, *239*
2:33, *85*
2:36, *24*
3:15, *239*
8:16, *92*
10:43, *91*
11:16, *88*
11:18, *100*
14:15, *300*
14:23, *91*
19:4, *91*
19:5, *92*
19:21, *88*
20:21, *91*
20:22, *88*
20:27, *81*
24:24, *91*
26:16, *239*
26:18, *91*

**Romans**
1-4, *253*
1:2, *255*
1:3, *12*
1:3-4, *12, 14*
1:4, *51*
1:5, *15*
1:9, *90*
1:17, *253, 255*
1:20, *13*
3:23, *58*
3:25, *284*
4:17-25, *255*
4:25, *258, 265, 284*
5, *266*
5:1, *113*
5:5, *179*
5:10, *94, 95*
5:12, *85*
5:12-19, *203*
5:12-21, *255*
5:15, *204*
5:17, *93*
5:19, *204*
6, *260, 295*
6:1-11, *265*
6:3-4, *5*
6:4, *85*
6:5, *96*
6:6, *204*
6:7, *260*
6:23, *257*
7:7-21, *256*
8, *248, 260*
8:1-2, *255, 265*
8:1-10, *255*
8:1-11, *247*
8:1-17, *39*
8:3, *12*
8:6-7, *225*
8:9, *88, 90*
8:9-10, *90*
8:10, *90, 93, 257, 265*
8:10-11, *257, 260*
8:11, *257*
8:14-17, *260*
8:15, *88, 227*
8:16, *90, 226, 286*
8:23, *260*
8:27, *225*
8:28-30, *248*
8:29, *3, 97, 165, 228*
8:30, *228*
8:34, *4*
9:1, *87, 88*
10:9, *298*
10:14, *91*
11:17, *51*
11:17-24, *39, 44, 46, 47*
11:24, *51*
12, *20, 37*
12:2, *236*
12:4-5, *21, 233*
13:14, *196*
14:17, *87*
15:16, *88*

**1 Corinthians**
2:11-15, *90*
3:9, *262*
3:23, *7*
6:11, *87, 88*
6:17, *128*
6:19, *301*
8:5-8, *7*
8:6, *14*
10, *12*
10:4, *13*
12, *20, 37*
12:3, *88*
12:9, *88*
12:12, *18, 34, 45*
12:12-13, *31*
12:12-27, *233*
12:13, *88*
12:27, *21*
14, *238*
14:2, *88*
14:4, *233*
14:26, *233*
15, *247*
15:3, *85*
15:10, *229*
15:20-28, *203*
15:24-28, *15*
15:28, *7, 15, 23, 28*
15:45, *88, 204*
15:47, *204*

**2 Corinthians**
2:13, *88*
3:3-9, *257*
3:3-18, *247*
3:6-9, *255, 256, 265*
3:17, *88, 208*
3:17-18, *226*
3:18, *4, 15, 157, 200, 201, 224, 226*
4:4, *201, 226*
4:7, *301*
5:1-5, *247*
5:17, *203*
8:9, *14, 57*
12:18, *88*
13:5, *93*
13:13, *248*

**Galatians**
2:15-21, *253, 255*
2:15-3:21, *255*
2:16, *91*
2:16-21, *255, 265*
2:19-20, *265*
2:20, *3, 49, 93, 226, 255*
2:21, *5*
3-4, *260*
3:7, *284*
3:10-11, *256*
3:10-14, *255*
3:11, *253*
3:17, *284*
3:21, *255, 256*
3:26, *15*
4, *248*
4:4, *4, 12, 85*
4:19, *93, 219, 228, 235*
4:26, *68, 69*
5:22, *46, 47*
5:24-25, *6*
6:14-15, *6*

**Ephesians**
1:20-21, *205*
2, *204*
2:6, *205*
2:8, *113*
2:14-15, *204*
2:15, *51*
2:18, *88*
2:22, *88*
3:5, *88*
3:16-17, *236*
3:19, *159*
4, *233*
4:3, *46, 47*

## Scripture Index

4:12-13, *220*
4:12-16, *233, 235*
4:13, *204*
4:15, *98*
4:15-16, *204*
4:16, *21*
4:18, *99, 133*
4:22, *204*
4:23, *88*
5:1, *7, 208*
5:18, *88*
6:18, *88, 298*

**Philippians**
1:21, *226, 235*
1:29, *91*
2, *13, 177, 311*
2:1, *248*
2:5, *12*
2:5-11, *11, 13*
2:6, *4, 11, 12, 13*
2:6-11, *11*
2:8, *237*
2:9, *4*
2:12-13, *229*
3:8-11, *12*
3:10, *5, 295*
3:10-11, *4, 11*
3:11, *5*

**Colossians**
1:8, *88*
1:10, *100*
1:15, *201, 224*
1:15-20, *203*
1:28, *219*
2:5, *88, 91*
2:9, *4, 158*
2:19, *100, 101*
3:3-4, *129*
3:9-11, *204*

**1 Thessalonians**
1:5, *89*
5:17, *298*
5:23, *90*

**2 Thessalonians**
1:12, *208*

**1 Timothy**
3:16, *228, 258, 265*
6:11, *236*

**2 Timothy**
2:22, *298*

**Titus**
3:5-7, *283*

**Hebrews**
1:1-4, *201*
2:10, *228*
2:14, *142*
2:17, *202*
3:1, *202*
4:12, *90*
4:14-15, *202*
4:15, *57*
5:8, *325*
6:4, *248*
11:1, *197*
12:10, *231*

**1 Peter**
1:2, *85*
1:3, *51*
1:8, *91*
1:15-16, *231*
1:21, *91*
2:5, *231*
2:9, *200, 202, 231, 233*
3:5, *231*
4:6, *88*
5:8, *225*

**2 Peter**
1:2-8, *247*
1:4, *57, 87, 105, 106,*
 *132, 134, 159, 171, 201,*
 *208, 214, 226, 231,*
 *232, 248, 280, 300*
3:18, *101*

**1 John**
3:1, *226*
3:2, *57, 70, 226*
4:12, *57*
4:16, *236*
5:10, *91*
5:12, *94, 201, 300*
5:13, *91*

**Jude**
19, *90*
20, *87*

**Revelation**
1:6, *202*
1:10, *88*
3:12, *39*
3:21, *205*
4:2, *88*
5:10, *202, 233*
17:3, *88*
20–22, *85*
20:4-6, *202*
21, *65, 69, 71, 73,*
 *75, 77*
21–22, *64, 65, 71,*
 *73, 79*
21:1-2, *66, 202*
21:2, *49, 53*
21:6-7, *71*
21:7, *66, 73*
21:10, *88*
21:10-11, *66*
21:12, *70*
21:15, *70*
21:19, *66*
22:1-2, *70*
22:1-5, *202*
22:3-4, *66*
22:4, *73, 78*
22:14, *70*

Printed in the USA
CPSIA information can be obtained
at www.ICGtesting.com
CBHW021559251024
16398CB00005B/309